VINTAGE WORTHING

Published in England by Rob Blann
Worthing, West Sussex BN11 5QF
e-mail: rob@rob-blann.co.uk

Part of the proceeds from the sale of this publication are donated to the Children's Chestnut Hospice Appeal and the Royal National Lifeboat Institution (RNLI)

1st Edition 2001

British Library Cataloguing-in-Publication Data
A catalogue record for this book is available from
The British Library

ISBN 0-9516277-3-2

Design, scanning and layout by
David Blann Design, Worthing
01903 600806

'Now' photographs by
Andrew Mardell Photography, Lancing
01903 765770

Printed by
Ashmore Press Ltd, Worthing
01903 506735

VINTAGE WORTHING

Images of a Lifeboat Town

1914-1945

ROB BLANN

Rob Blann

This book is dedicated to the memory
of my cousin Colin Foggett,
a keen yachtsman.

◆ INTRODUCTION ◆

Vintage Worthing makes essential reading for those interested in Worthing's history, both onshore and offshore. It is the third of a trilogy of books written by Rob Blann to commemorate Worthing's involvement with lifeboats, the three volumes together forming an illustrated record of the town's seafaring history and much, much more. Details of the other two earlier books can be found on the inside back cover.

Using a central theme of Worthing's lifeboat service and the people involved with it, *Vintage Worthing* seeks to explore the social development and expansion of the town as well as providing a unique pictorial record of the era.

This book guides the reader through many notable and memorable events spanning the thirty years from the start of the First World War to the end of the Second World War. It contains thirteen chapters, beautifully illustrated with 276 authentic period photographs, most of which are being published for the first time. It also includes numerous 'Then' and 'Now' photographs to demonstrate how lives and times have changed.

◆ CONTENTS ◆

◆ ABOUT THE AUTHOR ◆

Born and bred in Worthing, West Sussex, England on 9 February 1951, Rob Blann was educated at the town's Technical High School.

In 1970 he started a garden contracting business which has grown into the well-established comprehensive service that it is today.

Having descended from an old lifeboat family, it was not surprising that in 1988, Rob endeavoured to obtain the old Worthing Lifeboat House to re-establish a Lifeboat Showpiece Museum there, dedicated to the history of the town's valliant lifeboatmen. *(Daily Telegraph 14.9.88 page 2)*

With conservation and preservation high on his agenda, Rob was elected to lead the movement to save and enhance one of the world's oldest working picture houses – Worthing's Dome Cinema – a demanding task which he carried through with great vigour for 7 years from 1989 until 1996. *(The Independent 10.6.89; The Times 4.3.96 page 3; Daily Telegraph 11.6.96)*

Other books written by Rob, include one for the European Library, which has since sold out, as well as the trilogy of books on Worthing as a lifeboat town, which are still available.

Rob started the original weekly '*Remember When*' features in the *West Sussex Gazette* and has written for the paper for many years.

At the start of the millennium he launched the website *www.YourMemories.co.uk* with a worldwide appeal on the internet for the public's nostalgic memories of Britain. It has been a huge success and now the website has grown into an illustrated database of fond memories of growing up in Britain.

Following that success, Rob is developing a sister site *www.HeritageToday.co.uk.* as an online guide for tourists to find information on the best of British heritage sights and places to visit.

Rob's own personal website *www.rob-blann.co.uk* gives an overview of his activities.

Married to Jo since 1980, he has daughters from a previous marriage, and granddaughters too.

◆ PREFACE ◆

In the summer of 1914, the so-called 'Golden Years' of the Edwardian era were coming to a close, soon to be gone forever. Europe was to be drawn into a war of the most devastating proportions.

Yet life by the seaside at 'Sunny Worthing' carried on as normal, at least to start with. Holidaymakers continued to arrive, keeping local boatmen busy taking out parties for sailing and fishing trips; promenaders strolled along the seafront, taking the fresh air as it breezed in from the Channel; a plough, pulled by a pair of horses, worked the sands below, speeding up drainage and improving the facility for holidaymakers; swimmers enjoyed a specially designated area at West Worthing, screened off as a recognised public bathing station; and the town's professional fishermen enjoyed a successful season – one fisherman's catch alone amounted to as many as 4,000 bass on one particular day.

Long-skirted holidaymakers at leisure on the beach east of Worthing pier around 1914.

A carefree beach scene in an idyllic summer and all that it represented was soon to be relegated to the history books to become pure nostalgia, reminiscent of that bygone age.

Local boatmen, the Marshall brothers, prepare their sail-rigged Jolly Sailor *for another pleasure trip, c 1914.*

◆ CHAPTER 1 ◆

War Looms

One morning in July 1914, a loud and distant droning sound coming from the west caught the attention of fishermen on the beach, who began to search the distant, hazy horizon. Squinting through salty eyes, amazement spread over their leathery faces when a large, winged monster appeared in the sky, followed by another, and another, until there were four, all seaplanes, flying high above the water and approaching fast.

A minute or so later, the engine on the trailing aircraft faltered!

In a hasty descent it plunged into the sea just beyond the uncompleted Hotel Metropole (now Dolphin Lodge) at the bottom of Grand Avenue, casting water and spray up in the air.

The wrecked Naval seaplane No. 115 plunged into the sea off Grand Avenue after developing engine trouble on 22 July 1914.

Immediately, local watermen put off in a number of boats to rescue the two occupants, who, by then, sat perched on one of the aircraft's floats.

One of the other seaplanes turned back and circled over the damaged plane to ascertain that the two crew were in no immediate danger before the pilot continued flying eastward.

Some time later, the wrecked seaplane was towed into shallow water. The two ditched airmen introduced themselves as Leading Telegraphist Stirling, and Flight Commander Rathbone of the Royal Naval Air Service, who had been flying from Portsmouth to Felixstowe.

During the afternoon, a recovery flotilla consisting of a destroyer, a torpedo boat and an Admiralty tug arrived from Portsmouth, but they discovered that the seaplane was too badly damaged to be towed back to the Solent. Instead, it was dismantled during the evening by some local mechanics from Wades Garage in Chapel Road, who sent the engine and other valuable components onto Felixstowe by train.

Excitement grew that month, with the sighting of the Royal Navy's Home Battle Fleet off the Sussex coast. Hundreds of sightseers assembled on the seafront to watch eight vessels of the First Battle Squadron, which had sailed from Portsmouth, to dock at Brighton. When the flotilla reached Brighton, the ships dropped anchor, and ablaze with lights, they created a magnificently illuminated offshore spectacle after dark. Officers and crew enjoyed two days of festivities on shore before the vessels steamed on via Eastbourne before arriving in Deal.

At low tide crowds of people flocked around the wreckage under the watchful gaze of a local policeman.

As international hostilities in Europe increased dramatically, Admiral Sir John Jellicoe assumed supreme command of the Home Fleet.

By the end of July, the countdown to all-out war began, following Austria's declaration of war on Serbia. A scheduled debate in the House of Commons was postponed on account of the gravity of the European situation.

In a last futile attempt to prevent war, King George V sent a telegram to his cousin Czar Nicholas on 31July, but this failed to stop Germany declaring war on Russia the next day – Monday 1 August 1914.

- Sunday 2 August: British Fleet mobilised.
- Monday 3 August: Germany declared war against France; British Army mobilised.
- Tuesday 4 August: Germany invaded Belgium. A state of war came into being between Britain and Germany, and the Great British Empire was drawn into the conflict.

Meanwhile in Worthing, the Committee of Licensed Watermen met in a crisis session before announcing the postponement of their annual regatta.

To prepare for the war ahead, the government required 140,000 horses to be made immediately available for the war effort in Europe.

The Worthing requirement was directed by a Captain Prentice, who acted on instructions from London. A veterinary surgeon by the name of Percival Carter assisted in selecting the best local horses.

All kinds of horse-drawn vehicles were stopped in Worthing's streets. Carts, vans and wagons belonging to local tradesmen, and the horses were immediately removed from the shafts for inspection. Even private stables did not escape the far-reaching powers of Captain Prentice, they too were visited and subjected to the same scrutiny. Payment was made on the spot, and the horse owners ordered to take their animals to the Steyne School playing field in Brighton Road.

...the government required 140,000 horses to be made immediately available for the war effort in Europe...

Giving way to military priorities became the order of the day, such intrusions being accepted in patriotic spirit by the vast majority of Worthingites.

At the beginning of the war, Worthing had been blessed with hot, sunny weather, but as autumn approached, the weather deteriorated. Fierce gales uprooted trees on land and endangered shipping at sea.

In the midst of a severe storm on the morning of 15 November (1914), a barge was spotted in distress off Shoreham Harbour. Then shortly after 9 am,

Topical postcard of 1914 featuring the famous battleship.

a coastguard positioned on the pier head at Worthing observed a vessel about two miles or so east, off Lancing, dragging its anchor and being driven ashore by strong winds.

Spotting a distress signal flying from the mast, the coastguard notified the lifeboat authorities, whereupon chairman Hargood of the Worthing branch of the RNLI, immediately authorised the launching of the town's 13 year old lifeboat, the *Richard Coleman*.

At 9.30 am the mortar boomed, not just once as for routine quarterly practice, but twice, which meant an urgent call to duty. And before long, excited onlookers braved driving rain, and battled against a powerful south south-westerly gale blasting onshore to congregate on the promenade opposite the lifeboat house.

Those lifeboat crew who had been standing-by drew back the tall, heavy doors as quickly as they could, while other colleagues, on hearing the signal, arrived at the double to join them.

As so many horses had been whisked away for the war effort, man-power was the most practical alternative for pulling the lifeboat to the beach. With ample help from numerous volunteers, pulling on two lengthy ropes attached to its carriage, the lifeboat was hauled manually along the seafront towards the pier. Only too eager to help, no fewer than sixty two men volunteered for this back-breaking task.

Moving slowly at first, until the huge craftsmen-built boat and carriage weighing several tons, gathered momentum and they were soon rushing along.

With chains clanking, the carriage, with its important load, thundered up a purpose-built slope in front of the pier and onto the promenade.

There, the men succeeded in gradually slowing its impetus, bringing it to a halt; whereupon with the boat still securely chained, the carriage of wood and metal construction was reversed down the shelving, stony beach, simultaneously encouraged by an enthusiastic crowd, who had been following them the third of a mile from the boathouse.

Meanwhile, the haul-off rope on the pier had been rigged, passed through the pulley block, attached to the pierhead, and the end of the thick hemp hawser fastened to the bow of the *Richard Coleman*, in readiness for the launch.

High tide had peaked some 45 minutes earlier, but the uncaring, mighty breakers were still hurling themselves onto the beach, at a point where the flints met the smooth sand.

In spite of the gusting, forceful wind and a high, surging sea, the lifeboat was successfully hauled off its carriage and into the crashing breakers.

...the lifeboat was successfully hauled off its carriage and into the crashing breakers...

Inspired by the throng of spectators braving the elements, the lifeboat crew went forth on their mission, not knowing what they were to face.

The sail was soon set, and the lifeboat made off eastward towards the distressed sailing barge that was rolling in the heavy swell.

Many feared that the lifeboat would not reach the casualty in time!

Concerned onlookers hoped and prayed.

Suddenly, their prayers were answered. The wind changed direction, veering westerly, the crew of the barge hoisted the mainsail, and the coastguard

This grassland between the sea and the back of Beachfield was used by the Steyne School as part of their playing field

Catherine Marsh's Convalescent Home. which occupied the uniquely designed Beachfield in Brighton Road, was later demolished and the Aquarena swimming baths built.

THEN

The same grassland as top left being used for a games lesson by Steyne School...

NOW

...and as it is eighty seven years later, a boating pool next to the Aquarena swimming pool with New Parade in the distance.

breathed a sigh of relief as it drew away from the looming shore and out to sea.

From his position in the lifeboat, which was riding high on the crest of a wave one moment, and the next minute plunging to the depths of a trough, constantly surrounded by thick weather and rainy squalls, Coxswain Harry Marshall could not see the barge disappearing seaward.

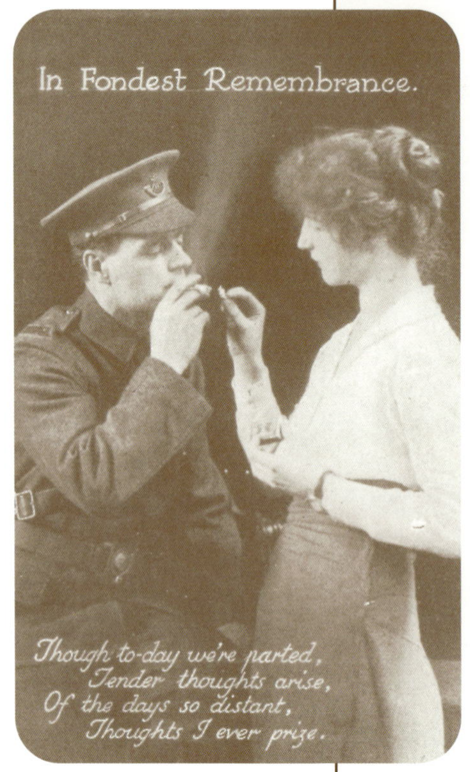

Following the declaration of the Great War, men enlisted in their droves and depended on postcards, such as this very apt one, to keep in touch with their loved ones

Ironically, the search continued to beyond the entrance to Shoreham Harbour, but finding no sign of a distressed vessel, the *Richard Coleman* sailed back to Worthing, returning ashore by the pier at 1.30 pm, having been at sea for almost four hours.

In the mean time, the Shoreham lifeboat, which had been launched some 30 minutes behind its neighbouring counterpart, found the barge, put five hands on board, and then escorted her to Newhaven Harbour.

At Worthing pier, it took the efforts of the vast number of assistants to haul up the *Richard Coleman* and reposition her on the carriage. No less than 63 volunteers each received 4s.6d. for their reliable services.

Four hours had elapsed since the firing of the lifeboat cannon, during which time it had been possible to obtain no less than the full complement of eight horses required for driving the carriage and lifeboat back to the boathouse. By 2.15 pm the *Richard Coleman* was re-stationed and made ready for the next maritime drama. A smith was brought in to oil and grease the carriage for which he was paid 4s.6d.

Under Coxswain Harry Marshall, a veteran of 15 services, and Second Coxswain Bill Blann, noted for his experience on 12 missions, were 11 other crewmen, all 13 were paid the standard rate of 15 shillings per man.

During the war, the Royal National Lifeboat Institution (RNLI) proved extremely effective around the British Isles. In the short period between 23 August and 12 November 1914, for example, lifeboats were launched on no fewer than 27 occasions to render assistance to His Majesty's ships and seaplanes, including *HMS Pathfinder*, *HMS Dryad*, *HMS Niger*, the hospital ship *Rohilla*, mine sweepers, Admiralty seaplanes, and a transport steamer, as well as fishing trawlers, two Belgian fishing boats, and other unknown vessels reported mined.

The lifeboat stations involved with these services were Broughty Ferry, Newhaven, St. Abbs, Margate, Harborough, Cromer, Lowestoft, Stromness, Hunstanton, Portrush, Greencastle, Tynemouth, Whitby, Robin Hoods Bay, Upgang, Scarborough, Teesmouth, Caister and North Deal.

A warm Worthing welcome in which the tall coastguard mast at the top of the beach can just be seen

Over the course of those 81 days, about 140 people were saved by the lifeboats, seven of which were among the first of the Institution's motor craft.

Meanwhile, defensive forces were on the alert for invaders from the English Channel. On Sunday 11 November, shots were fired at a fishing boat off Worthing. Harry Marshall and some fellow fishermen, night fishing in a small herring boat close in shore, had a close shave.

Using only a small lantern to guide them, they had been riding on their nets when London Territorials patrolling the beach spotted the rocking motion of their light. Their suspicion aroused, the soldiers challenged the boat.

There being no immediate response, the military opened fire. Four or five shots

Uniformed members of the Steyne School Cadets trained with a field gun on their playing field. (Behind the trees stands Beach House.)

THEN

Sports Day c 1914 for the Steyne School at their playing field some distance away in Brighton Road...

NOW

...now the site is occupied by the paddling pool next to the Aquarena.

skimmed over the fishermen's heads. Luckily no one was hit.

Brave Harry then risked his life wading ashore, only to find the Territorials waiting for him with fixed bayonets!

Together with his colleagues, he was marched off to the commanding officer, whereupon he explained he had in fact called out "friend" when challenged, and furthermore, had been unable to leave the fishing nets straight away, as their haul of fish would have been lost.

They were released, but expressed deep annoyance at the incident, contending that the military should have been aware they were only pursuing their livelihood.

Discussions to ease the situation for the town's boatmen were instigated by Harry Hargood, who looked after the interests of Worthing's seafarers. He met with the military authorities; and a satisfactory understanding as to future fishing was agreed.

All over the country, men enlisted for the Army and Navy Reserves. Hundreds of Worthing men joined-up. Tearful goodbyes were commonplace at the railway station as loved ones parted company.

Off to war to defend King and country, men from all classes and all walks of life came together in a united effort, the scale of which had never been seen before.

THEN

Chapel Road photographed from the Ann Street junction looking north in the direction of Wades Garage, whose entrance is marked by an advertisement on the side of an adjacent shop (detail above).

NOW

The same view today with Ann Street now cut off from Chapel Road by the Guildbourne Centre shopping precinct.

The Lavender Sanitary Laundry & Dry Cleaning Works in Ham Road with its staff of thirty three women and ten men.

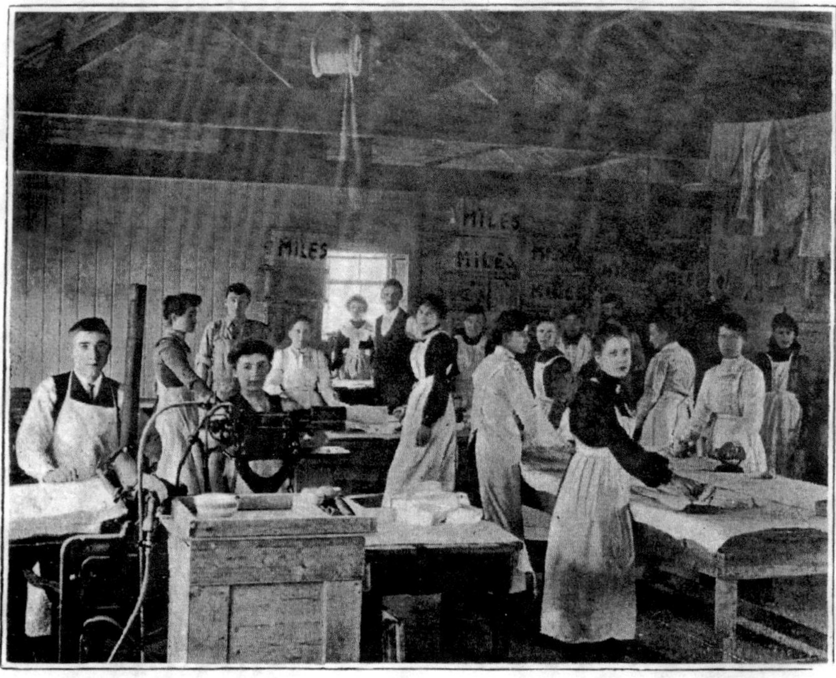

Inside the Lavender Laundry with the workers at their posts. An advertisement of the time claimed they used soft water, best quality soap and soda for the cleaning.

Lyndhurst Garage, Lyndhurst Road owned by Ernest Searle, opposite the original entrance to Worthing Hospital and near Park Road. The first taxis to be fitted with windscreens and roof racks.

An open-cockpit taxi and owner/driver Ernest Searle on a taxi rank by Worthing Pier and opposite advertising hoarding surrounding the site once occupied by the burnt out Royal Ho where The Arcade was to be built much later.

An aerial view of the town centre filmed from an early plane as it flew low over Worthing. The photograph dates after 1911 when the Dome, formally the Kursaal, was built (top left) and before 1925 when the two pier entrance kiosks were replaced by a pavilion.

Well-dressed workers holding the banner of The Workers' Union, Chichester & Worthing Districts.

THEN

NOW

Bridge Nursery with its glasshouses and beehives south of Ham Bridge Halt at East Worthing which has a wooden platform. The large house top left is today a rest home in Chesswood Road called Rosemary Mount, whereas the nursery has been developed into housing and is now Ashwood Close.

Feb 1915

◆ CHAPTER 2 ◆

DEATH ON DUTY! A LIFE FOR WHAT?

Terrible tragedies, occurring offshore from time to time, marred the serenity of life in the pleasant seaside town of Worthing.

On the afternoon of Wednesday 17 February, Worthingites faced another such grim reality after their gallant lifeboat crew had been beckoned towards the perils of the deep, reported the *Worthing Gazette*.

It had been an very rough morning. Mighty waves broke on the pebbled beach, while the wind continually howled around the coastguard station. Chief Officer Goldfinch, scanning the horizon through his telescope, glimpsed a westward bound schooner battling against the elements with most of its sails blown away.

She fought courageously against the south westerly gale, but by 1.35 pm, was driven shoreward out of control.

The lifeboat gun was fired twice in quick succession to muster the crew.

Simultaneously, it drew more people than usual to the seafront, for on this occasion the crowd included hundreds of soldiers billeted in the neighbourhood.

With no time to wait for horses, scores of soldiers, all heaving together on two

The Worthing Lifeboat Richard Coleman *barely visible as a fiercesome sea crashes over her, while a lone brave helper assists the launch from behind, photographed from the pier on 17 February 1915.*

Launching the Worthing Lifeboat Richard Coleman *in a rough sea. A band of strong men can be seen pushing her, while the haul-off rope from the pier head can be seen attached to the bow section; the dramatic scene being witnessed by a mass of people watching from the beach.*

long ropes, dragged the *Richard Coleman* on its carriage at a furious pace along the seafront and down to the launching point, east of the pier, in just ten minutes.

Warmheartedly praising the plucky lifeboatmen, who were facing the raging sea, protected only by their oilskins, kapok lifejackets and sou'westers, a young private remarked, "There's one advantage about our job, we've got a back door to get out of when things get too warm, but these chaps have no backway at all."

The rain was driving in, but the military helpers on the beach were not daunted. Others rushed onto the pier and laid hold of the haul-off warp.

With a force that had increased to almost hurricane strength, the wind roared through the iron framework supporting the pier. So rough was the sea, that to the watching crowd it seemed nigh impossible that any craft could survive.

As the tide peaked, waves broke with tremendous force on the beach and lashed furiously at the carriage. With considerable difficulty the lifeboat was launched – the command was given, and it eased off the carriage amid loud cheering from the soldiers, many of whom had never before witnessed such a scene, and were proud of the privilege. But then she grounded!

There she lay, being battered by the merciless, foaming waves. Conditions couldn't have been much worse. A couple of waves forced the boat around until she was almost broadside on. Excitement grew keener.

One moment she was on the crest of a breaker, the next she lay high and dry on the pebbles, but the soldiers stuck to their task.

Each time a spent breaker was sucked back into the sea, the soldiers enthusiastically rushed forward, wading into the water up to their shoulders in their struggle to get the boat off.

Then, the sea grew even angrier, wildly buffeting the rescue craft. A large wave came, and with many willing hands, the *Richard Coleman* took to the sea.

Such a melodramatic launch, yet only a quarter of an hour had elapsed since the lifeboat had left its station.

Determinedly all pulling together, the crew at the oars, and the helpers on the pier grasping the tow rope, the lifeboat was propelled past the pier head under the skilful command of Coxswain Marshall.

...so rough was the sea that to the watching crowd it seemed nigh impossible that any craft could survive...

The schooner Kings Hill *stranded at Goring on 17 February 1915; its crew survived but in a futile rescue attempt one lifeboatman was lost.*

Sails were quickly hoisted and the 35 foot long craft tacked westward into the prevailing wind, cheered on by the rain-sodden crowd, as it disappeared into the mist.

It was then, a question of anxious waiting for all those on the shore and lining the pier.

Coxswain Marshall later took up the story from this point: "I was continually cautioning the crew to hang onto the lifelines. Under the sea she went, taking it on the broadside all the time – and a tremendous sea it was too. The water flooded in and out like a sieve. The boat was full of water many times, but she emptied herself again." (As the automatic valve and pump system came into action.)

Harry had never had such a rough trip in all his 18 years experience as coxswain, and had not expected to get home alive.

In the treacherous conditions the boat made slow progress, so slow that after an hour at sea they were only about a mile and a half west south-west of the pier.

"All of a sudden an extraordinary big sea bore down on us. 'Hold onto your lifelines and attend to the sheets,' I bellowed, but it was too late! The gigantic wave swallowed us, boat an' all. The boat capsized, throwing us all into the water, all except one – my second coxswain, Bill Blann, who managed to secure a hold on the mizzen mast."

Being of the self-righting type, the boat immediately began to right herself.

"We scrambled back into the boat as best we could, then another huge sea broke over her. She capsized again, flinging us into the swirling sea once more.

When it righted itself again, I was thrown on the weather side, and the ruddy boat went right over me. The others were now on the opposite side of the boat, most managing to cling on, so that as she quickly came up again they too were brought up. As she did so, Bill Blann was still there hanging on to the mizzen mast (having been submerged, to complete a full circle back to the upright position). I could see the others managing to regain the boat, but I couldn't reach it. I was being swept away by the current! The next thing I know, a lifeline comes hurtling towards me, cast by Bill Blann. He saved my life."

Safely in the boat once more, Harry looked around and asked if all the crew were there, but one was missing – Burgess.

He was spotted more than 150 yards away. How could they reach him?

Everything was in disarray, all the oars had washed out, ropes entangled, and the sails had dropped and were hanging down. The lifeboat was all adrift. They tried to drop anchor but it was fouled. The running gear too had been rendered useless. The crew were frustrated at not being able to help their comrade, but at least his life jacket was keeping him afloat.

The *Richard Coleman* was being driven shoreward with oars floating adrift, but by the time they had recovered some to propel the boat, Burgess had gone.

...she capsized again, flinging us into the swirling sea once more...

Somehow, the distressed crew managed to re-establish some sort of control over the disabled lifeboat and headed for home.

Watching from the west side of the pier, an anxious crowd could see a vessel's masts in the distance – the original casualty, the schooner, by this time stranded at Goring. The returning lifeboat also came into view, just after 4 pm when the sea had calmed considerably.

As the lifeboat approached, its bowman lit a green flare as an indication of their return to the signalman standing on the beach, before the ailing *Richard Coleman* came ashore off West Street at 5 pm. Helpful soldiers once again eagerly rushed to assist, pulling the boat up the beach with a heavy rope.

Staggering from cramp and minor injuries, the lifeboat crew seemed broken to a man. Only twelve of the thirteen crew had returned.

Asked who was missing, a shaky voice answered, "Little Jack!"

Numb, and blue from the cold, their grim faces concealed the awful truth of what happened at sea.

It transpired that luckless Jack Burgess had been spotted drifting in the shallows some miles west of the town at 3.15 pm, and given urgent artificial respiration while dry clothes and blankets were sent down from the nearest house.

Doctor Morton had been sent for, and arrived at speed in his motor car.

After injecting powerful restoratives and continuing resuscitation attempts for a whole hour, the doctor could still find no pulse.

Edward Jack Burgess was dead!

His life was sacrificed in an attempt to save the four crew of the marooned schooner *Kings Hill*, who, in the end, managed to save themselves.

One had jumped overboard before the vessel, bound for Bideford with a cargo of 180 tons of manure packed in bags, had grounded. Rescued by some Territorials of the County of London Cyclist Regiment, stationed at Goring, he was taken to the old Goring Coastguard Station to recover. The remaining three stayed on board until low tide and then walked ashore across the Goring sands.

This postcard, produced in 1915 to commemorate the tragic death of lifeboatman Jack Burgess, made use of an earlier photograph when he was younger.

Worthing folk, deeply aroused by the bravery of Burgess (aged 37) and his fellow lifeboatmen, clearly demonstrated their feelings at his funeral when thousands lined the streets.

At a slow pace, the cortège left the Burgess home in Chandos Road to travel the short distance to Christ Church in Grafton Road. Recognised as the fishermen's church, the coffin, draped with the Union Jack, was placed inside for the service there.

Family mourners included his brother Gunner James Burgess and his brother-in-law Private William Harrison of the 2nd Royal Sussex Regiment, both in uniform.

Harrison, hobbling on crutches, had only recently returned from Netley Hospital where he'd had a leg amputated as a result of a war wound.

Following behind were not only the lifeboatmen with whom Burgess had been serving on that fateful day, but also the reserve crew.

At the cemetery in South Farm Road, many were unable to conceal their emotion, and very few eyes remained dry.

Innumerable, beautiful wreaths were placed on the ground in the vicinity of the boatman's last resting place, including floral tributes from Worthing Borough Fire Brigade, the town's Theatre Royal, and the Ethel Marie fishing party.

Meanwhile, the grounded *Kings Hill* was secured and its cargo removed.

Attempts to pull the stricken schooner out to sea with two motor boats failed, and it wasn't until 15 days after the fatal accident that she was eventually floated and towed to Littlehampton by the tug *Jumna*, hired for £4 an hour plus salvage rights.

The drowned Jack Burgess, or 'Jacko' as he was known by some, left a wife and four children without any financial support.

To offset the bereaved family's hardship, a local fund was opened by the Mayor, Alderman J White, JP, and simultaneously, the Worthing Gazette launched another appeal.

In addition, money was raised by individuals and organisations from all quarters of the community. Charity concerts brought in more cash.

Soldiers billeted in the town contributed over £100, bringing the total for the joint appeal to over £190.

The RNLI itself, awarded a further £250 directly to the dependants, and at the same time, presented Coxswain Marshall with its thanks inscribed on vellum, for the skilful manner in which he had handled the lifeboat in such severe weather conditions. They also granted an extra 10 shillings to each crewman on account of the arduous nature of their service, in addition to the double pay of 30 shillings that each crewman had already received.

On the seafront, a small flag, flying at half mast, fluttered in the breeze over a fisherman's 'box' which bore 'Jacko's name. For many years he had been a licensed waterman, in partnership with Harry Smith, their stand being immediately west of the bandstand. 'Jacko' had been a familiar figure on the seafront, where he had often been seen, from early spring to late autumn, attending his craft, both as a fisherman and a boatman. At other times, he had busied himself making his own nets, a sight which attracted many passers-by, to watch the intricacies of his craft.

In earlier days, when galley racing had been a feature of south coast regattas, 'Jacko' had been in demand as a coxswain, his many victories having led to him being sought after not just by local teams but even those as far away as Dover.

Latterly, to supplement his income from the sea, Jacko had been working on the erection of huts at Shoreham Camp. Ironically, had it not been pouring with rain on that fateful Wednesday morning, he would have been over there, and not available for the lifeboat.

Although 'Jacko' was the first Worthing lifeboatman to die at sea whilst on service, his was in fact the third death connected with the Worthing lifeboat since the RNLI took over the station in 1865.

The first, crewman George Riddles, had collapsed and died from a heart attack during an exercise in 1892. Three years later, lifeboatman Charles Lambeth had been run over and killed by the boat carriage whilst rushing to a rescue.

...innumerable, beautiful wreaths were placed on the ground in the vicinity of the boatman's last resting place...

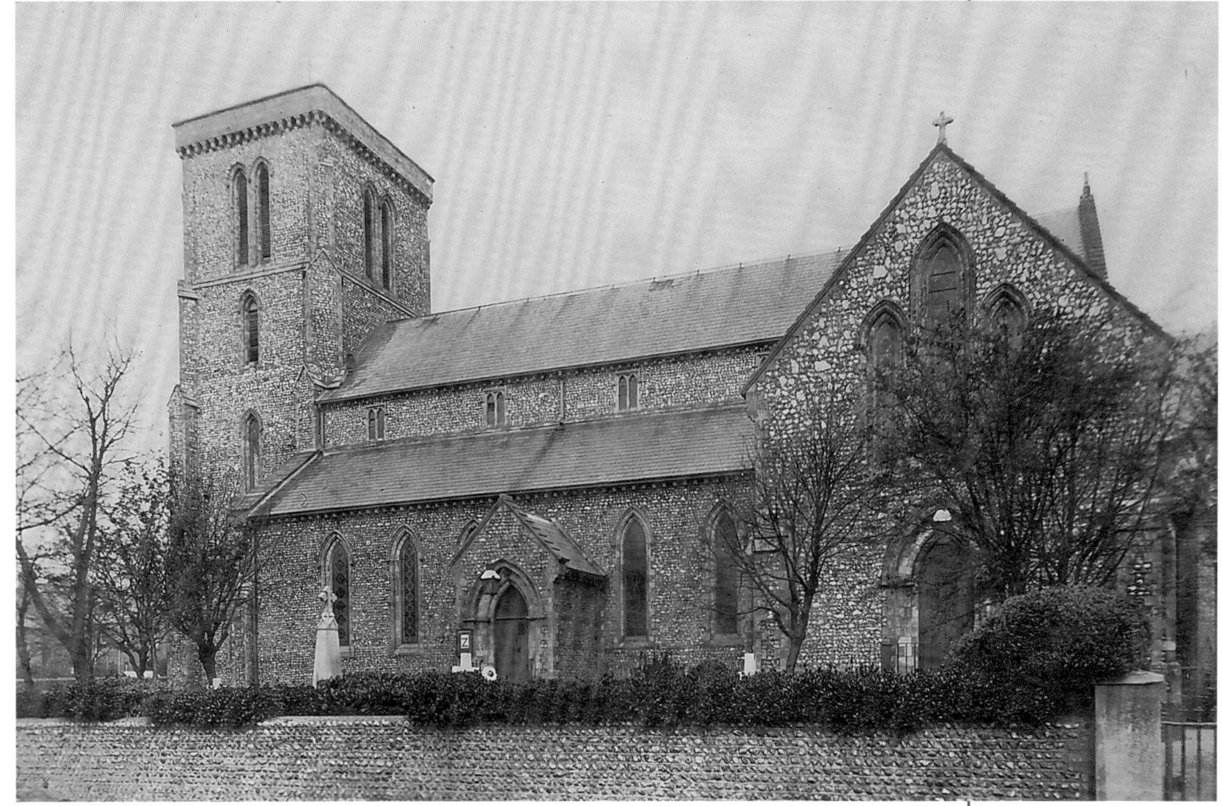

Worthing's Christ Church, Grafton Road, the town's traditional 'Fishermen's Church' where the funeral service for professional waterman and lifeboatman Jack Burgess was held in 1915

The interior of Christ Church where Jack Burgess's flag-draped coffin was placed for the memorial service in 1915

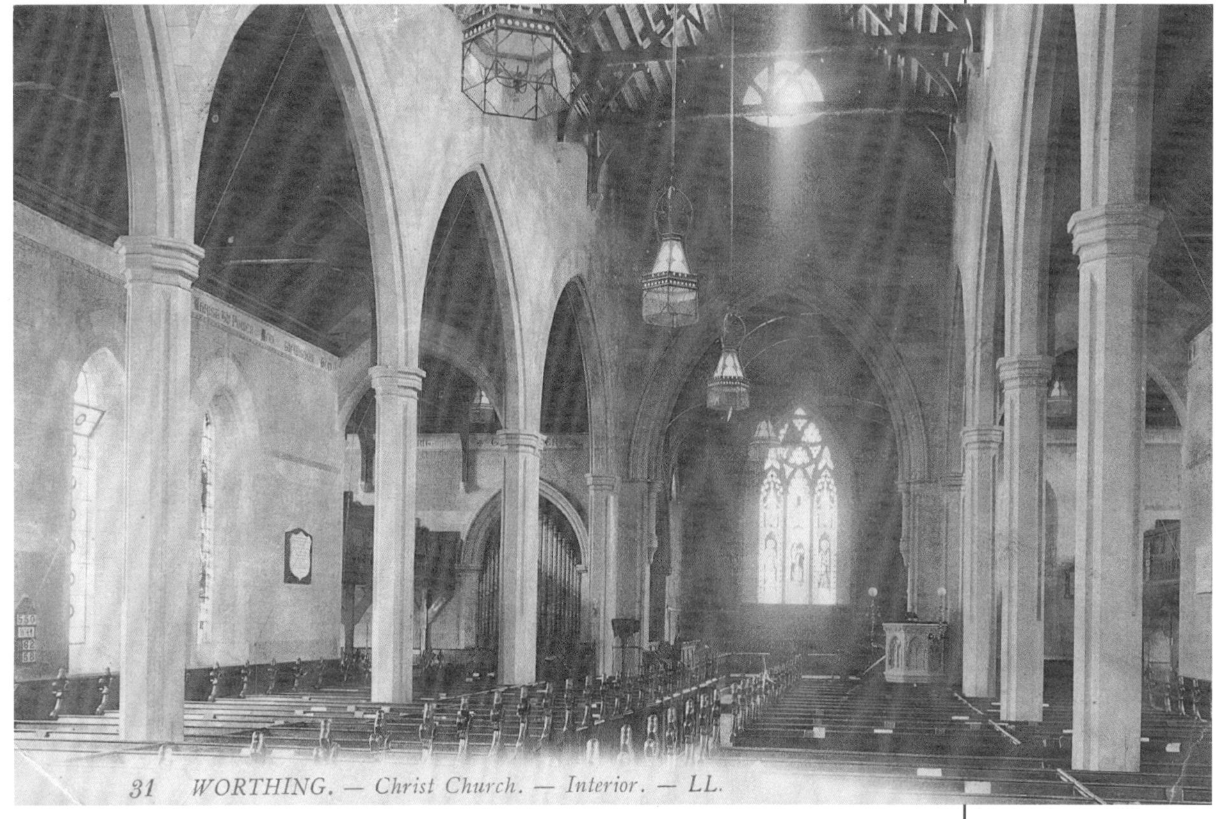

It was a sad coincidence that the late Lambeth had been the uncle of both the drowned Burgess and Harrison the amputee.

Troops stationed in the town had become so involved with the *Richard Coleman* and its crew, that two of the soldiers wrote a heartfelt poem dedicated to 'Jacko':

On the Front about mid-day in Worthing
Was a sight which one ne'er will forget;
At the sound of the mortar booming,
'Twas a signal, that there was a wreck.
Up ran the lads, with assistance,
As a call for the lifeboat was sent,
And a cheer went up as the gallant crew
Out to sea on their mission they went.

A family is now sorrowing silently,
Through our great and restless sea,
Which has taken from among them
A heart that was fearless and free.
He answered his call to duty
At a risk, it was thrilling to watch,
But was swept back to the land which he dwelt on.
Another life, for a life, that was lost.

W D and G G (of the Buffs)

On hearing about the tragedy, news reporters descended on the town. A journalist from London interviewed Coxswain Marshall and Second Coxswain Blann in the lifeboat house.

Climbing a ladder to the upstairs storeroom, Harry beckoned the newspaper man to follow. Standing in the room and surrounded by lifeboat gear, Harry gazed seaward through the window in the lookout turret and exclaimed, "My God it was rough out there!

With what's happened recently, and with the saving of 50 people over the 50 years that we've had an RNLI station here, you can see the necessity of keeping a lifeboat at Worthing."

Since being founded in 1824, the RNLI, as a national organisation, had been responsible for saving a grand total of 52,600 lives during its 91 years up to 1915. Of that figure, almost 1,000 had been rescued during the previous year alone, following the outbreak of war.

The entrance to Broadwater Cemetery in South Farm Road where boatman Jack Burgess was laid to rest surrounded by many wreaths and a multitude of moist eyes.

Soldiers like these billeted in Worthing during World War I hauled the lifeboat to its launching point when the maroon was fired.

Detailed close-up of three of the soldiers.

THEN

NOW

Broadwater Road looking north...

...towards The Downs.

The business card of Otto Brown, amusement caterer.

ENDLESS AMUSEMENT will be had if you
HIRE YOUR GAMES
From **OTTO BROWN,** Amusement Caterer,
Prospect Place Works, Worthing.

LARGE VARIETY OF HIGH-CLASS GAMES ON HIRE
— FOR —
Fetes, Galas, Flower Shows, & Carnivals,

Greyhound Racing, Loop Ball, Bubbles, Roll Ups, Darts, Skeeball, Electric Treasure Hunt, Electric Boards, Etc.

FETES ATTENDED. TERMS ON REQUEST.

THEN

Pictured here at the east side of the pier entrance is an amusement stall featuring a new game called Climbing Monkeys. It was owned by Otto Brown who was also a popular photographer of the time, the shed (far left) being a studio where he photographed holidaymakers and day-trippers.

NOW

The same view today, showing the Pier Pavilion (now called the Pavilion Theatre) which replaced the two entrance kiosks.

The bandstand enclosure (today called The Lido) with its original rectangular bandstand, which replaced the earlier birdcage bandstand.

A circus elephant being exercised on Worthing beach.

Children enjoying pony rides on the beach sand at low tide. The top of the original birdcage bandstand can be seen rising from behind the bandstand shelter (top left).

A local haulage contractor, Alfred O. Dell of Ruskin Road, driving his lorry in Poulters Lane, then known as Leafy Lane. Note the solid tyres and the spoked front wheels.

OPPOSITE PAGE:
Detail showing name and address on the side of his vehicle.

THEN

Durrington Lane looking south towards the thatch-roofed St Mary's Farmhouse (centre)...

NOW

...which still stands today, although the thatch has been replaced with tiles.

51. RUSKIN ROAD
BROADWATER
SUSSEX

THEN

Broadwater Street West looking south towards Broadwater School situated on the corner of Broadwater Green...

THEN

Durrington Lane looking north with a glasshouse nursery on the right.

NOW

NOW

...and the same view today.

THEN

Selden Terrace & Cleveland Terrace, Brighton Road, Worthing. 179

Brighton Road looking east from near where the Aquarena stands today. The glasshouses near the centre of the picture belonged to Feest, a local greengrocer.

NOW

1915-1916

◆ CHAPTER 3 ◆

Effects of War

Celebrating its jubilee year in 1915, the Worthing Branch of the RNLI boasted a particularly fine fund-raising record at its annual meeting.

Since its inception on 7 March 1865, the Branch had achieved the accolade of becoming one of the country's top fund-raisers. Worthing's contributions to the Institution's central funds had increased by a staggering 900% during the branch's 50 years, compared to the amount received at headquarters from all branches, which showed an increase of just 400% over the same period.

Well done Worthing!

Over the course of those same 50 years, the town's lifeboatmen had saved no fewer than 50 lives.

Held in the spacious lounge of Warne's seafront hotel, that year's annual meeting was addressed by a number of notable speakers including Sir Godfrey Baring, Bart, MP, a member of the (national) Committee of Management who had nothing but praise for the town: "We always regard Worthing as a model branch," he said, and continued, "in fact Worthing is model in everything, including its Corporation and its sunshine record." (A reference to 'Sunny Worthing'.)

Speaking of the effects of the war on the work of the Institution, he said, "The darkening of shore lights and the infamous policy of the German government in scattering mines indiscriminately has caused the number of lifeboat service launches to be abnormally large."

The country's lifeboatmen had risen to the occasion with patriotic fervour, manning the fleet of lifeboats dotted around Great Britain, which at that time totalled 267.

The meeting was chaired by Harry Hargood. The son of an admiral, he had made a life-long study of things nautical, and the cause of the lifeboat always claimed his close attention, for not only was he Branch Chairman, but he too, was a member of the (national) Committee of Management, which met regularly in London.

No-one was respected more by the coxswain and crew than the energetic chairman, who took a practical interest, for it was said that no launch, whether for service or practice, took place without Mr Hargood being on the beach to see the boat off, even in the roughest weather.

Philanthropic Mr. Harry Hargood, JP also devoted time to organise large fund-raising events in Worthing for another needy cause – the provision of comforts for wounded soldiers.

The number of injured being brought back to England increased dramatically in 1915. Temporary hospitals were set up, including one near Chichester – the West Sussex County Asylum at Graylingwell. Taken over by the War Office it was to look after thousands of casualties throughout the several years of bloodshed.

As well as being chairman of the hospital committee, industrious Harry Hargood, JP sat on the local Bench.

Convictions for drunkenness went down from 49 in 1914, to 30 in 1915, reduced to an average of little more than one person per thousand of Worthing's population. Yet only half were residents, the others being tramps.

Although drink abuse and related crimes were decreasing from their peak before the war, it may be surprising to learn that one third of all drunks were women!

Not only hampered by the familiar pattern of unsettled weather, sea fisheries were badly affected for the first part of the war by an Admiralty ban on most night fishing as well as a shortage of men due to enlistment in the Forces.

In an attempt to ease the situation, Worthing fishermen, in the latter part of 1915, won a concession following consultations between the Sussex Fishery Officer and the Admiralty Commander for the West Sussex District, whereby it was agreed to permit them to stand by their trammel nets at night – but only when their nets were endangered during bad weather. Not surprisingly, the compromise did little good, for many local boats were still unable to fish.

By contrast, the smaller boats which could be used for drift net fishing had a record season; and trawl net fishing, when the boats managed to get out, did remarkably well.

In November 1915, fishermen engaged in the herring season, took advantage of some particularly fine weather and brought in some rather large

Wartime restrictions on fishing were slightly eased when Worthing fishermen won a meagre concession from the Admiralty in 1915. Pictured here on the Blann stand are Harry, on the left and Bill, second from right, with the West Buildings turn off behind.

...it may be surprising to learn that one third of all drunks were women...

catches. Some prospered exceedingly well and secured a 'last' (11,000 herrings) at a catch, yet others managed only 1500 or even just 800 fish, which at other times would have been considered quite an achievement.

Despatched to different parts of the country, the fish fetched very good prices – as much as double the local market prices in some cases – earning between £60 and £70 a share for the luckier fishermen, an unexpected wartime bonus.

News of Worthing's windfall travelled fast. Three large buyers arrived on Worthing beach from Portsmouth to take part in the bidding, and an army lorry was sent down from the camp at Witley to collect fish for the soldiers. But alas, their journeys were wasted, for the next morning the fishing boats came in carrying very poor results – only a fraction of the previous large catches.

The Richard Coleman *returning from an exercise under sail and being hauled up wooden skids placed on the beach. Skids were used from 1916 onwards.*

Sprat fishing, with drift nets, met with poorer results than the previous season, and attempts to catch sprats with seine nets were a complete failure in 1915, mainly because of the unpredictable weather.

Other types of fishing – crab, lobster, prawn, seine net fishing for round and flat fish, as well as hook fishing – all met with unsatisfactory results, mainly because stormy south-westerly gales had disturbed the fish.

On the brighter side, river fishing for shellfish showed signs of a fair season, as a good supply of oysters and winkles were taken. Large numbers of people were engaged in gathering the winkles, providing work at an otherwise lean time of year.

An incident involving alleged 'dishonesty' in December 1915, resulted in a veteran fisherman suffering a heart attack whilst hiding timber found on the beach.

Seventy three year old Edward William Edwards, a senior member of one of Worthing's old seafaring families was collecting flotsam from the beach where considerable quantities of planking and other wreckage had washed ashore. Most of the timber was collected and stored under the supervision of the coastguard, but canny Edwards managed to secrete some to his home at Hillview, in Tarring Road, where he hurriedly sawed it up to stack it away from prying eyes. Tragically, while putting the wood away, he fell down and died almost immediately. Dr Howard of West Tarring was called in, but he had expired before he could save his life.

The Edwards family had been engaged in the fishing industry since well before the *Lalla Rookh* disaster of 1850 when two of Edward Edwards' forebears were among 11 drowned off Worthing, a terrible tragedy that had led to the setting up of the town's very first lifeboat establishment.

During 1916, an alternative method of launching the lifeboat was tried.

Difficulty and delay had been experienced since the regular horses, employed for the *Richard Coleman,* had been commandeered at the beginning of the war. Substitute horses did not show the same willingness to face the difficult task of entering a stormy sea.

Experimenting without horses, wooden skids were placed over the sloping, stony beach as an improvised slipway. When released from its carriage, the lifeboat

Soldiers on duty in Montague Street, photographed from Surrey Street.

Indian Wounded
at Worthing.

Wounded Indian soldiers, hailed as heroes, line up for a photo call in Montague Street, Worthing, where the Empire defenders were on a day out from Brighton's Royal Pavilion which had been set up as a temporary hospital specifically for the many hundreds of injured Indian troops.

Overington's on the corner of Salvington Road and Durrington Hill when it was a blacksmiths. It later became a garden and hardware shop and a lawnmower repair workshop was added behind. The premises have since been converted into residential accommodation.

Luff's sweet shop in Broadwater Street West, famous for its delicious home-made sweets, fulfilled orders from home and abroad.

THEN **NOW**

South Street looking towards the Pier; Montague Street is to the right.

Tarring Road looking west towards West Worthing Station with Down View Terrace of shops on the left and an undeveloped area on the right, filled with beautiful trees and backing onto the railway line, an area on which shops called New Broadway were to be built in the 1930s .

Goring Lane looking south towards the level crossing with mature elm trees lining the west side of the road.

Ferring Street looking south-east towards the war memorial opposite the garage which is now John Cooper's.

Well-known fishmonger F Stubbs' delivery van parked outside his Montague Street shop.

THEN **NOW**

Looking west along Salvington Road, the John Selden Inn (Right) stands on the corner of Half Moon Lane.

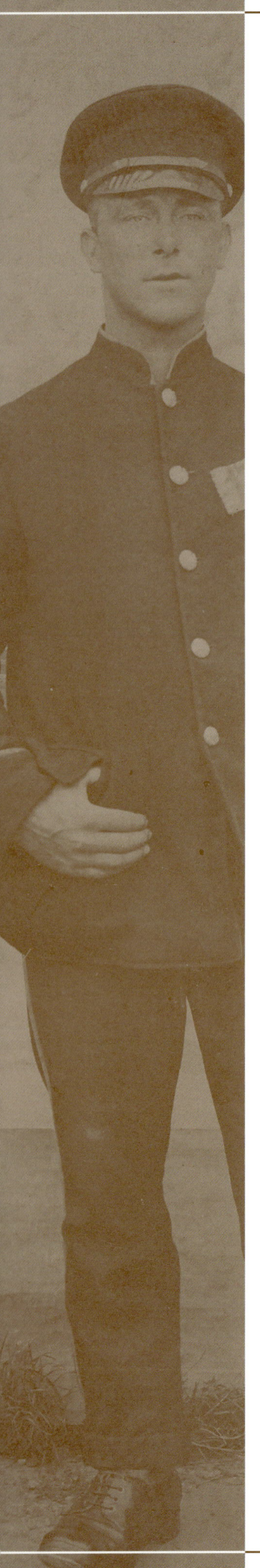

1918-1920

◆ CHAPTER 4 ◆

PEACE IN A CHANGING WORLD

Many skirmishes took place in the Channel during the four years of the 'Great War', resulting in a host of sunken steamships doomed to lie amongst their former wind-propelled counterparts rotting on the seabed.

Of those First World War casualties, probably the nearest to Worthing is the wreck of the *Shirala* about five miles off Littlehampton.

On 2 July 1918, the British India steamship had been bound for India carrying general freight and a cargo of ammunition, together with a few passengers. Weather conditions were described as perfect that afternoon as she steamed along the Channel.

On 2 July 1918 the British steamship Shirala, *bound for India carrying general freight and a cargo of ammunition, together with a few passengers was torpedoed and sank off Littlehampton.*

Using the 'safer' inshore route recommended by the Admiralty, and tactically manouevring to avoid possible enemy torpedoes, Captain E G Murray Dickinson was oblivious to the German submarine UB 57 that was already tailing them.

Captain of the U-boat, Ober-Leutnant Johann Lohs, had the Shirala firmly in his periscope sights.

At 5.12 pm, without warning, a torpedo blasted into the 5,306 ton steel British ship. The stricken vessel was soon spotted by an airship, fortunately a British one patrolling the Channel, which wirelessed for help. The message was answered and several small naval craft went to the scene to pick up survivors, resulting in what must have ranked among the first 'air-sea rescues' to have ever taken place.

Buckled amidship until bow and stern rose out of the water, it was almost an hour before the crippled steamship finally disappeared below the surface.

Eight of her crew were killed in the attack.

Four long years of bitter and bloody hostilities finally came to an end on 11 November 1918 when an Armistice with Germany was signed by Marshall Foch and Admiral Wemyss for the Allies.

In front of Worthing Town Hall, which was still in South Street at that time, a large crowd gathered. As the Mayor announced the wonderful news from the top of the steps, the excited crowd at first fell silent in remembrance until three rousing cheers were called for the King. Citizens began to celebrate, flags appeared and a great sense of victory was in the air.

Events were organised, such as aquatic sports which included 'Walking the Greasy Pole' and high diving competitions off the pierhead.

Six hundred and sixty-nine Worthing men had been killed in the 1914–18 war.

The most prominent reminder of the Borough's great sacrifice can be seen at the corner of Chapel Road and Stoke Abbot Road – the municipal memorial crafted in Portland stone and surmounted by a life-size bronze statue of a British soldier.

Two other memorials can also be found in the town. One , a beautiful alabaster stone tablet made by stonemason Francis Tate of North Street (the firm survives today) is to be found inside Christ Church, on the west wall close to the main entrance from Portland Road. The other, a brass plate, is at Worthing Football Club in Woodside Road, and is inscribed with the names of 17 of its members who died in the armed services between 1914 and 1918. Both were officially unveiled by Mr H Hargood OBE, JP, a Deputy Lord Lieutenant of the county, and a man of many public interests.

The RNLI, which had played a significant role throughout the war in rescuing survivors in home waters, had also helped save no fewer than 179 ships and their vital freight, including many cargoes of important food supplies. Around the coast, the vigilant lifeboat crews saved a total of 5,200 personnel from distressed sea-going vessels, as well as another 22 from ditched aircraft.

The Worthing Branch was advised to be extra vigilant in the months ahead. At its annual meeting in 1919, the Mayor, Alderman J Farquarson-Whyte, warned the station to be ready to render assistance to vessels damaged by mines, and indicated the probability of increased calls on the lifeboat as flying boat services developed.

Held on Thursday afternoon, 8 May, at the Connaught Hall, the meeting saw a special honour bestowed upon Mr Harry Hargood. A committee member for over

...at 5.12 pm without warning, a torpedo blasted into the 5,306 ton steel British ship...

The Richard Coleman, *drawn by six horses lent by local hauliers Hall & Co, was the main attraction in a parade on Worthing's very first Lifeboat Flag Day, 2 August 1919, held as part of a national appeal to raise funds for 50 motor lifeboats. The procession is seen moving along the seafront towards the lifeboat house.*

half a century and its chairman for more than forty years, Mr Hargood was unanimously elected president. Although into his seventies by this time, the energetic Mr Hargood remained on the (national) Committee of Management.

As part of a national appeal to raise funds for 50 motor lifeboats, Worthing's very first Lifeboat Flag Day took place on 2 August 1919.

The highlight of the day's proceedings was a procession through the town, and in particular the sturdy *Richard Coleman*, fully manned and drawn by six horses kindly lent by local hauliers Hall & Co. Thousands of enthusiastic supporters lined the streets.

On passing the seafront bandstand, the lifeboatmen were patriotically acknowledged by the Royal Engineers playing there, who struck up Rule Britannia. At the Town Hall, the procession marched past a number of dignitaries, including the Mayor and the Bishop of London.

Hard working ladies went throughout the Borough and surrounding villages collecting donations. Over 30,000 cardboard badges, decorated with brass and silk trimmings ordered for the occasion quickly ran out, and a further supply had to be telegraphed for from the manufacturers.

The response was truly magnificent, the day's activities, which included a charity concert, realised a total sum in excess of £250 for lifeboat funds.

...over 30,000 cardboard badges decorated with brass and silk trimmings ordered for the occasion quickly ran out...

One crewman's lengthy period of serving on the lifeboat drew to a close at the end of 1919. After 22 years as Worthing coxswain, Harry Marshall retired, having spent most of his life on the boat in one way or another. Before being made up to coxswain in 1897 he had served a period of six years as second coxswain.

Granted a pension by the Institution, the retiring coxswain was honoured by the RNLI with a double presentation in recognition of his many years of devoted service. He was presented with a framed certificate on vellum, and an aneroid barometer at the Branch's annual meeting in 1920, presented to him by the Mayoress.

From this time, Second Coxswain Bill Blann, at the mature age of 59, took over command of the *Richard Coleman*. (It is interesting to note that the retirement age on today's all weather lifeboats is 55, and on open inshore rescue boats it is even lower at 40.)

On 12 April 1920, Bill's leadership was put to the test in a curious rescue bid where no sooner did the stricken sailors board the lifeboat, than they clambered back onto their distressed vessel.

Weather conditions were appalling. By 6.30 am, the duty coastguard had spotted a barque-rigged sailing ship in trouble. Some four miles west of Worthing pier and about a mile offshore, the eastbound barque was experiencing considerable difficulty in the prevailing conditions. It tried to put about, but failed, then dropped her anchors, but it was too late, she was aground in the shallows off Ferring.

At 7.00 am the lifeboat mortar was fired. A quick turnout of lifeboatmen and willing helpers, despite a drenching south south-easterly downpour, pulled the *Richard Coleman* along to the pier where it was launched at 7.30 am.

The lifeboat reached the beleaguered vessel at 8.30 am, which turned out to be the *Pierre Antonine* of Naples, of about 1,500 tons and in ballast.

On reaching her, bowman Harry Blann threw a line to the stricken crew, who then set about pulling the *Richard Coleman* alongside. All wearing lifebelts, the stranded sailors started to abandon ship.

One sailor got in the lifeboat and two others descended a rope ladder over the side of the vessel until the captain espied a tug approaching from the east.

He instantly recalled his crew from the lifeboat, which then took the end of the tug's towing hawser to the marooned ship. At 1.00 pm, the tug, the *Alert* from Newhaven, succeeded in floating the Italian ship and towed it away eastward.

Mission accomplished, the *Richard Coleman* sailed back to Worthing.

During the day, the veteran president of the Worthing branch, Mr Hargood, had been in attendance at the station, true to his tradition, despite his advancing years.

Compelled to find an alternative to horses available prior to the First World War, the RNLI selected the Worthing lifeboat to experiment with tractor-drawing in May 1920, watched by many sightseers from the pier and on the beach.

The 13 crewmen, half of them having been on active service for the first time, each received 12s 6d, while no fewer than 43 volunteers were paid 3s 6d per man for helping to launch and later haul-up the lifeboat, a signalman who had been on duty for over eight hours got 6s 6d.

A total of £15 19s 6d was spent on this service, one that was to be the last to a large sailing vessel.

Not only in Worthing, but throughout the country, obtaining horses suitable for drawing lifeboats to their launching spots and into the sea, had become so difficult with the advancement of motor transport, that the RNLI was compelled to experiment with motor traction. Trials on the east coast with a 35 hp tractor proved that motive power on open sandy beaches could be adopted to replace horses, but the usefulness of a tractor on a stony beach was still an unknown entity.

To this end, Worthing was selected for an experiment in May 1920, under the watchful gaze of many of the Institution's top brass as well as the Chief Inspector of the Dutch Lifeboat Society.

Hundreds of sightseers gathered on the east side of the pier and on the promenade in front of the Dome Cinema to watch. Film operators and press photographers came down from London. So many people swelled the crowd that a large number of police were required to keep control, under the charge of Superintendent Pennicott and Inspector White.

Trials commenced, but problems soon arose. The *Richard Coleman* and its carriage, together weighing about eight tons, became embedded in the stones and had to be pulled out by volunteers. When the lifeboat and carriage eventually reached the sands, the wheels sank to such a depth that the boat had to be taken off before the carriage could be dug out.

Not the favourable outcome anticipated, it was abundantly clear that whatever the success on the east coast the tractor would not replace the old method of launching at Worthing, or anywhere with a similar beach.

Worthing's stony beach had coped with large boats in the past. There was a time in the 19th century when thirty luggers would go out from Worthing, each carrying six men and a boy, and come back laden with fish. The fishing industry had flourished at Worthing, but by 1920 only about 19 boats took part in the herring fishing.

Another great change by this time was that fishing was only local, not like the old days when Worthing had been one of the chief centres on the south coast for

The tractor trials went badly, lifeboat and carriage got stuck in the stones and had to be pulled out by oilskin-clad lifeboatmen and other volunteers on the beach opposite the Dome Cinema.

deep sea fishing, when boats went as far as Plymouth or even Penzance to catch mackerel, and to Yarmouth and Lowestoft for herrings. Motor and steam boats were largely responsible for the demise.

It was a similar story with prawn-trawling. Whereas some eight or nine boats used to engage in prawn-trawling, only the odd boat ventured out on this enterprise in 1920. But it wasn't due to poor fish stocks, there were no lack of prawns in 1920. Mackerel, herrings, lobsters, bass and mullet were all plentiful as well, while near the remains of the Indiana wreck off Worthing, there were any amount of whiting. Despite this abundance of stock, Worthing's lucrative fishing industry declined because of the poor returns offered to fishermen, who received little money for such a hard-working life.

Photographed by his captors in a German POW camp, former fisherman and lifeboat crewman Bill Blann junior died there during the closing days of the First World War after Harry Blann in Clifton Road received this photographic card with the simple message 'My dearest uncle and aunt from your ever loving nephew Bill, xxx'.

Costs had increased tremendously. Before the First World War, a net would cost £1 2s 6d, but by the 1920s, it had risen more than four-fold to as much as £5 2s 0d, while the price of oil required for preserving the nets had rocketed from 2s 3d to 12s 6d. – more than a five-fold increase!

Many a waterman found it easier to make a living from hiring out pleasure boats during the holiday season, so it is not surprising that by 1918 the quantity of fish being landed amounted to less than 27 tons, a mere fraction of what the fish market used to cope with. By 1920 it was even less.

Throughout the twenties, Harry Hargood consistently appealed for the revival of local fisheries, for he could remember the time in the 19th century when it was a thriving industry.

Another sign of the times was when Worthing's lifeboat, powered by the energy of men and force of wind was called upon to rescue one of those newfangled motor-boats running on a foul-smelling liquid – petrol.

A high south, south-easterly wind on the morning of 23 July 1920 increased to a strong force nine gale in the afternoon, making the sea very rough indeed. Anticipating the adverse conditions most boatmen had beached their craft, but one was still anchored out in the offing east of the pier. It was the *Shamrock II* owned by Mrs Charlotte Mary Challis of Fairlawn, Church Walk. Watchful of the worsening weather, the boat's master, Mr A Dunford of 5 Selden Lane, anxious to get the boat ashore, put off from the beach in a small dinghy with a man named Elliott of Broadwater. Together they boarded the *Shamrock* and attempted to start the engine, but without success. In the squally conditions, water had found its way into the carburettor.

The sea became even more turbulent. The anchor didn't hold and the boat began to drift. They were then at the mercy of the powerful sea.

The helpless motor-boat was driven towards a thickly-groyned part of the beach about two miles east of the pier, where a very heavy sea was breaking.

Seeing the boat's two occupants in great danger, onlookers on the promenade alerted the local lifeboat secretary, who ordered the lifeboat gun to be fired at 4.15 pm.

Taking to the water with Coxswain Bill Blann at the helm, the *Richard Coleman* headed for the *Shamrock* which by this time was off the Half Brick Inn at East Worthing.

Within 25 minutes the lifeboat was alongside, and the two endangered men, both in a sorry state, were taken off.

After securing the motor-boat with fresh anchors, the dinghy was towed back and anchored off the pier.

Many hundreds of people watched from the beach. So many that a number of policemen were called in to effect crowd control. Members of the second lifeboat crew cunningly went among the crowd with collecting boxes.

By 7.00 pm in the evening, the lifeboat was re-housed and ready for its next errand of mercy.

Yet another proud entry was painted on the station's service board – two lives saved – and the very first rescue of a motor vessel!

For this latest service each crewman was paid 15 shillings, 42 volunteers received four shillings each, for manually hauling the heavy carriage and handling the cumbersome lifeboat. The signalman was rewarded with four shillings for three hours duty. Totalling £18 7s 0d, the expenditure was largely offset by the magnificent sum of £18 collected from the huge crowd.

It was ageing Fred Marshall's last active duty on the lifeboat, for after a magnificent record of 17 actual service launches to his credit he was soon to retire from the crew.

The Connaught Hall (pictured left) was just two years old when the Worthing Branch RNLI held its annual meeting there in 1919. The first floor Chapel Road venue, which was used as a concert hall and theatre, then later as a ballroom, faces Ambrose Place. Today it is called The Ritz.

Worthing lifeboat the Richard Coleman *being launched for practice from the beach between the pier and the Dome Cinema. Hundreds of people turned out to watch the saviours of the sea when the lifeboat gun was fired to summon the crew.*

Worthing pier on Regatta Day, prettily decorated with colourful flags and bunting.

THE PIER, WORTHING 464.

Lifeboat practice around 1919. The three men standing in the stern were Harry Marshall (cox), Bill Blann (2nd cox) and a Lifeboat Inspector.

A rare photograph showing the Richard Coleman *under full sail.*

Holy Trinity Schoolboys pictured with their teacher Mr Stone. To his right is Fred Simpson, born 1912.

Worthing Borough Fire Brigade with their first two motor fire appliances outside the Central Fire Station on the east side of High Street on the corner of Charlecote Road. Built in 1903, the station was first equipped with two horse-drawn manual pumps and a hose-cart. The brigade received its first motor appliance in 1911, the Dennis Escape Unit (right). A Ford Baico (left) was purchased in 1922 for £500. Today the site is marked by a modern office block called Crown House.

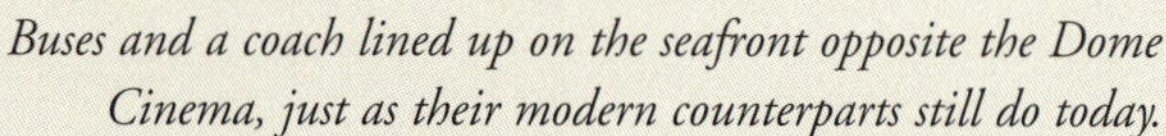

Buses and a coach lined up on the seafront opposite the Dome Cinema, just as their modern counterparts still do today.

LEFT: *The lodge and gateway situated at the north east corner of the Offington Hall estate, c 1920.*

BELOW: *Another view of the lodge and gateway at Offington Corner. The cameraman was standing in Warren Road looking past the horse and cart towards Crockhurst Hill. The turning on the right is Findon Road and the turning on the left (behind the hedge) is Offington Lane. Today the junction is a busy roundabout where the A24 crosses the A27.*

Fine details from the above photograph.

1921-1922

There is no braver company of men performing duties fraught with danger less ostentatiously than the tireless crews who man our lifeboats.

◆ CHAPTER 5 ◆

MOTORS AND LADIES MAKE THEIR DEBUT

Motor lifeboats were beginning to make their mark in the Lifeboat Service after the 'Great War'. By 1921, 25 out of 256 stations had been equipped with them, thereby replacing almost double that number of the old type with sails and oars; 13 more were approaching completion, and it was intended to provide at least 30 others without delay.

However, the engineering advancements brought with them escalating costs. Whereas in earlier days it had been possible to provide a lifeboat and set up a station for £1,000, it now cost from £7,000 for a smaller type of motor lifeboat and up to £15,000 for the latest design. That was apart from provision of a boathouse or slipway.

Technology may have changed the lifeboats, but the men who crewed them remained resilient to a man.

Modesty, the salient characteristic of lifeboatmen, was typical of Coxswain Bill Blann, who had served longest with the Worthing lifeboat – in 1921 his lengthy association with the service amounted to some 43 years since being a lad of 18. His quietly spoken manner belied a track record which was little short of an epic one.

Not one to make a fuss, Bill's rather reserved nature led to a walk-out by some of his crew later that same year, 1921. It happened

Coxswain Bill Blann aged 60 pictured in 1921 in front of the Richard Coleman on its carriage at the lifeboat house and dressed for action in oilskins, sou'wester and kapok lifejacket.

following a public protest by Worthing watermen, who found themselves in dispute with boatmen from a neighbouring port. The problem had arisen when the fishing industry became more and more depleted, and former fishermen were now using their boats for excursions as a living, resulting in too many men chasing the same work; and when that profession too became threatened, there was outrage in Worthing.

Worthing Town Council proposed to grant licences to Littlehampton boatmen to ply for hire with their motor launches carrying 60 or 70 passengers from the pier-head. Not surprisingly, Worthing boatmen objected strongly about unfair competition to their smaller boats.

The boatmen had no objection to the large paddlesteamers that collected passengers from the pier as they were not competing with them.

A protest meeting was held by all those who feared their trade would be poached, and they petitioned the Council relentlessly.

Nevertheless, Worthing licences were granted to the Littlehampton boatmen. As a direct result of that action, Worthing boatmen withdrew from any active part in that year's regatta, and some of them even went so far as to refuse the Regatta Committee the use of their small boats on the day for starting and marshalling.

One waterman, however, took a softer line than the others, and entered two of his boats for one of the sailing races. It was Bill Blann, the lifeboat coxswain, and

Paddlesteamers offered coastal excursions, a regular visitor to Worthing Pier in the 1920s was the two-funnelled Devonia.

Rebuilt in 1922, the paddlesteamer Brighton Belle *(pictured) was a frequent caller at Worthing pier during pleasure trips. The 200 foot-long paddler was later lost at Dunkirk in 1940.*

THEN

The Public Library, Museum and Art Gallery in Chapel Road ably run by the pioneering curator Miss Marion Frost.

NOW

The museum and art gallery entrance is through the portico on the right (see photograph above), while to its left is what is now the entrance to the Tourist Information Office – it initially housed the public library.

as a consequence, some of the lifeboat crew resigned.

The role of women was to become doubly important since millions of menfolk had been sacrificed in the 'War to end all wars'. The nation's census taken in 1921 showed that females numbered nearly 2,000 000 more than males, and showed only half of the usual increase in the country's population. Worthing's count also showed only a modest addition, totalling 35,224 citizens in 1921 compared with 30,305 at the previous 1911 census.

A hard-working woman who did a lot for the profile of Worthing was Miss Marion Frost, curator of the town museum and art gallery in Chapel Road.

A display at the art gallery that year, featured a fascinating collection of lifeboat models and apparatus rarely seen outside of London, arranged through the untiring efforts of Miss Frost, ably backed up by 78 year old Mr Hargood. Kindly loaned by the RNLI, the exhibits included showcases containing replicas of all kinds of lifeboats, such as the *Caroline Richardson* tubular boat stationed at Rhyl, and the hydraulic steam lifeboat Duke of Northumberland, stationed at Holyhead.

Worthing pier first erected in 1862 by the Worthing Pier Company at a cost of £6,500 and subsequently greatly improved over the years was purchased in 1921 by Worthing Corporation for £20,000. Note the seaweed on the beach – a persistent perennial problem.

Paintings displayed, included *The Storm Warriors* by Worthing artist F J Aldridge, while photographs, portraying the Worthing lifeboat, its crews and their work, brought back memories to many. A prestigious garden fete was staged by the Ladies' Committee, one of the invited nobility being the Duchess of Portland, president of the newly-formed Ladies Guild of the RNLI.

Held in the beautiful grounds of 'Tisree', Wykeham Road, on a glorious sunny afternoon, the event attracted many fashionable people. Bright frocks and brilliantly-coloured sunshades added to the cheerful setting, while an oriental touch was provided by two pretty Japanese girls selling chocolates and cream from their trays as they mingled with the crowd of gentry.

The event was very popular, with a succession of motor-cars coming and going until late in the day. It proved to be a success, and established the ladies as important fund-raisers for the lifeboat.

• • •

The Worthing lifeboat had used the pier as a breakwater to give some measure of protection during stormy launches ever since the structure had first been erected in 1862. Built by the Worthing Pier Company at a cost of £6,500, raised by selling £1 shares, it was taken into public ownership 59 years later in 1920/1921. After many years of discussions, Worthing Corporation eventually purchased the

Worthing's seafront Dome (left) whose ground floor Coronation Hall was converted from a roller skating rink into a 'luxurious' cinema in 1921. Opened 10 years earlier as the Kursaal (its Germanic name was changed during the war), the Edwardian complex had been showing films on the first floor.

...the Dome is one of the most splendid examples of an early cinema...

Victorian pier for around £20,000, realising its importance as an asset to the town and its tourist trade, for it had been considerably improved over the years.

Further east to the pier, stands Worthing's seafront Dome Cinema, which was converted into a working cinema in 1921.

When opened in 1911 as the Kursaal (its Germanic name was changed during the war), the Edwardian complex operated an 'Electric Theatre' on the first floor showing 'animated pictures'.

As audiences had increased, the 'pictures' moved down to the ground-floor Coronation Hall, which had been used as a roller skating rink.

The popularity of cinema continued to increase, so rapidly in fact that the Dome's owner, Carl Seebold, decided to convert the Coronation Hall into a permanent, and what was described at the time as luxurious, cinema.

The side galleries were retained, but at the southern end, theatre boxes were constructed. A raked floor was constructed with tip-up seats for 950 or so patrons. The Edwardian building's exposed roof trusses were covered with a new ceiling in which large and small domes were incorporated, to dramatic effect.

Little has changed since that 1921 conversion, costing around £8,000. The Dome is one of the most splendid examples of an early cinema building anywhere in the country, its heritage value being greatly cherished by the people of Worthing, who have fought for its preservation. It is still showing films after all these years.

Situated directly on the seafront, it was not unusual to find fishermen enjoying

Worthing's memorial to those of the borough who sacrificed their lives in the Great War, pictured during the unveiling ceremony on 11 April 1922 when Field Marshall Sir William Robertson carried out the honours. Today the Town Hall stands behind the memorial.

Worthing Borough Fire Brigade in the yard of the Central Fire Station, High Street. Charlecote Road houses can be seen in the background.

One of Searle's taxis pictured at his garage in Park Road. Denton Motors now occupies the site.

the occasional film there in 'the flea pit' as it was then known (a name applied to most cinemas in those days); and it had been known for the management to announce "wreck", on hearing the lifeboat gun, whereupon those lifeboat crew present would leap to their feet and be off at the double to the boathouse.

The services of the town's lifeboatmen were next called upon on 2nd July 1922, to go the aid of a motor launch foundering in appalling conditions while competing with others in the British Motor Club Cabin Cruiser race.

When the organisers held their annual cabin-cruiser race, they could not have anticipated the necessary involvement of the Worthing lifeboat. The 180 mile course from Greenhithe, on the River Thames, around the south-east coast to Cowes in the Isle of Wight, provided stiff competition for the 'Splash' Gold Challenge Cup, valued at 200 guineas.

Eight competing boats started the handicap race on Saturday 1st July 1922. At the Nore lightship they met with adverse weather conditions, which gradually worsened.

Very wisely, each boat put into its nearest port, all except shipowner Sir Walter Runciman's new launch, the *Lavengra*. A Thornycroft production with a 70 hp engine, the boat was caught in increasingly high seas after passing Beachy Head, and shipping water, the engine coughed and spluttered before giving up completely.

At the mercy of the prevailing gale, the swamped motor-boat drifted shoreward until the pilot dropped anchor.

She was now off Worthing.

When the sea moderated early the next day, two of the occupants, Mr R Thornycroft and Lord Douglas, paddled themselves ashore in a dinghy, and were made comfortable at the Warnes Hotel. Could it be that this was the same Lord Douglas who had achieved notoriety at the time of the trial of Oscar Wilde? If indeed it was, what a coincidence that he was cared for at the Warnes Hotel, only a few hundred yards away from where Oscar Wilde had previously stayed in the 1890s!

During the day, the weather worsened again. The south south-westerly wind increased once more to moderate gale force. In the afternoon, James Groves, a boatman and lifeboat crewman, reported the motor-boat to be in imminent danger of being driven onto the long sewer outfall pipe at East Worthing (opposite what is now Brooklands boating lake).

The lifeboat was called out and found three crewmen still on board the stricken boat. Transferred to the lifeboat, which then forged homeward to Worthing pier, the rescued were landed amid cheers from a large body of spectators.

The 15 ton motor launch was eventually taken in tow that evening by a motor tug to Shoreham harbour.

The survivors all being distinguished men, competing in a national race, the rescue attracted wider media coverage than usual – Worthing's lifeboatmen had again snatched lives from the cruel clutches of the sea.

...at the mercy of the prevailing gale the swamped motor-boat drifted shorewards...

NEXT PAGE: *Warnes, Worthing's premier hotel of the inter-war years, situated between Steyne Gardens to the left and darker boarding houses on its right. On 2 July 1922, Lord Douglas and Mr R Thorneycroft rowed themselves ashore and were put up at the hotel after being caught in terrible weather during the British Motor Boat Club's annual race from the Thames to the Isle of Wight.*

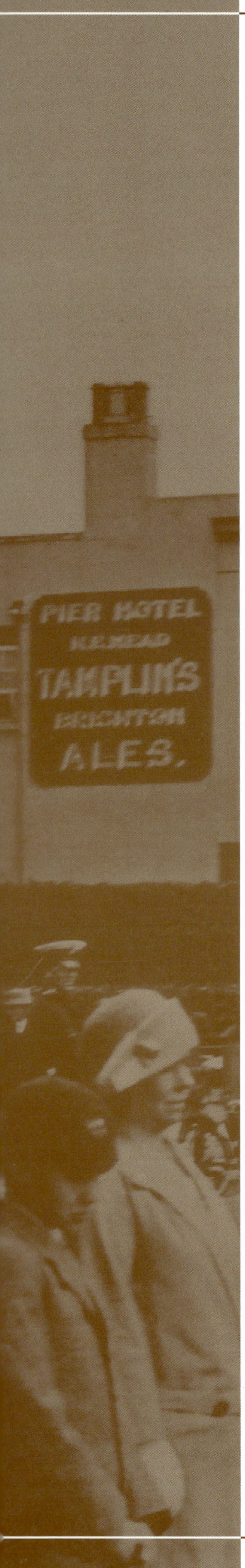

1923-1928

◆ CHAPTER 6 ◆

COMMEMORATION AND DEVELOPMENT

The highest honorary position in the RNLI was bestowed upon Harry Hargood when he was elected a national Vice-President in 1923. At the grand age of 81, his 60 years of experience working voluntarily for the Institution were still greatly valued, for despite his age, Mr Hargood, OBE, JP continued his work on the RNLI Committee of Management.

On Monday 13 August that same year, he accompanied the Mayor at a civic reception for a visiting novel lifeboat of extraordinary proportions moored at Worthing Pier.

Billed as a 'super lifeboat' she was 60 feet long and 15 feet across the beam, and was fitted with two screws powered by two six-cylinder 90 hp engines. Capable of 9-10 knots, this new craft, described at the time as the largest lifeboat in the world, carried a small amount of auxiliary sail. She was on her maiden trip – a round-Britain-cruise. This was the first British motor lifeboat to have cabins, two in fact, capable of holding about 50 people, while the total capacity of the whole boat was in the region of 150 persons.

Not surprisingly, Worthing became the focus of attention once more, as reporters and cameramen from national newspapers descended on the town to see this massive lifeboat. Built by Messrs J Samuel White & Co. at Cowes, on the Isle of Wight, at a cost of around £20,000, the boat had been designed by Mr J R Barnett of Messrs G L Watson & Co, the RNLI'S consultant naval architect.

While the country's first super-lifeboat was visiting Worthing, the town's first super-cinema was under construction.

The inspiration of impresario Carl Seebold, who had previously built the Kursaal (later the Dome) as well as the Picturedrome (later converted into the Connaught Theatre), his latest venture, the Rivoli, opened on 10 March 1924. The focal point at the junction of Chapel Road and North Street, it was built on the site of Worthing Lodge.

Finished to a high standard, the picture-house cost more than £75,000 to complete. From a commodious foyer which was capable of holding 200 patrons, one climbed a staircase to a large tea room on the floor above overlooking the foyer. Seating was provided for 1,200 viewers in the auditorium and for a further 500 in the balcony; additional accommodation was available in six ground floor boxes.

Published in a 1922 local newspaper, its caption read 'Lifeboat coxswains past, present and future'; Bill Blann (aged 61) left, his grandson Louis (Jim) Blann, his brother Harry Blann (aged 64) centre, his father Tom Blann (aged 89) seated, and George Newman, right.

Two postcards of Worthing lifeboat station and the Richard Coleman *published by the RNLI in 1924 to mark the centenary of the Institution. Inside, the walls are lined with pictorial displays of the many exciting rescues.*

A remarkable feature of the Rivoli was its sliding roof, which could be opened on hot evenings to provide extra ventilation and exhaust the tobacco smoke.

(Sadly the Rivoli caught fire on 19 January 1960, destroying the auditorium. The foyer remained standing and was used as an auction room until its demolition on 29 April 1984 for road widening. The Rivoli stood to the north-east of the roundabout near the present Town Hall.)

Speeding to the launch: the Richard Coleman *being pulled past the Arcade by a band of enthusiastic men using hauling ropes attached to its carriage. The leading men were at the foot of a ramp sloping up to the raised promenade from where it would be reversed down the stony beach and into the water, bow first.*

The town centre reverberated to the sounds of military bands when the RNLI celebrated its centenary in 1924, commemorating 100 years of maritime rescue work since it was founded as the National Lifeboat Institution in 1824.

The *Richard Coleman* was paraded through the town, its crew, wearing kapok lifejackets and ceremonial red woolly hats, sat in the boat up high on its carriage.

Headed by two mounted policemen, the procession included detachments and bands from the 3rd London Infantry Brigade, who were camped, some 1,400 strong, in Offington Park northwest of the town (now developed into a high class housing estate).

On reaching the pier, the lifeboat was ceremoniously launched into a sea that was generously gentle when compared to the rough conditions experienced on its missions of mercy.

As the boat took to the water, the bands played the *National Anthem, God Bless the Prince of Wales,* and *Rule Britannia,* while the Territorials stood to attention.

Coxswain Blann, standing aft, instructed his crew to "pull on the whites" and then "pull on the blues". The colour of a lifeboat's oars differed from one side to the other, white for port and blue for starboard, a necessary distinction to avoid using nautical terms which could baffle the volunteer crews.

Curiously, this was the first practice launch which Mr. Hargood had missed in all his 60 odd years of association with lifeboat work. But he could be excused, for as a Vice-President of the RNLI and a member of its Executive he was representing headquarters at the naming ceremony of Selsey's new motor lifeboat.

In 1924, Worthing's lifeboat was launched twice within three months for service, on both occasions in answer to distress rockets. But each time a Channel search in the *Richard Coleman* failed to find any sign of a distressed vessel.

On one of these abortive rescue missions a sizeable proportion of the lifeboat crew, five out of 13, came from just one family alone - the Bashfords - an outstanding example of the close family ties which existed in the lifeboat service generally.

Ready to launch: Worthing lifeboat crew wearing flat caps in the Richard Coleman. *Standing right - Coxswain Bill Blann, standing left - George Benn, centre facing camera - John Wells.*

A quarterly practice filmed in 1927

1) The mortar boomed once and the Richard Coleman *was hauled from the lifeboat house and eastward along the seafront*

2) Further along the seafront the manually drawn lifeboat followed by eager spectators of all ages passed the Stanhoe Hotel (demolished in 1948 and currently replaced by grass next to the multi-storey car park) on the corner of Augusta Place.

3) Launching from the beach east of the pier with Coxswain Bill Blann standing in the stern and controlling the rudder.

4) An extremely rare picture of the Richard Coleman *returning under sail watched by eager spectators on the pier.*

The seafront has undergone many changes over the course of time, some of the most significant this century taking place in the mid twenties.

Denton Gardens looking south from the Brighton Road entrance across the sunken garden and lily pond, photographed between 1924 and 1927.

A municipal leisure facility opened in 1924 to the west of Beach House and next to the boat clubhouse situated at Splash Point. Taking the form of a small two acre park, laid out with two putting greens and an ornamental garden, it was named Denton Gardens in recognition of businessman Alderman James G Denton who had given the town £1,500 to purchase the land two years earlier.

The northern end featured (and still does) a sunken garden and lily pond, while at the sea end, double-sided shelters on a raised terrace facing the sea on one side and the greens on the other provide shelter on a blustery day.

The east boundary of Denton Gardens was the unbroken, tall, flint garden wall of Beach House, which at that time was still privately owned.

Another parcel of land connected with Beach House was destined for pleasure purposes. To the north of Beach House and beyond Brighton Road, the ten acre plot, originally a grass meadow enclosure belonging to the house, was purchased by the local authority in 1922, laid out with bowling greens and more ornamental gardens, and that too was opened to the public in 1924.

Called Beach House Park, its main entrance is right opposite the house from which it took its name.

Beach House Park looking north from its Brighton Road entrance across the ornamental gardens towards the bowling greens, photographed by a cameraman at the top of Beach House soon after being opened in 1924.

The crowded Bandstand Enclosure.

Children being taken for a ride in the Worthing lifeboat Richard Coleman *as it was being drawn westward along the coast road past Arcade Buildings opposite the pier.*

A family with their fashionable car of the time pictured in Brooklyn Road, West Worthing in 1927 when the road was only a rough track.

...construction of a pavilion; completed at a cost of £35,000...

Three spectacular and quite separate seafront developments, each within a stone's throw of the other, and all erected by the same local builders, were to set the scene for the seaside town of Worthing as we know it today – The Arcade, the Bandstand & Enclosure, and the Pier Pavilion.

Firstly, The Arcade was built at the southwest corner of South Street, on a site which had lain vacant for almost a quarter of a century. Until 1901, the Royal Hotel had stood there before being destroyed by fire. After a long space of some 24 years, the site and surrounding buildings were redeveloped into an elegant post-Edwardian shopping arcade. Designed by Eastbourne architect Peter Stonham in a classical, Art Deco style, it was constructed by Worthing-based builders Frank Sandell & Sons on behalf of the Worthing Development Company, and opened in 1925.

Apart from the substitution of modern shopfronts, The Arcade has remained much the same until the present day, standing proudly at the junction of one of the town centre's busiest thoroughfares.

The Duke and Duchess of York (later George VI and Queen Elizabeth, now the Queen Mother) pictured outside the newly built Pier Pavilion with the Mayor, Alderman William Thomas Frost, on 30 May 1928. In the background are the Marine Hotel and Pier Hotel. The visit was in connection with an appeal for the Prince Albert Convalescent Home, a seafront site now occupied by the Beach Hotel.

To the west of the pier, the Victorian birdcage bandstand and associated shelters were replaced in this same year by a rectangular bandstand and walled enclosure to shield listeners from the prevailing winds, construction work again being carried out by Sandells. Costing the local authority £25,000 for a structure exceeding 200 feet and extending 150 feet over the beach on steel piles, the enclosure had the capacity to accommodate 2,200 people, 800 of the seats being under cover.

The new stage with its extending canopy was itself replaced some four years later in 1929 by a circular domed bandstand, which is still there today. Later, as the popularity of band music waned, a swimming pool was sunk into the enclosure, and the premises renamed the Lido. This in turn was boarded over in 1990 when the use changed again and the enclosure was altered to house Garry Smart's amusements.

In 1925, the two octagonal kiosks at the pier entrance were demolished to make way for the construction of a pavilion. Completed at a cost of £35,000, it opened as a concert hall with seating for 1,200 people – another local authority project. Today, it is called the Pavilion Theatre – the third major seafront construction to be erected by Sandells in the twenties. The style of this new pavilion's roof was designed to reflect that of its Victorian counterpart at the pierhead.

The year 1925 saw the 75th anniversary of one of the most tragic events in the history of Worthing, when in 1850, 11 of the town's fishermen were drowned attempting to render assistance to the distressed barque *Lalla Rookh*, which was disabled in a severe gale off Worthing. *(See chapter one of* A Town's Pride*, the first book in this trilogy.)*

On the commemorative day, the only two people still alive who witnessed the fatal event 75 years earlier were 83 year old Harry Hargood and 92 year old Tom Blann, the latter having very nearly joined the fated crew and become a statistic of the disaster.

The seafront between the Paragon Street turn off (left) and the Portland Road junction (right) photographed c 1920 when the Victorian 'bird cage' bandstand was still there. Between the two side streets stood Marlborough House, Grafton House and Grafton Mansions, all of which have now been replaced, both roads included, by today's multi-storey car park and Marks & Spencer.

The interior of the new (northern) Pier Pavilion completed in 1925; the open steel framework was later covered over.

A rare postcard of Worthing Pier showing both the north and south pavilions built in the same style. The landward pavilion was built in 1925 to reflect the Victorian design of its counterpart, but this 'two bookends' scenario existed for only six years as the original seaward pavilion burnt down in 1933.

Old folks' Dinner: Tom and Fanny Blann pictured in their nineties being entertained by local dignitaries.

Tom recalled, "I was just a youngster of 17 then, keen to join the fishermen going to help the ailing barque. We'd dragged the open ferry boat into the water and was about to jump in when my girlfriend's father, John Belville, stopped me. I was the last person to see him alive, and I owe my life to him. I married his daughter and we've kept his memory alive by christening one of our grandsons with Belville as a middle name."

A special service of remembrance was held at West Tarring Church.

Local churches played an all-important triennial role in fund-raising for the RNLI by taking collections for the Institution. Once every three years, Lifeboat Sunday, as it was called, involved all the churches in Worthing and the neighbourhood. Sermons were preached emphasising the needy charitable work of the Lifeboat Institution.

Lifeboat Day was revived on 14 July 1926, after a gap of several years. Unfortunately, the 25 year old *Richard Coleman* was away being overhauled at the time, so to arouse interest, the four year old Selsey motor lifeboat was invited over to Worthing and moored at the pier's landing stage. The 40 foot boat was of the type that the Worthing branch longed for – self-righting, and with all the latest equipment, including a line-throwing gun, and with an endurance of 15 hours, using four gallons of petrol an hour.

The last effective rescue by the Worthing lifeboat took place in September 1928 when distressed sailors were plucked from a stormy sea.

At 7.20 pm on 6 September, distress rockets were spotted some three miles southeast of the lifeboat house. Twenty five minutes later, the lifeboat entered the sea and floated easily, even though the tide was halfway out and the water shallow. Thrilled holidaymakers waited on the beach for the lifeboat to return.

The sea was fairly calm inshore, but further out it became lumpy, agitated by a moderate westerly breeze. It took the lifeboat crew nearly two hours to find the distressed vessel, a motor yacht with a broken rudder and taking in water.

Coxswain Blann was asked by its owner, a Londoner by the name of H L Edwin, to tow them back to Shoreham.

The lifeboatmen obliged, but the tide was too low to enter the harbour, and so the lifeboat anchored off the harbour mouth and made fast to the yacht until there was sufficient depth of water to enter.

It was not until 3.30 am that the patience of the still-waiting holidaymakers on Worthing beach was rewarded, by the sight of the returning *Richard Coleman* coming in smoothly and grinding to a halt on the pebbles.

This last rescue of three men and a boat by the Worthing lifeboat, was a classic irony. The *Richard Coleman*, with its crewmen pulling on the oars and tending the sails, towed a broken-down motor yacht powered by an engine intended to supersede the natural resources of wind and human strength.

A triumph of manpower over mechanical engineering!

THEN NOW

A family snap of 1927 looking east from the coast road opposite the Pier. There are four hotels in the picture: the Marine far left with the Pier Hotel next to it; with the Steyne and Warne's Hotels in the distance. The large space in the road is today occupied by a traffic roundabout and all the hotels have gone.

THEN

TOWN HALL, SOUTH STREET, WORTHING. 10

The original Town Hall stood proudly at the top of South Street providing a marvellous focal point looking northward from the seafront. It was sadly demolished in the 1960s...

NOW

...to make way for pedestrianisation and the Guildbourne shopping Centre!

A view of Montague Street westward from Montague Place taken by a 'Sunny Snaps' street photographer in 1927. The subject of the picture was Leonard Stenning.

A view of Brighton Road looking in the direction of Denton Gardens (left), with the Warwick Road turn off on the right. Note the AA patrolman standing in the middle of the road saluting as an unknown dignitary is driven by watched by waving spectators.

NOW

And as it is today… the houses in the background long since gone.

A Tramocar pictured on the seafront by the pier. Peculiar to Worthing these solid-tyred vehicles operated on a circular route from the pier, incorporating the seafront, Grand Avenue, West Worthing Railway Station and Mill Road.

THEN

The Arcade and South Street, Worthing

The Arcade (left) photographed from the promenade was built at the bottom of South Street in 1925, while on the opposite corner stood the Marine Hotel (later demolished).

NOW

The arcade on the left, remains architecturally unspoilt, whilst the shops opposite have been replaced by 'modern' counter-parts.

Trinity Football Club team of 1923.

Girls from Elm Grove School photographed in 1925. Right to left: Betty Baker, Winnie Welch, Evie Ellis, Pauline Simpson, Kathy Kinshott, Lizzie Welch, Gladys Horne, W. Forest, Bertha Simpson (nee Damp).

The 4th Worthing (Broadwater) Girl Guides pictured in 1923.

One of the two infant classes at Elm Grove School in old wooden WWI huts behind the main building, c 1929. The pupils are: Edna Wright, Richard Luder, Jack Manville, Doris Randell, Mabel Collier, Alan Botting, Joan Chessell, Grace Horn, Victor Blake, Ailene Pleasance, Eric Warner (his father was a chimney sweep), Rita Jacobs.

Major repairs being carried out on a Southdown Bus in the road in 1928.

Worthing firemen pictured around 1929 in their brass helmets on the newly acquired Leyland appliance in front of the Central Fire Station in High Street. The names of the crew were: (Driver) F/m S Vaughan, Chief Officer H J Jones, 2nd Officer A Lyne, Sub/Officer H Humphrey, F/m Jago, F/m D Arseneau, F/m W Taylor, F/m S Watkins, F/m H Blann and F/m G Humphreys.

Standing in front are the six members of the Fire Brigade Committee who are: Councillor Mr Whittington, Councillor Mr D'Eath, Councillor Mrs Knight, Councillor Major Barnes, Councillor Mr E A Brackley, Councillor Mr H W Symonds.

1929-1931

◆ CHAPTER 7 ◆

Countdown to Closure

The very last launch of the *Richard Coleman* on active service ended without a positive result. It was on 20 March 1929, after the coastguard received an urgent SOS message in the early hours, from a Portuguese steamer called *Sines*, whose position was calculated to be around 22 miles west south-west of the lifeboat house.

At 2.45 am, the lifeboat was launched, but a lengthy search through thick fog in the vicinity of the *Owers* Lightship found no trace of a distressed ship, so the lifeboat headed back to Worthing about seven hours later.

Subsequently, a Japanese steamer reported a ship's lifeboat drifting, about one degree west of the position reported earlier. This time a Navy destroyer from Portsmouth was deployed to search.

It took the *Richard Coleman* all of seven hours to sail back to Worthing from its final call of duty, in weather that was foggy, although not exactly the stormy conditions to which the crew had become accustomed.

On Tuesday 21 May 1929 a carnival atmosphere gripped the town. Worthingites, and day-trippers too, had gathered in vast numbers to welcome a visiting dignitary of high esteem. The occasion was the visit in state by the Lord Mayor of London, Lieutenant-Colonel Sir J E Kynaston Studd to celebrate the extension of the Worthing Borough boundaries to include the villages of Goring and Durrington.

With sun shining brightly, thousands lined the colourfully decorated procession route from the railway station to the Pier Pavilion, where an official open-air ceremony took place. For many of the sightseers, this was the second time they had witnessed such a spectacle in honour of a Lord Mayor of London, for it was just 15 years earlier that Sir T Vansittart Bowater had presided over the official opening of Worthing Pier after it had been rebuilt following its momentous collapse in 1913.

The township of Worthing was 'relatively new', as the earliest record of it as a town dates back only as far as 1803 when a special Act of Parliament was passed constituting a body of 72 Commissioners as the local governing authority.

Forty-nine years later in 1852, the first Local Board of Health was formed, at a time when there were about 5,000 inhabitants and the size of the town amounted to 784 acres.

It was in 1890, that Worthing was incorporated as a borough by Royal Charter, by which time the population had increased to around 16,000 in an area that had

1) From the lifeboat house (its first floor/rooftop lookout turret can just be seen to the left of the boat) the Richard Coleman *is drawn by lengthy ropes along the seafront road, watched and closely followed by hundreds of keen onlookers*

2) Drawn by eager helpers and surrounded by crewmen, the lifeboat on its sturdy carriage passes the Berkeley Hotel as a policeman controls the traffic

expanded to 1,790 acres governed by a 24-member Council.

By 1901 the number of citizens had grown to more than 20,000, and it was in the following year that the boundaries were extended to include the villages of Broadwater and Tarring, bringing the total area up to 2,988 acres and expanding the Council to 32 members.

The census taken in 1921, indicated that despite the wholesale slaughter of young men in the 'Great War', Worthing's population showed a marked rise to over 35,000.

The further extension of the boundaries which took place on 1 April 1929 to include both Durrington and Goring created what became known as Greater Worthing, an area occupying 7,845 acres and was inhabited by a large number of residents in excess of 44,000. The newly extended local government grew to number 40 Councillors – relatively small compared to the 72 Commissioners thought necessary when the population was well under 5,000.

Worthing has had its fair share of storms and flooding over the centuries, indeed, some would say more than a fair share, but one particular freak of nature stands out boldly in the memories of those Worthingites who experienced it – a tidal wave!

The only one ever reported at Worthing, it occurred on 20 July 1929. One who witnessed the incident was a young seven year old boy called Bill Blann (the author's father). Now aged 79, he recalls what happened on that summer's day.

"I was only seven at the time, and being a Saturday which meant no school, I went to play on the beach opposite the Half Brick Hotel with my sister Mabel, five years my senior. The tide was right out, probably about 200 yards, and we were shrimping in the shallows."

Referring to the first indication of what was to come, he said, "Out at sea we saw a long band of white stretching right across the horizon. Mabel, realising the magnitude of this wall of foam surging towards us, instantly grabbed my hand, and together we ran for the safety of the shingle beach. The sea followed us, right up to the high water mark."

Frightened by their ordeal, Mabel and Bill made their way home and didn't return to the beach that day. It was only by sheer quick-thinking that neither they,

...out at sea we saw a long band of white stretching right across the horizon...

nor any of the other beachgoers, were injured or washed away.

Three months later, Worthing's neighbouring lifeboatmen at Shoreham Harbour enjoyed a double celebration. The station there which had closed five years earlier in 1924 due to silting up, re-opened on 19 October 1929. At the same time, Shoreham's old rowing and sailing lifeboat was replaced by a motor lifeboat.

A grand gala occasion to welcome the boat was organised concurrently with Flag Day. Boats in Shoreham Harbour were hung with pennants and bunting to create a carnival atmosphere. A welcoming reception at the Canal Lock was organised by a Major H L Philips, and included three notable Worthingites: Mr Hargood, OBE, JP, DL, as a national representative of the RNLI, Worthing Mayor Alderman H F Carmichael and Deputy Mayor Alderman W T Frost. Officers of the Shoreham branch included: Earl Winterton, MP, P C (president), Mr Harold Brown (chairman) and the Shoreham Harbour Master, Commander A R T Williams (hon sec).

Some seven weeks later, the Worthing lifeboat crew were called out just one more time, to assemble in readiness for a rescue mission, but ultimately their services were not to be required.

It was on 6 December 1929. At 9.40 pm a message was received that a Hungarian ship three miles off the *Owers* Lightship and drifting shoreward, even with two anchors out, need assistance; and that the cable ship *Telconia* was proceeding to assist from 10 miles west south-west of *Owers*.

Coxswain Blann immediately assembled his crew, who donned their lifejackets ready for service, and stood by. In the event they weren't required immediately as the faster motor lifeboats from Selsey and Shoreham had been dispatched but the Worthing lifeboatmen were kept on standby waiting for the distressed vessel to drift closer.

It wasn't until shortly before midnight, that the Worthing Coastguard received a message from the Commander-in-Chief at Portsmouth saying: "The wind has slightly veered, vessel able to get clear, danger past. A tug has been sent to position".

Worthing's lifeboatmen were then stood down, all apart from one, who, together with the head launcher and one helper, was retained at the boathouse in case circumstances changed.

As 1929 drew to a close, Worthingites reflected on the closure of the New Theatre Royal that year, the Bath Place establishment that Carl Seebold had taken over and vastly improved in Edwardian times, where contemporary plays with famous actors, and in some cases first productions, were staged. Films had been shown there as well as live shows, but with stiff competition from cinemas the theatre had fallen into decline.

A closure in 1930, which was to change the way of life experienced by generation after generation of townsfolk, was announced by the RNLI.

With the stationing of a motor lifeboat at Shoreham, the Committee of Management at headquarters decided it was no longer necessary to maintain a lifeboat at Worthing, thinking that Worthing was adequately covered by the Shoreham motor lifeboat six miles to the east and the Selsey motor lifeboat about 20 miles west.

...but local feelings ran high, for Worthing had had a lifeboat stationed here for nearly 80 years...

But local feelings ran high, for Worthing had had a lifeboat stationed here for nearly 80 years. Coxswain Bill Blann told a *Worthing Gazette* reporter, "Still there are times when a lifeboat is required here. I know it takes a little while to float our carriage-launched boat, but Shoreham and Selsey have to come many miles to get here."

Quite obviously, Worthing was known as a lifeboat town; it was an integral and

Class 3 of West Tarring Infants' School in the building behind the Reading Room, c 1930.

The gardening class at Durrington School in Salvington Road, c 1930.

Durrington School in Salvington Road c 1930 before the road was made up and before it was encircled by development.

OPPOSITE PAGE: *An aerial view of the Bath Hotel looking south east towards Heene Terrace.*

Twenty two members of Worthing's two Lifeboat crews pictured at a special dinner on 22 January 1931 to mark their disbandment.

Fisherman Harry Blann repairing a sail next to his boat on the beach opposite New Street.

important part of life for everyone; whenever the lifeboat gun was fired, the whole place came alive with excitement.

"I'm sorry there won't be any more quarterly practices," said Bill Blann when interviewed by the press about the impending closure, "because people take a lot of interest in these launches, and they bring the money in. People like the practices – I'm always being asked when they're coming off – and in the summer many who come to watch us have never seen a lifeboat launched before."

The Worthing lifeboat had been launched on service 36 times and rescued 58 people since it was taken under the wing of the RNLI in 1865. Prior to that, the Worthing Lifeboat Establishment, which had started with a Littlehampton-built self-righter in 1853, was locally organised and funded by donations.

To mark the end of an era, a special dinner in honour of the Worthing lifeboatmen was given by Worthing Branch RNLI on 22 January 1931. The lifeboat crewmen, some of whom had been in lifeboat service for more than 50 years, enjoyed a tasty repast at Barnes Cafe, at The Arcade.

Just eight weeks later at the annual meeting of the Worthing Branch on 20 March, 15 certificates of service were awarded to Coxswain Blann and his crew by Sir Godfrey Baring, Bart, chairman of the RNLI's Committee of Management. The combined service of the 15 men totalled 312 years. In addition, Bill Blann and his assistant coxswain each received a small pension.

...in the summer many who come to watch us have never seen a lifeboat launched before...

The lifeboat *Richard Coleman*, with its valves and launching gear removed, was kept at the lifeboat house as an exhibit to raise funds for the RNLI. This museum which commemorated nearly 80 years of lifeboat service at Worthing was enthusiastically looked after by the last coxswain, Bill Blann.

Going back to the mid 19th century for a moment, the inaugural meeting of the lifeboat committee had been held at the home of Admiral William Hargood, and it was his son Mr H. Hargood who had become chairman of the branch in 1866, remaining in that office until 1919 when he was made president.

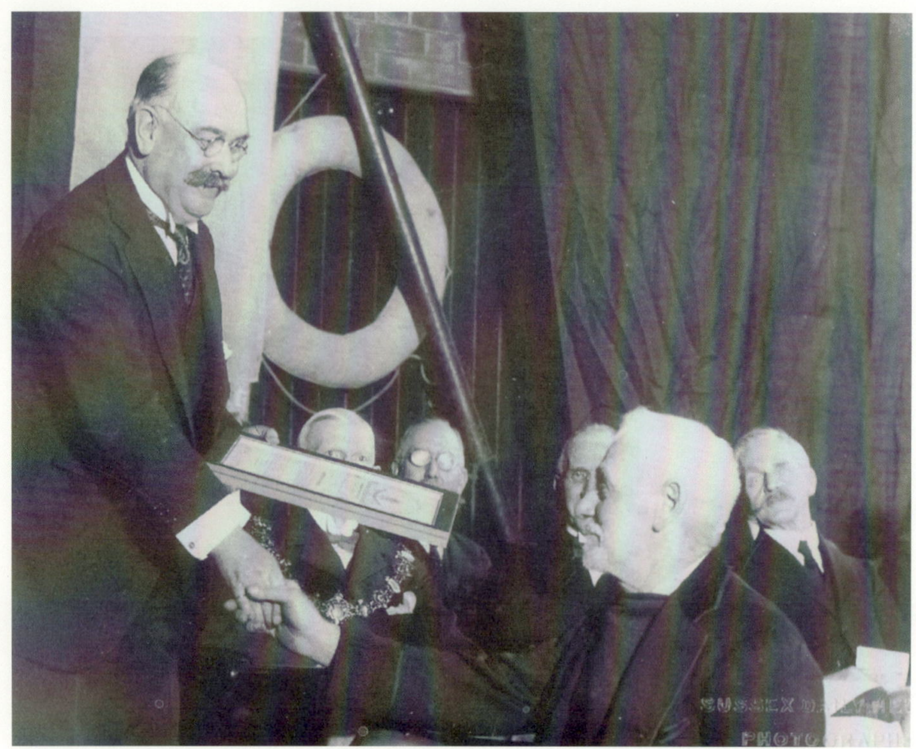

Coxswain Bill Blann being presented with a framed Vellum Certificate of Service by Sir Godfrey Baring, Bt (chairman of the national Management Committee of the RNLI) at the annual meeting of the Worthing branch on 20 March 1931.

...he contributed so much to public life that Worthing bestowed upon him the unofficial title of the Grand Old Man...

A born philanthropist, his name was synonymous with many public bodies. In 1890, Worthing-born Harry Hargood had helped form the Worthing District Nursing Association; he was a magistrate for 39 years; had been one of the original aldermen of the West Sussex County Council; and for more than 20 years had been president of Worthing Swimming Club.

He contributed so much to public life that Worthing bestowed upon him the unofficial title of the 'Grand Old Man'. Sadly, he died on 4 March 1932, just eight days before his 90th birthday, having fulfilled his numerous public duties until the end.

Otto Brown's permanent funfair on the seafront opposite the bandstand.

The Bath Hotel in Bath Road. The site is today marked by a development of flats.

The first police motorcycle patrolman in West Sussex: PC Bill 'Tiny' Dear, proudly wearing a merit stripe above his cuff, pictured on the first police motorbike, a Sunbeam.

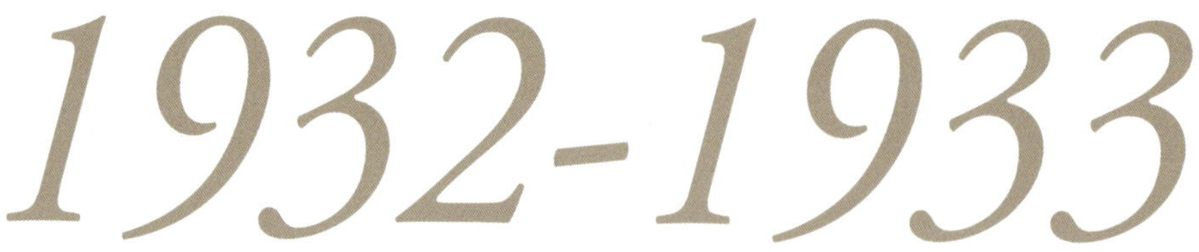

1932-1933

◆ CHAPTER 8 ◆

TRAGEDIES UNITE TOWNSFOLK

Life wasn't easy for the working classes in the Great Depression of the 1930's. Coal ,delivered by local hauliers Hall & Co at 50/- a ton, was a severe strain on many household budgets. In those pre-television days most homes had a radio; a Philco five valve radio could be bought for 18 guineas, the equivalent of a month's wages for many. For the small minority of very well off residents, a motor car was a must; a Rover Family Ten from Moody's Motors of The Broadway, West Worthing would have set them back £179.

Horse-drawn coal deliveries in Lansdowne Road in 1935. Note the pneumatic tyres.

For pure pleasure, and the viewing of newsreels, there was a choice of three cinemas in the town – the Picturedrome, the Dome and the Rivoli – all still under the personal management of impresario Carl Seebold.

A more adventurous form of pleasure, sailing, although more fulfilling was not without risk. But if accompanied by an experienced high-ranking Royal Naval Reserve officer that risk would surely be minimised.

Such was the case on a perfectly normal, late Saturday afternoon at the end of April 1932. The time was gone 6.00 pm. It was windy but not gusty, ideal sailing conditions, when Kenneth Howden (aged 23) was taken out for what was meant to be just a short sail from West Worthing by 38 year old Lieutenant-Commander Gerald Stewart Blenkins, RNR.

A female friend of the naval officer, Miss Evelyn Thompson, of Rose Walk, Goring had intended to go with them in the small 13 foot boat, but fortunately for her she changed her mind at the last minute and decided to wait for them on the beach with her sister Margaret.

Not long after putting off, the two men adjusted the sail until they were sailing well. Yet after only a quarter of an hour at sea, things went disastrously wrong.

Without warning, the boat capsized. By this time they were about a mile and a half off Wallace Avenue.

The two sisters watched in horror. Unable to help apart from summoning assistance they rushed along to the coastguard station where the coastguard immediately telephoned for the Shoreham lifeboat.

Then the girls went to find local waterman Reg Paine. He set out at once with fishermen Tim Sullivan and C Bashford in his motor boat, kept on the beach near the pier, heading in a southwest direction. The time was 6.55 pm.

Time was passing quickly. Their friends were in mortal danger. Still the lifeboat did not come.

Fearing for their men friends' lives, the sisters stopped a promenader and got him to go and phone for the Shoreham lifeboat again.

About a quarter of an hour after the capsize, both men were seen in the choppy water clinging precariously to the boat, observed through binoculars by motor mechanic Gordon Brown Rowson.

"I could just make out what looked like heads by the keel of the boat," said Mr Rowson, of Sea Home, Goring who happened to be on the beach at Goring when he saw the boat capsize. He too had previously gone for help.

Around 7.10 pm, about half an hour after the accident, Reg Paine's fishing boat reached the spot. Another hour later and the Shoreham lifeboat was still on its way, having only got as far as the pier.

The fishermen steamed about for several hours searching for survivors. "We had no lamps but we kept stopping our engines hoping to hear a cry."

The Shoreham lifeboat did not arrive at the spot until 8 pm. After an hour-long search it pulled up to Reg Paine's fishing boat to liaise with the local fishermen. They too had found nothing. Widening the search they went to the west because they knew the tide was running.

At 11.20 pm, a mile off Kingston, the fishermen found the boat floating stern up with the sails still fully set, some three miles west of where it capsized and nearly five hours after, but there was no sign of any survivors.

"We tore the sail to get the boat up. There were no reefs in the sail. The sheet was fast. We could not see if this was only accidental because we had to cut it."

After towing the boat back to Worthing, Reg and his two fellow fishermen heard the Town Hall clock in South Street strike 3 am as they walked home.

The next day, questions were being asked. Why did the Shoreham lifeboat take so long arriving? Could the two sailors have been saved if the Worthing lifeboat was still functional? Public feeling was running high.

An inquest on Lieutenant-Commander Gerald Blenkins was held in the small parlour at the Henty Arms, Ferring, by the Deputy Coroner for West Sussex Mr F. Haddocks. It was so crowded that there was hardly any standing space. After hearing the various witnesses, Mr Haddocks summed up: "If he could have held on a little longer or if help had come a little quicker, they might both have been saved. He was a big, strong man. If the lifeboat at Worthing had been in commission they might have been saved. It seems to me that there should be some craft at Worthing kept where it could be got at quickly".

The other victim was not recovered until 12 May, 12 days after the accident, when the body of young Kenneth Howden was washed ashore at Sea Lane, Goring.

At 11.20 pm, a mile off Kingston, the fishermen found the boat floating stern up with the sails still fully set...

...a series of three tragedies resulting in the loss of five lives...

Julian Howden, the grieving father of Kenneth, was so incensed that his son could have been saved had help arrived more quickly, that he set up a committee to organise the stationing of a rescue boat at Worthing.

The first meeting was held at his home, 54 Mill Road, where it was proposed to purchase and maintain some sort of light boat which could be launched at any time in case of accident. Mr Howden offered to give a substantial sum of money towards the purchase of a boat and equipment, if the rest could be raised by public subscription, and began by enlisting the support of Mayor, Alderman F A Watts.

Two months later, on 18 July, another boating disaster occurred, when a rowing boat capsized off Lancing, drowning Welsh labourer Rowland Gunter who lived in the village. He was in a party of three on a fishing trip. One of his companions, Arthur Blaker, was blind and was fortunately rescued by the third member of the party Mr C White.

Once more there was no quick response rescue craft available to rescue Gunter.

Just four weeks further into summer, on 15 August, there was yet another catastrophic capsizing of a sailing boat. Cruising along the coast, both of its occupants were drowned – Reginald Connolly (aged 15) of 14 St George's Road and Ronald Rowland of 121 Brighton Road.

Still there was no rescue boat at Worthing!

Citizens were deeply moved by the series of three tragedies resulting in the loss of five lives. Donations poured into the Rescue Boat Appeal and by the end of August the funds collected by the hon sec Mr C M Butcher of 3 Abbot's Close totalled over £520, but that still was not enough.

The campaign was given further publicity when a design for the proposed rescue boat was submitted by Messrs John I Thorneycroft & Co Ltd, who incidentally, had never before built a rescue boat, and was to be quite a novelty.

Bill Blann in the doorway of the lifeboat house pictured with the boy from next door, c 1933. Note the lifeboat-shaped collection box.

Measuring 25 ft in length with a beam of 7ft 6in and a draft of only 2 ft, and fitted with a drop keel that would automatically lift on striking an underwater object, the craft was to be powered by a four cylinder engine developing 30 bhp, with an internal water cooling system allowing the engine to be started with the boat still on the beach.

Its large propeller, running in a tunnel to protect survivors in the sea, would provide sufficient thrust to guarantee a speed of eight knots.

Controls were to be positioned next to the steering wheel so that the boat could be manoeuvred single-handedly, leaving the rest of the crew free for rescue work.

A mast and ample sail in a simply designed rig, requiring just two or three hands were to be provided, and rescue equipment was to include a powerful searchlight for night use. A towing post would be fitted, and life-lines with cork floats would encircle the hull.

The hull would be planked on the double diagonal system, with oiled fabric stretched between two skins of mahogany to ensure watertightness. The keel, stern and deadwoods were to be of English oak. Such a construction ensuring strength with lightness and at the same time durability. Buoyancy tanks would render her practically unsinkable.

Attention was paid to the launching of the craft. Thorneycroft's recommended a light cradle, low slung and mounted on one large wheel either side, with broad rims to prevent the cradle from sinking into the shingle or sand. The estimated time for launching the boat was five minutes.

A fire-proof and water-proof casing would cover the engine, which would be electrically started. To avoid any possibility of mechanical failure, there would be duplicate starters and magnetos, twin bilge pumps and two fuel feeds.

Thorneycroft's had reduced the draft of the boat to the lowest possible figure consistent with stability and sea-going qualities. In their opinion this boat was the smallest type suitable for rescue work at that time.

In January 1933, the Rescue Boat Committee applied to the Council for

An aerial view of the seafront between the Bandstand Enclosure and the Pier Pavilion. Detail below.

planning permission to erect a timber boathouse 34 feet long immediately behind the rear of the relief map that stood to the east of the pier pavilion, but the application was rejected on the grounds that the beach should be kept as an open space. A further application for a smaller boathouse was also rejected, but arrangements were made for the boat to be permanently housed in new premises about to be built at Splash Point for the Worthing Amateur Boat Club, part of which would be leased to the Rescue Boat Committee.

By the following Spring, the new boat was completed at Thorneycroft's yard at Hampton-on-Thames. The boat-builders invited a number of dignitaries from Worthing, including the Mayor Councillor Thomas Ernest Hawkins and his wife the Mayoress, to a special lunch on Monday 26 April 1933, to be followed immediately by the official launching of the rescue boat.

Given at the Mitre Hotel, Hampton Court, guests of honour to the lunch, from Worthing, included three councillors, the police chief and the Rescue Boat Committee, together with their wives. They were Cllrs Brackley, Mason and Budd, Police Superintendent Bristow, and committee members A W Buckingham (chairman), C M Butcher (secretary), Holloway, Howden, D L Dick, D Dick, S Hales and R S Paine (coxswain).

For Thorneycrofts, Commander Leyland, manager of their Marine Department, expressed the hope that the presence of the new boat at Worthing would prevent any further fatalities.

After the lunch, at the slipway, 30 or 40 Worthing people witnessed the Mayor starting the boat's engine while the Mayoress cut the tape to complete the official launch. The boat, built to the aforementioned specifications, slid into the water accompanied by loud cheering, which must have made the people of Kingston wonder what was going on in their midst.

The rescue craft was described by some as a 'pocket' lifeboat, yet it carried 25 people and a crew of four without difficulty. Apart from its size the other noticeable thing that made it differ from a lifeboat was its colour; it was painted white instead of the RNLI blue, and she had a red rubbing streak marked around her hull.

Whilst under construction, several other towns showed an interest in the rescue boat and for Thorneycrofts it looked as though Worthing's would be the first of a chain of these craft around the coast.

This launching ceremony was intended only to be a preliminary one, as the actual christening was to follow at Worthing at a later date when a boathouse site had been decided upon. She would be named the *Kenneth and Gerald* to commemorate the names of Kenneth Howden and Gerald Blenkins whose deaths by drowning led to the start of the rescue boat scheme.

Two days after the launch, Coxswain Paine and his four crew sailed some 200 miles, going down the Thames estuary and around the Kent coast on their way to Newhaven harbour, where the boat was to be kept until a suitable boathouse could be obtained.

Local fund-raising continued, and was further boosted by the proceeds from two plays put on at the Durrington Institute on 6 May by amateur players *The Adventurers*.

Exactly one year had passed since the rescue boat fund had been launched and the generosity of Worthing citizens was reflected in the total subscribed which stood in the region of £1,000, probably enough to cover the cost of the craft.

...the rescue craft was described by some as a 'pocket' lifeboat...

A junior class at Elm Grove School in 1932/3. Some of the known children are: Harold Shaw, Les Grout, Ron Short, Doug Davies (became Workshop Manager, Hall & Co), Joyce King, Dorothy Dawson (became a teacher), Andrew Pace, Margaret Simmons, Joyce Jackson, Brity Peres and Muriel Wright.

Brass helmeted Worthing firemen on their appliances taking part in an August Bank Holiday parade pictured in Warwick Road. Note the old Tower Brewery in the background.

Listening to the band: The circular bandstand viewed from inside the Enclosure.

Looking across a crowded promenade towards the Bandstand Enclosure.

South Farm Road level crossing, photographed from Cross Street looking northwest.

OPPOSITE PAGE: *Detail showing the van belonging to fishmonger F Stubbs waiting while a steam locomotive puffed by.*

F. STUBBS

1933

◆ CHAPTER 9 ◆

A Prince and a Pauper

The Gypsy Moth that was sighted over Lancing College shortly before noon on Monday 22 May, 1933 was no ordinary biplane, reported *The Worthing Gazette*. Guided by an Avian flown by none other than aviation pioneer Cecil Pashley, the Moth made a perfect landing at Shoreham Aerodrome.

Witnessed only by a handful of spectators on the field, a few men working on the overlooking railway embankment, several reporters and policemen, this modest welcoming party belied the visitor's importance.

A small car ferried the visitor along the rough cart-track by the edge of the airfield heading southward to the subway underneath the railway. Here he was transferred into an official car which was too large to have passed through the rural subway.

As the car approached Chapel Road in Worthing on this still and sunny summer's day, prettily coloured flags and bunting could be seen hanging from buildings in the vicinity of the recently completed new Town Hall, built to the north of the Museum, which was soon to be officially opened.

As far as the eye could see, the pavements on both sides of the road were massed with people anxious for a glimpse of the special visitor, while on the upper floors, each open window had its full complement of eagerly waiting faces. Several youths even perched precariously on the roof of the Rivoli Cinema commanding an unobstructed view of the enclosure cordoned off in front of the Town Hall for the privileged few. Opposite the dignitaries, stood the Territorials forming a guard-of-honour from 228th (H) Sussex Field Battery, and either side was lined with members of the British Legion, of the Legion of Frontiersmen, Scouts, Guides and Cubs as well as schoolchildren.

The sound of cheering further down Chapel Road warned the thousands of waiting spectators of the approaching guest.

A mounted patrol rode up to the arena, followed almost immediately by two black police cars, one of which was carrying the Chief Constable of West Sussex, Mr A S Williams.

Seconds later a saloon car drew up and out stepped Lord Winterton acting as deputy for the Lord Lieutenant of Sussex, who stood aside as the Royal visitor followed him out of the car.

Wearing a red carnation on his grey suit, Prince George (who later became

King George VI) smiled in acknowledgement as a roar of welcome swelled from the patiently waiting crowd.

While the excitement was still at its height, Major J E Rodocanachi, commanding the guard-of-honour, ordered the Royal Salute to be given, whereupon the Territorial band of the 57th Home Counties Brigade played the first six bars of the National Anthem.

Before performing the opening ceremony the Prince was briefly introduced to local dignitaries as well as the designer of the Town Hall, architect Mr C Cowles-Voysey, and Mr A B H Colls whose company Trollope & Colls Ltd had built the 'municipal mansion'. However, the Prince took time to speak at length to the foreman Mr H Westwood, representing the workmen, who had physically constructed the building.

Striding up the steps, his Royal Highness inserted the key in the lock and swung back the great bronze doors, declaring the Town Hall open.

The whole scene was bathed in glorious sunshine, so hot that people started collapsing and had to be stretchered off by police and St John's Ambulance men to the clinic behind the Town Hall. But so many fainted in the heat (more than 100 altogether) that patients had to be laid on a grass area which existed at the side of Stoke Abbott Road at that time.

Like all members of the Royal family, Prince George took a special interest in ex-Service men, and whilst in Worthing, lost no time in speaking to those in the guard-of-honour who had seen service overseas in the Great War. Sergeant A A Hunt of 58 Howard Street, who had served in the Royal Artillery in Mesopotamia and India, said after the opening ceremony: "You would never have realised that it was a Prince of England talking to you. He was more like one of our own pals."

Local character Charles 'Punch' Riddles would have been in the crowd watching the Prince had it not been for his untimely death just three days earlier. A familiar figure on the beach, he looked the part of a fisherman in his entirety. Out in the open in all conditions, he had a weather-beaten tan which was the envy of many inland visitors.

Punch was a typical old beachcomber and odd-job man, and had been known to every boatman on the seafront for many years. As a longshoreman, his rowing and sailing skills were second to none, knowledge which he eagerly passed on to novices.

He had friends in all walks of life, including many rich ones. Like all old salts of his type, he had the habit of exchanging experiences with all those who cared to stop for a chat.

Curiously, he earned a reputation as a reliable weather forecaster, for if asked very early in the morning what the day's weather would be, he invariably answered with the most uncanny accuracy.

Like many old salts he could be trusted, but in his case his trustworthiness was absolute, for when one of Riddles' old friends was asked for the most impressive feature of his character, the reply was: "If I had £1,000 which I wanted to place in safekeeping for a time I should have given it to Punch to keep for me".

Aged 79, he died a pauper at the East Preston Public Assistance Institution (better known as the Workhouse), but a number of his close friends took steps to see that he was buried in private ground.

...like all old salts of his type he had the habit of exchanging experiences with all those who cared to stop for a chat...

A horse-drawn wagon of the Southern Railway collecting or delivering luggage to a house in Lansdowne Road in 1935.

Road accidents were commonplace in the 1930s. This Austin 16 police ambulance was used to ferry Worthing's injured to hospital.

THEN

NOW

Wide road junction: taken from the Norfolk Hotel (now a public house and night club) on the corner of Newlands Road, this view looking northward shows a lorry (centre) driving up the old Broadwater Bridge. The road seen on the left is Railway Approach (now the site of a multi-storey car park).

The new Town Hall in Chapel Road, opened in 1933, by the junction with Stoke Abbot Road (right). Note the war memorial on the corner, erected in memory of those men of the Borough who sacrificed their lives in the Great War.

1933

◆ CHAPTER 10 ◆

New Rescue Boat in Action

Almost without warning, Worthing's new rescue boat arrived off the town on Monday evening 31 July, reported the *Worthing Gazette*. No announcement had been made, save for the placing of a blackboard outside the pier entrance stating that the boat was arriving that evening and would be welcomed by the Mayor and Mayoress. As there was nowhere to house the craft, its sudden appearance came as quite a surprise.

The Worthing Rescue Boat Kenneth & Gerald *of the 1930s, was funded by private subscriptions.*

Having left Shoreham Harbour just after 6.00 pm, the *Kenneth and Gerald*, crewed by Reg Paine, Tim Sullivan and Charlie Bashford, the same crew incidentally who discovered the capsized craft in which Lieutenant-Commander Gerald Stewart Blenkins RNR and Mr Kenneth Howden had met their death in the April of the previous year.

Despite the lack of publicity, word of mouth travelled fast and hundreds turned out to welcome the new 'pocket lifeboat'. Among the principal guests were Kenneth's parents, Mr Robert C Paine (chairman of Worthing Boat Club), Mr G E Spencer (representing boatbuilders Messrs John I Thorneycroft & Co Ltd), and a number of Aldermen and Councillors. Massed on Worthing Pier and lining the prom, the crowds almost prevented Piermaster Mr R C Paine from reaching the Deputy Mayor, Alderman F A Watts (Chapel Road shoe shop proprietor) standing in for the Mayor.

As the *Kenneth and Gerald* drew alongside the landing stage, Mrs A W Buckingham (wife of the rescue boat committee chairman) threw a bunch of white heather to the coxswain (Reg Paine). A floral replica of the boat was presented by Messrs W Simpson and afterwards sent to the Mayoress.

After a short cruise westward in the new craft, Alderman Watts addressed the

Playing Hoopla at a fairground

attentive crowd from the boat, to announce how glad he was that the people of Worthing appreciated their new rescue boat.

A number of ladies made a collection for the fund during the evening, and later a donation box was fixed to the boat.

For launching purposes, a two wheel cradle costing £75 and modelled on the lines of that used for *Miss England III* (Sir Henry Seagrave's world water speed record-breaking boat) was installed the next morning, on the beach immediately east of the Bandstand Enclosure, near boats belonging to Reg Paine, the Rescue Boat coxswain.

Later that week a further appeal was made in local newspapers for continued financial support from Worthing citizens to keep the boat running and well-maintained.

The following week it was used as the safety boat at the annual regatta, held on the Wednesday afternoon to coincide with half-day shop closing, where it gave sterling service during the rowing races when several boats, bobbing up and down in the heavy sea, filled with water.

Competitors for the sailing and rowing races came from as far away as Southampton, Deal and Herne Bay. There were races for canoes, outboard motor boats and speed boats too. Worthing Swimming Club contributed to the success of the fixture with men's, women's and boys' contests.

For the first time in some years, a running commentary was broadcast from the pier, and at the conclusion of the day's events the Mayoress presented the prizes.

Six weeks after being stationed on Worthing beach the Rescue Boat was called out in answer to distress signals seen out to sea at about 9.30 pm on Thursday 14 September.

Quickly mustering his two crewmen, Coxswain Paine enlisted help from the crowds of willing holidaymakers, who had gathered around on hearing the maroons fired, to launch the *Kenneth and Gerald*.

Within minutes, the fishing boat *Britannia* also put off with Worthing watermen W Belton, W Bashford, W J Bashford and E Wells.

At first the Rescue Boat made for a light due south of the pier, but it turned out

...six weeks after being stationed on Worthing beach the Rescue Boat was called out in answer to distress signals...

to be a trawler that had noticed nothing unusual.

St John Ambulance men on parade at the Little High Street Drill Hall, rushed down to the beach as soon as they heard the maroons. Under the command of Ambulance Officer W Child, they fetched their oxygen respiratory apparatus from the first-aid hut by the pier, and stood by in case their services were needed.

The rumour of a vessel in distress had drawn huge crowds down to the beach where they waited patiently until the *Britannia* returned about 11.30 pm, when Mr Belton revealed that despite searching many miles between East Worthing and Littlehampton they found nothing unusual.

The Rescue Boat, whose powerful searchlight, combing the Channel, could be seen from the shore, landed back again at midnight, and was drawn up the shingle with the help of the many spectators.

Although the Rescue Boat failed to locate anything, the speedy and commendable launch had created a big impression.

As the two boats had found nothing, had distress signals really been sighted? Shoreham Coastguard reported seeing something resembling two shooting stars out to sea. Worthing Police claimed, the following morning, that the supposed signals were actually caused by bombing practice at sea. But a Worthing man reported having seen a splendid meteor from the seafront just after 9.30 pm, about the time the Rescue Boat was called out. Mr A E Hills of 12 Byron Road said it was visible for only about three seconds, beginning as a faint streak of light and rapidly enlarging into a seemingly large yellow and green sphere with a long tapering tail before breaking up into two or three fragments which then simply faded away. Could it have been that this meteor was mistaken for distress signals?

A goods train chugging across West Worthing level crossing. An unusual view captured from the top of newly built flat-roofed shops in New Broadway, Tarring Road, looking westward towards the station and the train shed beyond.

BEST
MENS·BOYS WEAR
Gales
MARSHALL
TARRING CROSSING
TOBACCONIS
NEWSAGEN
EXCHANGE IT
NEW FORD

The west elevation of Charmandean private school. After the school closed, the building fell into disrepair, and shortly before its demolition in the 1960s a young lad playing in the building fell through the floor and was killed.

Proprietor of the Dome and Rivoli Cinemas, Carl Seebold, pictured in his later years.

The turretted lifeboat house annexed to the adjacent Armitage Blind Home (which has since been converted into residential apartments called Claydon Court).

Worthing had many chain stores including the International.

THEN

Marine Parade looking westward past the Marlborough Hotel (right)...

NOW

...which was demolished along with adjacent properties to allow for modern development including the multi-storey car park and Marks & Spencer.

1933-1934

◆ CHAPTER 11 ◆

Fire and Five Flicks

Worthing pier's original Victorian Southern Pavilion ablaze on 10 September 1933.

Disaster struck Worthing pier once more on 10 September 1933. (In 1913 it collapsed at the height of a ferocious storm – see *Edwardian Worthing* - the second book of this trilogy.)

The first indication to promenaders out for an afternoon stroll in their 'Sunday best', came when smoke drifted westward over the sea, its source being the southern pavilion.

Tea was being served when the hall suddenly filled with smoke. Flames appeared through the floor and people abandoned their tea to rush for the exits.

A huge blaze soon developed. Flames leapt into the air, some as much as 60 feet high, could be seen for miles along the coast and by pleasure boats and ships at sea.

Hundreds of people were on the pier at the time and hundreds more rushed to the spot.

Urgent calls to the fire brigade and the police station brought firemen and police speeding to the scene, but they were powerless to save the pavilion, for the strong wind from the east fanned the flames steadily and in an hour it was reduced to a charred mass.

Blazing pieces of decking began falling into the sea. Too late to save the far end of the pier, the firemen concentrated on preventing the flames from creeping along the planking to the other pavilion, just seven years old, at the landward end.

Holidaymakers, some dressed only in bathing costumes, volunteered to help the emergency services. Armed with picks and crowbars they set to work tearing up the decking planks.

An aerial shot of the pier following the fire of 10 September 1933. All that remained of the Southern Pavilion was the metal pier girders surrounded by the iron landing stage.

The plan worked. One pavilion was saved but nothing remained of its original Victorian counterpart. Although built about 40 years apart, they had been designed in matching styles. For a short period of only seven years they had both graced opposing ends of the pier, just like a pair of book-ends.

The blaze and the destruction made headlines nationally, even taking up the entire front page of the *Daily Mirror*, which boasted of being the largest selling daily picture newspaper.

The Rescue Boat Committee made headlines locally when they 'dropped a bombshell' over the proposed housing of the *Kenneth and Gerald* Rescue Boat. Agreement between Rescue Boat and Amateur Boat Club committees could not be reached over the proposal to rent part of the latter's forthcoming new premises at Splash Point, and in November the former decided to pull out. And so the *Kenneth and Gerald* was destined to stay even longer on the open beach.

In December, the Council invited tenders for the erection of the new club-house which was to be leased to the Boat Club.

Buildings for another type of leisure pursuit, that of watching films, were not council owned. Worthing at this time had just three cinemas, all still run by impresario Carl Seebold: the Dome, Rivoli and Picturedrome.

Two more cinemas were under construction: the Odeon in Liverpool Road where steelwork had begun in September; and the Plaza in Rowlands Road.

The latter was built in record time by Andrew Gibbs Ltd of London, employing more than 200 men on the site each day, mainly locals from Worthing and Brighton. Once the steel framework was in position, it took less than 16 weeks to complete the building. The magnitude of the operation was immense: 1,500 tons of soil were excavated, 600 tons of structural steelwork were erected, 700,000 bricks and 500 tons of cement were used; wired with sixty miles of cable, the building was illuminated by 10,000 lamps; while 1,000 gallons of gold, silver and other cellulose paint decorated the place. The modern Art Deco building, lit from cunningly concealed recesses in walls and ceilings, even boasted air-conditioning.

...both graced opposing ends of the pier, just like a pair of book-ends...

Opened by the Mayor, Alderman H T Duffield JP, on Thursday evening 14 December 1933, in the presence of a 2,000 strong audience, the Plaza was built for Louis Morris at a cost of £80,000. Equipped for the provision of first-class stage plays, as well as screening films, the 'Super-Cinema', as it was then called, was a tribute to the skill of architect Mr H Weston, M Inst R A, M Inst SE, FIAS.

The opening programme contained two outstanding items: an organ selection by Dando on the £4,000 John Compton organ, the first instrument of its kind; and the showing of Santa's Workshop, the most costly Walt Disney coloured 'Silly Symphony', seen in Worthing before its London release.

After the performance, a reception for 350 guests was held in the finely appointed first floor ballroom.

(The cinema closed in 1968, and is currently a bingo and social club, while the ballroom has been used as a discotheque night club.)

The Mayor had a varied life. Two months later on 15 February 1934, in his role as a magistrate, he heard the case of a tall, attractive girl charged with attempting suicide by throwing herself off the end of the pier. It soon became apparent that her action was the result of a broken love affair with a married man, Harold Dawson. Exposed as having lived with him, and having a seven month old baby by him, her 'scandalous' behaviour made headlines. Sentencing Mercia Moreton, she was bound over, while Dawson lost his job as a cellist with the Municipal Orchestra, ousted by the fear of a wave of public feeling against him.

Dawson then became another statistic joining the 477 unemployed in Worthing drawing benefit – 365 men and 112 women – but fortunately the job situation following the Great Depression was improving, as the number of claimants was 228 lower than the previous year's figure of 705.

Even most of those fortunate enough to be in work received only minimal wages, a fact borne out by the very few Worthing homes having a telephone: only 7% of residents could afford to be connected.

One of the civic duties undertaken by the Mayor was to preside over the annual meeting of the Worthing branch of the RNLI. At the 1934 gathering held at the old Town Hall, South Street on Monday 5 March, chairman Lieutenant-Colonel A F Randolph, CMG,DSO, reported a remarkable success in raising more than £190 on Lifeboat Day alone, an increase of around 35% on the previous year, and a record for many years past.

Three weeks later, at the annual meeting of another local maritime organisation, the Worthing Regatta, the Mayor was elected president. Addressing the assembly in Mitchell's Chapel Road Cafe he remarked, "I can remember regattas in Worthing more than 60 years ago. Although, perhaps, they were somewhat different then compared with what they are now, they are still just as interesting. Furthermore, the fixture is one of the town's best advertisements."

Three days earlier, the Mayor had officiated at the grand gala opening of the Odeon Cinema on Saturday 24 March 1934. Famous British film stars were there, and a large crowd had to be controlled by police. Anne Grey, a striking blonde, became the centre of attention, and there was a rush to glimpse the four other stars: Molly Lamont, Dave Burnaby, Kenneth Kove and Dorothy Boyd.

The picture house, set back from Montague Street in Liverpool Road, was actually opened by Lord Winterton who drew attention to a paragraph in the

...the cinema closed in 1968 and is currently a bingo and social club...

souvenir programme which said that as far as possible the directors would screen only British films, and everything made for the Odeon was British.

One of the few purpose-built Odeons to have an organ installed, possibly to compete with the recently opened Plaza, Henry Wingfield was at the console of the British Compton 3/6. It was on a lift, and featured a special illuminated glass surround in which such illusions as 'snowfalls' and 'flame effects' could be produced at the flick of a button.

Designed by architects Whinney, Son and Austen Hall, the building boasted a circular-ended projection by the entrance, housing tea rooms on both ground and first floor levels.

The south-facing front of the building and the tower were coloured cream to contrast with the remaining brickwork.

...famous British film stars were there...

The Arcade's northern entrance on the corner of South Street and Montague Street.

The view remains virtually unchanged today.

...brought the total number of working cinemas in Worthing at this time to five...

The auditorium and balcony seated 1600 patrons. Air-conditioning was provided. A special feature of the Art Deco interior was the lighting, and there was a band of light around the proscenium opening, providing varying effects using three-coloured lighting.

(The Odeon closed in 1986, and the popular and familiar landmark was demolished by Humphrey Avon to make way for his Montague Centre complex.)

Together with the Dome, the Rivoli, the Picturedrome and the Plaza, the Odeon brought the total number of working cinemas in Worthing at this time to five. The town boasted two theatres as well: the Pier Pavilion and the Connaught Theatre. (The latter at this time was not at the same venue as it is today but at the adjacent premises now known as The Ritz. The Connaught Theatre moved into the old Picturedrome building when the cinema closed in 1935.)

The town's natural open air theatre – the beach – played host to the annual regatta which included a thrilling bombing event by members of the Southern Aero Club, who targeted the occupants of a motor boat with bags of flour and soot. Held on Wednesday 15 August 1934, a day which old sailing hands considered to be the best for sailing in 20 years, the sporting fixture was enjoyed by dense crowds watching from the promenade and the pier.

Worthing Amateur Boat Club used their new galley, the *Endeavour*, for the first time, but the club enjoyed only moderate success.

Their performance over the season as a whole, however, gave them much credit: the club rowed at ten regattas in a total of 33 races, securing seven firsts, six seconds, 11 thirds and two fourths; they even won the Sexton Cup back from Shoreham who had held it for the previous five years.

The Worthing Rescue Boat stored on the beach opposite Bedford Row.

The Worthing club's newly built Art Deco premises at Splash Point were officially opened on Wednesday 19 September that year, by the Mayor (Alderman H T Duffield J P) who had been a member since 1880 when the club had been founded by Sir Robert Loader.

Recalling the early days of the club, the Mayor said, "I remember quite well getting up at four and five o'clock in the morning and coming down to Worthing from Tarring to put in an hour's rowing before breakfast," and reminiscing over some past successes his worship called to mind, "In the years 1923-24-25 we did wonderful things at Worthing, and we were the rowing champions of the South Coast."

During the evening, members had a jolly good time at a dance held in their new premises, a clubhouse with improved facilities not only for rowing but for social events.

There was ample room in the building, for it was originally intended to house the Worthing Rescue Boat as well, before the latter's committee had suddenly decided against it, probably through lack of continuing funds to pay the rent on the

Ferring Lane, Ferring, looking northward past the Henty Arms pub sign (right).

A view from Splash Point showing Denton Gardens' shelters (right) and the newly built Art Deco Boat Club premises (left).

The newly built Bandstand Enclosure and Pier Pavilion in the background, together with the prominent domed turret of the Dome Cinema. Photographed just before the Arcade was built.

proposed lease. The *Kenneth and Gerald* which had then started its working life on the beach just east of the Bandstand Enclosure, was later moved to a position east of the pier.

Put into action again on Sunday 21 October when a vessel got into difficulties beyond the pier, the Rescue Boat went to the aid of the converted submarine chaser *Sorcha* that had run out of petrol. Drifting, she was in danger of grounding.

When the *Kenneth and Gerald* was called out, it too got into difficulties. As soon as it was afloat, it developed engine trouble and was delayed for half an hour before the fault was rectified. It then towed the Sorcha, which was en route from Southampton to Shoreham Harbour, to its destination. Subsequently, a donation was made to the Rescue Boat Fund on behalf of the owners, the Southampton Launch Works.

Rescue Boat coxswain Reg Paine reflected upon the recent past, when up until just four years earlier, the Worthing lifeboat had still been in use. Powered by wind and human energy, the rowing and sailing craft could never have suffered from engine failure.

Professional boatman Reg lived at Western Place, and the short walk home each day from his pitch on the beach by the Bandstand Enclosure took him towards the Lifeboat House overlooking the sea.

During the day, its tall doors were wide open exposing the sturdy *Richard Coleman,* while the last coxswain of the lifeboat, Bill Blann, was on hand to guide members of the public up to a specially constructed gallery overlooking the boat and to answer questions on the various exhibits and framed photographs of thrilling and dangerous services undertaken in the Worthing lifeboat.

Only the most tactful approaches could induce Bill to talk of his personal bravery. He spoke unassumingly and appeared to think that by reason of its frequent recurrence, his taking his life into his own hands had been a commonplace matter.

Modest Bill unpretentiously dismissed suggestions of his individual brevity by expressing:

"It was all in a day's work."

...the Rescue Boat went to the aid of the converted submarine chaser Sorcha that had run out of petrol...

The Convent of the Holy Rood which stood on the north side of Stoke Abbott Road.

The author would like to hear from anyone who has been to St. Dunstan's School which used to be in West Worthing.

Children frolicking in the shallows where a small boat lies anchored. Note the conspicuous Dome Cinema which was, and still is used as a navigational point by local fishermen and boatmen.

Two pictures of F G Searle's Motor Show held in Montague Street's Literary Institute in 1934.

Ham Road Garage at Pages Corner featuring a badly damaged car being towed in by its breakdown truck.

Ferringham Lane, Ferring.

THEN

Looking north from Downview Road towards West Worthing level crossing with the Down View Hotel on the left.

NOW

Tarring Crossing today. A busy junction with an automated level crossing.

1935-1938

◆ CHAPTER 12 ◆

Times to Celebrate

Following the pier fire of 1933, the sub-structure was rebuilt the following year, and a new southern pavilion constructed in an attractive Art Deco style of the period. Opened in 1935, the building included a small dance hall, cafe, sun lounges and balcony, and the total cost of the works was put at £18,000. (Today that same pavilion houses a night-club.)

Worthing pier showing part of the new Art Deco Southern Pavilion, built following the destruction of its Victorian predecessor by fire.

Another opening ceremony with a maritime connection took place in that same year of 1935. It was the Hargood Room at Worthing Museum, built using £1,500 bequeathed to the town by the late Mr H Hargood who had championed so many causes for fishermen as well as the RNLI.

A further civic building was also completed during that busy year – the Assembly Hall in Stoke Abbott Road, linked to the adjacent Town Hall in Chapel Road. Officially opened by an Alderman and Honorary Freeman of the Borough, James Gurney Denton, who contributed the massive sum of £40,000 to cover most of its cost, the Hall was another great asset to the town to be built in the inter-war years. This was his second gift to the town. He had previously given the Town Council the site for Denton Gardens next to Beach House in Brighton Road in 1922. Denton, four times Mayor, was unable to be present at the opening ceremony due to his recovery from a fall some five months earlier which had made him seriously ill. Even though he was not able to attend, he still managed to carry out the official duty by pressing a button at his home, Selden Lodge in Selden Road. Via some ingenious wiring, the switch was connected to an electronic device which opened the massive bronze doors of the public building. Just two years later in 1937, the elderly gentleman died. In many ways he had been a generous benefactor to the town of his adoption where he had amassed a personal fortune through his business interests.

A significant change in the field of local entertainment came in 1935 with the closing of the Picturedrome cinema in Union Place on Sunday 16 June. The following day alterations began to convert it into the Connaught Theatre that we know today. When it reopened, the theatre was run initially by Messrs Charles Bell and W Simpson Fraser who leased the building. (The latter became known as Bill Fraser who played Snudge in television's *Bootsie & Snudge*.)

The year of 1935 will be remembered as Jubilee year if nothing else. George V with his queen, Mary, celebrated 25 years on the throne. As with other towns, Worthing engaged in a busy programme of events to mark the royal occasion.

Thousands flocked to Worthing to participate in the carnival atmosphere, many even came down on the train from London. It was estimated that more than 30,000 people turned out for the Silver Jubilee. Such a vast crowd had never before been seen in the town. Through streets, lavishly decorated with bunting draped and flags flying from every possible vantage point, snaked a mile-long procession of imaginative tableaux as well as military contingents and representatives of local organisations, that formed the backbone of the Borough's celebrations. The carnival-type floats were representative of Great Britain and her Dominions, and formed a combined tribute to King George and his queen from the many and various groups representing the Borough. The procession was so long that the first float was entering Montague Street before the last had left North Street, the whole pageant taking about 20 minutes in all to pass slowly by.

The author's father, Bill Blann, a youngster at the time being educated at the local Sussex Road School, remembers singing in a large choir of school-children near the steps at the entrance to the Pier Pavilion. Close by, was a battery of guns of the Artillery Corps which nearly deafened them when they fired the salute. Each child was given a commemorative mug as a memento.

Celebrations concluded that evening with fireworks and dancing, and a huge bonfire was lit on Cissbury Hill as a beacon.

...and a huge bonfire was lit on Cissbury Hill as a beacon....

THEN **NOW**

Goring bypass (Goring Way) under construction, 1938.

The turning to the right in front of the Conservative Working Men's Club is an extension of Mulberry Lane.

...streets adorned with all sorts of colourful streamers, flags and evergreens....

All the flags and bunting came out again just two years later in May 1937 when George VI was crowned. Bill Blann had left school by then and was working in his first job as a boy assistant at Blackwells gents outfitters on the corner of Teville Road and South Farm Road. He recollects that Mr Blackwell bought in bales of red, white and blue bunting to be sold by the yard from rolls, hundreds of Union flags of various sizes, and coloured gold crowns and royal crests stamped out of cardboard.

People were still very patriotic in those days despite the high unemployment and shortage of money. At times business was so poor that in one of the worst periods remembered, the weekly takings at Blackwells were down to just £12!

Yet, townsfolk surpassed themselves in decorating the town so patriotically, for not only were the streets adorned with all sorts of colourful streamers, flags and evergreens but around 200 shops had magnificent Coronation displays in their windows. Some visitors to the town claimed that Worthing was among the best-decorated towns in the country.

The largest feature of the Coronation celebrations was the town procession, followed in the evening by fireworks and a an open-air dance in Homefield Park. At the pier pavilion a Coronation Dance under the patronage of the Mayor went on until the early hours of the next morning.

The old people of the Borough were not left out, 350 of them were invited by the Mayor to tea at the Town Hall two days later. Entertainment followed and finally each guest was presented with either a souvenir canister of tea or tobacco.

'Follow the Coronation in your own home,' urged an advertisement in a local paper, 'on an up-to-date all-wave all-mains Superhet receiver. List price £13 2s 6d, Radioline Ltd, 52 Tarring Road will rent this set at less than 2/- a week.

Pictures of the Coronation were shown at the Rivoli Cinema at the junction of Chapel Road and North Street. The week long special programme included the Paramount British News film of the Coronation and the Fox British Movietone Pictures in Technicolor. Two main features of the programme were *Our Royal Heritage* and *Dear Old London*, creating a profoundly patriotic atmosphere.

In 1937, further building work took place on the pier, adding the amusement hall about halfway along the promenade length in time for the summer season. At the same time, action was taken to protect strollers from strong winds by the erection of the present central windshield along the promenade length of the Pier, effectively connecting the new amusement hall to the north and south pavilions.

The housing boom of the 1930s was self-evident in the Borough with new estates going up everywhere. At the western end of the Borough 'seaside residences on the beautiful Goring Hall Estate' were advertised at £950 in 1937, while the Goring Hall itself was up for sale at £6,500.

'Attractive Georgian style residence approached by a carriage drive, containing five reception rooms, 19 bedrooms, four bathrooms, garages, three cottages, well laid out gardens, tennis courts, etc. Total area five acres. Pleasant wooded walk to the beach. Would suit use as a school.'

Goring Hall was subsequently used to house a private school, before being turned into the present private hospital.

To the north of the Borough, Hasler Estates offered 'Delightful detached residences at Offington Park with old world charm for £1,075. Modern bungalows £675.'

A special Coronation cake and local residents in St Anselms Road, 1937.

Teville Road during the snow of December 1938.

But home ownership was out of the question for the working classes who continued to rent. To put into perspective the typical earnings for a female in service, one need look no further than the situations vacant column in local newspapers:

'Housemaid wanted for modern house, two in family. Wages £45.' Bearing in mind that this was an annual sum, her earnings amounted to less than a pound a week!

The rise of these new affluent estates brought more wealth to the town, for those middle class families moving in, needed to furnish their homes. Quick off the mark to exploit this new found opportunity was the Electricity Board, who unveiled their new showrooms in Chapel Road, officially opened by Earl Winterton, MP on Monday 10 May 1937.

With an abundance of visitors to Worthing, the hostelry business was also booming. The seafront Pier Hotel on the corner of Marine Place and standing next to the Marine Hotel, underwent a complete transformation which took a year and a half to accomplish. Building work was completed by May 1937. Only the name remained the same, for everything else had changed beyond recognition. What had originally been a little two-storey building, had metamorphasised into an Art Deco three-storey construction of enviable proportions. Boasting eight double rooms and six single rooms, its main entrance was in the Marine Place side street.

By 1938 the ever-increasing resident population of Worthing topped 62,700. Not only was there an influx of new inhabitants, but the actual Borough boundaries themselves had been extended on no less than three occasions during the course of the century. The first in 1902 when the ancient parishes of Broadwater and Tarring were incorporated, the second in 1929 when the villages of Durrington and Goring were taken in, and the third in 1933 when parts of the parish of Findon to the north, and Sompting to the north-east were included.

The Jubilee Procession of 1935 travelling southward down Chapel Road.

Looking northward up Chapel Road past a policeman on point duty by the old Town Hall (right).

THEN

Warwick Street decorated for the Royal festivities.

NOW

The pedestrianised version it is today.

Worthing Borough Fire Brigade Annual Christmas Party 1935 at Central Fire Station for the firemen's children and their friends. During the War, the auxiliary firemen assisted the Borough Brigade in keeping the party going.

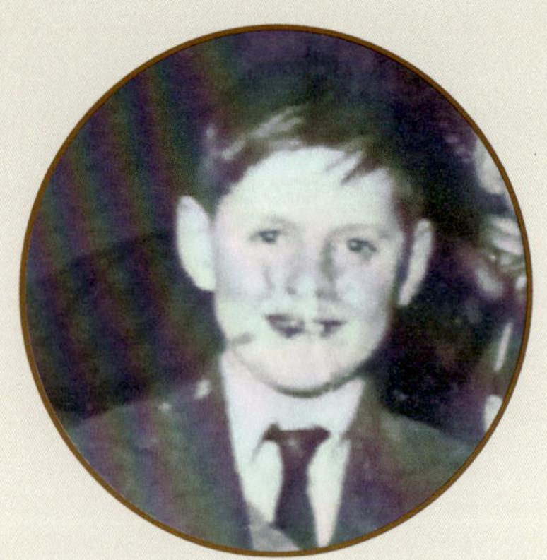

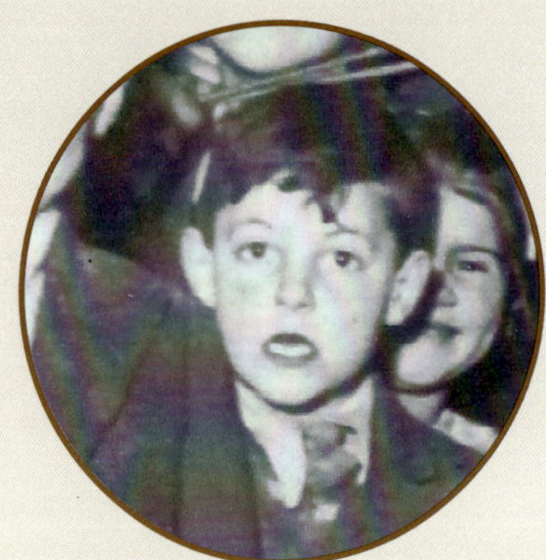

◆ WHO ARE THEY? WHERE ARE THEY NOW? ◆

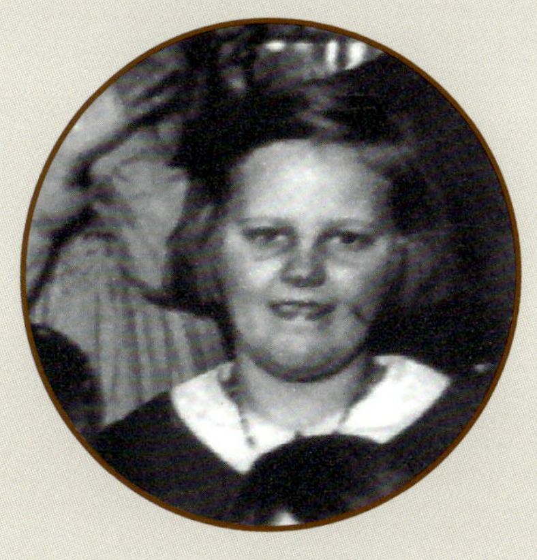

IF YOU RECOGNISE ANY OF THESE FACES...

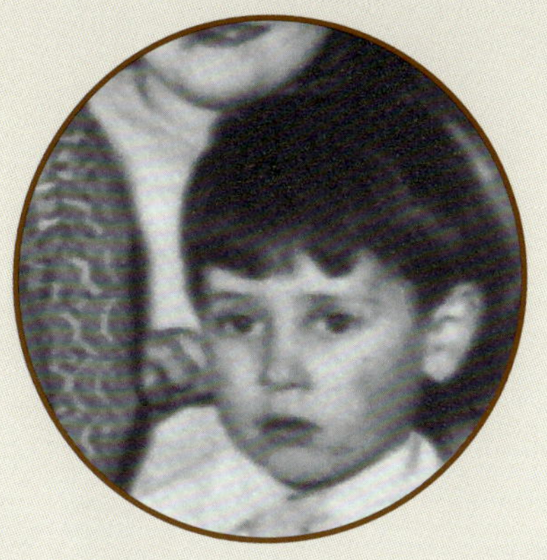

...CONTACT THE AUTHOR AT...

www.yourmemories.co.uk

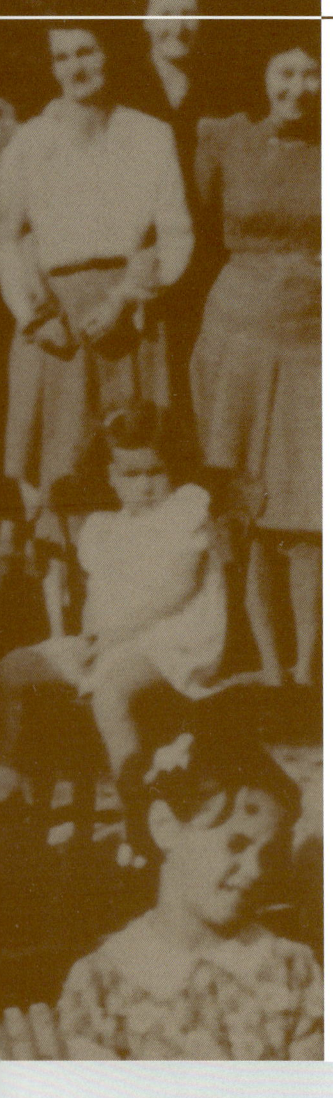

1939-1945

◆ CHAPTER 13 ◆

TIMES OF LOSS

To assist sea-going holidaymakers and townsfolk who found themselves in danger, the town's Rescue Boat *Kenneth and Gerald* was always at hand for an emergency, and remained on the beach to the east of the pier. But the demand upon its services gradually dwindled and it was sold to a Shoreham boatyard in the late 1930s.

After the lifeboat station closed in 1930, the lifeboat *Richard Coleman*, still without its valves and launching gear, was kept on at the Lifeboat House as an exhibit to raise funds for the RNLI. This museum continued to be looked after by the last coxswain, Bill Blann (the author's great grandfather's brother), a task he readily undertook without any absenteeism, even during inclement weather. Unfortunately, it was this tenacity that was probably his downfall, and eventually brought on an illness from which he died, on 3 January 1939 aged 77. His son Jim took over as caretaker.

The Gloucester Place terraced houses seen here, were demolished in the 1960s and a multi-storey car park built on this site between Buckingham Road and Graham Road.

Worthing was left with neither a lifeboat nor a Rescue Boat. It was now up to local fishermen and boatmen to rescue those in distress in their own small boats. Such a rescue took place on 3 June 1939 when George Bashford of 19 New Street saw a sailing dinghy capsize in a moderately rough sea. He immediately rowed his boat out with a strong offshore wind behind him and, with considerable difficulty, succeeded in picking up the beleaguered yachtsman, Mr A G Olby, who was clinging to the upturned hull, and took him safely to the shore. His prompt action was commended by the RNLI who wrote to him and conveyed their appreciation.

For several reasons the year of 1939 was a particularly memorable one for the other Bill Blann, my father. He changed jobs and went to work at the newly opened branch of the Fifty Shilling Tailors (on the corner of Montague Street and Liverpool

Two-way traffic in Montague Street (looking east from its junction with Montague Place). Note the Fifty Shilling Tailors top left.

Road), so called because you could buy suits there from 50/-. The shop was very busy because people were stocking up with clothing for fear of another war. A large percentage of the population had experienced the shortages of the Great War and therefore were being prepared for what they anticipated could be lean years ahead.

That same year, at the age of 17, Bill joined the newly-formed Air Defence Cadet Corps (ADCC, that later became the Air Training Corps, ATC). Young lads were keen to join, for to them it was a great adventure. But without doubt his most poignant memory of 1939 was of a social evening held in the Odd Fellows Hall, Clifton Road. For it was there that he met a certain pretty young lady for the first time – Betty Kent – who was later to become his wife and the author's mother.

Towards the end of the 1930s there was increasing talk about Hitler and the rise in German forces. Then on Sunday, 3 September 1939, came that inevitable broadcast. All gathered around their wireless set, Bill, together with his brothers, sisters and their parents, listened intently as the Prime Minister, Neville Chamberlain, announced that we were at war with Germany. On hearing that devastating announcement, Bill's mother Annie was reduced to tears, as memories of the loss and bloodshed of the last war, just 21 years earlier, came flooding back, and of how almost every family in the land had been affected by death or injury. A few minutes later they were startled by the shrill wailing of the air raid sirens, followed later by the sounding of the All-Clear, thankfully, this time it had been a false alarm.

On Sunday mornings the Air Cadets embarked on local route marches for three or four miles. One of their duties was to carry communications between the air raid centre under the new Town Hall and the various temporary fire stations set up at various places around the Borough.

"All good fun to us lads who couldn't wait to throw our weight against the evil Hitler," recalled Bill. "At first we had no uniforms but after some months were kitted out and really felt that we were doing our bit."

Rationing became the order of the day, and shops had a terrible time. Morale was probably at its lowest when France fell to the advancing German Army who forced the evacuation of our troops at Dunkirk, leaving just the English Channel between us and them.

...minutes later they were startled by the shrill wailing of the air raid sirens....

...we will fight them on the beaches...

Many frightened Worthing people thought that an invasion was imminent. Then, Churchill broadcast his now-famous speech: "We will fight them on the beaches..."

The very next morning the spirit of Worthingites changed. People dragged beach huts into side turnings off the seafront and filled them with shingle, in an attempt to hinder any invading Germans. Only a futile effort, but nevertheless the spirit was there.

Proper coastal defences were soon put in place. Every boat was removed from Worthing beach and stored on waste ground at the eastern end of the borough, where Brooklands boating lake has since been created.

Worthing pier had already suffered two disasters, it had been blown down in 1913, burnt down in 1933, and in 1940, it was about to suffer its third disaster in a relatively short 37 year span of its 137 year existence. It was about to be blown up! A central section of the promenade of the pier was tactically destroyed by explosives, thus isolating the landing stage at the far end. Workmen busied themselves casting concrete blocks known as 'tank traps' along the promenade itself and surrounded them with barbed wire. The beach was mined by the military.

A huge gun emplacement was built at Splash Point and another on the prom opposite the end of Grand Avenue. Worthing got its first taste of enemy bombing in 1940, resulting in many houses being demolished and residents being sadly killed or injured.

The No. 5 Southdown Bus bound for Tarring towing a wartime gas trailer which fuelled the engine.

Some buses in the streets of Worthing no longer ran on petrol and oil but on coal gas, produced in a trailer towed behind. This often caused them to struggle up Broadwater Bridge, stop, the conductor jump off, rush to the rear and stoke up a little, before rushing back on to the bus which gallantly struggled on!

Air raids continued, often caused by German planes jettisoning bombs left from their London targets as they screeched over the coast on their way back to France and Germany, some falling on the Downs as well as on Worthing and other coastal towns. People still had to be careful how they travelled around and always had to have their identity cards on them at all times, more so as there was a very large military build-up in Worthing taking place in readiness for the invasion of France.

Then in June, during the night of the 5/6th June the noise of planes continuously passing overhead, hour after hour, kept some residents awake. They were conveying the 6th Airborne Division over Worthing. Next morning they learned from the radio that the British and American Armies had landed in Normandy and were doing well.

That same month a Lancaster bomber, on its way to bomb Germany, but losing height due to engine trouble, just missed the crowded Plaza Cinema in Rowlands Road before crashing on the shore opposite the bottom of Heene Road. Bursting into flames, its load of bombs and ammunition exploded intermittently with

A German Heinkel III Grief shot down at Cote Street, 16 August 1940. Its two crew were found dead.

Cutting a blanking-off card with a small hole in the middle for vehicle side lights.

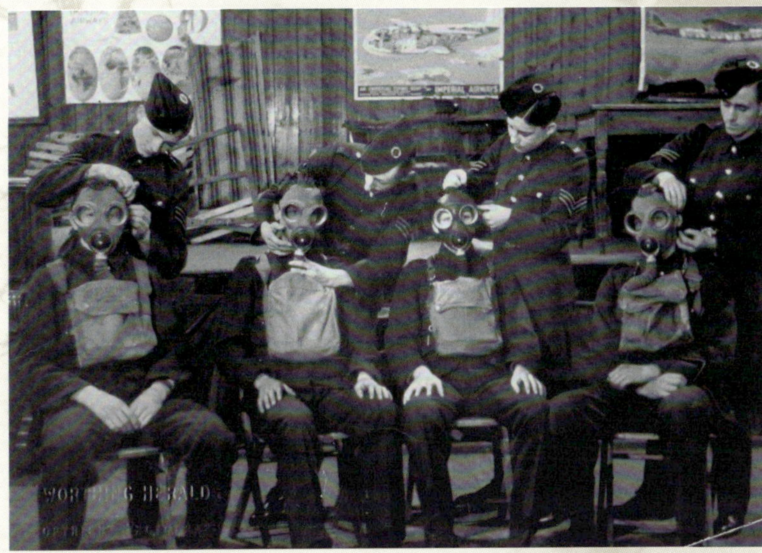

Cadets of the Air Training Corps practising with gas masks

A happy victory photo taken at the Oddfellows Hall, Clifton Road at the King Street party to celebrate the cessation of war and the return of our local service men and women. New Year 1945/6.

War Weapons Week parade making its way northward along Chapel Road past the Town Hall, 22 February 1941.

An air raid shelter built next to a shop at the top of Sompting Road. The Downlands Hotel in Upper Brighton Road can be seen far right in this view taken on 9 February 1946.

The same view today, with the air raid shelter replaced by two further shops.

Blackout precautions: workmen spraying three white bands around the base of a tree to show up in the dark.

Home Guard: An anti-invasion exercise at the approach to Worthing Pier by members of the 12th Sussex (Southdown Motor Transport) Battalion using a track laying military vehicle on 3 August 1941.

Home Guard on exercise on Worthing Pier by the northern pavilion.

Masking headlights for the blackout using a special metal mask with three horizontal slits for casting light downward across the road, January 1940.

Auxiliary Fire Service officers filling up a static water tank from a fire hydrant. These tanks were placed in strategic positions mainly for firewatchers to douse incendiaries.

Members of the Auxiliary Fire Service on parade in Charlecote Road in September 1939, opposite the Central Fire Station on the corner of High Street. Chief Officer Jones is in command.

Brighton Road looking east from the top of the newly built Onslow Court on 9 March 1938 towards the site of the present petrol station, beyond which is marshland where the boats were stored when removed from the beach for the duration of the war. The marshland was later turned into Brooklands Boating Park.

A fire engine and stores staff pictured at St Ronan's School, Mill Road, B Division HQ of the National Fire Service stationed there for the duration of the war. The site is now part of the College Gardens development.

Chapel Road looking north. The lorry is at the foot of the old Broadwater Railway Bridge, to the left is Railway Approach (now the site of a multi-storey car park). On the right of the picture is IKC's Grocery Warehouse, long since gone. The site is now occupied by a Co-op superstore.

THEN

Broadwater Road looking south towards railway bridge.

THEN

Goring Street, looking north towards Littlehampton Road and Titnore Lane.

NOW

Today, the simple road junction is a busy roundabout on the A27.

NOW

...and the same view today.

THEN

Broadwater Road looking north from Ivy Arch Road.

NOW

Now widened into a dual carriageway, it is the main inland route out of Worthing.

A circus elephant on the south slope of the old Broadwater Railway Bridge, photographed from Railway Approach. On the left is the IKC's Grocery Warehouse (now a Co-op Superstore) and on the right is the Norfolk Hotel (now a pub and night club).

West side of Chapel Road (today part of the Teville Gate development) south of railway bridge - Bus Stop for nos. 7, 7A. 7B and 8.

West side of Chapel Road (today part of the Teville Gate development) south of railway bridge - Bus Stop for nos. 3, 4, 9 & 10.

A traditional horse-drawn milk float of Oaklands Farm Dairy, pictured at the end of its round in West Worthing.

◆ EPILOGUE ◆

Changing Times

After the war, the rebuilding of housing and essential buildings took priority over the repairs to the pier, and it was not until 1949 that the pier reopened to the public.

Jim Blann was still the caretaker of the lifeboat showpiece museum, proudly polishing the artefacts for posterity and showing visitors and holidaymakers around the station.

But in the late 1940's, the RNLI bosses decided to sell off the period lifeboat house. Even though visitors to the historic station made donations and, the RNLI took a short-sighted view and wanted a lump sum straight away.

The promenade section of Worthing pier being rebuilt between 1947 and 1949, having been blown up to hinder a German invasion during the war.

Worthing was a 'lifeboat town', it is steeped in historic tales of its brave and heroic lifeboatmen, men who often drove themselves to the very edge of their physical and mental exertion in atrocious conditions attempting to rescue those in danger on the frequently violent sea.

Nevertheless, the RNLI stuck to its guns and sold the quaint Victorian lifeboat house in 1950, and the *Richard Coleman* lifeboat was removed, to be taken to the Greenwich Maritime Museum as an exhibition piece.

It happened one sad May morning without any pomp, without any ceremony and without any high ranking officials to oversee the operation. It was as if the gallant vessel and the townsfolk were being chastised for some reason unknown. Early on Thursday May 12 she left Worthing quietly, in stark contrast to that exciting day some forty nine years earlier in 1901 when she was welcomed to Worthing by a marching band and paraded through streets lined with thousands of townspeople *(see Edwardian Worthing)*.

A lorry tractor unit arrived to haul the *Richard Coleman* away, but she would not shift. The ever-faithful lifeboat did not want to leave her home. A gang of council workmen nearby were called upon to assist and with their help she was dragged quite reluctantly out of her boathouse.

Visitors to the special Lifeboat exhibition at Greenwich, pictured by the Richard Coleman, *The Mayor and Mayoress of Greenwich, Lady Kinahan, Vice-Admiral Sir Harold Kinahan, Mr L C H Cave a member of the RNLI Committee of Management, and Mr Frank Carr director of the museum.*

Still on her own carriage, she was pulled by the lorry to the goods yard by Worthing Railway Station. The slow journey was watched by the curious and inquisitive, as she was hauled eastward along Marine Parade before turning left into South Street and up Chapel Road. At the goods yard a crane there was utilised to lift her weighty bulk unceremoniously onto a lorry to be transported to Greenwich Maritime Museum, where she was to be displayed at a special lifeboat exhibition from 16 May to 10 June 1950.

The small number of bystanders who wished her goodbye could be heard muttering, "That's another link with old Worthing gone."

Back inside the lifeboat house the space looked so large without its lengthy occupant. Framed and treasured pictures still hung on the walls, pictorial mementoes of daring rescues and of thrilling parades.

It had all begun exactly 100 years earlier, in 1850, when Worthing's need for a lifeboat focused on the drowning of 11 of the town's best fishermen while attempting to render assistance to a gale-damaged barque at the mercy of the high sea. Those 11 brave souls had unwittingly left behind no less than 48 dependants with no means of support. Friends, relatives, and the more philanthropic-minded among the well-to-do classes rallied round and mustered support. The fund that was set up, collected an absolutely enormous number of donations that amounted to a staggering total of more than £5,000, which today would be equivalent to more like £750,000 after taking inflation into account.

It was that shining spirit of wanting to help those in need that had compelled those 11 brave fishermen to venture into the stormy waters that fateful day, a quality that led ensuing generations of fishermen and lifeboatmen to consistently risk their own lives for the sake of others that were in peril.

...another link with old Worthing gone...

The Worthing Lifeboat Station had been held in high esteem by the top men at the RNLI and had been frequently used as a shining example to others, no doubt the

A view of Worthing seafront showing the conspicuously unique turret of the lifeboat house (above the car on the right). This picture was taken after the building and the adjacent one to the left had been sold to the Armitage Blind Home in 1950. An oblique balcony was added to realign the two buildings. On the left of the picture the coastguards' flagmast can be seen in the distance. This popular landmark remained in position until 1968.

reasoning behind Worthing's selection as the Station to be used in making promotional lifeboat films on more than one occasion around the turn of the century.

But this was the end of an era. The finish to 100 years of lifeboating at Worthing where the lifeboat had been almost part of daily life. Folk mourned. Worthing could no longer use the prefix and be called... *'A Lifeboat Town'*.

But its long list of lifeboatmen will always be warmly remembered as... *'A Town's Pride'*.

The lifeboat house's new owners, the Armitage Blind Home next door, used it as an annexe. It was they who removed the tall double doors and constructed an oblique balcony across the front in an attempt to align the two quite separately designed buildings.

The Denton Lounge was built onto the west side of the pier's north pavilion in the late 1950s, and the information kiosk east of the pavilion was put up in 1963.

With the increase in boating as a leisure pursuit in the 1960s an inshore rescue scheme was devised in which local boat-owners participated in conjunction with the Coastguards and the RNLI. Worthing's link in this arrangement received its first emergency call in September 1963 when a Worthing Yacht Club safety boat went to the aid of a disabled cabin-cruiser anchored about 500 yards west of the Pier.

The cabin-cruiser, had five people aboard: Mr and Mrs Bob Samet; their two children, Sally and Frank; and Mr Samet's American cousin. They had left Southampton four days earlier bound for Newhaven, and developed engine trouble. With both of its twin engines out of action, it was in danger of being blown ashore and holed on the rock beds.

The distress call was received by Yacht Club member Eddie Dunhill at 8.00 pm on a wet and windy evening. Without hesitation he mustered a volunteer crew to launch the boat, but unfortunately, because the tide was right out, around 45 minutes were expended on reaching the distraught craft.

An attempt by the small safety boat to tow the nine ton stricken vessel to Shoreham Harbour failed, so the mother and children were taken ashore. At this point the Shoreham Coastguards dispatched their standby motor boat, *Knight Errant*, but apparently, owing to the complication of insurance laws, it was unable to take the beleaguered cruiser in tow.

Next morning, Mr Samet managed to start one of the engines, but after about a mile it just petered out. Not long after, a yacht from the French coast which had lost its way in the early morning fog just happened to come across the cruiser and hove to. Luckily the owner was a mechanic and offered to examine the boat's engines. He managed to get up enough power for the cruiser to limp into Shoreham.

Although Worthing's last offshore lifeboat was withdrawn from service in 1930, an RNLI inshore rescue boat (IRB) of the inflatable type was stationed in Worthing

The Richard Coleman *being drawn out of the boathouse for the very last time on 12 May 1950.*

The Richard Coleman *on its carriage being pulled by a lorry tractor unit, seen here navigating the roundabout at the bottom of South Street, observed by curious onlookers.*

The Richard Coleman *on its carriage, displayed outside the Greenwich Maritime Museum from 16 May to 10th June 1950.*

...there was nothing left to save. She was gone forever...

from 1964 (for eight months each year) and proved to be of great value in rescuing the increasing number of small pleasure craft that got into difficulties. Even though it was kept in a boathouse on the beach to the east of the pier it was not entirely safe from perpetrators of wilful destruction. In 1967, largely due to the effects of vandalism, the IRB was withdrawn from service.

The tall flagmast which had stood on the prom opposite the old Victorian lifeboat house for many years was removed in 1968, Worthing Borough Council giving the reason as 'the substantial cost of maintenance.'

But many considered it an act of municipal vandalism upon a popular landmark, which sported a weather vane at the top and flew a red warning flag when the sea was too rough for swimming.

As for the *Richard Coleman*, it was removed from the Greenwich Maritime Museum and put on show at Margate and Southend. Then came a golden opportunity in 1967. Worthing was offered the return of its historic pulling and sailing lifeboat, but Worthing Borough Council refused. As a result, that important piece of our heritage was stored on the open beach near the *Kursaal* at Southend.

Sadly, in 1972, the *Richard Coleman* was set alight and destroyed by vandals; there was nothing left to save. She was gone forever.

The lifeboat house changed hands several times over the years and has had various uses including an art gallery and an aromatherapy clinic, until in 1988 it was put up for sale by auction. At that time the author instigated and spearheaded a campaign, which extended to television and the national media, to reinstate the lifeboat house as a showpiece museum complete with an authentic and historic rowing and sailing lifeboat, a plan which would have reached fruition had it not been for insufficient funding and lack of timely interest from Worthing Borough Council.

During the following year, the town's old lifeboat house, which had served the community, as well as coastal shipping, from 1875, and had been the centre of so much attention over the course of time, was converted into a house – the end of not only an era but of much more, for it symbolised a way of life and a community spirit in which everyone had pulled together to help others.

That way of life has now been recorded by the author in a trilogy of books on Worthing and its lifeboats. 1990 saw the launch of the first book *A Town's Pride* and a year later came the second volume *Edwardian Worthing*.

To commemorate the author's earlier literary works on local lifeboatmen, a Worthing pub was renamed 'A Town's Pride' in 1992, a gesture which he considered a great honour. Formerly the Beachcomber in New Street, the inn featured a vast array of photographs reproduced from the first two books but since the inn changed hands, the photographs and the lifeboat theme have now been removed.

Part of the proceeds from the first two books were donated to the RNLI. Television celebrity and RNLI Vice-President Raymond Baxter came to Worthing for a donation presentation from the author.

Since the RNLI closed the station, Worthing has maintained strong links with the Institution through its keen and devoted fund-raising branch, because the sea has conveyed to us a great heritage, and it is up to us to maintain that heritage. We can all do so by helping that great organisation, the Royal National Lifeboat Institution, without whom, those who depend on the sea for a living or those who use the sea for pleasure, would be very vulnerable and at the mercy of nature's forces.

The culmination of unique co-operation between a publican, an author and the RNLI. The Naming Ceremony of 'A Town's Pride' public house, New Street, took place on 2 May 1991 when entertainment was provided by the internationally-famed Kenny Baker and the Riverside Jazz Band.

Standing: Simon Power (pub owner), Rob Blann, Les Fuller (RNLI IRB Coxswain 1964–1967), Peter Sim (pub manager), Joan Power (wife of owner); Front: Kenny Baker, Linda Sim (pub manageress).
Eight years later in 1999, the pub changed hands and the lifeboat theme was done away with. The dozens of enlarged and framed lifeboat sepia photographs were taken down and the pub signs altered.

The scene outside W H Smith in Worthing when television celebrity Raymond Baxter (RNLI Vice-President) arrived in a vintage car (sponsored by Pavilion Car Rental, Worthing) to accept a donation from the proceeds of the author's book Edwardian Worthing. *The author is accompanied by members of Worthing Edwardians in period costume.*

◆ INDEX ◆

BLANN LINEAGE

EDMUND
(landlord of Nelson Inn 1803)
|
HENRY
(smuggler - see *A Town's Pride*)

EDWIN (drowned in boating accident see Ch.2 of *A Town's Pride*) — TOM (lifeboat 2nd cox)

BILL (lifeboat cox) — HARRY (lifeboat bowman)
|
BILL, JUNIOR (died POW camp WW1)

JESSE (carpenter)

HARRY (retained fireman) — BILL (gents' outfitter)
|
ROB
(author & garden contractor)

Welcome...

"Many enthusiast photographers dream of making a career from their hobby and combine their passion and skill for picture-taking with earning a living from it too. While many are able to turn this dream into a reality, the harsh truth is that for the majority of amateur photographers, the opportunity to 'live the dream' and take pictures full-time is one that eludes us. However, that's not a reason to be disheartened as there still remains lots of opportunities to profit from your photos, even if you're not a professional photographer. From working part-time as a photographer to taking pictures to sell as stock, the chances are there for you to earn money from your images and in this comprehensive guide, our experts will show you how. We've dedicated a large portion of this Magbook to social and portrait photography, which is where the greatest opportunities lie to earn money on a part-time or full-time basis, but we've covered other areas too. We've also extensive ideas and information relevant to all photographers on the basics needed to be a successful photographer, from creating a brand for your business to the role social media plays to how you should conduct yourself to ensure you're seen as a dedicated and conscientious photographer. If you've always wanted to make a success of your photography and believe you could make money from your images, then this guide has the information you need to succeed. All the best!"

DANIEL LEZANO, EDITOR

Why you should aim to profit from your photos

"For most of us hooked on photography as a hobby, there comes a point when people tell you that you should do it for a living. Chances are your first instincts are riddled with self-doubt, then comes a turning point when you've developed your skills and confidence to a level that you start to think its the next natural step. Unfortunately, for some it can be a long, tough journey between this bout of determination and actually making photography a full-time living, especially if you go about it the wrong way. But, do it the right way and you'll find you can earn and learn along the way. I'm sure everyone can agree that there's nothing more appealing or motivating than the thought of being able to do what you love and be paid well for the privilege. Some refer to it as 'living the dream' and while this Magbook has been compiled to help readers reach that goal, we've gone to great lengths to ensure that we provide you with the reality of that dream, so you have all the information you need for a strong start in a competitive industry. Over the last two years, we've investigated the profitability of different money-making routes so we can tell you, in detail and with authority, the best ways to maximise profit and where to invest your time and money for the biggest return. We've also rigorously researched different areas of the market and been given invaluable advice and insight from leading professionals, industry and business experts on how you can make money and build a successful career. However, don't lose sight of the real reason you're trying these new ventures: your love of photography and the satisfaction of people liking your work enough to pay for it. Good luck!"

CAROLINE WILKINSON, ASSISTANT EDITOR, MAKING MONEY FROM PHOTOGRAPHY

MAKING MONEY FROM PHOTOGRAPHY
Produced by *Digital SLR Photography* at:
6 Swan Court, Cygnet Park,
Peterborough, Cambs PE7 8GX
Phone: 01733 567401. Fax 01733 352650
Email: enquiries@digitalslrphoto.com
Online: www.digitalslrphoto.com

Editorial
To contact editorial phone: 01733 567401
Editor **Daniel Lezano**
daniel_lezano@dennis.co.uk
Art Editor **Luke Marsh**
luke_marsh@dennis.co.uk
Features Editor **Caroline Wilkinson**
caroline_wilkinson@dennis.co.uk
Designer **Luke Medler**
luke_medler@dennis.co.uk
Editorial Co-ordinator **Jo Lezano**
jo_lezano@dennis.co.uk
Editorial contributors:
Stuart Cooper, Brett Harkness, Ross Hoddinott, Lee Frost, Esther Ling and Martyn Moore

Advertising & Production
Display & Classified Sales: 0207 907 6651
Advertising Sales **Guy Scott-Wilson**
guy_scott-wilson@dennis.co.uk
Sales Executive **Joshua Rouse**
joshua_rouse@dennis.co.uk
Production Controller **Dan Stark**
dan_stark@dennis.co.uk

Publishing & Marketing
NICKY BAKER DIGITAL PRODUCTION MANAGER
DHARMESH MISTRY BOOKAZINE MANAGER
ROBIN RYAN PRODUCTION DIRECTOR
JULIAN LLOYD-EVANS MD OF ADVERTISING
DAVID BARKER NEWSTRADE DIRECTOR
JOHN GAREWAL PUBLISHING DIRECTOR
IAN WESTWOOD MD TECHNOLOGY
BRETT REYNOLDS CHIEF OPERATING OFFICER
IAN LEGGETT GROUP FINANCE DIRECTOR
JAMES TYE CHIEF EXECUTIVE
FELIX DENNIS CHAIRMAN

For licensing contact Hannah Heagney on +44 (0)20 7907 6134 or email hannah_heagney@dennis.co.uk
For syndication contact Anj Dosaj-Halai on +44 (0)20 7907 6132 or email Anj_Dosaj-Halai@dennis.co.uk

The paper used within this Magbook is produced from sustainable fibre, manufactured by mills with a valid chain of custody.
Making Money from Photography ISBN 1-907779-79-5
Printed by Benham Goodhead Print (BGP)

CONTENTS

TURN TO PAGE 130 TO FIND OUT ABOUT OUR FANTASTIC SUBSCRIPTION OFFERS

132 PAGES
OF EXPERT ADVICE AND INSIGHT

WANT TO TURN YOUR PICTURES INTO PROFIT?

Are you serious about making money from your photographs or contemplating turning pro? Then take your time, ensure you're well prepared and don't rush into anything until you've got all the facts. Here we provides you with the key factors you need to think about

FOR MOST OF US who ponder on the prospect of generating an income from our photography, what stops us is the thought of an oversaturated market combined with our own self-doubt and not knowing how to get started. Now, if we told you making money from your photography would be easy, we would be lying. However, in this new series, we aim to equip you with everything you could possibly need to know about how to improve your chances of generating an income and, more importantly, keep the money coming in. What you do with this information is down to you. You might adore your day job and want to make a little extra cash to fund what can be an expensive hobby, take the first steps towards becoming a semi-pro or a weekend photographer, or it may give you the tools and the confidence to take the plunge and turn professional. Whatever your intention, there will be plenty for you to take on board in this guide and apply to your own money-making schemes. We'll take a look at the hard-core fundamentals of building a business, with advice from accountants and industry experts, as well as providing you with insight into the types of photography-related jobs that are on offer. And for those of you who simply want to earn a little extra pocket money, we'll be investigating the ways you can sell your images directly and indirectly to customers so you know where to invest your precious personal time and turn a profit. So stick with us as we not only build up your photography skills, but also your bank balance.

For those of you who would eventually like to make photography a full-time or part-time career, our first nugget of advice is to make sure you get at least a few fully-paid photography jobs before you pack in the nine-to-five. Take the time to research the routes to establishing a photographic business and talk to professional photographers already working in your field of choice. Find out not only ways to get work but if there's even enough work out there, as many sectors are shrinking. Try to hear first hand what life is like as a semi- or full-time pro. While digital may have made professional image quality more attainable, it's also made competition fierce in nearly every sector. So while making a bit of pocket money could be quite achievable, if you want to make it so that half or even all your income comes from photography, you'll need to be prepared to put in the work, as it won't be easy. Chances are that you will spend more time in front of a computer than you will a camera, editing pictures, chasing clients and uploading images, not to mention managing your accounts and marketing material. And if you're a weekend photographer, it will be even tougher as you'll have to find a way of doing all that while balancing a full-time job.

A sensible photographer, however, will keep their day job and work weekends and evenings, building their client base, experience and portfolio. It would be foolish to believe that if you turn professional you will instantly be on the receiving end of a full-time income, unless of course you manage to secure yourself one of the rare salaried photographic jobs in the industry. The vast majority of photographers, however, will have to earn their money through self-employment, which means starting a business. Not only does this come with a plethora of factors to consider such as taxes, banking, branding, marketing and insurance, you need to be prepared not to turn a profit in the first three years, as very few new businesses do. However, if photography is really your passion, what's three years of working hard to build a business you love when it could lead to a lifetime of living the dream?

Digital cameras and the internet have opened up many more avenues for all levels of photographers to potentially make money, so the opportunities are definitely there to cash in on. Though to really maximise the benefits, you need to be prepared to put in the time to develop your photography skills and market knowledge as well as sustain an unyielding determination to improve and succeed. Too often talented photographers struggle to make money from their photography,

> "To really maximise the benefits, you need to be prepared to put in the time to develop your photography skills and market knowledge"

ISTOCK PHOTO

while other mediocre photographers manage to have a profitable career all because they have the business acumen and perseverance. The title 'professional' is not necessarily a reflection of technical ability or creativity, it only means that you try to make most of your money from photography. There are many gifted amateurs whose images are capable of rivalling a professional photographer's, so, for this reason, just because you might not be a professional shouldn't discourage you from pitching yourself as a photographer worth paying for, if you think your images are good enough. However, if you feel that you do not have the skills yet to go semi- or full-time pro, concentrate on your technique, building up experience, and start trying to make money slowly.

If you're ready to make some serious money and to put the effort in, you may want to start thinking about setting up a business. For anyone who's never been self-employed this can seem like a very daunting prospect, but it's actually rather simple. The first step applies to nearly everyone reading this, who earns more than £6,475 a year and is intending to sell their work to make a profit, however small, and that is to register with HM Revenue & Customs. You need to register with them once you've received your first pay cheque, and are therefore actively trading. You can either register as a sole trader, as a partner or as a member of a limited liability partnership or company. If you fail to let HM Revenue & Customs know within three months of trading, you might be slapped ➤

Key contacts & resources

- **Business Link:** For personalised, free advice for how to set up a business, contact Business Link: www.businesslink.gov.uk
- **The Tax Office:** For advice on filing your yearly tax return call 0845 3000627
- **HM Revenue & Customs:** To register as newly self-employed: 0845 9154515
- **Companies House:** To register your business name or set up a limited company, contact: www.companieshouse.gov.uk
- **Rights:** For information on your rights read the UK Photographers Rights Guide: www.sirimo.co.uk/2009/05/14/uk-photographers-rights-v2
- **Essential read:** *The Freelance Photographer's Market Handbook 2012*

ISTOCK PHOTO

"You need to think about the type of insurance you need for your equipment and whether you need public liability and professional indemnity insurance too"

with a £100 penalty fee, and if you do not register at all, and therefore neglect to pay tax on your new earnings, chances are you'll pay a lot more than this in fines and possibly even jail time. We'll be covering topics including registration options, types of businesses you can own, tax and write-offs in more detail in the *Business Matters* section of this guide. But for the moment, generally speaking, registering as a sole trader is the way to go for most photographers who are making a little extra money, and semi-professionals. It requires no registration fees, you keep all your profits once they're taxed as income and accounts are fairly straightforward to keep. The only downfall is that you'll be personally liable for any debt that your business runs up.

If you'll be requiring business loans and a fair bit of investment, you might want to keep your business debt separate from your personal finances by registering as a private limited company. However, while this means that if your business goes bust you're not personally liable, it will open you up to additional fees, requirements and responsibilities, including registering with Companies House. Finally, for those of you wanting to shift career paths in one go and be your own boss, but need support to run a business, you could invest in a photography franchise. You buy the licence to use the established brand name, products, services and management support. Depending on the terms of the franchise agreement, you might have to pay an initial fee, ongoing management fees or a percentage of your turnover to the franchiser, and the way you operate your business might also be dictated, but at least you do not have to start a business from scratch.

Alongside registering, it's worth arranging an appointment with your bank to discuss setting up a business account and potential funding sources that you might need for set-up costs such as photography equipment, computers, software and even business premises like a studio. Even though you may only be doing the odd weekend wedding or selling a few images via a stock library, it will be a lot easier to manage your income and expenses from a dedicated account, saving you time and stress when it comes to filling out your end of year tax return. (See page 106 for more advice on banking and funding.) You'll also need to think about the type of insurance you need for your equipment and, depending on the field of photography you're working in, whether you need public liability and professional indemnity insurance too. Finally, you can get to the creative, and arguably much more enjoyable, part of building a business: building a brand and marketing yourself (see page 14 for more information on how to do this).

Now, at this point, you're either excited and raring to get going, or terrified by the level of commitment needed, and questioning whether you're ready to go part-time or full-time pro. Our advice is, if you're not sure, start slow and pick out the information that can gradually start to make you money – be it small amounts at first – until you're confident you can take it a step further. But remember to keep this guide in a safe place for when you're ready to refer back to it later. To make it easier for you to distinguish what stage you're at, and what information to take on board, read our photographers' profiles and then look for your symbol in parts of this guide that offer you custom advice. ■

Which type of photographer are you?

This guide will prove essential to all levels of photographer, but relating yourself to one of the three main types below will help you identify the information in the guide that's most relevant to you

HAVE A READ OF OUR three main types of photographer. By identifying with one of them, you will quickly and easily be able to see how the information in our guide relates to you and how your chances of success vary according to the areas and topics of photography that we are covering. You may find similarities in more than one description, so make sure to read all of our advice as it will help greatly improve your chances of making money from your photographs.

BEGINNER INEXPERIENCED AMATEUR

You've probably been taking snapshots on a compact for a while, but haven't had a DSLR for long. You've caught the photo bug and love taking pictures of anything and everything, but get frustrated that you don't have all the fundamental knowledge needed to take full control of your photos. So, you often shoot in a fully automatic mode when you want to be sure you get a decent shot, while experimenting with the various modes and learning from your mistakes. You regularly photograph your family and friends and you try to dedicate some spare time to shooting interests, such as the garden, landscapes or portraits. In terms of gear, you've the basics: an entry-level DSLR with a kit lens, possibly a budget telephoto like the 55-200mm. You've a nice little gadget bag, a basic tripod but few if any specialist bits of kit like a flashgun. You rate your photographic skills as 'OK, but could do more', but among your many near misses, you've some shots you rate as 'very good' to 'excellent'.

ENTHUSIAST ADVANCED AMATEUR

You've used a DSLR for a number of years and quite possibly owned a 35mm DSLR too. You rate yourself as a very competent photographer who knows most, if not all, of the basic requirements to get a perfectly sharp, well-exposed image. You're recognised by those you know as a very good photographer and most likely have been asked not only for copies of your images, but also to take some shots of friends and family too. Your passion for photography is as strong as ever and while you've a good level of expertise, you crave new ideas, techniques and skills to learn, to help expand your talents. You don't earn significant amounts of money from your photos, but you've a strong idea that you could do based on comparing your work to others, from what you've been told and from your modest successes so far, which could involve shooting the odd weekend wedding to selling images on stock libraries.

You've a decent camera outfit based around a mid-range DSLR (with possibly an older, entry-level model as a back-up). Your lenses are all good quality and as well as a good standard zoom, you've a telezoom, an ultra wide-angle and possibly a specialist lens like a macro, as well as a 50mm f/1.8 and a creative option like a Lensbaby. You've a flashgun, sturdy tripod, a good quality gadget bag or backpack and quite possible have, or are thinking of getting, a lighting system. You are fairly competent in Photoshop and other digital techniques and print your best images on a high quality inkjet printer.

SEMI-PRO ADVANCED ENTHUSIAST

You may not have a full-time job as a photographer, but you know you have the creative skills and competency to make serious money from photography. Taking pictures is a major passion in your life and you rarely go anywhere without your DSLR, as it would pain you to see a great photo opportunity and not be able to capture it. For this reason, you own a premium compact that you can carry around with you for when a DSLR isn't practical. You want to live the dream of going pro but unfortunately, for whatever reason, the time isn't quite right, but you have a rough plan and a strong desire to one day make a living as a pro. You're skilled at most photo techniques, but read photo magazines for inspiration and ideas and to see how others earn a crust. You regularly enter photo competitions not only to try to win, but as a challenge to help you improve your skills. You earn a modest but good income from the odd job, such as portrait or wedding shoots, selling images to local businesses and from commissions from online stock libraries. You're on your second or third DSLR, having upgraded to a model you're now satisfied delivers the quality you need. You've a good mix of lenses, with some if not all being premium optics. Among your f/2.8 zooms you have a 50mm, 100mm macro, a premium wide-angle and maybe a teleconverter and/or set of extension tubes too. You've a decent collection of photo accessories including reflectors, lighting, a remote release, a couple of tripods and gels/diffusers to use with your dedicated flashgun.

SHOOTING FOR SUCCESS

With so many areas of photography to choose from, it can be difficult to know where to invest your time, resources and energy for the best chance of a return. We take a closer look at what areas of photography offer you the best opportunities to earn money

EVERY GOOD IMAGE that you capture has the potential to make you money, it's just a case of knowing how and where to sell it. By our reckoning, there are three main areas that a photographer can make money from: services, products and stock. Each one lends itself to some fields of photography more than others and, depending on the types of images you're selling, has varying profit potential.

Services refers to commissions, whether it's shooting a wedding, a portrait shoot, for a newspaper or for the National Trust. Normally this will be a flat fee, however, if it's a commercial shoot, it's usually an hourly rate, normally amounting to between £500 and £1,000 a day. Services can also be extended to teaching photo courses, which hold huge earning potential for those photographers with the experience and expertise to run them. Products are where the money can really be made, especially in social photography, as you may often find that clients spend just as much – if not more – buying their images in their various guises as they do on the actual shoot. For many photographers, such as landscape, travel and fine-art photographers, selling images is their main source of revenue, whether that's online, in stores or directly to customers. Stock is fairly self-explanatory, but we'll be going into that in more depth over the next couple of pages.

The very first thing you need to do is decide what field of photography you want to concentrate on. There are several areas of photography that are harder to get into than others and suit full-time pros rather than enthusiasts. For instance commercial photography, be it fashion, food, products or beauty, normally requires a few years working as an assistant before getting to know the right people and tools for breaking into the business. You could start learning the trade as a part-time assistant if you're willing to wait even longer and probably not earn much money in the process. Photojournalism, again, is a difficult job to get into by relying on commissions from newspapers and magazines, but a good way of kick-starting this career is to fund your own assignment and then pitch it to publications when you return. Other areas of interest might be film stills, press, beauty or corporate photography – there are a lot of different avenues to investigate, each with different types of rewards to be reaped.

Target the people who pay

If it's money you want, the biggest earner has to be social photography, which includes weddings, portraits and events. Not only will you be paid for the service, but the potential for selling products is massive because you have a captive audience wanting to pay for the images. While photographing weddings is a huge responsibility and shouldn't be done unless you're confident about your abilities, a family portrait session is more fun to do and you don't need a studio: lifestyle portraits are perfect for the outdoors where kids can enjoy themselves and relax. Or you could invest in a lighting system and go to your clients' house for the shoot. Depending on how involved you want to get, selling albums and prints, rather than giving clients a DVD of images can be a real moneymaker and it ensures that everyone they show your photos to is seeing them at their best. Often, if you're trading, you can be eligible for trade prices on printing and presentation methods too, which can leave you room to apply a healthy mark-up for the customers, making you a tidy profit. How much you charge is up to you, there are no rules or regulations to guide you, but it's a good idea to check out the local competition as you don't want to price yourself out of the market. Weddings can range from £600 to £3,000+ depending on the package offered and the duration of the wedding. Even as a weekend photographer you have the potential to earn several thousand pounds a year.

The myriad of events you can photograph is endless but sometimes seasonal, for instance football tournaments, Christmas parties, proms and school dances. So, grab yourself a portable printer and your camera, take shots of people on the night, print them immediately and sell them for £10 each. Normally the venue owner takes a slice of your profits, but you'll still potentially walk away with a healthy sum.

EARNING POTENTIAL: SOCIAL

BEGINNER .... ●●●●●●○○○○
Do a shoot for friend and family for £50

ENTHUSIAST ...... ●●●●●●●●●○○
Earn thousands doing a few shoots a year

SEMI-PRO .... ●●●●●●●●●●○
You're only limited by how hard you work

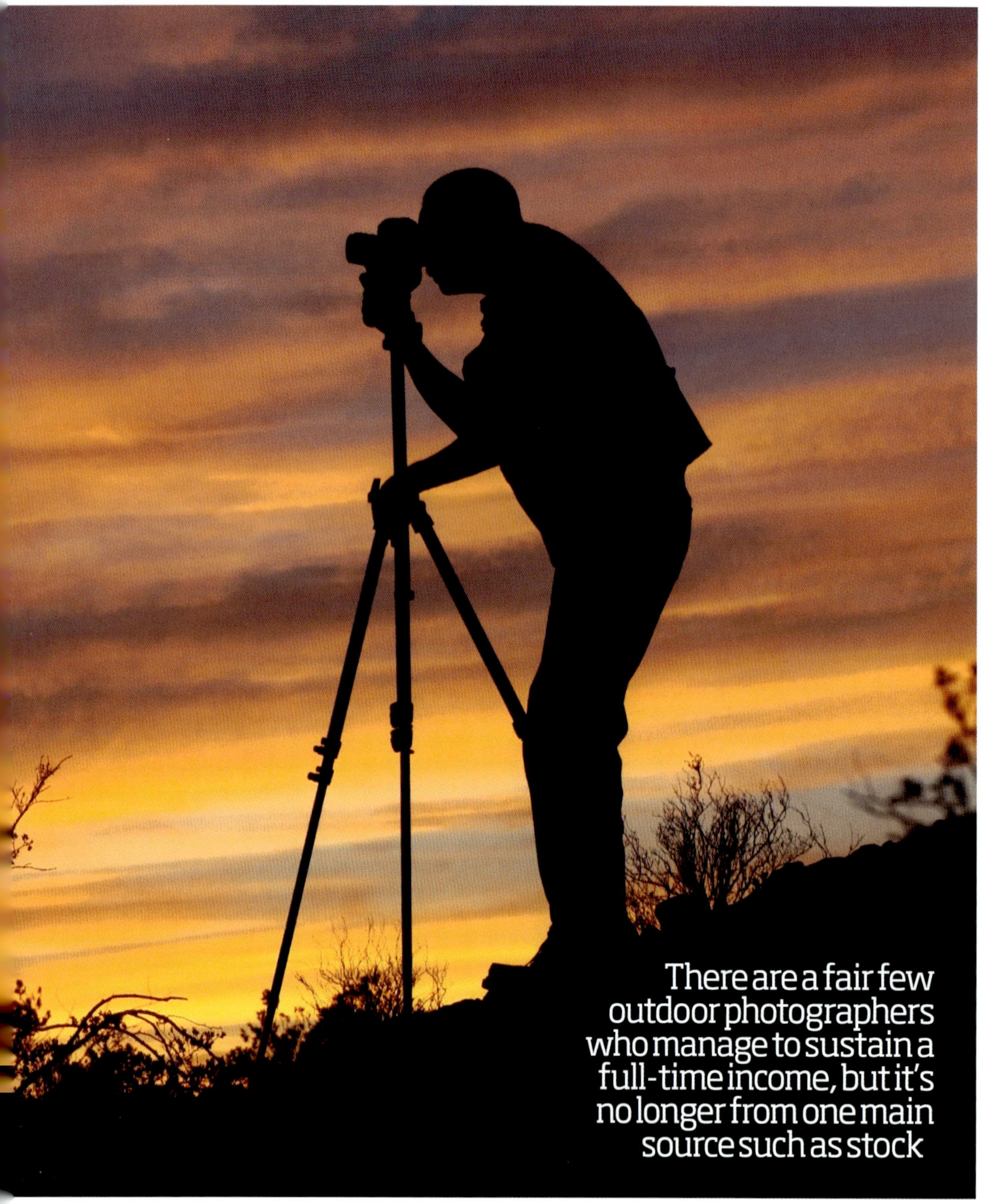

ISTOCK PHOTO

There are a fair few outdoor photographers who manage to sustain a full-time income, but it's no longer from one main source such as stock

Case studies

Adam Burton

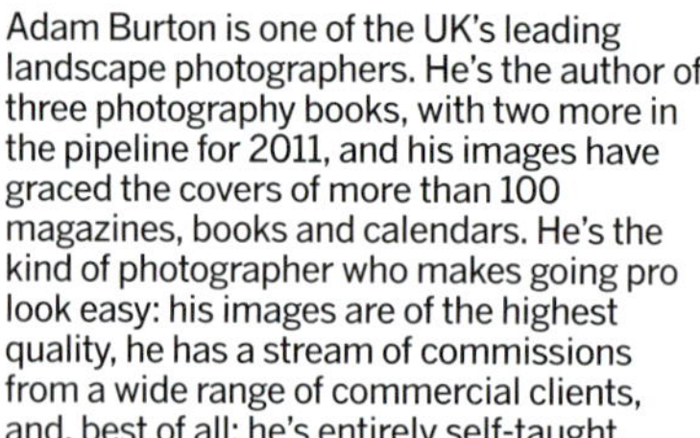

FULL-TIME LANDSCAPE PHOTOGRAPHER

Adam Burton is one of the UK's leading landscape photographers. He's the author of three photography books, with two more in the pipeline for 2011, and his images have graced the covers of more than 100 magazines, books and calendars. He's the kind of photographer who makes going pro look easy: his images are of the highest quality, he has a stream of commissions from a wide range of commercial clients, and, best of all; he's entirely self-taught.

Learning the nuts and bolts of photography from reading magazines and putting the techniques into practice, Adam went from novice photographer to a leading professional in under eight years but says it's still incredibly difficult to sustain an income, especially from landscapes, as there's so many people doing it. "The best route for me has been to try lots of different things. While I still make money from stock, it's not as much as I did: now I sell pictures through Getty for as low as £1.40. I produce photography books, do tutoring, sell prints through my website and license images for various uses such as greeting cards, calendars, brochures and books.

"To make money from photography you have to be flexible, have plenty of clients and lots of different revenue streams. You have to be a good business person and really efficient to help your business stand out from the crowd. Building a good reputation is important too as once you become recognised as a good photographer, that's when things start to get easier."

A tough market to crack

Of all the different types of photography, landscapes is probably one of the most popular to practice, but also one of the toughest to make money from. Too many photographers shoot landscapes as a hobby and then practically give their images away, reducing the need for companies to buy them.

It used to be that landscape, wildlife and travel photographers could rely on stock agencies to supply them a solid income. But as this part of the industry is now overwhelmed by mind-blowing submissions from enthusiasts and amateurs, as well as the professionals, it has driven the price of stock down, making it difficult to earn a living from. There are some talented photographers who have managed to make these types of photography a full-time career, for instance travel photographer and regular contributor Jon Hicks jet sets around the world for the stock library Corbis Images. There are also a fair few outdoor photographers who manage to sustain a full-time income, but it's no longer from one main source such as stock libraries. However, it still has the potential to earn photographers a few hundred or thousand pounds over time.

For pros to keep their head above water, they have to bring in different revenue streams. Some photographers do courses and workshops at home and abroad, get publishing deals or self-publish photo books and calendars, or work for photography magazines and the National Trust, while others try newer avenues such as selling their images printed on roller blinds. It takes initiative and funding to get ideas and products like this off the ground, but you could try pitching your images to companies that can create, or at least sell, the products for you, such as interior design firms or The Art Group. Check out www.55Max.com for really inspiring and affordable ideas.

EARNING POTENTIAL: OUTDOOR

BEGINNER .... ●●●●●●○○○○
Earn a few hundred from selling stock

ENTHUSIAST ...... ●●●●●●○○○○
Sell your images on a market stall

SEMI-PRO .... ●●●●●●●○○○
Keep your fingers in lots of pies!

ISTOCK PHOTO

Take stock of your image bank

You could be sitting on a gold mine and not even know it. OK, well maybe not a gold mine, but at least the funds for a new lens or digital camera. Most of us will have some great images stored on memory cards or on a hard drive that we've forgotten about, because we do not know what to do with them, but the stock photo marketplace is an ideal way to put these generic images to work for you.

Joining a stock agency normally requires you to register and submit a selection of your best work. The agency will then judge the quality of the images and decide whether to allow you to contribute. If all goes well and your images are accepted, they will show your best picture on their website for companies and individuals to license. You'll get a cut of the client's licensing fee, but how much varies from agency to agency. Alamy offers 60% of the sale, which is generous.

While the industry is saturated by stock photo agencies, most are owned by Getty Images and Corbis Images, each with their own image standards and requirements, licensing rules (rights-managed or royalty-free) and prices. These big agencies can be very selective of who they work with, normally sticking to pros who have been providing them stock for several years. Microstock sites, on the other hand, such as iStockPhoto and ShutterStock, are open to all levels of photographer and reach a huge audience, however they pay less than the bigger agencies. As long as your images pass the site's technical requirements for image quality, Microstock can be one of the easiest ways to make money, especially if you have the volume. You might only earn £1 per picture, but if you sell 1,000 images a year that's a fair bit of money in your pocket. One way you could get involved with Getty Images is via its Flickr Collection. Instead of submitting images directly to Getty, click on the ***Request to License*** link on your photo page and Getty will assess your portfolio for their collection. It's known for some contributors to have earned thousands through this partnership.

> "Microstock can be one of the easiest ways to make money. You might only earn £10 per shot but if you sell 1,000 in a year that's a fair bit of money"

EARNING POTENTIAL: STOCK PHOTOS

BEGINNER..........
Stock is easy to earn a little money from

ENTHUSIAST......
It's a good platform for selling pictures

SEMI-PRO..........
It won't be your main moneymaker

Where to sell images online

The internet has created a brilliant platform for selling pictures, whether it be via stock libraries, third-party websites such as Red Bubble, eBay or your own website. There are several companies that enable you to set up a facility to sell your pictures through your website, for instance, Clikpic and Livebooks.

Top pocket-money tip

Try getting your photographs on the walls of businesses such as galleries, cafés, banks and offices – anywhere that could capture the interest of your target market. You might also want to try setting up a market stall or selling greeting cards in a local art shop. Read ***Profitable Projects*** for more details.

BUILD YOUR BRAND

How you market your photography is arguably as important as your skills as a photographer in shaping your success. Read on for expert advice about branding your business and essential marketing tools

DESPITE THE IDIOM 'don't judge a book by its cover', most of us still prejudge the quality of a product on how professional it looks. It's the same with photography: in a market that's bursting with excellent photographers – amateurs and professionals alike – it's difficult for consumers to know where to spend their money for quality and value. So, before they even look at your work, rightly or wrongly, they'll judge you on your brand and it has to effectively communicate what your all about.

"As a photographer, getting the brand right has got to be the most important thing, after knowing how to take a half-decent shot," says Nige Burton, managing director of Freebird New Media, which specialises in brands for photographers. "Photography is one of the rare trades these days that can make a really good business, despite the economic climate, if the formula [for branding and marketing] is followed correctly.

"Everything that a photographer puts out about their business should be of the highest quality to reflect their service and images. If you give out a cheap, tacky business card, people think: cheap, tacky pictures. It's better to have few, great promotional products than lots of average ones" says Burton. Regardless of what level of photographer you are, no element of your business should appear 'amateurish'. It must all look professional, slick and from the same camp. Invest in business cards made from a heavy stock – they're not very expensive – and a well-designed logo with company colours that feature across all your promotional material. You don't have to spend a fortune, you just need to make it look as if you have.

With word of mouth generating the most amount of business, it's not unusual for your website to be a client's first point of contact with your work. It therefore needs to represent you and the image quality they can expect from hiring you. Again, you do not have to spend much on a website, just follow these few pointers. Make sure you have a strong homepage that displays your best images to hook them in, that it runs efficiently and is easy to navigate. If someone has to wait for a website to load and isn't 'wowed' by a striking image from the outset, they'll get bored and move on before you've even had a chance to show them what you can offer. You have about three seconds before a viewer decides whether they're going to look any further in to your website or move on, according to Burton. That's not a lot of time to make a good first impression, so make it count.

"A good website allows potential clients to react to your images. The website should be doing its job in the background, allowing the imagery to speak for itself." It shouldn't be too plain as it won't enhance the imagery and it shouldn't be so complicated that it jars the viewer and overwhelms the images. You need to find a balance that enables your website to be a platform that encourages people to browse through your images.

You should also be very selective about what images you display. Too many photographers try to cram in as many pictures as they can on their website, most of which are average at best. If you use 12 or 14 fantastic images, people will think you take every image like that.

> "Everything that a photographer gives out about their business should be of the highest quality to reflect their service and pictures"

When a client visits a website, says Burton, they want to see your images, then they look for your brand to assure them it's a quality, professional service. If they're still interested, this is when they'll move on to read about you. Tell them a little about yourself, but don't give them information they don't need like the fact you have a dog called Chipper and like cheese on toast. Keep it strictly business, relating everything back to why they might want to hire you. If you struggle with this side of the website, consider hiring a copywriter to do it for you. Finally, make it easy for them to contact you and make sure the website is search engine-friendly, as it's your number one marketing tool.

"We often get clients who want to charge £1,500 for a wedding but spend £200 on a website, and they cannot do it – it doesn't work as it doesn't reflect the quality that's expected of a photographer charging £1,500. You get what you pay for and while people do need to watch their pennies, it's important that they get the best brand they can for their budget.

What makes a good brand?

As photography, especially portraiture and weddings, is a bespoke service, a brand should reflect something of the individual photographer's personality and how they take pictures. It also needs to be designed to target the type of people who make up the broadest part of your market. For instance, 90% of the time, it's the woman who selects her wedding photographer or family portrait photographer, so you have to pick a branding and logo that appeals to women the same way a car or sports photographer should have a logo that appeals to men. The only generic field of photography is wildlife and landscapes as this is all about the quality of imagery and less about the photographer.

A good place to start creating your own brand is to build a mood board comprising images, words and colours that you like and you think represent your style of photography and personality. From there you can ask yourself the difficult questions to help define your company's identity:

1. Who are your customers (i.e. age ranges and 'type' of person)?
2. What adjectives would you use to describe your company? For example. friendly, professional, innovative, safe, funky, relaxed, efficient etc.
3. What makes your business different from your competitors?
4. What areas of your business do you want to bring to the foreground?
5. What do you want your company colours to be? (For swatches visit: kuler.adobe.com)
6. What are you going to call your brand or company?

The worst logos, according to Burton, are those featuring Clip Art "it's the kind of thing you'd see in newspaper adverts in the late '80s and early '90s." Getting your company's name right is equally, if not more important than the logo design. "We've found what works really well is just to have the person's name with the word 'photography' after it. It sounds simple but a lot of photographers tend to come up ➤

rosshoddinott
PHOTOGRAPHY

"If you want to create a lasting brand, one that encourages people to look at it, then use strong colours but tone them down with muted colours to set it off"

with really contrived names and we have to force them to think what that's saying to a potential client. Some names suit a company's name more than others, for instance you might be called Paul Pratt, and Paul Pratt Photography isn't the best. But if you use the middle name instead, it becomes a more professional Paul Mark Photography. It's all about what a name conjures up in the mind of a client.

"When choosing fonts for your brand, you have to think about how it will look on screen. It's not so important with your logo, but with your website, there are a few fonts you should stick to so it's easy to read, one of which is a strong Sans Serif. With a logo, the biggest mistake I see is people mix too many fonts: there shouldn't be more than two really. Sometimes people have four words with four fonts and it jars. It's a case of stepping back from the logo and asking yourself, like you would with a picture, is it balanced right, is it pleasing? For colours, you should avoid bright yellows and reds. There's quite a bit of colour psychology that goes in to picking a brand's colours, and while yellow and red are bright and vibrant to get your attention, they soon make you feel uncomfortable and you don't look at it for long. If you want to create a lasting brand, one that encourages people to look at it for a while, then use a strong colour but tone it down by adding muted colours to set it off, rather than two strong colours that can jar against each other."

While you can create your own logo and brand, don't underestimate its power of persuasion so make sure it reflects your worth. If you really want to grow your photography business, think seriously about investing in a professional brand as it will pay dividends in the long run.

If you want feedback on your own logo design or website, you can contact Freebird for their opinion and advice, or another design company, but you may need to pay a small fee for the service.

What should I do?

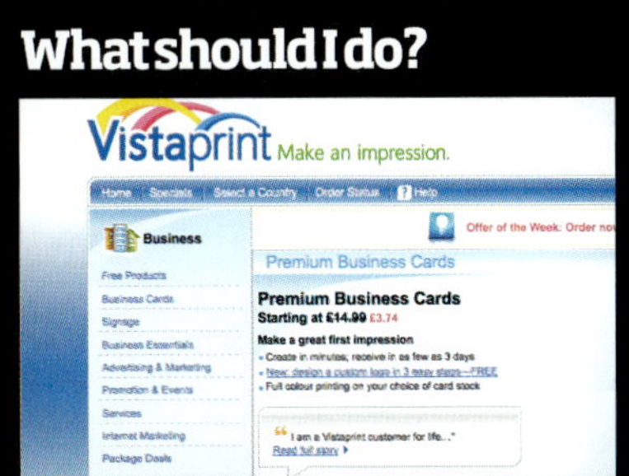

Beginner (£25 - £50)

Design your own logo using Photoshop or use a generic logo that you can download from companies such as www.vistaprint.com and network on Facebook and Twitter. If you want to start marketing in other avenues, then invest in some business cards and a templated website, from the likes of www.clikpic.com, so people can view your work and contact you.

Enthusiast (£100 - £300)

If you're a dab hand at Photoshop and have a creative eye, try designing your own logo or contact your local university or college to see if a graphic design student can do one for you. You may need to pay them but you can expect it to be a fraction of what a professional would charge. You may also want to try contacting design companies such as Freebird to discuss what they can offer you for your budget. If you only have £100 to spend, it may be that they can design you a brilliant logo and then you can opt for a templated website instead of a more expensive custom-built site. As you're serious about your photography, get a business card that says it; www.moo.com offer very affordable and high-quality business cards. You'll probably need to get some letterheads and return address labels too, which you can get relatively cheaply from www.vistaprint.com.

rosshoddinott
PHOTOGRAPHY

Semi-pro and professional (£500 - several thousand)

Depending on your budget, and how much income you're generating from your photography, you should look to get a professional design company such as Clock or Freebird to create you a complete brand. Most companies do packages that include custom logo design and website design as well as print media such as brochures, pamphlets, letterheads, compliment slips and business cards. But, most importantly, you'll get one-to-one contact with a designer and copywriter as you're developing the brand together. Doing this will really give your business a strong start.

Marketing tips

Getting people talking about your photography is the easiest, cheapest and most efficient way of promoting your business. We give you some advice on the best ways of getting your business noticed

WHILE BRANDING gives you a foothold in the market, a solid marketing strategy will give your photography business a leg up. The best way of making marketing work for you is to have lots of fingers in lots of pies and, if you're serious about developing your photography business, create a year's marketing plan, doing something new each month to expand your contact base and bring in clients.

Some of the best photographers are highly self-critical, always striving to do better and are rarely satisfied with their images, which can make it very difficult for them to promote their work. As a result, too many amateurs and enthusiasts undersell their services. The solution is simple: either find ways of building up your confidence, such as winning competitions or getting more on-the-job experience, or get someone else to be your alter ego and push the business for you. We're not suggesting you hire an agent, but milk your friends and family as they're likely to be some of your biggest and most loyal fans. Then once you get some clients, provide them personal and professional service and they'll become your mouthpiece. As most business comes from word of mouth, its time to get people talking...

Be social

Get involved and connected with local businesses. Join business networking groups as they can offer an abundance of support and contacts to help develop your business. Offer your photography services to them for free in exchange for them promoting your business. For instance, approach a new restaurant or venue to see if they need images to hang on their walls or offer to do promotional pictures for a child's clothing store, as long as they recommend your children's portrait business to their customers. If you're a wedding or events photographer, try and build relationships with local venues and event decorators. Give them images you've taken of their work while at an event and the next time someone asks them to recommend a photographer, your name will be the first to roll off their tongue.

Have an online presence

A website that's searchable via Google is crucial for giving your business a platform to showcase your work. A blog is a really important part of your website as not only will it make your site more searchable, it's a place where you can brag about all your latest photography work that may not relate to your main business. You should look to update your blog at least twice a week, even if it's just a strapline and a couple of images (turn to p20 for advice on increasing your web hits). Don't underestimate the power of social networking sites either. Set up a company Facebook and Twitter account to keep your followers updated with your latest work and link it to your website and also other businesses from your networking groups for cross promotion.

Get free exposure

Unless you try to get a commission from a magazine, it's unlikely you'll get paid to feature your images on their pages. However, don't let this put you off. Submit your images to a suitable magazine and ask for a credit for instant exposure. If you're a wedding photographer, think about all those brides-to-be and mothers you're showing your images to. Look at local magazines too, such as *Hertfordshire Life*, to see if there's any content you can contribute. Having your images published also gives you instant credibility, it's like winning a competition. There are endless magazines in the market from gardening and travel to hiking and country living, just take a visit to your local newsagent and sift through the shelves. Research the magazine thoroughly and pick the pictures that best suit their content, then submit them to the Features Editor in the form of a contact sheet, with details of who you are and what you want. Once you've been published, shout about it: add it to your blog, Twitter and Facebook!

> "If you're serious about developing your business, create a year's marketing plan, doing something new each month to expand your contact base"

Get your work seen

Displaying your images at trade shows are a brilliant way of having your work seen by new people, but often it requires a hefty outlay in terms of renting a pitch and promotional material, so make sure you invest your time and money in the right one. Do some research about the show that interests you to find out whether the people that attend are the types who might hire you. For instance, if you mainly do portraiture, go to the shows where you know families attend. Provide visitors with some brochures or folded pamphlets that they can take home with them and attract them to your display by offering balloons to children and a prize draw for the adults. To begin with, avoid national shows; they may be bigger and attract more people, but competition is fierce. You're better off staying local, as this is more likely where your clients will be. Check out country shows and craft fairs too, and try to do a large regional event at least once a year.

Keep in touch

Even though your commission may have ended, it doesn't mean your relationship with the client has to. If you shoot weddings, for instance, send the couple a custom-made anniversary card and send all your clients company branded Christmas cards. If you're a social photographer, send your cards out by the latest the end of November, giving time for people to hire you for a portrait shoot before Christmas. Setting up an email newsletter is also an excellent way of keeping your business at the forefront of people's minds: send them regular updates of your latest work with links to your website and blog.

Market yourself

You are your best marketing tool, so you need to sell yourself just as much as your talents as a photographer. Remember that people buy people, if they like your attitude and feel comfortable around you, chances are they'll hire you. Make sure you know your business, be presentable, personable and professional as well as flexible to your clients' needs. Even if you're not 100% satisfied with your work, don't let anyone else know that. Pick only the images you love to put in your portfolio; being proud of the selection will make selling your images much easier. Clients will pick up on your attitude towards your work, so make sure it's positive. As you market yourself more, you'll hopefully draw attention to your work but it won't all be positive. Don't let feedback knock your confidence or take it too personally, everyone will have an opinion, but do keep an open mind to ways you can improve too.

HOW TO CREATE YOUR OWN LOGO IN PHOTOSHOP

If you're looking for a simple logo to promote your part-time enterprise, there's no need to pay for a professional designer. Follow our tips for creating your own branded logo

ONCE YOU'VE come up with ideas for your company's identity, including its name, a logo, perhaps a slogan too, and some key words that define your business, it's time to put these ideas into action. For the purpose of this step-by-step we'll use the name, Caroline Ann, and the word Photography to give the logo context. But before you start designing yours, here are a few things you should bear in mind...

- **Keep It Simple:** Unless you're a wiz with Adobe Photoshop or Adobe Illustrator, it's best to keep your logo clean and clear: leave the complex designs, images and illustrations to the design pros and concentrate on the text.
- **Don't opt for style over substance:** Experiment with different fonts, font sizes, colours and the positioning of words, finding a balance between readability and a style that gives clients the right impression about you and your business.
- **Test if you're using the right font:** Ask a friend to say the first thing that comes to mind when they see your logo: if it's child-like, and you're going for professional, or vice versa, then you know you're on the wrong track and giving clients the wrong impression.
- **Give the company's name prominence:** Make sure the important parts of the logo are bigger and better than the less important words, for instance Photography shouldn't overpower the company's name, in this case Caroline Ann.
- **Avoid gimmicks:** If you double-click on a text layer in the Layers palette, it will open a Layer Style dialogue box that offers loads of style options such as adding shadows, bevels and embossing. These can easily be overdone, making your logo look cheap and 'amateurish' so best to steer clear. The same with the Warp Text too in the top toolbar.

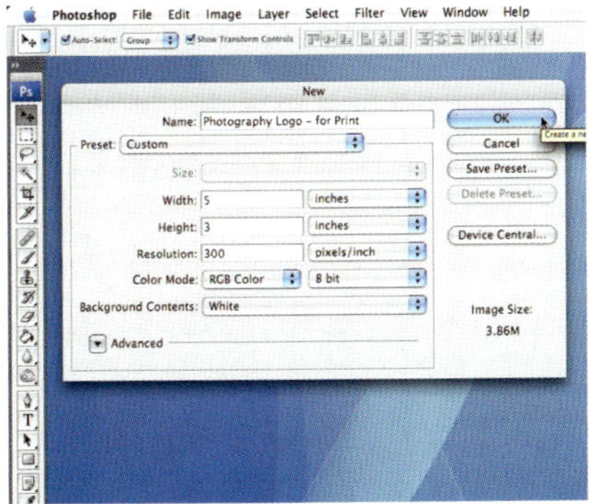

1) Create your canvas

Click *File>New*. As this logo is intended for print, ensure the *Resolution* is 300 pixel/inch; *Color Mode*: RGB; *Width*: 5 inch; and *Height* 3 inch. You want a file size of at least 2MB (look in the bottom right-hand corner of the dialogue box for the *Image Size* and adjust the width and height to see it increase or decrease). Name the file, in this case 'Photography logo – for print' and then click *OK*.

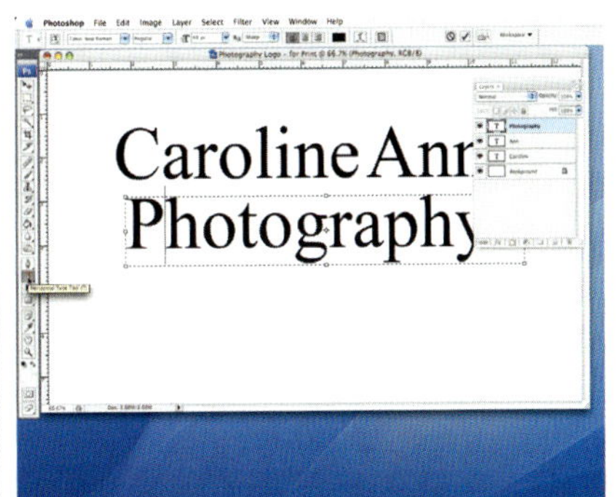

2) Work on different layers

Select the *Text Tool* and create a text box on your canvas. Instead of using one text box to hold all the text for the logo, create separate text boxes for each word so you can alter the size and position of the words using the *Move Tool*. We create one text box for 'Caroline', one for 'Ann' and one for 'Photography'. This also creates different layers in the Layers palette, which allow me to edit each part separately.

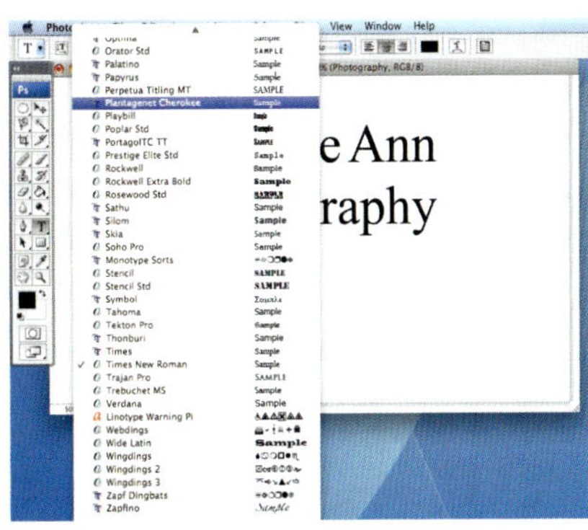

3) Pick your font

Our default font type is Times New Roman, which looks rather boring, so using the top toolbar, experiment with different fonts and font types (Bold, Regular Italic), sizes and colours. If you have more than one part to the logo, for instance two or three words, you could try varying the font and style for each word but make sure they work well together. See the panel for examples of what to avoid.

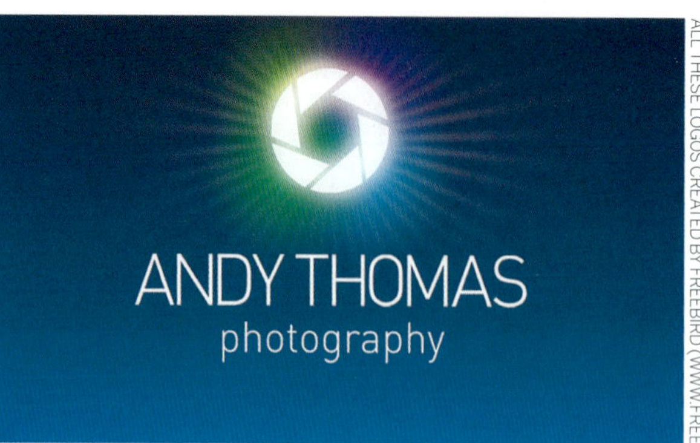

ALL THESE LOGOS CREATED BY FREEBIRD (WWW.FREEBIRD.CO.UK)

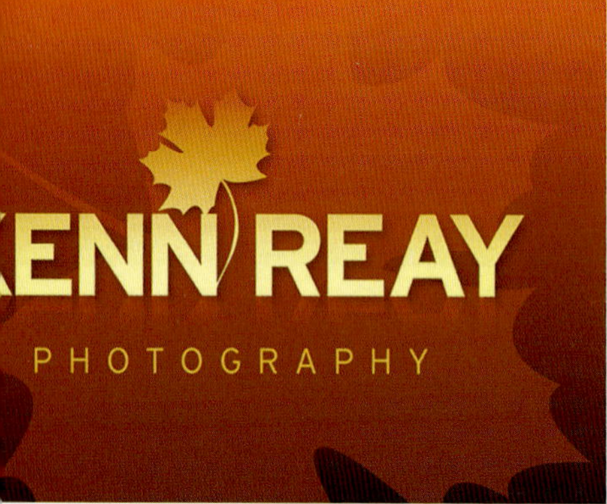

ord+martin
=photography

What works?

Here are some examples of type to use and what type to avoid:

☒ Avoid calligraphy; it's very dated.

Caroline Ann
kids * fun * photography

☒ Unless your company is focused on kids' portraiture, for instance, use fonts like this in moderation as they rarely look professional or appeal to an adult market.

Caroline Ann
Photography
CarolineAnn
Photography

☑ Try mixing different fonts and text types

☑ Use shapes to make your logo more dynamic. For simple shapes use the Elliptical or Rectangular Marquee Tool

4) Get more creative

To make the logo a little more individual, we pick out the A that's in Caroline and Ann to make a feature of it. We use the *Move Tool* to reposition elements in the logo, clicking on the correct layers, and also changing the size of individual letters. **Wrong:** Keeping the 'C' as small as the 'roline' and 'ann' makes it illegible. **Right:** Making the 'C' as big as the 'A' adds balance and improves readability.

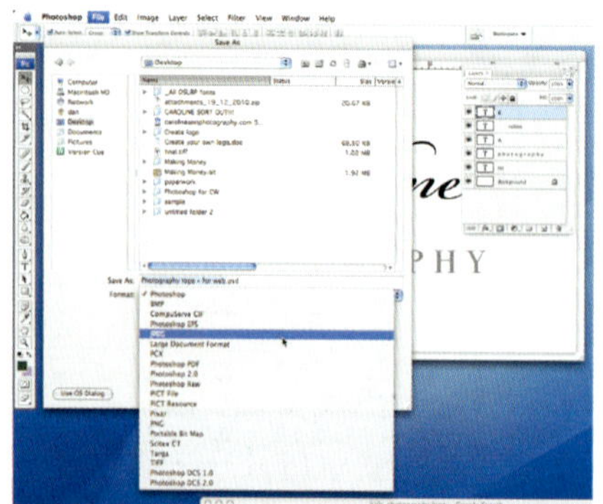

5) Save for print and web

You should save three versions of the logo: a .psd file so you can edit the logo later; a JPEG version of the high resolution logo for print; and a lower resolution image for your website. Your current logo should already be in a .psd format, so to save it as a JPEG go to *File>Save As* and select JPEG from the *Save As*: drop-down menu. Now close the .psd file and open the JPEG image, then go to *File>Save As* and rename it 'Photography logo – for web'. Now click *Image>Image Size* and change the *Resolution* to 72 and select *Bicubic Sharper* (best for reduction) from the *Resample Image* drop-down menu to preserve image quality. Click *OK* and save the changes (*File>Save*).

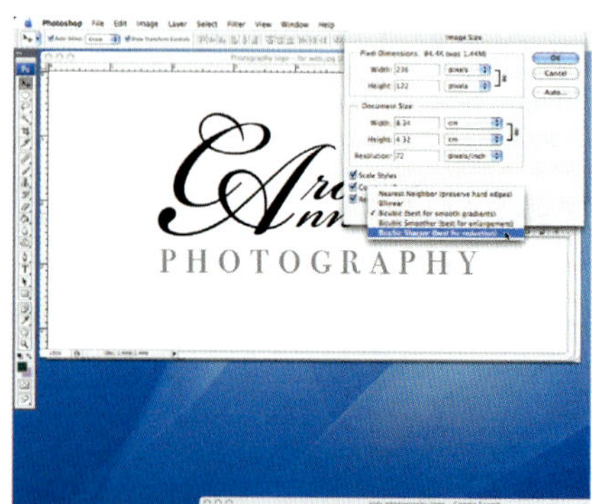

When applying your logo to your website or promotional material, make sure it's in the top left-hand corner as this is where the eye is drawn to first.

INVEST IN THE WEB

You may be a fantastic photographer, but if no one sees your pictures, how will you ever get noticed? Having a website presents your photography to the world and is easier and more affordable than ever!

DO YOU HAVE A WEBSITE? If the answer is no, then the next thing you need to do is book a day off work and dedicate the time to setting one up and uploading your images. Sure, you may have a Facebook account or have images uploaded to Flickr, but if you want people to take you seriously as a photographer worth paying for, then you need to have your own dedicated website.

It's worth pointing out right at the start that having your own website is far easier and much more affordable than you might think. Uploading images from your computer to your website is as easy as downloading from your camera to your computer, while the annual fee for a great-looking website to proudly display them on can cost the same as a couple of memory cards.

Why have a website?

Along with your camera kit, a website may prove to be the best investment you make for helping you make money from your photos, so you need to build one that reflects the quality of your photography and your brand.

As photographers, the main purpose for having a website is to be able to showcase our best images. Before the arrival of the internet, we could only do this by exhibiting work on gallery walls, or in magazines. Now, we have the potential to allow a worldwide audience access to our photos. However, that's just the start of what a website can offer photographers. Regardless of whether you're a hobbyist, an enthusiast or a pro, you can set it up so that visitors have the opportunity to buy prints from you. In its most basic form, this could be by providing a contact email address. Better still is a simple automated set-up where visitors choose the size of print they require before ordering and paying online.

Of course, if you are serious about wanting to earn money from your photography, you'll want to have a website that works harder at selling your services as a photographer than just selling images you may have already captured. In other words, you want potential clients to visit your website and, having seen the standard of your work, want to book you to take pictures for them. Your website, therefore, should be viewed as the most powerful brand extension that you have to offer, so you need to be sure it sells you as a photographer the best it can.

The most sophisticated websites have private areas, accessed via password, that allow clients to log in and view their image galleries and to select their favourite images. Your website also enables you to promote how busy you are and the diversity of your work. While image galleries allow you to do this to some extent, a far better way is to have a blog where you regularly comment on your shoots, allowing clients to add their comments too. It's also worth having a site that has links to your Twitter and Facebook account and check that it's iPhone compatible, so prospective clients can look at your site and be updated with your latest work on the go. It's a brilliant way to reinforce how busy and popular you are!

Setting up your own website

Thankfully, you don't need to construct your own website as there are various options available that leave you time to concentrate on choosing the images you wish to upload and the accompanying text.

1 READY-MADE TEMPLATE FAST & AFFORDABLE WEBSITES

If you want your own website, by far the easiest option is to take advantage of one of the many companies offering ready-made website templates for photographers. With this option, you simply choose your favourite template, pay an annual fee and then upload your favourite images. Depending on the package you opt for, you can add extra options, for instance, more galleries, a shopping basket allowing visitors to order prints, email forwarding, client areas and so on. It's the easiest option and also the most affordable, making it by far the most desirable choice for amateur and enthusiast photographers. Those looking for a more professional website may need to consider one of the firms that produce bespoke websites.

However, that said, many professionals use this option and have done well by it. Regular contributors to *Digital SLR Photography* magazine Mark Bauer and Helen Dixon are both successful landscape photographers who use Clikpic to host their websites. In fact, they became contributors by being discovered on Clikpic. Many social photographers also use the likes of Bludomain for a more sophisticated offering. Either way, remember to check what the technical support services are like and how easy it is to manage the site's content yourself.

Verdict: This option is affordable and the latest templates in general are attractive and professional looking. It's definitely the best choice as a first website. Most offer a free trial period too!

SUITABILITY: TEMPLATES

BEGINNER 10/10
Affordable, easy to set-up and maintain

ENTHUSIAST 9/10
A good solution if you're testing the waters

SEMI-PRO 8/10
Looks professional but is unlikely to match your business's brand

Check out the following...

CLIKPIC: WWW.CLIKPIC.COM:
From £35 per year. Free 14-day trial.

AMAZING INTERNET: WWW.AMAZINGINTERNET.COM
From £25 per month. Free 30-day trial.

FOLIOPIC: WWW.FOLIOPIC.COM
From £13 per year. Free 14-day trial.

PHOTIUM: WWW.PHOTIUM.COM
From £44 per year. Free 30-day trial.

BLU DOMAIN: WWW.BLUDOMAIN.COM
From $50 per year. One-off payment.

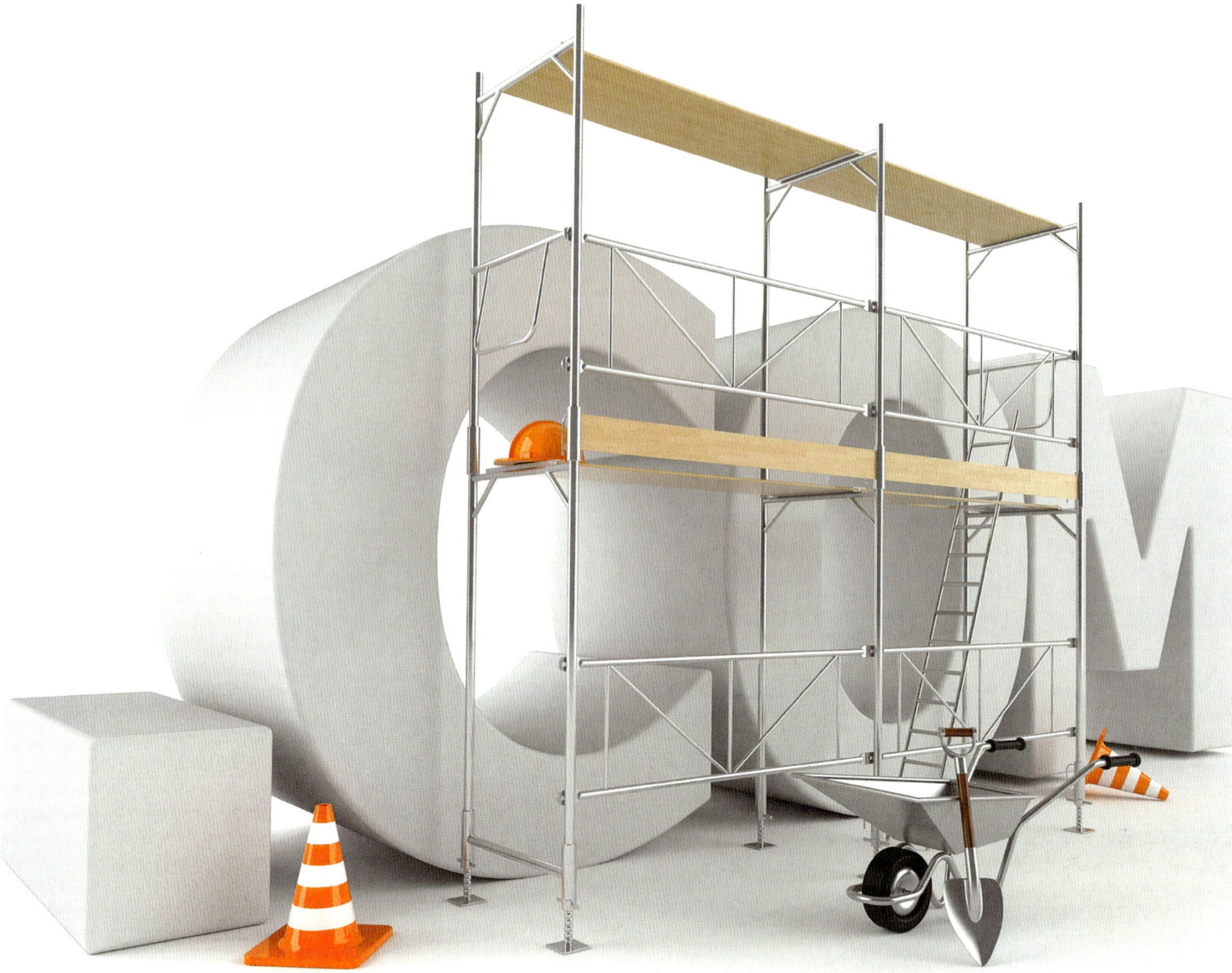

Time trial: Three hours to create a website using Clikpic

Daniel Lezano takes up Clikpic's free trial offer to see how easy it is to set up a website.

Probably like most of you reading this, I've wanted my own website for quite a while but never had the time to set it up. I still haven't the time, but this article has forced me into it! I'm trying out Clikpic, one of the UK's most popular with photographers, to see how fast and easy it is to set up my own website.

I register for my free trial, click on the automated email and quickly set up my account and password. I download the comprehensive User Guide PDF, following the steps in section two and three on how to add words and images. I prepare a selection of images to upload and decide to divide my website into images taken on a DSLR and some of my favourites shot using the Hipstamatic app on my Apple iPhone 4. From start to finish, it took three hours to set up a basic website with three gallery pages – proof that Clikpic's system is fast, works well and delivers on its promise.

I've still to determine what domain name to give my site, but for now, you can visit the website at: www7.clikpic.com/daniellez

1) Add words

2) Upload images

3) Check it works

4) Website ready!

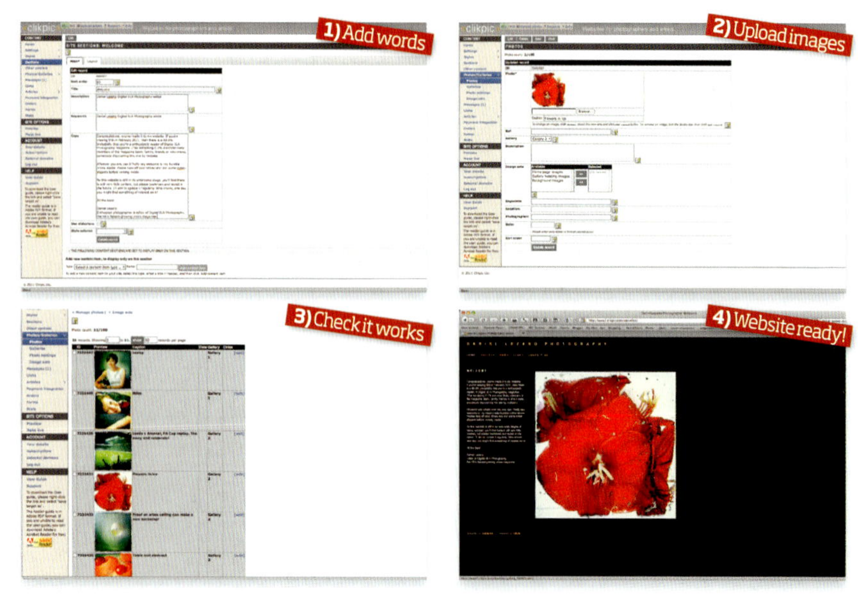

2 BESPOKE WEBSITE UNIQUE BUT EXPENSIVE

The template option is one that will suit the needs (and budgets!) of most amateur and enthusiast photographers, but those looking for a one-off design that reflects their individuality and customer appeal, may need to dig a little deeper and pay out for a website to be custom made. The benefit is that you can have a website that looks like no other. As with option one, there are a number of firms that can build photographers a bespoke website to suit their needs, but they are considerably more expensive, often ranging from several hundred to thousands of pounds, depending on how elaborate it is. But if you feel that your photographic business will benefit and flourish from a totally unique website, then it could be money well spent. You'll be dealing with companies that have produced websites for other photographers, so you can expect them to have a good appreciation of your needs and be able to deliver a website with the facilities you require to make it the best possible online shop window for your business. Bear in mind when shopping for a designer that you want one that offers continual technical support once the site has gone live, and a management interface that's easy for you to use. After all, you don't want a website that looks fantastic but where you haven't an idea how to figure out how to update its content.

Verdict: An option for those photographers who want to emphasise their unique style and provide the impression they're successful and at the top of their game. It's expensive, so you'll need to be confident that it's an investment that will reap rewards.

SUITABILITY: BESPOKE WEBSITE

BEGINNER .... (3/10)
Your money is better spent on camera kit

ENTHUSIAST .... (5/10)
A little OTT until you're making money

SEMI-PRO .... (8/10)
First impressions count, so consider it

Check out the following...

AMAZING INTERNET: WWW.AMAZINGINTERNET.COM
Various options, starting around £1,000

FREEBIRD: WWW.FREEBIRD.CO.UK
Various packages, starting around £1,200

PHOTOGRAPHYWEBSITEDESIGN.CO.UK
Flexible packages, starting from £595

3 WEBSITE CREATION SOFTWARE MOST INVOLVED OPTION

The other option of course, is to create your own website. It's obviously by far the most time-intensive and we'd only recommend considering it if the template option doesn't appeal or you don't fancy paying out a large amount to another company to create it for you. While it's possible to build a website using Photoshop, there are a number of software packages available designed specifically for this purpose. They vary in features, flexibility, the amount of web hosting space provided and, of course, price, but all will demand your time, so think long and hard before you choose this option. We've listed below four of the more popular website creation packages.

Verdict

While the initial cost may be attractive, you'll need to dedicate considerable time and need a high level of expertise to understand the fundamentals of web creation. The exception is Apple's iWeb, a superb, attractive and easy to use package.

SUITABILITY: BUILD YOUR OWN

BEGINNER .... (2/10)
Seriously? You should be taking photos

ENTHUSIAST .... (5/10)
Only try this is you've lots of free time

SEMI-PRO .... (4/10)
Unless you have the know-how, your time is better spent developing your business

Check out the following...

MR SITE'S TAKEAWAY WEBSITE FROM £20
WWW.MRSITE.COM
On offer are three packages (Beginner, Standard and Pro) each offering additional features and online storage space. With the Beginner packages on sale for as little as £13 and the Pro package available for around £50 (its guide price is £100); Mr Site has proven quite popular, although a fair amount of know-how, patience and free time will be required.

MAGIX WEBSITE MAKER 4 £40
WWW.MAGIX.COM
This package isn't aimed at photographers, but has enjoyed success with those who want Flash animations and static images. As with most of these packages, its interface is more than most novices can handle, but for those wanting an animated website, it's a good choice, especially as it can be found for £20.

APPLE IWEB (ILIFE '11 £46)
WWW.APPLE.COM
It's no surprise to discover that the easiest web creation package for Mac users comes from Apple. iWeb would normally be recommended, but Apple announced it would be switching off the MobileMe service handling iWeb, making it defunct.

ADOBE DREAMWEAVER CS5 £400
WWW.ADOBE.COM/UK
This sister package to Lightroom and Photoshop offers incredible power and sophistication, but unless you're an expert with cash to burn, we'd suggest you steer clear of this £400 package.

RECOMMENDED READING
BUILD A BETTER WEBSITE £7.99
From the publishers of *Digital SLR Photography*, this Magbook offers expert advice for computer-savvy individuals keen to build their own website. You can order a copy of the 2011 edition for £6.96 from www.magbooks.com

Top ten do's & don'ts

However you create your website, here are our golden rules to follow:

1) Display a selection of stunning images rather than lots of average ones. Always choose quality over quantity.
2) Flash animation and slideshows may look great, but HTML loads faster and is handled better by Google.
3) Do what you can to improve your SEO – see panel opposite.
4) Keep the site's design simple and professional; avoid texturised and busy backgrounds.
5) Make the navigation simple, visible and all thumbnail images clickable. Functionality is key to keeping viewers on your site.
6) Make sure it's easy for people to contact you.
7) Choose an obvious domain name – your name followed by 'photography' for instance.
8) Add elements that make people want to return, such as a blog.
9) Make money from your site by adding a shopping basket.
10) Add links to Facebook, Twitter and RSS.

Jargon buster

Domain name: The web address people will type in, eg: www.joebloggsphotography.com.

Email forwarding: A facility that allows any messages typed into your website to be forwarded by email to you.

Flash: Software used to create sophisticated animated graphics for websites.

Hosting: Your website and all the elements within it, such as the images, will need to be stored on a computer known as the 'host'. If you're uploading lots of high-res images, ensure your website host offers a package with a suitably large capacity – 2GB should be the minimum.

HTML: The code used to construct websites.

SEO (Search Engine Optimisation): A mechanism that raises your website up in Google's rankings – vital if your business relies on your website being seen

Template: The core design of your website, although it's often customisable.

Make sure your website is seen by all the right people by following these simple steps...

Domain name and hosting

Two important considerations when preparing to have your own website are what it will be called (domain name) and who you have to host it (web hosting company). Think carefully about what name you give your website. Most photographers use their name, with the word photography or something similar after it. Spend a little time working out some options. As well as what comes before the dot, you need to think about what comes after: do you want .co.uk, .org, .com or one of several other options? We'd suggest you buy both .co.uk and .com for your website. You can discover if your choice of domain name is free using one of the web hosting websites listed below. Expect to pay around £4 a year for a .co.uk domain and £10 per year for a .com. You'll need a company to host your website and while you may opt to go with the same company that designed your website, make sure you can take your domain name with you when you leave. Most hosting companies provide you with options to choose the amount of web space you require, a number of email addresses, decent mailbox capacity and 24/7 web support. We've listed a selection of the most popular below, visit their websites for details of the packages they offer.

1&1: www.1and1.co.uk
The Image File: www.theimagefile.com
Fasthosts: www.fasthosts.co.uk
Webfusion: www.webfusion.co.uk

Search Engine Optimisation (SEO)

If you want your website to be seen by as many people as possible, you need to spend time improving your SEO. It's a mechanism that can help your website appear higher up the rankings of Google and other search engines. You can pay firms specialising in SEO, but we'd suggest you give it a go yourself first by following our tips:

Use keywords (words that people might use when searching for your site or images) to each page. Check their searchability on Google Adwords. And use the most important words first.

Install Google Analytics on your site so you can track how it is performing in searches, monitor your website's traffic and where viewers are coming from. It can be particularly useful if you want to know how effective your marketing is.

Add your business to Google Places.

Make sure you include descriptive text on your website about your services and products for search engines to index.

Use descriptive page titles for the top of your web browser using keywords you'd expect people to search with, along with your name. Eg: Beautiful portrait photography, Peterborough | Joe Bloggs.

Use HTML on your site rather than Flash – Google is much better at recognising HTML – or at least have a HTML mirror site.

Maintain a blog regularly to generate traffic to your site and new searchable content.

Get as many reputable websites to post links back to your website to improve traffic.

A few more things to consider...

Your brand is important, so ensure you have a decent logo design and place it in the top left corner of your screen.

Make sure you use a well-known font and that its legible. We recommend Verdana, Georgia and Times New Roman, in that order.

Flash technology doesn't display correctly on many devices, and there is very little content for search engines to find. The use of Flash also means that the site takes too long to load, which often discourages users from staying on the site (on average, a user will wait ten seconds for content to load before moving on).

Alternate the home page image so every time someone revisits, they see a different image, and don't have the same image visible when they click through to the site to avoid repetition. Try showing a selection of your images on your homepage, but avoid introductory Flash slideshows; viewers are likely to lose interest if they have to sit through it.

If you've not completed certain pages, ensure they're removed from the website's navigation.

Avoid using music on your website as it can prove distracting, repetitive and intrusive. Alternatively, turn the music off as default, giving the user the option to switch it on.

Finally, pick your strongest images that reflect your talent, brand and services and have them fill as much of the web page as possible for maximum impact.

BOOST BUSINESS WITH SOCIAL MEDIA

Understanding social networking and using it to your advantage can be of huge benefit to your business. So love it or loathe it, online social networking is here to stay and we say if you can't beat it– why not join it?

A FEW YEARS AGO websites were the new thing everyone had to have and few people knew how to get one. Now websites are an essential commodity for anyone wanting to run a successful business and especially for photographers who want to promote their work. Making phone calls and submitting images on disk has become outdated as the world of emails, FTPs and websites have revolutionised the way we interact.

Now there's a new revolution: social media. It's become the way we share news, develop relationships with strangers, conduct debates and promote our products and services, to name just a few. Of course, there's no substitute for face-to-face communication for building valuable relationships, but the inception of social media has made it far easier to connect with more people globally than ever before. Social media gives you the scope for reaching more people, particularly potential clients, without necessarily having to leave your office. Most consumers or industry professionals such as photo editors expect you to have an online presence in the form of at least a website. It used to be that when someone made a referral it would be followed up with a phone call, but now it's usually with a web search. And it's highly likely if you've no web presence a potential client will doubt the validity, professionalism and quality of your business, perhaps enough not to take the enquiry any further.

Working with social media sites is a daunting prospect, especially if you're not that computer literate or web savvy, as for many it's difficult to know where to start, let alone how to make a productive marketing tool out of it. There are three main social networking sites you should be getting involved with: Twitter, Facebook and LinkedIn – but the most important resource for building an online presence is your blog, which in many respects is what you're trying to drive traffic to via those other social sites.

In this section, we'll try to help you get your head around why you should be using social media, how to use it to grow your business and the pitfalls you should avoid. Swiftly folllowed by invaluable information about how to create and manage perhaps the most important aspect of your social media empire: your blog.

Twitter

If you thought Twitter was for celebrities and their stalkers, you're not entirely wrong. It's also used by the likes of politicians, who want to effectively communicate their campaign messages, magazines that want a quick way to connect with an audience and photographers looking to promote their work.

As a marketing tool, Twitter's wide social net has the potential to explode a business. It's an extremely powerful way to connect with people and share information, to build new relationships and stimulate interest in your photography and services. You can use Twitter to keep abreast of trends, what your industry peers are up to, equipment launches and discussions on topics you care about. You can also use it to drive new traffic to your website and blog, build relationships with potential clients, announce achievements and generally generate interest in you.

Joining Twitter is easy and takes minutes. Simply go to www.twitter.com and click 'sign up now', follow the instructions and you're ready to tweet. OK, there's a little bit more consideration needed than that but that's basically it. When you come to choose your username, make it memorable, use keywords you think people will use when searching for you on Google, for instance your business name, and keep it short. Enter your profile information, such as your website and blog URL, a short biography and then upload a photo to personalise your profile and to put a face to your business.

Start out by finding people you'd like to follow, such as friends and family members, photographers you admire and publications you enjoy reading. If you want to find topics that interest you, type the topic in to the Twitter search box. If you want to tweet, write a message into the box at the top of the Twitter page and if you want to comment on a post by a user simply post the message the same way but add the username. For instance, @DigitalSLRPhoto, thanks for this fantastic Magbook! Now people can click on the username to go to that user's page. Before you start tweeting, though, read Twitter's section on Rules and Best Practices as breaking these rules might result in your account being suspended.

While it's good to have followers, opt for quality over quantity; people who you can contribute to and can contribute to you and your business. The best way of doing this is to target your tweets to a specific audience so you know the content you're posting will be of interest to the majority of your followers and that they're likely to retweet to their followers, building your database of contacts. You'll find it easier to attract and retain these followers if your voice is clear and simple – not muddled with content that doesn't relate to them. If you need to target multiple audiences, say you do fashion and lifestyle photography, consider running separate Twitter accounts.

Twitter top tips

1) Follow the top Twitter users or big names in photography to watch how they use Twitter and the type of content they post.

2) To get the most from Twitter you need to be an active member. The more people you help, the more interesting resources you post for your followers and the more you contribute to conversations, the more other members will help you. Before you bombard followers with updates about your latest shoots and expect them to take notice, establish yourself as a valued member.

3) Join Google Analytics for free to monitor your success at driving traffic from Twitter to your blog or website. You could also join TwitterCounter (at a cost) to keep track of how many new followers you get daily.

Useful Twitter resources

Bit.ly Lets you shorten your URLs (links) to cut down the characters for your tweets.

TweetPhoto.com or TwitPic.com Use these to share your photos on Twitter.

TweetReach.com See how many Twitter members saw your post and shared it.

Twitterfeed.com Feed Twitter with posts from your blog, Facebook page or any other networking site with an RSS feed.

WeFollow.com Find out the top people to follow in photography in terms of influence and their number of followers.

Keep on top of tweets
It's easier to tweet regularly if you do it from a mobile device such as a smart phone or an iPad, as you often have instant access to Twitter to make real-time updates.
Follow us on Twitter: @DigitalSLRPhoto

ISTOCK PHOTO

Q&A: Getting the most from Twitter

A little birdie tells me to join Twitter, but what is it and how does it work?
In short, it's a mini blog, or microblog as it's known by IT experts. It's a form of social messaging centred around you posting (or 'tweeting') comments, updates about your business or personal life in no more than 140 characters for your 'followers' (people who subscribe to your updates) to read. Its purpose is different for different people. Some use it to keep in touch with friends and family, the media use it to keep the public informed by reporting news, while writers and photographers use it as a business and marketing tool to build up a fan base and industry connections.

How often should I use Twitter?
It's best if you get involved with Twitter as much as you can, and not just to post about yourself. It's all about building relationships and you can only do this by staying connected, therefore try to tweet at least two or three times a day – but make sure it's something of value to your followers, not just that you had eggs for breakfast. Unless someone is looking for your tweets, chances are they will quite quickly get buried under all the other updates they receive from the other people they follow, so it helps to constantly put up fresh content.

Can I use the same account for personal tweets and business updates? It's good to show some personality in your tweets but you need to tweet content that's valuable, and not just about your personal life, to keep followers interested. The exception would be if you're a high-flying, living the dream photographer with stories that everyone wants to read. If that's the case though, chances are you wouldn't be reading this article!

How can I increase my number of followers? Remember it's quality over quantity, and you want your quality followers to be spreading the word about your content to their quality followers, and so on, to expand your reach. Do this by encouraging your subscribers to retweet your comments and pictures by posting something interesting. It's important to fill out your biography too as anyone accessing your profile will want to learn about you before they click *Follow It*, adding you to Twitter's Suggested Users page so more people can add you. Contributing to conversations will also expose you to more people. The beauty of Twitter is that anyone can contribute to any conversation, so don't be afraid to chime in on a conversation between users, even if they're big names in the photography world. Just make sure what you say is of value as you'll have more followers watching you than you might if you were posting to your camera club.

How can I learn about current trends?
Participate in Twitter's Trending Topics to join global public conversations and to find out what topics are being tweeted about the most. Trending Topics are listed on the sidebar on the right of your homepage.

Can I select who follows me? Your Twitter profile is public by default, so everyone can read your updates whether they follow you or not. If you want to restrict who can read your updates you can protect your tweets by approving each and every person who requests to follow you. You can do this by going in to your *Account Settings>Settings* and checking the box *Protect my Tweets*. You can also block people you don't want following you but it won't stop them from reading your profile if it remains public.

Q How can I link my Twitter account to my website? Get the HTML code off Twitter to create a link. This way i someone reading your blog wants to subscribe to your tweets, they only need to click on the link. For details on how to do this, visit Twitter's Help Centre.

Facebook

Chances are if you don't already have a Facebook account, you've at least heard of it, even if you're not entirely sure what it is. Facebook is more than a fad, there's even been a movie made about its founding and close to 700 million people are active members, using it to connect with friends, family and business contacts. Most people use Facebook to post pictures, promote events, broadcast details about their lives and keep tabs on just about everything and anything from their Facebook 'friends' to companies and organisations. 50% of users log on to Facebook daily, making it a great marketing venue for businesses and easy to maintain regular channels of communication with people who love your work and can help to develop your fan base.

There are several similarities between Facebook and Twitter, but Facebook blurs that line between personal and professional as customers often share much more information about their everyday lives on Facebook. Not everybody is a member of Twitter, or actively tweets, but many more people are members on Facebook, which means more customers – especially if your photography business mainly deals with the public. It has huge referral potential too, as now more than ever people refer to their social networks for recommendations, and clients share your work and their experiences with their online network, which is usually full of local people – ideal if you photograph portraits or lifestyle images, local sports or local landscape photography.

As well as being able to promote your work via your personal Facebook page, there are infinite numbers of groups on Facebook that act as platforms for discussing topics, exchanging advice, critiquing images and to generally generate a buzz about your work.

ISTOCK PHOTO

Why use Facebook?

Why marketing your business through Facebook can have huge benefits:

- There are 700 million active users on Facebook, with 50% logging in daily.
- The average user has 130 friends.
- 700 billion minutes per month are spent on Facebook.
- The average user is connected to 80 community pages, groups and events.
- Entrepreneurs and developers from more than 190 countries build their business with a Facebook platform.

ISTOCK PHOTO

"Now more than ever people refer to their social networks for recommendations and clients share your work and their experiences with their online network"

And if you can't find the right group for you, create your own.

When getting established, you can't rely on editors to publish your work or for big commissions to come your way, so you need to find ways of self-publishing your work. Facebook is one way of doing this and can act as an avenue that sends people to your blog. There have also been instances when photographers, pros and amateurs alike, have found that by posting their images of newsworthy events on sites like Facebook or Flickr, they can get picked up by the press because they've gone viral.

As with Twitter, the key to promoting your work via Facebook is to understand the community you're targeting and what motivates them to connect with you. Once you know that, you can work on engaging with them and building relationships and an awareness of your work. While you could do this from your personal profile page, eventually you might start to struggle as you attract more business contacts and it becomes difficult to maintain relationships with friends while still appearing professional. In 2010, Facebook launched a page for businesses called Fan Page specifically so that brands could promote themselves for free. It was a fortunate move for photographers as it meant you could try to distance the personal from the professional.

You can customise your business page with content to target prospective clients, such as adding photographs and behind-the-scenes videos to your shoots, linking to your blog or Twitter, hosting photography-related discussions or even launching studio promotions and offering exclusive discounts.

It's quite simple to create a Fan Page: go to www.facebook.com/pages/create.php and you'll be faced with different options for your business, but the three you want to choose from depending on your set-up are: 'Local Business or Place', 'Artist, Band or Public Figure' or 'Company, Organisation or Institution' and follow the step-by-step instructions. You need to upload a profile picture, but unlike your personal page, this doesn't have to be a picture of you. It could be the image you use on your promotional material and business cards, or just a beautiful image you've taken that you hope will catch someone's eye. It's an opportunity to promote your business's brand.

Setting a page up won't be enough to entice people to join you. You need to market your page by mentioning it everywhere possible: post updates on your blog and your other social networking sites. It's even worth adding a note to your business cards or other promotional material inviting people to join you on Facebook and follow you on Twitter.

This should help to get the people you do

How do I get a custom URL?

By default, Facebook assigns a long, complicated string of numbers and letters to your Fan Page URL, which isn't ideal if you want to direct traffic to your site. To get around this you can create a custom, or branded, URL for your page such as facebook.com/your business name. Firstly verify your account. Then you need to get 25 different fans to click ***Like*** on your page, and you will be eligible for a branded URL. This should be fairly easy to do, especially if you've got a profile page, as you could get 25 friends and family members to do it for you. Now go to www.facebook.com/username and apply for your URL.

Social media: Useful resources

TweetDeck.com If you work with more than one site, this tool will help organise your activity on Twitter, Facebook, LinkedIn etc to make it easier to handle.

Twitter App Automatically loads your tweets to your Facebook status.

Seesmic.com Make your life easier by managing all your social networking from one place, your desktop or mobile device.

know on board but how do you access those other 700,000,000 members waiting for an invitation? Word of mouth, I'm sure we can agree, is the most powerful way to gain new business, so the benefits of connecting with a small fraction of these members are huge. The best way to do this is to give your current members something to talk about, something of value that interests them, because as soon as they click the ***Like*** button for your post, it shows up on their newsfeed where every one of their followers can read it. Another way is to target a broad audience by joining discussions in various groups or communities. If you're an outdoor photographer, for instance, instead of just trying to find those elusive editors, National Trust big wigs or tourist board contacts, link in with nature photography groups, landscape appreciation groups and even local groups who like to photograph the same locations as you. It's these places that your potential clients are likely to search if they're looking for new talent. If you're a portrait photographer, it's a similar situation: join communities for portrait photography and contribute to local groups not specific to portraits, such as those for new mums or mother and toddler groups, as this is where you might pick up customers who live in your area. Most photographic associations like the MPA, magazines and photography companies have Facebook pages where you can contribute to the community and learn from their members. Like Twitter, depending on what type of photography you do and whom you want to target, it's a good idea to set up different Fan Pages. For instance, *Digital SLR Photography* contributor Ross Hoddinott has a Fan Page for his own work but also a Fan Page to promote his courses with photographer Mark Bauer.

ISTOCK PHOTO

And the rest...

While Facebook and Twitter are the major workers when it comes to building your posse of dedicated followers, there are a few others to consider too. LinkedIn, which launched in 2003, is a dedicated networking site for professionals to connect with colleagues and professional contacts. Similarly to Facebook's Fan Page, you can create a company page, join professional groups and make yourself known to potential business contacts in the trade and clients. It's a great method for marketing and to expand your contact and client base. Unlike Twitter and Facebook, it's invitation-only so you control who you connect with by accepting their invitation. It's something worth considering if you want to connect with magazine editors, photo editors or art buyers, not to mention any of the 23,325 members in the Photography Industry Professionals networking, Canon EOS or Nikon photography group. Posting status updates here can be a very effective way to keep in touch with editors you've worked with in the past, especially if they move companies, and for new editors to find you.

Other websites you might want to consider include Flickr, which is fantastic for building up contacts with photographers and improving your Google rating and is increasingly the place where publications go to find great pictures. Google is also currently launching Google+, which is designed to rival Facebook, so that's worth keeping an eye on. There's also YouTube for posting behind-the-scenes videos or tutorials. Forums are also brilliant as you can contribute to conversations, get advice from fellow photographers and invite more people to follow you on Twitter, Facebook and to read your blog. Good sites include ePHOTOzine.com, digitalslrphoto.com, Redbubble.com and DeviantArt.com.

Once you've built a strong online network of contacts, you'll be amazed at what you pick up and who gets in touch. You'll have access to new ideas, current trends and contacts to help develop your business, and be able to connect with people around the world who you wouldn't otherwise have been able to. You'll not only have a network of people marketing your business for you, you'll have a global support group ready to help answer any photography or business-related questions. Social networking sites are fantastic learning platforms, places you can watch and learn from your favourite photographers, view their latest work, read their opinions, and even ask them questions. Do we have you convinced yet?

If you're new to social media, hopefully it all seems a little less daunting than before you started reading this article, but it's worth remembering too that all the strings to your online presence have to tie in together for maximum benefit. Social networking sites are primarily used to drive traffic to your website and blog, so more people can see your images. It's therefore crucial that your website, and the photography featured on it, is good enough to clinch the deal that your online networking has been selling. It's no easy task and takes daily maintenance to stay on top of it and to develop relationships, but in many ways it's made building and expanding your business easier than ever.

Beware: Protect your images!

There's always a down side to every up side and while social media has its benefits, posting your images to these sites isn't without risks. Most predominantly it's the potential for misuse of your photos. The best way to limit this risk is to resize them to 72dpi and 700 pixels on the longest side, with a watermark logo. It might not stop someone stealing them, but it's an effective deterrent and it means you know that even if the image was stolen it could never end up on a billboard. Another option is to link the images in your post directly to your own website instead of uploading photos to the Facebook or Twitter site.

Case study: Lindsay Adler

Lindsay Adler is an NYC-based fashion and portrait photographer, and author of *The Linked Photographers' Guide to Online Marketing and Social Media*. Caroline Wilkinson finds out about the impact social media has had on her business and the pitfalls to watch out for

"THE SINGLE most important thing I have done for my career is to use social media. When asked what two pieces of advice I'd give any new professional photographer, I always say the first is don't be afraid to ask. Don't be afraid to ask advice from that photographer you admire on Twitter, don't be afraid to ask that gallery you think your work would be qualified to be in or to ask a publication if they'd be interested in featuring some of your pieces. And two, build relationships via social media. The biggest way to getting jobs is through recommendations and social media makes that much easier.

"Within six months of using social media, it became a moneymaker for me. People like to connect through online media now. Once it was by letter, phone and then email – now it's the likes of Twitter, Flickr, Facebook and LinkedIn. By posting new work on Twitter or my blog, I've sparked the interest of magazines and publications, and I've even had clients schedule appointments via Facebook. If someone hears about you and is interested in learning more about your work, you have to provide somewhere they can go online. For established photographers, someone that's been around for 30-40 years, social media is not as important as they've already built a reputation, so while it can still help grow their business they could make do with a website. But for people just getting started, online social networking is essential to get people connected to you and your work.

"When I moved to London to become a fashion photographer, it quickly became clear that it would be no easy task. I'd send good pictures to magazines, but nothing ever came of them, so I started a blog and used good keywords to describe my images. Within two months a magazine got in touch with me having come across some of my beauty photographs while researching for a feature about body art. When my visa came to an end, I moved back to New York City to do fashion photography, but before that I posted on Twitter: 'Moving to New York in a week, can't wait.' Someone replied back 'I'm in New York, I have a studio, do you want to share it?' It's extremely difficult to find a studio in NYC and to have someone approach me would never have happened without the scope of social media. Twitter also works well if I'm looking to buy new equipment as I 'tweet' for advice and I'll usually get 15-30 responses from people suggesting what I need.

"I 'tweet' two or three times a day about various things. One of the benefits of Twitter is it makes conversations really easy and casual. I've had magazines that follow me and post ' hey, love your pictures, would you be interested in doing something for us?' I've found interns on Twitter by posting what I'm doing and asking if anyone wants to help. I can follow a very successful photographer, watch what they're doing and learn from them. Usually if they're using Twitter the way it should be used, and I ask an insightful question, typically they'd respond to me. How often do you send an email to somebody and it gets ignored? As Twitter only requires a 140-character response, it's really quick and easy to get back to people.

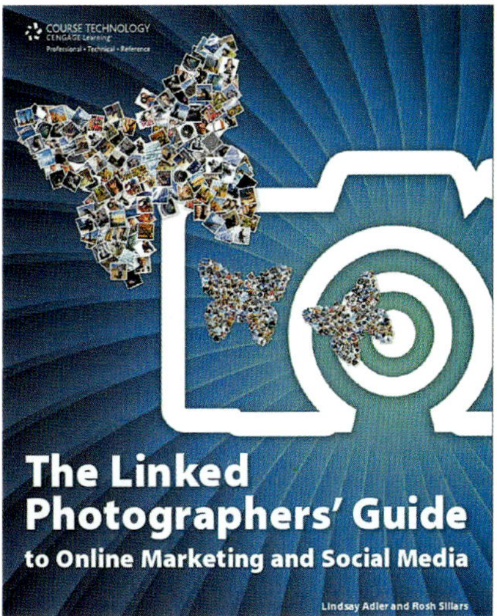

The missing link? Lindsay's book offers helpful advice and insight and is on sale for £10.99.

"To get a feel for Twitter I started by following the big names in photography to see how they did it and then followed their lead. I tend to passively follow someone until they say something of interest and then comment. For instance, I'll follow certain magazine editors, keeping quiet for a while. I watch until they say something that relates to what I'm doing or inspires me and then I I'll 'tweet' an insightful comment. If they think it's interesting, they'll usually respond, starting a memorable conversation so this person now knows who I am.

"When posting your own content on any social media site, it's important to target a specific audience and to create a social networking presence that appeals to them. For instance, in the US, graduation pictures are really popular, so when I was working as a portrait photographer, I contacted students in my local area offering them high-end fashion-style portraits. I posted the images on Facebook and offered free pictures to anyone who shared the link with their friends. Within six weeks I had more business than I could handle as I had reached out to people in the area and given them something they'd like to talk about.

"While there are benefits to social media, it has its perils too, and over-sharing is one of them. There are some people who share absolutely everything that's going on in their life and they're very successful because people connect with them as a person. It is, however, a very risky thing to do because when you have something important to say about your recent work, awards or your musings on your field of work, it can get lost in the noise. It's a strange balance as while you need to remain professional, you also want to show your personality, express your likes and dislikes and the type of person you are. No one wants to have a conversation with a business, they want a conversation and build a relationship with a person. There's a fine line between the two.

"You can also lose your private identity online. If something's annoying me and I want to put it on Facebook, I can't any more as some of my clients might follow me and as a business I don't want to offend or upset anyone. Maybe I went to a party and have great pictures of my friends, but as it's not a professional presentation of myself I wouldn't necessarily put those pictures on Facebook. Even if you have a Facebook Fan Page, you can never guarantee your clients aren't going to look at your personal page. My Fan Page is a great tool for me as I don't share any business-related topics or recent shoots on my personal page. But I get a lot of clients who request my friendship on Facebook. It's commonplace now, if you meet someone you like, to add them as a friend on Facebook to keep in touch and an eye on what they're doing. So sometimes it's a little challenging because if you reject a client's request, what's that saying to them? You can change a lot of privacy settings to restrict access to the content of your personal page but Facebook changes its rules all the time and when they do that it means everyone can see everything on your page until you reset your setting.

"Having some kind of content on YouTube can also be useful. While most searches are done via Google, the second highest number of searches are done on

LINDSAY ADLER

"Within six weeks I had more business than I could handle as I had reached out to people in the area and given them something they'd like to talk about"

YouTube. I've had people contact me because they found a behind-the-scenes video to one of my shoots, an introduction to a class I was teaching or a gallery showing something I did. It's putting extra content out there. You don't have to spend ages on it, but YouTube is highly linkable and people really like videos and also like to share them with friends and family. If you're in the videos it also helps people connect with you, as they can watch you talk and put a face to your business.

"The most important part of your social media is your blog because it is a way to show your personality and that you're consistently producing high-quality work. You should be sharing stories about your work, successful shoots, something people can interact with. If they're looking at your photos on Facebook their interest can get diverted to another page or if someone posts a comment, but if you get them to your blog they're exposed to your branded identity. They're able to experience your brand and your photos the way you want them to without distraction. There are many other reasons why a blog is important, but it's a great way to communicate your brand.

"If you're going to create content for your blog, share a resource that someone would want. For instance, as a wedding photographer you could post your 'top ten tips for looking great in your wedding photos'. It doesn't necessarily do much for you as a photographer, but if a bride sees it and likes it, she'll share it with another bride or her bridesmaids and now you've got all these people and potential clients looking at your blog because you've created something useful for them, something they would want to link to.

"The mantra is figure out who your audience is and what you want to say to them and where you can find them online. For example, as a wedding photographer my audience is female, engaged 18-40 year-old women. So where can I find them online? Maybe you have a local bridal magazine and maybe it has a blog: if so, put a guest post on that blog to drive traffic to your site. Or perhaps target certain groups for brides on Facebook. You could also place an ad on Facebook as it allows you to directly target women in a certain age group in a certain geographic area as soon as they switch their relationship status from single to engaged.
I try to segment all my target audiences and then I try to figure out what content is most important to them.

"You want people to be able to connect with you in as many forms as you can, but I always try to lead people back to my blog and try to make it obvious what my Twitter link is, what my Facebook link is and LinkedIn link is. On Twitter it's not always easy to get people to look at your other work, so I have it linked to my site and blog. Whenever I add to my blog I always post an update on my Twitter or Facebook Fan Page to say ' Hey I've posted pictures of my recent beauty shoot on my blog, check out the new photos' with a link to my blog. You can activate automated Facebook or Twitter posts for when you update your blog but they're rarely descriptive. Doing it yourself gives you a chance to inject some personality in to the post.

"If you're focused and provide good content to the right audience, you'll see a return, which is one reason I wrote the book. When I tried to build a network I made lots of mistakes and wasted time not knowing what was the right content. As I'm not particularly tech-savvy, I forced myself to learn about blogging, URL shorteners, Twitter, etc and the best practices for using social media. Putting it all in a book meant that other people can find success quicker and get back to what they love: photography. The usefulness of social networking for getting people interested in your work shouldn't be underestimated, as the more people who know you, the more business you'll get."

BLOGS: STEPS TO SUCCESS

Learn the basics of blogging to give your business the best chance of success by providing yourself with a platform to be loud and proud about your latest news and images

IT SHOULD BE at the centre of your network, it's the destination you want to drive all traffic to, the place you can showcase your brand and personality, and clinch those clients. It's the ever so powerful, inexpensive – yet priceless – new media champion: The Blog. If you're asking: 'What's a blog?', we're wondering where you've been hiding and you obviously didn't read our article on social networking for your business. If you did read it, however, you'll have an idea how the whole social media monster operates and the key role a blog plays. The next step is to learn how to create one, the guidelines to maintaining it and to using it efficiently for building your profile and traffic to your website.

The beauty of blogs is that they enable you to self-publish. No longer do you have to wait for that magazine commission or book deal to raise your profile. Blogs can help grow your audience by connecting with current and potential clients. One way it does this is by turbocharging your Search Engine Optimisation (SEO): your ranking when someone searches for you online, for instance via Google. Even without the blog being read, search engines index new content to help people find you if they search for content you've written about. Aside from this, a blog can boost your profile by offering viewers a deeper insight into your work and your brand – you can use it as your marketing mouthpiece. Ultimately, a blog helps you to build an audience who shares your content by backlinking (posting links to your blog on their site: one of the most powerful ways to boost SEO), increasing the visibility of your brand.

To do any of this successfully, you need to provide content that's compelling for your clients, whether that's via inspiring or cutting-edge imagery, humour-fuelled tales about your shoots or practical advice: it's for you to decide what best fits your brand. While images are an essential commodity for a photo blog, they shouldn't be the only commodity; which is usually the pitfall of most portfolio websites. Giving your audience content of value or a resource that they will want to share with their contacts will help with your SEO and expand your reach. You can use a blog to disseminate thought-provoking commentary on the industry and pose questions to your audience, inviting them to comment as another way to get them connected to your brand. Photographer Chase Jarvis (blog.chasejarvis.com/blog/) does this well – take a look for yourself.

It's the same with product reviews. A well-written review of new photo gear can generate interest, especially if you accompany it with images taken on a shoot while using the kit – or, even better, a behind-the-scene video that's linked to YouTube. People want to hear from people who know what they're talking about but, to sustain interest, it's something you have to do quite regularly. 'How-to' articles and lists are another effective way of delivering useful content. For example, 'How to pose for your wedding pictures', '20 portrait ideas' or a list of your top photographers compels readers to post links to your blog. If you want to take the lead from a pro, look at Joey Lawrence (www.joeyl.com/blog/). In addition to posting detailed explanations and insights into his shoots, he writes in-depth articles – his latest being 'How to create a photography portfolio'. Photographers will love it as it gives them free, expert, practical advice (perfect for promoting his tutorial DVD). I'm sure the companies he plugs love it enough to link the article to their website too, and it also adds to his credibility as a high-end pro for his commercial clients. All in all, creating a buzz about him, his work and business, as well as boosting his SEO by creating additional links to his website. That's what we call blogging for success!

Email marketing

A blog is great for delivering information and showcasing your latest photography, but you're relying on your audience to take the time to visit your blog or to react to your updates on Twitter, Facebook or LinkedIn to see it. One way around this is to invest in email marketing, which enables you to send the content directly to your contacts. By packaging up your blog posts and sending them via email, you can keep old clients abreast of your new work and push yourself in front of potential new clients, too. It's often not a free service, and takes time to construct, so it's worth doing right, otherwise you risk your investment heading to the trash. It sounds obvious, but the best way to get someone to read it is to give them something they want to read by tailoring the content to their interests.

Email service providers

- **MailChimp** [mailchimp.com]
- **Vertical Response** [www.verticalresponse.com]
- **DotMailer** [www.dotmailer.co.uk]
- **Vistaprint** [www.vistaprint.co.uk]

Analyse that
Use Google Analytics to monitor the frequency and type of traffic reading your blog and visiting your website from your blog. Find it at: www.google.com/analytics/

Our tips for email marketing

- Keep your marketing message consistent by designing the newsletter the same as your website and other branded material.
- Use your business name in the 'Subject' field so it's easily identifiable.
- Avoid sending the email Mondays or Fridays as it's likely to be given less attention than if it was sent midweek.
- Send the email monthly or bi-monthly to keep your audience engaged.
- Have someone proofread your newsletter and test all the links before sending it – you don't want your first impression to be poor.

ISTOCK PHOTO

Blog platforms

You don't need to pay for a custom blog or know how to communicate in HTML to have a brilliant blog these days. Of course, paying a little extra or having that technical knowledge can make your operation slicker, but it's not essential, especially when you're first starting out. With quite a few free blog services available, it's worth taking the time to investigate the different options, to find out what they do and don't offer, and what 'free' really means. Do make sure that, whichever service provider you go with, you have the features to develop a good design, build a community and communicate your brand and work effectively. Here are a few we feel are worth looking at: most are free, while a few require a monthly subscription.

WordPress / www.wordpress.com
This is one of the most widely used blogging platforms. For basic templates, it's free to use, but with the option of payable upgrades, you can install various plug-ins to extend the blog's functionality, widgets and customise the blog to suit your content. It has an easy-to-follow set-up and interface to make managing and updating your blog a breeze, but you can't use your domain name.

WordPress (self-install)/ www.wordpress.org
If you host your own server, you can download the WordPress software and install it yourself so you can use your own domain name and enhance your SEO. This requires some technical knowledge.

Blogger / www.blogger.com
One of the first blogging services to be launched in 1999, Blogger – now owned by Google – is free to use, but requires you to create a Google account. It's a basic blog with limited customisation capabilities compared with other platforms, but as it's connected to Google, it ties in well with other Google products, such as Google Adwords.

FotoJournal / www.myfotojournal.com
Although specifically designed with professional photographers in mind, FotoJournal is a new blogging service, so only currently offers a handful of designs to pick from. Like most services, it can link to your Facebook, Twitter, Flickr and other social networking sites with ease. The downside is if you want some of the more advanced features, like Google Analytics, more storage or Priority Support services, you have to be willing to pay for the privilege (up to £9.70/$16 a month).

TypePad / www.typepad.com
An easy-to-use blogging service that can be connected with your LinkedIn profile so your professional contacts get regular automatic updates of your posts. You get similar benefits to WordPress, such as widgets for your Facebook and Twitter account, customisable design and templates, and an easy-to-manage interface. You also have the ability to view statistics that help you monitor where your readers are coming from and their activity, as well as a customer support team of expert bloggers waiting to answer any of your questions and provide help when needed. A free trial is available, otherwise membership starts from £5.43/$8.95 a month.

Tumblr / www.tumblr.com
Featuring an abundance of customisable design templates, you're sure to find something to fit your style and brand. If you have HTML know-how, you can even formulate your own design. Tumblr is one platform that has social and mobile networking nailed: you can blog using an iPhone app or even via email, you can automatically update your Twitter when you post and publish to Facebook – and, best of all, it's free to use.

Lara Jade

www.larajade.co.uk/blog

A british-born, 22-year-old fashion and advertising photographer, now residing in New York City, Lara Jade uses her blog to provide her international followers with an insight into her work and life as a photographer in the Big Apple. Since establishing her business at the young age of 17, Lara has built a solid social media network that's now bursting with millions of other photographers and artists who follow her work as a source of inspiration.

Lara shares with us why she thinks blogging has played such a large part in her social media success: "It keeps my followers interested and gives me a platform to immediately show new content and behind-the-scenes images of my shoots and training days. For me, blogging provides followers with insight into the life and work of photographers, enabling them to connect with the person – not just the photographer's product."

LARA'S TIP: Keep the design of your blog consistent with your website and link it to your Twitter, Facebook and LinkedIn accounts to maximise marketing potential. Blogging is an excellent way to develop interest in your work. Offer followers an insight by posting behind-the-scenes images and reports.

LARA JADE

Brett Harkness

www.brettharknessphotography.com

Social and commercial photographer Brett Harkness recently relaunched his website having had his portfolio site converted into a 'blog-site', replacing many of his image galleries with blogs, thanks to design firm Flosites. Here's what Brett had to say about his change of approach: "I used to update my website twice a year, but I'd update my blogs four times a week, so it seemed logical to use this platform instead of the usual gallery, which we now feel is a little old hat. People are now used to working with blogs and having relevant and current information instantly accessible. So we have a wedding and lifestyle 'blog-site', a training 'blog-site' and galleries only for our commercial, fashion and travel work. Since relaunching our site, our traffic has doubled. As soon as we blog about a wedding, we link the blog to the venue of the shoot, they link back to us, we put a link to the blog post on Facebook and Twitter – it's all driving traffic to it. If someone rings us asking to see images from a certain venue, we only need to send them the link to that blog post and it's on their desktop. I've designed a couple of blogs before and wanted to jump out the window, so, for this one, I knew exactly what I wanted, but asked Flosite to design it as it was quite technical and part of an extensive refurbishment of the site."

BRETT'S TIP: Don't put too much on the blog at once: limit it to ten pictures. I've seen blogs where they've posted 30-40 pictures showing the best of the wedding, but it leaves no surprises for the clients. Keep it updated because if people visit a blog to see it's not been updated for a month, it puts them off - it also helps your Google ranking. Make sure you rename your images with your name and the place they got married - not the couple's name (eg Joe&Jane2011.jpg), as it helps search engines.

BRETT HARKNESS

Karan Kapoor

www.karankapoor.com

Advertising photographer Karan Kapoor is new to blogging this year, but he has already seen his website traffic almost treble as a result. "I can use it to post information about my shoots and images that won't necessarily make it into my portfolio. For instance, if I'm abroad doing a shoot, I might post one picture with a caption saying: 'I'm in Barcelona shooting for 'X', what an experience!', or I might post a more extensive story with a selection of images from a shoot. People in the imaging business like to see what photographers have been doing. I try to post at least once every month and I also use sites like LinkedIn and Behance.net – it's quite phenomenal how many hits I get on my blog from contacts reading my updates on these sites.

I try to keep my posts business-related, such as awards and latest photography projects, personal and commissioned."

KARAN'S TIP: Keep your blog posts short and relevant to your readers. Think about what your audience will want to read. Posting reviews of photography gear is great for your photographer followers and might mean they share your post with others, but make sure you accompany it with beautiful images from the shoot. Your prospective clients won't be interested in the specs of a piece of kit, but they will be interested in seeing the work you've created with it.

KARAN KAPOOR

Blog platforms

While it's not essential for you to have a bespoke blog, Nige Burton, director of design company Freebird, gives us his views and advice for managing a photo blog.

"Having a professionally designed blog is as important as having a professionally designed website if your customers are to take you seriously. A blog is a great way to keep in touch with existing clients as well as attracting searches for potential new ones. It's always best to design something bespoke but then integrate it with a tried-and-trusted platform like WordPress, as it's designed to be easy to use and has built-in SEO advantages.

"It's vital, if you go down the route of having a blog that you keep it regularly updated. I'd recommend a minimum of once a week, but more if possible. There's nothing worse than your clients looking at a blog that hasn't been updated for six months. Diarising this for the same time every week often works and is as important as anything else that makes it into your schedule. A blog post doesn't have to be long, but a few paragraphs of sharply written, relevant copy are worth their weight in gold.

"Remember what people are expecting from a photography business, and keep it image-heavy but with some order, and feature only your absolute best work. Make sure it remains completely corporate and within your established brand. Remember: a blog for business is not the same as a blog for pleasure, and your audiences will be quite different. Mix them up at your peril."

SOCIAL PHOTOGRAPHY

Learn all you need to know about running a portrait or wedding photography business

IT'S TIME TO ACT LIKE A PRO

You don't have to be a pro to act like one. We take a closer look at how some of the most successful UK social photographers conduct business and build their reputation alongside their bank balances

"WE DO NOT DO photography for the money: it's our passion," says Kristie Harkness, co-owner of Brett Harkness Photography. While this statement is probably true for most photographers, it's an easier sentiment to swallow for those who have a profitable career in photography than for those struggling to fund their passion. Whether you're trying to pay for your weekend tech-habit, give yourself a bit of disposable income or hope to earn enough to support your family, money is a major motivator. And I'm sure we can all agree that the more we earn the better.

No matter what the scale of your business, or how long you've been selling your images, the way you conduct yourself and your services puts a price on your value and influences how much clients are willing to pay. If you look like an amateur and behave like one, people will think you're an amateur and want to pay you accordingly. If you want to maximise your income by charging professional prices, even if you're a part-timer, you need to be prepared to deliver a consistent professional service. It's a reason why some photographers are enviably lucrative, while equally talented photographers flounder.

Every arena of photography has its own professional code of conduct, but social photography like weddings and portraits is a service-driven sector, so just as much emphasis should be placed on the customer experience as on image quality. If you demand hundreds of pounds for a wedding but expect to turn up on the day having done no preparation, wearing jeans and a T-shirt, take a few snaps and give them a disc of non-edited images, then don't expect much work in the future. And frankly, if some sucker does hire you, it's unlikely to result in referrals or to help you develop a reputation for quality.

Your reputation is your ticket to higher earnings, but it's also fragile and easily tainted so you need to deliver high quality service consistently. Once you've built a reputation for quality, you'll be more in demand and eventually be able to do fewer shoots for more money. If you work hard, you may even be able to afford the same attitude as Brett and Kristie.

The customer experience should start from the moment you answer the phone to a prospective client. To give the air of professionalism the Harknesses want to convey, Kristie makes sure she's at her desk in the studio ready to answer business calls at 9am. Not walking around a busy Tesco. While very few of us can afford the luxury of a studio and will initially at least be shooting alongside our day job, we can follow pro photographer Esther Ling's lead and simply answer the phone with your name and a smile on your face. "It makes you sound happy and people like to hear from happy people. If you answer the phone miserable, it's not a great start."

After initial contact send the prospective client a brochure, invite them to look at your website and to meet with you to discuss what it is that they're looking for. "How quickly you correspond with people, whether through brochures, email or phone is really important for securing the client," says Kristie. For your business to appear professional, your brand and what it represents needs to be reflected in the way you deliver service and be backed up by your blog, website, portfolio, promotional material and brochures, to form one streamlined package.

Investing time to develop a relationship with your client will pay dividends in the long run too. Set up a meeting with them to discuss what it is they want and expect and, where a wedding is concerned, make regular contact to see if you can help with their planning and to arrange a pre-wedding shoot that prepares you both for the big day.

Dot the I's and cross the T's

Depending on the type of photography, there is a certain amount of paperwork to be aware of to protect both parties. A verbal contract with a deposit at booking is enough for a portrait shoot. However, a wedding photographer needs a written contract to ensure both parties are covered in case anything unforeseen were to happen. It doesn't have to be anything big or scary, just a few terms and conditions. A lot of weddings get booked a year in advance, so if the couple decide not to go through with it at short notice you could be left out of pocket. This safety net has proved valuable for Brett Harkness:

"We've just had a wedding cancelled and we had already turned work away. This is why in our contract we specify a non-refundable deposit and in our cancellation clause it says if they cancel between 100 and 90 days before the wedding, they still have to pay 50% of the balance," explains Kristie Harkness. Their contract also requires the balance to be paid four weeks before the wedding and states that they retain all copyright of the images. It also says that do whatever they can to find a replacement photographer if for any reason Brett can't make the shoot (this is why having a posse of photographers in your network pays off!).

Even if you plan to do the occasional wedding, make sure you get the clients to sign a contract, no matter how nominal the fee. While a cancellation policy might not be a concern for you, outlining the image rights should be. Even if it's friends or family that you're doing the wedding for,

> "Your reputation is your ticket to higher earnings, but it's also fragile and easily tainted, so you need to offer high-quality service consistently"

you never know what might happen in the future, and good friends should understand that business is business. While the photographer owns all copyright, often clients will want to know whether they can get their images on disk. Detailing the copyright in the T&Cs means you can stipulate their terms of use, including making them aware that you can use the images for your marketing material. However, if you plan to submit images to magazines, be courteous and ask them for their permission anyway. If you do give images on disk, Esther Ling advises putting a clause in the contract that stipulates that they can print the images for personal use but they cannot resell them, nor can they edit the images in any way. By doing this, you're asserting at least some control over how your images might be seen by prospective clients. Esther bundles her T&Cs in with her booking form, making it less intimidating for clients. Here she has the bride and groom write down all the key details of what's been agreed for their wedding: date, time, cost as well as ceremony and reception venues to make sure everything is in black & white.

Although contracts aren't necessary for small portrait shoots, you do need to have your clients sign a model release form if you think you'll want to use any of the pictures commercially. And if you're photographing children under 18 years old, you will need to get parental permission to allow use of the images in magazines too. For commercial, landscape and fashion shoots, on the other hand, a contract is very specific to a client, and should detail the length of the image licence and terms of use, for instance whether the images are to be used worldwide or just in the UK.

With the web being such a vast resource, you can find all these documents online or, if you're struggling, photography forums are brilliant if you need help. A lot of photographers are willing to share their contracts. Similarly, if you join professional bodies like the Master Photographers Association (MPA), you get access to their legal advisors and documents such as model releases and contracts. The website of the Association of Photographers is a good place to start to download T&Cs, commissioning invoices or usage guidelines for commercial shoots too.

Professional practice

Most jobs come from recommendations, so while you're on a shoot you're also marketing yourself to all the guests. Expect your images to be seen by friends and family, and make sure you're always representing your best work. If you're shooting a wedding, dress smart but comfortable – black shoes, trousers and a shirt and tie as basic. Esther Ling goes as far as dressing like a guest, as she finds people are less intimidated by a guest with a fancy camera, enabling her to get much more relaxed reportage shots. Lifestyle photography is rather different in that it's a much less formal environment, but still warrants looking smart/casual.

Every photographer will develop their own rules, for instance professional photographer Stuart Cooper never barks orders at wedding guests or tells them they can't shoot over his shoulder because, for him, it's important not to bring negativity into the wedding day.

When working with children on a portrait shoot, Stuart leaves his camera in the car and spends time with the children so that they get used to him before he even starts trying to take pictures. There's also no time limit on the shoot, he dedicates a day to a client so there's no pressure to rush, encouraging them to relax, which helps him get better pictures. Also when it comes to boudoir or maternity shoots, he's very careful to find out what the client is comfortable with: "I always makes sure Anna, my wife, comes on these shoots with me and we show the client a portfolio of maternity pictures from fully clothed to nudes to get a feel for what they're looking for and comfortable with doing. Rather than just coming out with 'so, do you want to strip off or not', as that's just uncomfortable." Stuart never touches a model either. Instead if he wants them to get into a particular pose he'll demonstrate it first, turning his back to offer some privacy while the model gets in position.

Post-shoot protocol

From start to finish, the aim is to exceed clients' expectations and the best way to do this is to manage them. In the same way you show the client examples of your work before they book to make sure they know what to expect, you should try to under-promise and over-deliver where possible. Stuart Cooper, for instance, tells his customers their album will be done in eight to ten weeks, but delivers in six.

The viewing is a chance for clients to relive the shoot and is a process that shouldn't be rushed. It can take anywhere up to three hours, sometimes longer, to select their images and decide what products they want to buy. "While a lot of photographers cannot afford their own studio to hold viewings, a lot of very successful photography companies bring slideshows and products to a client's house, or network with hotels so they can use a conference room for a small fee or in exchange for images of the venue," says Kristie Harkness. You can use a room in your house to host client viewings too, but make sure it's private and away from family life. However you go about it, presentation is key.

Projectors can be picked up for around £200, but initially, if you're starting out and say spent your last penny on a new lens, you could hook your laptop up to a TV, burn the slideshow to a DVD or borrow a projector. "There are loads of ways you can do it if you're resourceful," says Kristie. Not everyone does a viewing either, although they do offer the best opportunity to make more money by up-selling products. As an alternative, you could make a proof book, upload a slideshow online or have the client select the pictures off your website. "It's about finding what best defines your business and the type of market you want to cater to. Similarly with products, some people want it on a disc and that's it, others want to give a product," she adds. There are many album companies on the market to suit all levels of product, from small photobooks to large hand-mounted albums. Check out the likes of Bespoke Photobooks, Loxley Colour and Graphistudio for more details. If you do decide to include or sell products, invest in at least one sample album, ideally with your images in or with the cover products, so clients can see what's on offer. You can then build on this as your business grows. It also helps to have a few framed or canvas prints on the walls to give clients ideas of how finished products will look. If this is out of your budget, opt for a chevron package from companies like Kaleidoscope Framing Limited to give the clients at least some visual options.

"If you see them struggling, try to offer advice on the types of products you think suit them," suggests Esther. "For instance, will the album be living on a shelf most of

Top ten tips

1) It's all too easy nowadays to conduct business by email – but don't! Pick up the phone or arrange to meet with the client as it will help build a better relationship.

2) Don't leave anything to chance. Prepare thoroughly by taking time to get to know your clients and what it is that they want.

3) Happy clients lead to future clients. By delivering the best service you can and exceeding their expectations, you're setting yourself up for referrals.

4) When you arrange to meet your clients for a chat or viewing, make sure the venue is comfortable yet professional. If it's at your home or studio, ply them with tea, coffee and biscuits. If it's a wedding viewing, round off their experience with glasses of champagne.

5) Always be early to a shoot and generous with your time.

6) Aim to under-promise and over-deliver.

7) Always carry business cards with you everywhere you go.

8) Invest in promotional material like brochures and branded folders for your booking form and contracts.

9) Be business-like but also open and approachable so your clients feel relaxed and comfortable during the shoot.

10) Always conduct yourself professionally, whether you're with friends or other photographers, as you never really know who you're talking to.

> "The customer service shouldn't end once the shoot's finished or when they've received their beautifully presented products. Maintaining the relationship is crucial"

the time or would they like a coffee table book that's suited to being on show? Tell them what covers wear better than others and what sizes suit their types of images."

The customer service shouldn't end once the shoot's finished or when they've received their beautifully presented products. Maintaining the relationship is crucial to get referrals and repeated business. Esther Ling sends her clients anniversary and birthday cards to reconnect and as a gentle reminder that she's around. She's found it often results in repeat business such as maternity, baby or family portrait shoots.

If you're serious about making money from your photography you might want to consider joining a professional body like the MPA, the British Institute of Photography or the Society of Wedding and Portrait Photographers for support. They each have their own codes of professional conduct that they expect members to adhere to. But even if you're not a member, following their standards (details are available on their websites) can be good business practice. Clauses such as client confidentiality, upholding the standard of your work and dealing fairly, honestly and helpfully with clients and suppliers are pretty basic principles that can only help your burgeoning reputation and, hopefully, your bank balance. ■

HOW TO PROFIT FROM PORTRAIT PHOTOGRAPHY

Looking for a new career and love taking portraits of friends and family? Perhaps contemporary portrait photography is the way to go. Find out how to start up and run a successful lifestyle photography business with our realistic and expert advice from some of the country's leading professionals

IT'S ONE OF THE MOST popular types of photography in the market today, but what is lifestyle photography? To advertising agencies, who coined the term, it's photographically recreating a certain lifestyle for the purpose of selling. To some social photographers, it means photographing clients in their home going about their daily lives, or outdoors, to incorporate their style of life into the images. And for the high street studio photographer, it's delivering informal portraiture that fits with the client's life. For instance, it used to be that anyone going to a studio to have their picture taken would wear their best dress or suit, but more people now want photographs that reflect their lifestyle, and prefer to wear the likes of jeans, shirts and no shoes. But regardless of how you plan to conduct your business in a studio or a client's home, the important aspect of lifestyle photography is to capture emotions, personalities and the essence of clients' relationships in an artistic, facilitating fashion.

Words like 'relaxed', 'candid' and 'natural' are plastered across the websites of countless self-proclaimed 'lifestyle photographers', yet few reflect these adjectives in their work, with their portraits looking posed, formal, unprofessional or showing little to no signs of life. It's therefore clear that more and more, the term 'lifestyle photography' is being used as a marketing ploy to dress up photographers' work as contemporary portraiture. If you're to make it in this competitive market, and to set yourself apart from the hoards of other striving portrait photographers, you really have to do what it says on your tin and produce outstanding work, as well as deliver outstanding service.

Manchester-based photographer Brett Harkness believes that, in part, geography plays a large part in success. "If you're north of Watford then think about it seriously. The lifestyle market is a luxury right now – it's not at the top of people's list. To make a living from just photographing kids, for instance, you're going to have to be producing something that's got the 'wow' factor, if you're to get the clients in without selling your soul to the devil and giving everything away on disk. It's probably the hardest side of photographing society that there is now and certainly for the last 18 months."

If hearing this hasn't sent you running for the hills, then the first thing to do is consider joining a trade association such as the British Institute of Professional Photographers (BIPP) and/or The Master Photographers Association (MPA). You get access to awards, qualifications, promotions, training days and marketing advice. While you need to be a full-time photographer to join the MPA, you can be part-time and still get the support and some of the benefits of the BIPP while you work towards your first qualification.

> "You're going to have to produce something that's got the 'wow' factor if you're to get the clients in without giving everything away on disk"

Talking about what it takes to make it in this business, portrait photographer Frazer Visser, from Hamilton Studios in East Grinstead, West Sussex, makes an elementary but often neglected point: "What's fundamental to every portrait photography business is consistently good photography, whether you're presented with a screaming newborn or a family of 20, three difficult children and a dog. You have to constantly deliver high standards. The client knows whatever they bring to us, however grotty the children are, we will rise to the challenge and deliver consistently good pictures. If they've loved a large canvas print on their friend's walls, then they know that we will produce photography equally as good for them. They come in knowing what they're going to get; that confidence keeps the clients coming back and the referrals coming in."

A large part of lifestyle portraiture relies on the professional friendships you forge with the clients. To get great images, they need to be happy and relaxed. It's so important that you get along. You can start building that relationship at the time of booking by having a chat with them about their lifestyle and what they want from the shoot. You may find that your client is a London socialite who likes his designer fashion and spends his weekends at his family's stately home or that she's a farmer's wife who hates anything formal and wants photographs by her dilapidated barns. Clients need to be treated differently and many will welcome your advice on the best clothes to wear and insight in to how the shoot will go. You also need to think carefully about how you'll go about photographing them, as each client deserves the special treatment to get the best from the shoot. One way of doing this is to adapt your style to suit the subject, for instance you may take studio lights to the stately home but you wouldn't to photograph the farmer as it doesn't suit her organic style. Another way to keep the experience special is to dedicate the entire day to the client so as to concentrate on creating a beautiful array of images for them to potentially want to buy.

Meeting the client at their home before the shoot is a great way to gauge the client's lifestyle, tastes and what they want from the session, by getting a quick glimpse in to their lives and their characters from the way it's decorated. From a selling point of view, it's also a good opportunity to take note of what wall space they've got so that later, when they're seeing the images at the viewing, you can make gentle suggestions for where potential framed prints or canvases could work well. For instance, if the client's home is very minimalist, there are certain items that may suit their lifestyle and taste, such as perspex blocks and acrylics rather than big, embellished frames.

Sometimes, you have no choice but to arrive at a house cold and have to think on your feet, once you've had a look around. You may find that the clients apologise because they think their house is too small or feel that there's nowhere lovely inside or in the garden to use as a backdrop. You have to reassure them that it's not the case, as there's always somewhere. Sit them in front of a door or a garden gate if you have to, they may look at you a little strangely at first but because you'll use a wide aperture to blur the background, all you're looking for are colours and texture. Ideally the clients will have beautiful big ➤

BRETT HARKNESS/ WWW.BRETTHARKNESSPHOTOGRAPHY.COM

ESTHER LING: WWW.ESTHERLING.CO.UK

> "Spend time just observing their everyday interactions around the house to get them comfortable with the camera, then move them somewhere more unusual to them"

windows or french doors that flood their house with natural light, so all you need to use is a reflector. If, however, the client's home is less than ideal, head straight for the door. Not to leave but to use. Every house has a front or a back door and if you sit the subjects in the doorway, turn all the lights off indoors, and meter for the skin tones, the background turns black and you have gorgeous diffused light on their faces. The rest of the shoot you can then do outdoors. Or, if your style is more strobes than sunlight, take the studio to the client's home and use studioflash or flashguns to breath life in to the shoot.

Portrait photographer Esther Ling advises, if you can, to spend some time just observing their everyday interactions around the house to get them comfortable with the camera, then move them somewhere more unusual to them. This way you put them at ease as they know you have the shots that they want and the rest are just a bonus – even though nine times out of ten they'll buy your more artistic images. Try different angles and perspectives without making the subjects feel like they're performing for the camera. You may need to get them in position but it's by talking to them that you put them at ease and can elicit the natural reactions like laughter that make the best images. ■

BRETT HARKNESS

ESTHER LING

ESTHER LING

Professional advice and handy hints on how to tackle your three key clients...

Babies & children: Unless you want to specialise in photographing newborns and know how to do it well, you're better off waiting until the child can hold its head up or sit up, otherwise there are only so many things you can do. Try to use natural light as much as possible, as using flash around a baby is not a great idea, but if you have to do it, do it quickly and only take a few shots as you can damage their eyes. Babies also mimic you, so if you smile long enough at them eventually they'll smile back.

Toddlers are the best age of child to photograph as you can just have fun with them and they'll react much more to you. Take them out in to the garden or a field, have them run or jump in puddles. Make it a fun experience to keep their attention as it will be gone in a matter of minutes. You have to know what you want and you have to be in walking distance from your background. You'll probably have to use natural light most of the time because the children are always active and you can't be running after them with a flashgun. But if you do want to do a flash shot, save it to the end when they're exhausted and sitting down.

Some parents can be quite pushy, always telling their children to smile and looking over your shoulder, but while the big smile shots are important as the parents love them, try to also capture them while they're playing. Shots of them acting naturally and not looking at the camera or from behind will give the parents a choice when they come to the viewing. Nine times out of ten, the clients think they want just the big smiles, head and shoulders or full-length shots and tight facial crops, but when they see your more candid images they'll be blown away and spoilt for choice.

Teenagers: The age of a teen seems to be getting younger and younger. Every 11-year-old wants to be a teenager, so you need to gauge the child's maturity as this will help you decide whether you should be posing them in a fashion style or be playing games. If you shoot a teen with the family there, they'll react differently than if they were on their own.

Teenagers can be very self-aware and outwardly confident, they want to look good and usually want their photographs taken too so can be very willing models. While you might not have a make-up artist with you on the day, teenagers usually want to change looks quite frequently throughout the shoot, so start off by looking through their outfits and factor in time for costume changes.

BRETT HARKNESS

BRETT HARKNESS

ESTHER LING

If there's a group of teens, photograph them together first to get them relaxed and to capture some animation between their friends and/or siblings. Then leave the parents at home while you go for a walk around town with them individually to look for funky background and for more of a fashion shoot, if appropriate. With teenagers it's not about big smiles, it's the slightly sultry and moody shots that they see in magazines that they want taken of themselves.

Families: You need a lot more light when working with groups to be able to get enough depth-of-field. An old indoor favourite is the French doors as they're a great source of diffused natural light, or any door that's wide enough and opens up to an outdoor space. Why not try swinging the sofa around to face the French doors and positioning the family around the sofa so they're lit by the diffused sunlight coming through the door. If natural light is limited indoors, try mixing studioflash with the daylight by bouncing softbox-mounted flashes off the ceiling to give you the aperture you need (f/8 or f/11) to get the whole family sharp.

When dealing with groups try and opt for symmetry and balance where you can. For instance, don't put the widest person at the end unless there are two of them and they can act as bookends, otherwise place the biggest person in the middle of the composition and have them perhaps holding a child on their knee. If you decide to take the session outdoors, walking shots are great for families as they don't always have to be looking at the camera. Ask them all to look at your assistant or a plane in the sky, as this way they'll be more inclined to look in the same direction. If the kids don't want to walk, have the parents swing them to add energy to the pictures.

Become a studio-based photographer

Working from a studio is a different business from being on location. Here we provide insight and advice on ways to make a studio-based business work and how to use it to produce perfect portraits

THE BEAUTY OF BEING a lifestyle photographer is that you can run your business from anywhere as there's no need for a permanent studio.

If you're organised and prepared, you can turn the clients' home into your mobile studio as well as conducting the initial meeting and viewing there. But, if you're someone who likes to have the business come to them and prefers working in a controlled environment, you might want to consider being studio-based. You could rent a premises or convert a space, like your garage if you want to work from home. You will need more than a white backdrop and a basic studioflash set-up to look the professional, though. If your studio is at home, you'll need a separate area for clients to wait in before having their photos taken, a suitable dressing room with mirrors for clients to change in and a viewing room with plenty of pictures and products on display. Ideally all of these should be areas that can't be intruded upon by roaming children or disrupted by family life. Ideally, if you can, the studio should have a separate entrance entirely so that no clients have to walk through your home to reach your business.

The words 'Venture-style' photography are guaranteed to make discerning professional portrait photographers cringe, but as much as some may loath the franchise, you have to admire what they've pioneered and its popularity with the masses – apart from its price tag. White backgrounds, simple lighting set-ups and images full of colourful personality. It's an efficient and profitable business model, but one we wouldn't advise an independent to try. You need to build a business on relationships and you couldn't do this if you operated a daily conveyor belt of clients. Whether you work in a studio or a clients' home, it's best to limit yourself to one client a day so you can focus on delivering a great customer experience, without the pressure of a time schedule hindering your creativity.

As a studio portrait photographer, having a detailed knowledge of how your camera works is a benefit, but don't over-estimate the importance of this technical knowledge. Knowing what every button on your camera does won't make you a better studio photographer on its own. What's more important is knowing how to get what you want from the client, being able to interact with the clients effectively and getting the lighting and posing right to make the images so appealing that the client is willing to hand over lots of money for them.

Unless you know exactly what you want and how to get it, studio photography can be challenging as you have absolute control over the environment and you somehow have to elicit reactions that may not come as naturally as they do if the client was at home. This means singing, dancing – whatever it takes to get the shots you want in the studio.

It's really important to control the sitting too. Having children running around or jumping up and down, with you chasing behind them and snapping away, is not the best idea in a studio environment. Not only do you have to consider the safety hazards, but you also can't be changing the position of the studio lights every 30 seconds to keep up with the kids. You need to know what you want to achieve from a session and learn to manipulate the shoot to make sure the kids sit still and look at you long enough to get it. Remember, it's the eye contact that often makes the portrait.

Using a tripod is a really good way of drawing your subject's attention to you. As the camera is set up on a tripod, it means you can concentrate on engaging with the client, and there are various things

BRETT HARKNESS

"You can play peek-a-boo behind the camera, use tickle sticks, have toys falling off your head or bubbles popping on your nose – anything to get their attention"

you can to do that encourage them to look at you and get the right expressions. For instance, with a young baby, you need to get in very close to them, as they can't see far, and lock eye contact with them to get their attention. As they get older you can play peek-a-boo behind the camera, use tickle sticks, have toys falling off your head or have bubbles popping on your nose – do anything that gets their attention. If you had the camera to your eye the whole time, you wouldn't be able to interact with the client very well, while this way you can play with them while remotely taking the shot.

The more children you have in the picture, the more difficult it can be and it's even more important to be in control. There's nothing worse than if you're doing a shoot and there's granny in the background and parents to the side calling the children or telling them to smile. If this happens, try to encourage the adults to sit down out of the way so the focus is on you and the camera. It's important that all eyes are on you, and whether it's a smiley shot or not, their expressions are the same.

As well as lifestyle photography, you might want to offer other forms of portraiture too such as boudoir, pets or even fine-art photography, like British Professional Photographer of the Year winner Lisa Visser has done, but you have ➤

The essential kit list

Standard equipment

- ✔ A DSLR and back-up camera
- ✔ A telephoto zoom lens. We recommend a 70-200mm f/2.8 for supreme quality
- ✔ A portrait lens. The 50mm f/1.4 or f/1.8 would be perfect and cost-effective
- ✔ A wide-angle lens for the family portraits such as a 24-70mm f/2.8 is a good choice
- ✔ For shooting on location or in the client's home, you could opt for a portable flash system like Elinchrom's Quadra Ranger System, if your budget can stretch that far. Otherwise opt for a couple of flashguns, a Lastolite Ezybox and wireless triggers like those produced by Pocket Wizards.
- ✔ And don't forget some large reflectors!

Studio equipment

- ✔ Two or three studioflash heads with attachments such as barn doors, honeycomb grids and softboxes. We recommend Bowens or Elinchrom
- ✔ Props such as seats and rugs
- ✔ Backgrounds: Even though a white and black background should be a staple, variety is key so make use of your wall space to create different backgrounds. Perhaps invest in different coloured paper rolls, or even plaster a corner with patterned wallpaper while keeping another bare brick, or paint it white, for added texture.

Top tips

Ask an experienced professional photographer, someone you admire, to critique your work. It's important to find out what you're doing well but, more importantly, what could be improved. It might be demoralising but by picking your work to pieces, it means next time you go in to a shoot, at the back of your mind you'll know the things you have to watch and correct. It could be small details that you miss during shooting, like where the subject's hands are, or sitting them up higher that make all the difference. Joining trade associations like the MPA and BIPP are great for this reason as you'll be able to get your portfolio critiqued, often live, and receive invaluable feedback.

Top ten marketing tips:

Forget advertising, give yourself a jump-start by adding some of these cost-effective marketing methods into the mix:

1) Offer your customers an incentive for referrals such as a free print from their last shoot for every new customer they refer to you.

2) Sell products, not a disk. By controlling how your images are presented you're controlling how you're marketing yourself. Consider your client's home as your gallery and you'll be surprised at how many customers you get from seeing your work on someone else's wall.

3) Join local business networking groups. You never know whom you might meet: an owner of a play centre or a children's clothing store perhaps, or even other photographers. Creating these business links can be invaluable, as not only can you pick up new leads such as 'so and so' has had a new baby or is pregnant, but you could offer to shoot marketing material for these businesses in exchange for them referring you to their clients, putting a link to your website on theirs or distributing your marketing material.

4) Keep your blog and Facebook page up to date. Adding new content to your website will improve your search engine optimisation and encourage prospective and current clients to return to see your new work.

5) Create an email database of everyone who's been in contact with your business, from photographers and suppliers to current clients and enquiries. Create an e-newsletter to send out once a month with some of your most recent work and links to your blog.

6) Working from home, especially at the beginning when you may not have much business, can be lonely and unproductive. Take your laptop out for lunch or the afternoon and base yourself where you'll be interacting with other local businesses. Again, you never know who you might get chatting to and what prospective clients you might meet.

7) Subscribe to the RSS feeds of other photographers and photography websites to keep on top of latest work, marketing and changing trends and techniques.

8) Keep up with your continual professional development by going on courses, business and photographic, to develop your style, skills and to meet like-minded individuals.

9) Send handwritten thank you cards to every client along with birthday cards for their children and Christmas cards for the family. Enclose a voucher for a free sitting or product to entice them to come back.

10) Focus your business and marketing material towards delivering the best client experience possible, rather than centering it around your products and services, as this is what will get you new customers.

to be sure your style will sell. When Lisa first started developing her award-winning fine-art work she would have to start a shoot with the staple lifestyle images that she knew clients would buy and then throw a few of her fine-art shots in to the mix.

"I wasn't sure if people would like the style of the work I enter in to competitions, but it became really popular and the mums seemed to appreciate that side of photography. Eventually I would like to be doing 100% fine-art photography, but for the moment I'll suffice with 10% high street lifestyle and 90% fine-art.

"People want portraits for a lot of different reasons, sometimes it's a record for the family, other times it's a special occasion and sometimes it's for grandparents. The style of photography people want seems to change depending on its purpose, and the fine-art shots are because they want something different and stylish for their wall. They're not doing it for an updated shot and they're certainly not doing it as a present for grandma, they're doing it for themselves."

Lisa's business partner, Frazer Visser, continues: "If you come in to the market with a new and interesting style, it has to be something that people want to buy. You can't be arrogant about your niche, you have to be willing to adapt as otherwise you'll be stuck before you've started. As a studio, if we hadn't changed over the years we wouldn't be here now. If we were still doing the traditional handpainted background and potted plant in the corner, we would have fallen at the first hurdle." ■

"People want portraits for a lot of different reasons, sometimes it's a record for the family, other times it's a special occasion and sometimes it's for grandparents"

Top tips

Never give copyright to your clients. If you sell prints, you need to make it clear in your terms and conditions on your website that your clients are not allowed to duplicate any prints they buy from you. Never give them copyright, otherwise you won't be able to use any of the images for your marketing purposes and you can miss out on future sales. It's also a good idea to keep their images backed-up for at least a year in case they contact you wanting to buy more.

Your pre-business checklist

Before you set up shop, here are a few things to consider doing to give yourself a strong start:

1) Create a business plan and open a business bank account (see p106 for more details).

2) It sounds obvious, but make sure you have enough funds, or a second income, to support yourself while the business is growing. Contact a financial planner or your bank for advice on small business loans if needed.

3) Build a strong portrait portfolio using friends, family and test shoots.

4) Branding: Come up with your name and design yourself (or commission) a logo that reflects the quality of your work and the personality of your business.

5) Website: This is your number one marketing tool: it will be your shop window and is fundamental to attracting new business. Make sure it oozes personality and professionalism, leading with your images, and link it up to your business' new Facebook, blog and Twitter pages to increase your online presence.

6) Business cards: The second most important piece of marketing material. If you don't have much money to invest in marketing at the start, at the very least buy some business cards. Cost-effective companies include moo.com, Vistaprint.co.uk and Printexpress.co.uk.

7) Get adequate insurance to protect your equipment, business and clients, such as public liability and professional indemnity. Contact one of the major insurers such as Aaduki or Glover & Howe for advice on exactly what you need and check what permits you need if you're to run a business from your home.

8) Set up an accounting system so you can keep track of your expenses and income in anticipation for submitting your year end tax return once you register as self-employed.

9) Rent or buy the equipment that you need for the studio and/or location photography; post-production; premises, if you want to hire a studio; and even consider opting for a credit card machine for when you have to take that first big transaction.

10) Read the *Business Matters* section (starting on page 105) of this guide for details and advice on how to set up a photography business.

Master the products, pricing and profit

Like most artisans, photographers struggle when it comes to selling their work. We offer you some advice on how to make a profit a less painful process

BRETT HARKNESS

© IMAGE BY THE FRUITION TEAM/KALEIDOSCOPE FRAMING

Suggested suppliers

- **Folio Albums** www.folioalbums.com
- **Kaleidoscope Framing** www. frames4photographers.com
- **Loxley Colour** www.loxleycolour.com
- **OneVision** www.onevisionimaging.com
- **Queensberry** www.queensberry.com

LIFESTYLE PHOTOGRAPHY has huge potential to be a lucrative career but relies upon your ability to sell to be profitable. It's usual to charge a client between £50 and £200 as a non-refundable 'sitting fee' at the time of booking to cover the cost of your time but after that your income is based on how much the client is enticed to spend on their pictures. Before you decide what to charge, do some research and scope out the local competition to make sure you won't be undercutting or pricing yourself out of the market. Flexibility is important too, as if you're offering a session fee for £60 but your client wants you to travel 200 miles to meet them, chances are you'll barely cover your costs. Most lifestyle photographers assign a base rate for local and studio-based sessions, but put a disclaimer on their website to say this price might increase depending on the location of the shoot.

The next stage is pricing your products. It's not uncommon for photographers to put on average a 75% mark-up on the trade price of their products. You have to consider the time it takes for you to prepare and edit the images, postage and packaging, and other overheads for operating your business such as equipment, studio hire, insurance, marketing material, courses – and above all – the value of your talent and expertise. Figuring this out may seem like a tall order but it's even taller once you factor in your market. There's no point offering a Queensberry album from £500, or framed prints from £300, if it's not affordable for your clients. The same way a £50 coffee table book and £70 frames probably wouldn't convey the sense of quality a high-end client wants. Shop around for suppliers and products that reflect the quality of your photography and business but are also suitably affordable for the majority of your market. There are lots of suppliers to choose from so you won't be short on choice. Post the price list on your website so that clients know what they're getting.

Most photographers find they sell what they show, so make sure your viewing and sales areas are uncluttered with lots of big pictures on the wall in products you want to push. If you're doing the viewings at the client's home, then you need to take samples along with you. It is a pain to have to lug all the equipment with you but, on the flip side, it means you can literally show the client what the products will look like on their walls. Alternatively, Kaleidoscope Framing sells a Photographers Sales Box (£320 plus VAT), which is ideal for the mobile photographer and holds all your customised product samples. If you can help it, don't put your clients' images on your website for them to buy. It rarely works. Your best chance at making some money is at the viewing and allowing the client to buy products.

Being good at sales is really important if you want to be a social photographer. You can be the most fantastic artist in the world but if you can't close a deal, you'll end up penniless. Training courses can help if it doesn't come naturally to you, but one way to make it easier is to be acutely aware of what's selling, changing trends and tastes via people's reactions to certain photographs. Lisa and Frazer Visser advise posting new pictures on your business's Facebook page and observing which images get positive comments. You can do a similar thing during the viewing by recognising what images people are 'oooing' and 'ahhing' over, what products people are buying – and perhaps more importantly what they're not – and what pictures people are liking in your studio or website gallery. Then the most important step is to tailor your style to match the market, and this means keeping your style fresh by constantly developing new techniques to add to your repertoire, as if you do the same thing year in year out it's unlikely clients will come back. Try to create images that clients couldn't dream of producing, as this is where certain lifestyle photographers are failing. Photographing people in a field is one thing, but adding creative flash is another. You have to step it up a notch.

MAKE MONEY FROM WEDDINGS

In this comprehensive guide about wedding photography, explore your style and the basics of the business, learn the essentials of marketing and pricing and how to keep ahead of the competition

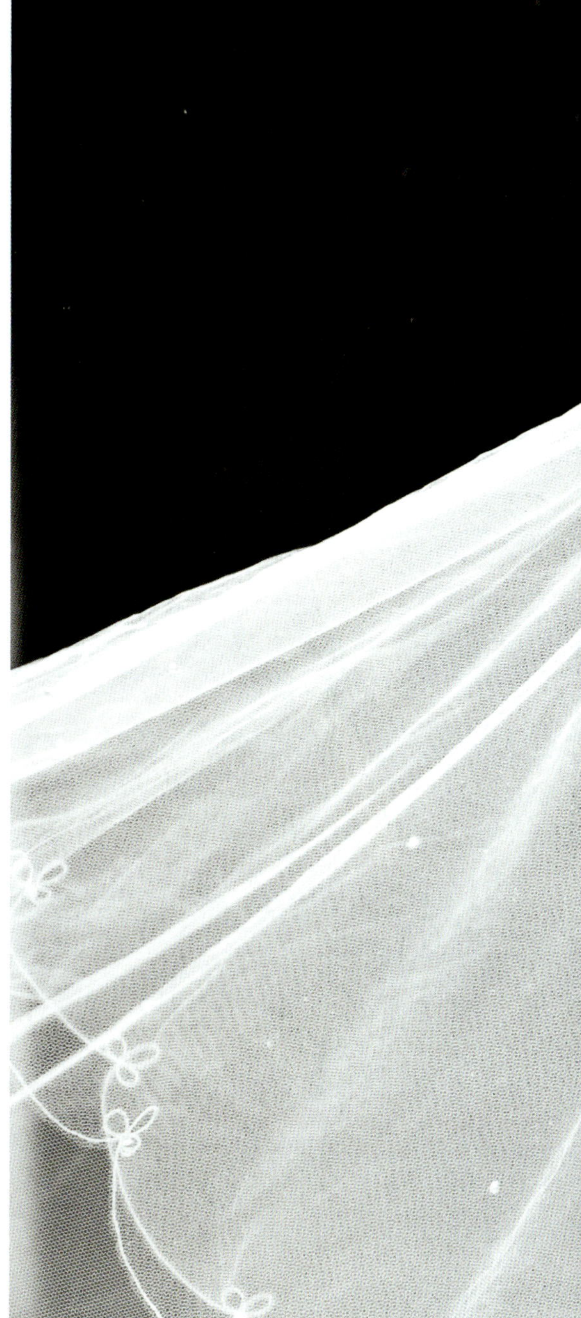

WEDDING PHOTOGRAPHY is an easy way to make a fortune, right? Wrong. Unfortunately this is the all-too-common, nonchalant misconception that many photographers have, and it often results at best in a business that struggles to get off the ground, and at worst some very unhappy clients and disastrous wedding photographs. We're not saying that wedding photography isn't profitable, it certainly can be, or that it's extremely difficult. The fact is though that it's not – contrary to popular belief – something that just anybody with a half-decent DSLR and a couple of lenses can do well. In this major section, we'll be equipping you with everything you need to know about wedding photography, from how to get started, securing clients and conducting wedding shoots, to post-production, workflow and album design. All that we hope is that by the end of it, if you still want to give weddings a go, you approach it with the right conscientious attitude and the respect that it and your clients deserve.

Few great wedding photographers will say they do it just for the money, as frankly the money's not enough to relieve the pressure of knowing you only have one shot at capturing a couple's special day. Wedding photography is a passion, a huge responsibility and commitment, though it's also very rewarding. There's such satisfaction in seeing a couple overjoyed with their pictures, and knowing that they'll be treasuring your work for a lifetime. It gives people so much pleasure, which is probably one reason why so many photographers don't mind doing weddings for free – at least initially.

Finding your footing

As the market is busting at the seams with wedding photographers, you have to be prepared to compete for clients. Talent's not enough in this market: a lot of brilliant photographers are struggling to make ends meet while average photographers flourish, and this is because too often photographers lack the essential business skills to market themselves properly.

"You've got to start off in a market that you're comfortable in" advises wedding photographer Brett Harkness. "It's important that you don't start targeting high-end clients and big budget weddings before you're ready for it. It only takes one mess-up and word will get around." Also, your charges have to be right for what you're delivering, so if you're charging a lot of money the customer experience has to reflect this, from the way you answer the phone and the brochures you send out, to the coffee you serve clients when you meet. It also determines your market, which in turns determines your brand and how much you need to invest in it.

Your brand should reflect you, your style of photography and your approach to weddings and business the way you want others to see it. You don't need to invest money in professional branding at first, in fact it's probably worth avoiding it for the first year while your business evolves, but if you come to make the business a full-time enterprise it's worth considering. It's important to make sure your brand is consistently and accurately represented

> "Few great wedding photographers say they do it just for the money, as frankly the money's not enough to relieve the pressure of only having one shot at capturing the special day"

throughout everything you do and your marketing material, as this is what helps you look like a professional, even if you're a weekend wedding photographer.

If you're going to spend money on anything though, you should look to invest in a decent website because as a social photographer, this is your shop window. Clients will make a decision whether to contact you within seconds based on how professional, sleek and functional your website is and how your online portfolio looks. Bland template websites simply won't cut it in this industry. The website should reflect your brand and style as a photographer, but you don't need to invest in an expensive custom website. Companies like Bludomain, Clikpic, Amazing Internet and Freebird all offer design-orientated templates or affordable bespoke websites specifically for photographers so they're polished and professional. Many of the websites also feature the all -important blogs, Twitter and Facebook links so that you can keep your clients and future clients updated with all your latest photographic work, personal and professional, adding to your authenticity and search engine ranking.

Networking with local suppliers like bridal stores, florists, wedding planners and venues are crucial for getting your business off the ground and to build your basis of referrals. You will need support, so join your local networking group to meet a variety of small business owners, as you

never know where it could lead and build up relationships with other local photographers. Networking with competition can prove to be a lifeline. Photographers are very supportive of one another and having contacts ready to support you when you need it means that if you ever have technical questions about kit, technique or business, you have like-minded people to bounce ideas off, and who can bail you out of a wedding if you fall sick or can't make it on the day. Getting on the preferred supplier list at wedding venues is also a superb way to draw in clients as they often make a decision based on a recommendation.

First of all, research the venues that you want to work with. Think about the type of clients they attract and whether it's the same client that you want to draw in. What types of weddings does the venue specialise in? Does it have a hook like a lake, a grand, charismatic interior or extensive grounds? How much does their typical customer pay to be married there? And be sure to suss out the standard and style of photographers they already recommend to see where you fit in – for instance if they only have traditional photographers and your work's more contemporary that might be the open door you need. Before you approach whoever is the gatekeeper, have your objectives clear. How many weddings a year would you like to do at this venue, what can you offer them – for instance are you willing to do promotional pictures to replace their tired marketing images and put a link to the venue on your website? Send them a formal letter with a contact sheet of your images, a business card and brochure then follow up with a phone call a couple of days later to set up a time to meet. Go equipped with branded business cards, brochures and your digital and soft-backed portfolio that sell your best images, so you can prove to them that your business fits with their brand and core values. If you learn to sell yourself and your services, always act the professional even if you only shoot the occasional wedding and be diligent with your networking, there's no reason why you can't develop a successful business on whatever scale suits your situation. ➤

How much should you charge?

When taking the first steps into a creative market that's highly competitive and unregulated, like wedding photography, one of the most difficult tasks is to put a monetary value on your service. Most photographers start at a low price because they have low confidence, then as their confidence grows with experience they charge a little bit more. But there are others who ooze confidence but have no experience and enter the market charging £1,500– £2,000 straight away. Knowing the value of your service and having the confidence to stand by your prices should be something you tackle early on. You can probably increase your prices by 20% a year without alienating your referrals, who are pre-sold on what you charged for your last wedding. But it could take years to get to a level where you can charge the 'going rate' that you deserve, which right now is around £1,500. And if you decide to drastically increase your prices overnight, you could be saying goodbye to all the hard work you've done building up a referral base in that market. You're actually much better off doing weddings for free with the purpose of building a portfolio and confidence then, when you're ready, start charging what you should be. But remember to tell those clients who you're shooting for free how much you would normally charge, that way if a friend asks them how much you were they know to say the right amount.

It's true that with a higher price tag comes higher expectations and this can be daunting for new wedding photographers. But by charging professional prices you'll appear more professional and probably attract more clients.

Finding your price bracket comes down to a lot of variables: you need to be competitive so that you're not undercutting or pricing yourself out of the local market and figure out how much you need to earn to be profitable – otherwise what's the point? There are lots of liabilities with weddings, so you need to factor in the cost of insurance as well as the wear and tear on kit, mileage, gear hire, an assistant, marketing; everything that it takes to run your business. Plus, and perhaps most importantly, your time and talent. One way of pricing this is by giving yourself an hourly rate, and not just for the wedding day but for the time it takes for post-production and album design too. The average is around £50 an hour.

The cost of an album can be as much as £600, depending on who you use, which you've also got to mark-up if you want to make a profit. So some photographers offer this as an optional extra and instead give the images on disk. While there are many arguments fore and against this, it really depends on how precious you are about your images and whether you want to risk clients editing the pictures and your work being misrepresented, or miss out on extra income from reprints. You could put a clause in your contract to protect your images but you still won't have control over the print quality. Alternatively, you could offer clients a free CD with the images from the album or at an extra cost. It really depends on how you want to conduct your business and the value for money you wish to offer clients. ■

"Finding your price comes down to a lot of variables: you need to be competitive in the local market and figure out how much you need to earn to be profitable - otherwise what's the point?"

What should you do if a friend asks you to shoot their wedding?

✔ **Manage their expectations** Ask them to show you images that they like and be honest with yourself, and them, as to whether you can produce pictures of a similar quality. If you don't feel you're up to the task, tell them but offer to be a second photographer on the day. This way you don't take the risk, they get extra images for free and you have a chance to gain some experience and pictures for your portfolio.

✔ **Prepare, prepare, prepare** Arrange a pre-wedding shoot with the couple so you both feel comfortable on the day knowing what to expect from one another. Scout out the wedding and reception venue in advance for backgrounds and natural light.

✔ **Be equipped** Read our section on wedding kit to find out what gear you need to rent or buy for your experience level.

✔ **Get a shot list** Have them write you a list of 'essential' pictures and use it as a reference on the day. There's nothing worse than realising too late that you didn't get a picture of the happy couple with grandma or a full-length picture of the bride in her dress.

✔ **Learn about lighting** Most wedding photographers rely on natural light for their shots, avoiding direct sunlight for the risk of bleaching details in the dress, ruining pictures with deep shadows and squinting subjects. So, learning how to control and diffuse natural light is essential. In case you have to use direct sunlight, or there's a lack of natural light, you also need to know how to use fill-in, bounce or off-camera flash.

✔ **Enlist help** Ask a friend, your partner, or a member of the wedding party (ideally an usher or best man) to help to organise the groups and to hold reflectors when needed. Having someone there to do crowd control is also an asset, this way when you're photographing the bride and groom there isn't a hoard of guest paparazzi distracting them from looking at your camera.

✔ **Play it safe** Set your camera to Raw and aperture-priority mode. You'll have greater flexibility and scope for recovery later in post-production if you get the exposure slightly wrong than if you were to use JPEG. Working in a fully- or semi-automatic mode, also enables you to focus on interacting with guests and capturing spontaneous moments that you'll miss fiddling with settings.

✔ **Be directive but not disruptive** As the photographer, it's your responsibility to get beautiful pictures that capture the day without interfering. For most of the day the photographer should be a fly on the wall, rarely seen or heard, so set your camera to Quiet mode if you can and draw out the inner photojournalist. The more guests are aware of you, the less likely you'll capture spontaneous moments and natural expressions. But when it comes to the couple's and group shoots, it's your time to take control. Don't be afraid to be bossy but also keep the atmosphere light and relaxed so you can fire through the shots while keeping everyone's spirits high.

✔ **Business cards** Most new work comes from word of mouth and referrals, so make sure you go equipped with business cards.

How to build your wedding portfolio

Potential clients judge your worth on the quality of your photography, so a decent portfolio is crucial. We explore the right and wrong ways to create and showcase your portfolio to maximise sales

STARTING OUT AS a wedding photographer can be a bit of a chicken and egg dilemma: to get paying clients you need a strong portfolio but to get the portfolio, you need the clients. This is probably why most new wedding photographers start out shooting the weddings of friends or family for free, or as a second shooter. It's a great way to build a portfolio but it doesn't always give you a chance to explore and develop your style or creativity as there's limited time at a wedding to experiment, and as a second shooter you're often restricted by what the main photographer wants.

Setting up a mock wedding shoot, also known as a test shoot, on the other hand can be a really effective means of building a portfolio that you think presents your talents and style in the best light to potential clients. It also gives you the opportunity to perfect your photography and lighting skills, as well as try out new techniques that you can later use at an actual wedding. As you're in control of the shoot, you can work slower and be more methodical about taking the shots perfectly than you would at an actual wedding, where you're governed by the day's schedule and capturing the couple's story. It's also far easier to push your boundaries and to trial-and-error your creativity when you don't have paying clients in front of you or looking over your shoulder, as you don't have to worry about looking incompetent or unprofessional.

Keeping your portfolio fresh and current is really important for staying ahead of the competition, as is pushing your photography skills, so test shoots are good practice for any photographer no matter what level they're at or however long they've been a wedding photographer for. Lifestyle and wedding photographer Stuart Cooper endeavours to do at least two or three a year, giving him an opportunity to update his portfolio with images that reflect the current wedding trends, as well as try out new creative ideas.

"Whenever you do a test shoot, it's worth doing them well and quite often it's good to get other people involved as part of a networking exercise too. The sky's the limit with what you can do and get from these types of shoots. If there's a venue's' recommended supplier' list, for instance, that you want to be on but you've yet to shoot any weddings there, approaching the management to ask if you can use the grounds for the test shoot in exchange for some of the images of the venue is a good way in," claims Stuart. Do the same for a hair stylist, make-up artist, attractive friends who you can use as models, and a local bridal store for a dress loan, and you've got yourself the makings of a test shoot. As everybody will be giving their time and services for free, make sure you reciprocate with images of their contributions, for instance close-ups of the flowers and dress, or beautiful portraits for the model and make-up artist. It's a really good opportunity to build relationships with local suppliers, get your images on other business's websites and it gives you something to blog about as well, which can be really beneficial according to Stuart. "A blog is a really useful marketing tool, for instance, if someone's getting married at a particular venue and you've just blogged about a test shoot you've just taken there, there's a good chance that when they type it in that the search engines will pick it up." Test shoots are an opportunity to use unusual locations or places you wouldn't be able to get to on a wedding day like National Trust properties, train stations, ruins or the coast. You can also use light and shoot at times of the day you might not normally have access to, for instance there's gorgeous light at 5am but you'd struggle to persuade a bride to get out of bed that early for pictures unless you were paying her!

If you want to use an exclusive venue and they won't let you do a shoot there for free, you might want to consider paying for it and look at it as an investment. Normally it can cost between £50 and £200, depending on how much of the venue you want to ➤

IMAGE © STUART COOPER PHOTOGRAPHY

> "Keeping your portfolio fresh and current is really important for staying ahead of the competition, as is pushing your photography skills with test photoshoots"

Get professional help

By joining professional associations like the Society of Wedding and Portrait Photographers (SWPP), you can access a wide range of professional advice and contacts in the industry that can help you organise test shoots. The SWPP also offer its members a mentoring programme, whereby you can receive training and one-to-one appraisals of your work with advice to help you progress. (For more information email: info@swpp.co.uk). There are also a few wedding photography courses on the market that can help you supplement your portfolio while you train. They organise the test shoot for you so it looks stylised and authentic, but you will often have to share the shoot with other photographers too. It's a good option if you want the professional training, but your shouldn't rely on just these images for your portfolio as it won't be an accurate reflection of your ability to shoot a wedding. We'd recommend you consider courses by Brett Harkness Photography and Aspire Photography Training.

Trash the dress

Another way to make your portfolio look contemporary, and to earn a little more money, is to offer clients a post-wedding shoot. A few years ago an American concept called 'Trash the Dress' crossed the Atlantic, causing a bit of a stir. Brides were swimming in the sea, walking on railway lines and being posed on haystacks and in gritty urban scenes, producing some really edgy editorial-style images. It was an intriguing idea, but there was something about potentially ruining a stunning £1,000 dress that didn't quite catch on in the UK. But the idea of taking the couple to an unusual or photogenic location, for a more stylised and creative approach, will only ever be a hit – after all what bride wouldn't want images of her in her wedding dress that look like they could be straight out of a bridal glossy. Even though there's no need to risk ruining their treasured dress, assess their attitude as you may find they're willing to be more adventurous than you think they are.

use and how long you need it for. But send them postcards of the images you shot there and you might be lucky to get on their list of preferred photographers. If that happens, the £200 investment is likely to be returned tenfold.

Stuart recommends a recce of the location before the shoot to find the best spots for natural light and to plan where you need to be at different times of day to get the best light. Introducing props into the shoot too can help give images an editorial edge and make them look more stylised. It also means you can get more mileage out of the images as you can post them on blogs like Rock n Roll Bride, Style Me Pretty and Rock My Wedding, or submit them to magazines for marketing and PR material.

Whether you arrange the shoot for a day or a couple of hours, you can do one of two things: go with the purpose to get one or two 'wow' shots or to get a bank of good images. It's always good to go armed with some tear sheets from magazines or download pictures on to your memory card so you have an idea of what you want to achieve or try. There's only so much you can do, so it helps to have visuals to make the most of your time and art-direct the shoot. Although you don't want to copy the images, they're your inspiration and can be helpful for giving guidance to the models. However, even though you should plan the shoot, leave room for spontaneity as you never know what might happen and it's a good opportunity to learn to be reactive as well as proactive, like you'd have to be at an actual wedding. You need to be able to get the best from any situation and take stunning impromptu pictures.

Your style of photography is partly what clinches you the client, which is why it's so important to truthfully represent yourself through your portfolio. Don't only use your test shoots as a chance to try something completely new and off the wall, use it to build a base of images. Staging glamorous or edgy shoots in incredible locations look amazing and can be invaluable for marketing, but make sure you also include realistic scenarios that couples can see themselves in. You might even want to consider doing a test shoot in the most diabolical weather, with a less photogenic model and a bland wedding venue; you won't use it as marketing material but it's reassuring to show prospective clients that you can make the best of even the worst situation and still take stunning pictures.

Use your first few test shoots as a chance to figure out your style and what you want to offer your clients. More traditional photographers focus on the classic poses and group shots, others opt for a relaxed fly-on-the-wall approach and some very dramatic stylised shots, often with heavy use of flash. If you're more of a traditionalist, be aware that as the world of

© STUART COOPER PHOTOGRAPHY

Sell, sell, sell

Be bold. Your portfolio is your strongest promotional tool and it should be treated as so. Show it off to everybody and anybody to generate buzz around your work. Have your portfolio accessible online via your website, but also consider getting a selection of your signature images printed in a portfolio book to show clients exactly what type of wedding photographer you are and the standard they can expect. You can order a beautiful portfolio from the likes of Blurb, Sim2000, Loxley Colour and Everleaf.

© ASPIRE PHOTOGRAPHY TRAINING

> "Recce the location before the shoot to find the best spots for natural light and to plan where you need to be at different times of day to get the best light"

wedding photography changes, this cookie-cutter approach is becoming less popular. Couples want creative wedding photography, often comprising a balance of the latter two styles; a documentary approach with photographs of the two of them interacting and being spontaneous combined with some interesting and creative portraiture. You may still need to do the odd classic portrait and formal shots, however, to appease the traditionalists in the family.

If you don't know what style of wedding photography you'd like to explore, research other wedding photographers online for inspiration or flick through bridal magazines, blogs and websites, then practice various set-ups and poses until you find your groove and what you're most comfortable doing. Find your strengths and develop them, but don't neglect your weaknesses too as most weddings require a little bit of everything.

Getting reportage shots in your portfolio can be a little tricky on a test shoot but not impossible. Obviously there will be a lack of guests, but try to capture pictures of the couple looking at each other or off camera, laughing together in between staged shots, or from a viewpoint that makes it look as if you're observing them from a distance, as this can create candid-looking images. It's also worth asking a local photographer if you could be a second shooter or approach a friend who's getting married to see if you can take some shots on the day too: as you won't be the main photographer your images will naturally look voyeuristic. Or, if you're a little bolder, drop in on a registry office armed with some business cards and catch the brides and grooms and their guests as they congregate outside. You'll need to get permission from anyone you photograph though if you want to use images of them in your portfolio or for marketing material.

Even if you opt against a test shoot, it's crucial to challenge your photography so you keep developing new skills. Learning how to use flash will definitely set you apart from the bride's uncle, giving you stylised, saleable images. It's too easy to slip in to a routine of taking set shots at a wedding, but keep your images and style fresh and you'll keep people talking about your work. ■

WORKING A WEDDING

In this section of the guide, learn the logistics of shooting a wedding, how to conduct and profit from a pre-wedding shoot and the techniques that will help you capture the shots that sell

"IN THE EARLY DAYS, I've exploded a bottle of champagne over the bride's mother, dropped lenses in a pond and smashed my 50mm f/1.2 lens moments before the bride entered a very dark synagogue, where flash wasn't allowed. I've had the shutter in my DSLRs collapse and had to have a camera shop courier a new body to the wedding by motorbike. I've even had to finish some weddings using film because my cameras have failed," recollects Brett Harkness, one of the UK's leading wedding photographers. "You have to pick yourself up, pull yourself together and get on with it – it's part and parcel of photographing weddings."

Wedding photography is more than lighting, aperture and composition: you need to be able to handle every eventuality while still appearing composed and in control – even if you're panicking inside. Until you have encountered every kind of wedding day disaster, kit malfunction and nightmare guest, and know instinctively how to handle it all, every wedding will pose new problems to overcome no matter how meticulously you plan. Which is why preparation is so essential. Covering the basics will put you in a much better position to cope with the unexpected when it happens. Until you become comfortable with the process of a wedding day, we advise you plan it like a military operation and try to identify problems as early as possible by having regular meetings with your clients. You want them to feel relaxed and confident that their photography is in capable hands, so it's your job to discuss their prospective plans as early in the process as you can to address any problems that could interfere with them getting the pictures they want. After all, with so much to contend with, it can be easy to miss out on crucial pictures or a part of their day because you didn't prepare for it properly. If this happens, not only could it knock your confidence but you could be feeling the financial effects of a damaged reputation for years to come.

Even before the clients book, you should be managing their expectations. Make sure they're happy with your style of photography and that they're fully aware of what to expect. Once they book with you, take a deposit (normally 25% of the total amount) to secure the date and ask them to review and sign a contract, nothing too heavy just something to protect you both (see pxx for more details). Even if you're shooting for friends and family, if money is changing hands, ask them to sign a contract outlining the use of the images and your cancellation policy.

In the lead up to the wedding, arrange a few meetings with the couple to discuss wedding day plans, what they want from you and their album, if they're having one. Ask them to bring along a few images they like from the web, magazines, or from your online portfolio, to show you the type of images they want and more importantly what they don't want. It's vital to build a rapport and trust with clients before the big day, so work with them at the planning stages to ensure they get what they want. The couple won't know how long you need for pictures and the best time to do them based on the time of year, so address these logistics five months before the wedding, rather than five weeks, when perhaps nothing can be done about it. ➤

"Get all your kit together the night before because inevitably you'll be in a rush the morning of and tend to forget things. Make sure all your lenses are clean, memory cards are clear and batteries are charged" *Esther Ling*

Top tip

You may find writing a shot list containing the essential images you need and want to capture a useful way to make sure you don't forget any pictures the bridal couple and you want for the album. There's nothing worse than getting home and realising you've forgotten to take a full-length portrait of the bride in her dress, a picture of all the bridesmaids or the groom with his 98-year-old grandfather. You may also find it helpful at the beginning to print off an inspirational contact sheet of images and poses you'd like to try on the day so if you get stuck, and have a sneaky second, you can refresh yourself.

Always think what if?...

Be prepared for anything you can think of. One minute it might be beautiful weather, the next it could be raining so make sure you have big white umbrellas at the ready. If you don't, chances are a guest will have a couple of large, unattractive golf umbrellas with logos on that not only look horrendous but give your couple an ugly colour cast. Have tissues to hand for crying guests and make sure you have back-up equipment and a plan B in case gear fails, you have to do the group shots indoors where there's limited light or a power cut forces the speeches and dinner to be done in candle light. It could happen!

Questions to ask the client...

- ✔ What's the schedule for the day?
- ✔ How many people in the wedding party?
- ✔ How many people at the ceremony and then at the reception?
- ✔ Where and when are you getting married and is the ceremony in the same location as the reception?
- ✔ Are you planning any surprises for the guests or individuals?
- ✔ Are you planning any surprises for each other? (Ask them each privately)
- ✔ What have you spent the most amount of money on and is there anything particularly sentimental?
- ✔ Who are the essential people you want photographed and photographed with?
- ✔ What is it about the venue that you love? (So you know to get photographs of it)
- ✔ How are you both arriving to ceremony/reception? (You'll need to approach photographing a horse and carriage differently to a classic car)
- ✔ Who is giving the bride away?

"Write down who everyone in the bridal party is and the essential shots on postcards so you can refer to it during the day. It's useful to include any notes on the day too, such as if there are members of the family who shouldn't be stood next to each other in the group shots, as with so much going on it's easy to forget on the day" *Stuart Cooper*

Your 'to do' list before any wedding day

- Visit the ceremony and reception venues at a similar time of day as they'll be used for the wedding to scout out the best lighting and backdrops. Look for big windows for natural light and areas of open shade that you could use for the group and bridal couple shots.
- Check what the venue's selling factors are, perhaps they have a grand staircase, a lakeside jetty or character features that attracted the couple, which you can use for photographs. If the venue is very basic, concentrate on finding uncluttered backdrops and areas of soft natural light like windows or even doorways so you can use the interior as a dark background.
- If the couple want a group shot with all the wedding guests, find out if there's a place in the venue that can give you a high vantage point like a balcony or open window over an area outdoors. If they don't, you know you may need to come equipped with a stepladder.
- If it's a church wedding, arrange to meet the vicar to discuss any restrictions on photography. Sometimes you won't be allowed to use flash during the ceremony or at specific times, like the exchanging of vows. The vicar should also be able to tell you the best places to stand to get photographs and where prior photographers have shot the groups. Ask the registrar if it's taking place in a registry office.
- Find out when the wedding before and after yours is happening so you know your window of opportunity to photograph guests arriving and after the ceremony.
- If the wedding's not too far away, do a test run of the journey from bride's hotel where she's getting ready to the ceremony and then to the reception venue. You may be surprised at how difficult some venues can be to find if they're off the beaten track or how your initial travel time is doubled by traffic at that time of day. If you have to go further afield for the wedding, travel up early and try to do this the day before the big day.
- Arrange a meeting with the couple's private or venue wedding coordinator to discuss the details of their wedding day and where events like the first dance, wedding breakfast, cutting of the cake and reception drinks will be held. If possible, get them to run through the wedding with you so you know exactly where you need to be and when to get the best angle for pictures.
- How big is the wedding? Do you need to hire a second shooter or an assistant to help you or can you rely on the best man and ushers to help coordinate people for the group shots?
- Introduce yourself to as many operators and suppliers for the wedding as possible, such as the florist, venue manager and wedding coordinator. By doing so, you can arrange to send them pictures you've taken of their work, which can help build up your contact base. If they like your images and decide to use them for their promotional material, you'll probably find you become one of the first wedding photographers they recommend to any of their clients.
- Speak to the DJ or band about how they plan to light the room for the first dance so you can decide if the ambient light will create enough atmosphere or if have to provide your own light and exactly how do you want to do this.
- Once you have a detailed schedule of how the day will go and an idea of the lighting conditions you'll have to work with, plan when and how your best chances are to get the shots you need and equip yourself for the task, be it learning or practising flash techniques or hiring equipment.

Create a detailed schedule of the day

Every wedding is different and should be treated as such, but by preparing for each one the way we advise you to, you'll be setting yourself up for success and reduce any of your wedding-day stress

WHEN COMING up with your schedule, be realistic about your journey times. How long will it take for you to get from the various venues, factoring in traffic and time of day. If you can, do the journey and time it or use Google Maps or Map Quest to plan the route. When you plan the day like we've done here, leave room to be flexible in case of the unexpected and, if you can, assign more time than is needed for the group shots and bridal portraits. If the bride is fashionably late to the ceremony, it will be your time with the bridal couple that is squeezed as everything else has to happen on time. If it's a long way to travel, you may even want to consider staying in a hotel near the wedding venue. It's a good excuse for a weekend away, you won't risk being caught in traffic, plus – best of all – it's tax deductible!

10.30am: Meet the bride at her hotel room to take pictures of her and the bridesmaids (Lily, Jen and Pippa) getting ready. If time, photograph the groom at home (the groom's house is 15mins from the hotel).
12.15pm: Get to the church ahead of the bride to photograph arriving guests and group shots of the groomsmen (Ben, Phil and George) if we didn't have time earlier. (Church is 20mins drive from hotel and five minute drive from groom's house).
12.55pm: Bride to arrive in horse and carriage with her father and bridesmaids.
1pm: Ceremony.
1.45pm: Ceremony finishes. Get confetti shot and guests with bride and groom outside the church.
1.55pm: Leave for reception venue before bride and groom (15min drive).
2.15pm: Bride and groom arrive at reception. Meet them at the entrance. Drinks and canapés on the lawn.
2.30pm: Have the ushers gather all the guests on to the lawn for a group shot.
2.40pm: With the help of the ushers, organise the group shots of the guests to be taken on the lawn.
2.55pm: Take group pictures of the bridal party. Use a different location to the group shots of the guests.
3.20pm: While the guests and wedding couple chat on terrace, take the time to capture the table details and decorations in the venue as well as documentary images of the guests.
3.45pm: Whisk the bride and groom away for their private portrait shoot.
4.30pm: Bride and groom must be back for their receiving line.
5.10pm: Speeches.
5.30pm: Wedding breakfast.
7.00pm: Cutting of the cake and evening guests arrive.
7.30pm: First dance.

© STUART COOPER

© ESTHER LING

© ESTHER LING

Pre-wedding shoots

An engagement, or pre-wedding, session is a fantastic way to get to know the client, for them to get to know you and for you to see how they slot together as a couple. To find out what they like, what they don't like about themselves and to build your relationship with them. The photography is actually the least important part of the pre-wed – it's all about encouraging a connection between you and the clients that can carry through into their wedding day. Keep it relaxed and relatively unstructured, with them dressed comfortably even if it's jeans and t-shirts so the images simply capture them being together and having a good time.

Different photographers have different approaches to a pre-wedding shoot, but they all consider the sessions to be an integral part of preparing clients for their wedding day. Professional photographer Esther Ling invites her clients to pick the location, be it at the beach, a local park or to meet them at their home. "I approach it like I would a lifestyle portrait shoot, whereby we go out for a wander and stop off to take pictures where the light is right and the backdrop is good. It usually takes no more than a couple of hours. The key is to make them comfortable and to keep the animation going by chatting to them all the time. Posing isn't usually necessary as if you make them feel comfortable you can often catch them as they fall in to poses, laughing and having a good time as opposed to having them sit quite stilted," says Esther. Some photographers prefer

to do the engagement shoot in a very different location to the wedding venue to increase the saleability of the pictures. However, if you're still a little daunted by shooting a wedding it might be worth arranging the pre-wed at the actual wedding venue to get accustomed to the setting, lighting and backdrops.

The engagement shoot is an ideal time to subtly find out if there are parts of the client or angles of themselves they don't like, as it's usually now that they'd say something like ' try not to get me from this side, it's not my best'. Log comments like this into your brain for the wedding day and be sensitive to their hang-ups; you might not understand why they hate their shoulders or nose but do what you can to conceal those areas and to find their most flattering angle as it could be the difference between them loving or hating their pictures. Most people don't like having their picture taken and need a lot of guidance to be made to feel comfortable, down to how to stand, where to look and even their smile. If you simply tell them to stand while you take pictures, without much interaction from you, the images may look stilted. If the subjects are hankering after some direction, try to be as descriptive and specific as possible. For instance, don't tell him to say something in her ear, as it's likely he won't know what to say. Instead tell him to whisper 'I love you' and photograph the huge grin that crosses her face or to nuzzle in to her neck as she glances towards the camera. By encouraging them to interact with each other, it will elicit some natural reactions. It's also a good chance to gauge their personalities. If they're quite shy and quiet you'll probably struggle to get them to do anything eccentric, but if the couple is outgoing and relaxed from the outset, it's a chance for you to get creative and have fun with your set-ups. A good way to start the shoot is to warm up with a few 'safe shots' (the type of images that consistently sell) such as them touching foreheads, a three-quarter crop with him holding her or a head and shoulders shot, and then try to loosen them up by having them walk, run or jump hand in hand and or even suggest they give each other piggy-back rides. If the couple have children, encourage them to come along to the pre-wed shoot too to make it more of a family photo session.

> **"Keep it easy: use one lens and a reflector. Leave flash for the wedding day"**
> *Brett Harkness*

While the main aim is to get to know the clients and to see how they photograph, there is potential to earn some extra money too. Most photographers include a complementary engagement shoot in their wedding packages but not the images, so there's room to sell off the back of it. Try to treat the pre-wedding shoot like you would a wedding: edit the images in the same way and present them to your client in a similar fashion. Don't sell yourself short by saving unedited images to a disc and posting them off to the clients, as you'll be missing a trick! ➤

Top tips

Before or after the shoot, take the couple somewhere they can relax over a cup of coffee like your studio – if you have one – or a quiet but chic cafe or bar. Somewhere you can chat without being interrupted. Use this time to recap on the plans for their wedding day. Run through your list of questions to find out who's who in the family, if there's any family members you need to get pictures of or family situations you need to be aware of, like new partners, divorced parents or widowed grandparents. Do the pre-wedding shoot at least three months before the wedding day, leaving plenty of time to provide them with framed prints or a signature board and for you to prepare for any wedding day changes that may have happened since your last meeting.

Remember it's all about delivering a professional service that reflects your brand. So, if you can, meet up with the client to view the pictures on a projector screen or computer, you could do this in your studio, at their home or hire a conference room in a hotel. If you do a viewing, try to be equipped with products you're trying to push, like mini albums, frames, canvases and acrylics in sizes you sell. Nine times out of ten, clients buy what they can see. As a gesture of good will for the bride and groom, you could do what Esther Ling does and make a note of the couple's favourite picture, get it framed and mounted so guests can sign it on the big day. Another option could be to do a guest book with pictures from the shoot, as some people prefer a book they can keep on a shelf. If the bride and groom are too busy to meet up for a viewing, you could load the images up in a private gallery on your website for them to view at their leisure. Some website companies like The ImageFile also enable you to sell prints and products directly from your website, so the clients can pick how they want their engagement pictures presented. ■

"Put branded vouchers in jewellers and florists for a free engagement shoot and prints as an incentive for new brides and grooms to test you out as a photographer. Chances are they'll book you off the back of it" *Bjorn Thomassen*

Boudoir and pre-bridal photography shoots

While your competition only offers one type of pre-wedding shoot, why not buck the trend by offering more variety for your clients and catering to the bride's saucier side as well as their more traditional

WHILE AN ENGAGEMENT shoot is about getting to know the bridal couple, professional photographer Bjorn Thomassen also offers pre-bridal shoots for just the bride. He turns the bride's trial for hair and make-up in to a private, stylised photoshoot where she puts on her dress to preview how it all looks on camera before the big day. Sometimes it's done in a studio, others on location or in a rented space. "It's a great opportunity to cultivate a relationship with the bride and has proved so popular that we built it in to our packages as a selling point," says Bjorn.

More and more brides are also interested in doing boudoir or fine-art nude sessions before or after the wedding to give to their new husband on their wedding day or as an anniversary present. This seductive yet tasteful style of photography is becoming increasingly popular and very profitable for wedding photographers, but for such intimate images brides often prefer to use a female photographer. So, if you're male

it's often reassuring for the brides to have a female assistant on the shoot too.

If you don't have or want to hire a studio, you could do the shoot at the bride's home or book a chic hotel suite. For this type of shoot, where the subject could feel really vulnerable and exposed, your priority should be to make them comfortable and relaxed, so a warm and safe environment where no one will interrupt is crucial. It's also important that she feels sexy and attractive so the images exude confidence, so you need to provide a lot of reassurance and possibly a hair stylist and make-up artist for the session too. You could also offer this type of photography shoot as an

alternative to the pre-wedding shoot; photographing her nude or in lingerie rather than her wedding dress, but still using the session as the trial for the bride's hair stylist and make-up artist.

The fundamentals of a wedding day shoot

Get a sense of how to shoot a wedding with our expert advice

THESE DAYS THE wedding photographer is one of dozens at a wedding with a high-end DSLR, so you've got to produce something that Uncle Tom can't. Everything from the way you work with natural light and flash, to composition and posing, as well as post-production, needs to be a cut above the average photographer with high-quality kit. Most photographers are hired for six to eight hours to cover the bride getting ready or the ceremony through to the cutting of the cake or first dance, but no matter how long you're booked for, you should shoot with the album in mind and capture the story of the day, from the little details to the big events and from the emotion-fuelled candids to the more posed portraits.

Getting ready

Some of the best candids can be captured while the bride and groom are getting ready. There's so much activity and emotions are running high that it's a wonderful opportunity to capture some relaxed shots of the bride with her mother and her bridesmaids. And if there's time, some posed pre-ceremony portraits of the bride. When you first arrive at where the bride is getting ready, introduce yourself to any parents that are around and start taking pictures unobtrusively. If the lighting isn't good enough, don't be afraid to move the bride and the mirror to a window for a few pictures to make the most of any naturally diffused and reflected light in the room. Normally it takes the bride at least two hours to have her hair and make-up done, and while you don't need to be there for the entire time, take the opportunity to photograph details for the album, ideally with a macro lens, such as the flowers, wedding fragrance, jewellery, dress details and shoes.

Typically, the bride's make-up will be applied last, so you need to make sure you're there to take photographs of that being done – focusing on details like her lips and eyes using a wide aperture or use differential focusing to capture her reflection in the mirror. Try to also get shots of her putting on her veil or tiara and doing her dress up. This is when being a female photographer or having a female assistant can help – male photographers may have to skip this.

If you have time to visit the groom before the ceremony, use it to document him getting ready too, ironing his shirts, putting on his cufflinks etc but also to grab a few portraits of him and his groomsmen. If you're too tight for time, you could take these shots while they're waiting for the bride to arrive at the ceremony venue. For the purpose of the album, ask him to adjust his cufflinks or buttonhole while you take a couple of close-ups or shot of him and with his best man and ushers. Use every opportunity you can to grab pictures.

It's times like this that a second shooter is helpful. One of you could be with the bride and/or groom, while the other is capturing candids of arriving guests. ➤

Camera settings and techniques

Set your camera to shoot Raw + JPEG to give you more flexibility when it comes to 'developing' your images later. If your DSLR has a dual card slot, instead of using the second memory card to store images that overflow from the first, use it as a back-up in case your first card fails. Set the back-up card to store only JPEGs so it won't fill up as fast and if you use a larger memory card, like a 16GB, you probably won't need to change it during the day. For the memory cards that hold the Raw files, don't use bigger than 8GB. You may need to switch the memory cards a few times during the day but it means you're not storing all your Raw files on one large capacity card, which if it becomes corrupted could mean you losing some or all of your images.

What exposure mode should you use? Some pro photographers argue that if you cannot shoot in manual, don't do weddings. But, then again, very successful photographers like Brett Harkness use program mode and manually adjust the exposure compensation for more control. It's whatever you're comfortable using but don't rely solely on the camera, digital technology is there to help you but you need to know how to take control if you have to in case of tricky lighting conditions. Aperture-priority mode works well if you're dealing with changing light levels and it allows precise control over depth-of-field to get the beautiful out of focus backgrounds wedding photographers love.

Leave your camera set to AWB (Auto White Balance), unless you're in a room with mixed lighting or with a strong colour cast – like a church – where you may need to quickly take a custom WB reading. And unless you've got a cracking camera that allows you to shoot at high ISOs with no noise, try to keep the ISO below 400 or convert the images to black & white as this often adds atmosphere to a grainy finish.

We'd advise you try to use ambient light as much as possible, using doorways, windows and areas shade for soft lighting. Learn how to use fill-in and bounced flash as well as how to balance off-camera flash with ambient light too though, as it opens up possibilities come the evening, shooting indoors or backlit subjects. High-speed flash is also a technique worth mastering as it enables you to shoot with wide apertures in bright sunshine for more creative results.

The ceremony

You should try to arrive at the ceremony at least 15 minutes before the bride to take some test exposures, capture the nervous groom, details such as the order of service, candles and flowers and arriving guests. The ceremony is one of the trickiest parts of the day to photograph due to low light and no-flash rules, so you may have to rely on fast lenses and open apertures. Position yourself to the side of the altar, or similar if it's a registry office, so you have a good view of the processional, the bride walking down the aisle and the mother of the bride at the front of the church. If you can, try to take a picture of the expression on the groom's face too. If you have a second photographer, position them at the back of the venue for a different view. During the ceremony, try to capture the key moments like the exchange of rings and tender looks between bride and groom.

© STUART COOPER

© STUART COOPER

© STUART COOPER

© BRETT HARKNESS

© BRETT HARKNESS

© BRETT HARKNESS

Bridal portraits

If the bride is running late, it's usually this part of the wedding day that gets squeezed to compensate so you need to be able to get the most out of what little time you've got to work with. Normally 20 minutes is sufficient, but you should try to plan your shots so that one pose flows in to another easily and you're able to get different pictures from one pose simply by changing angles, having them look at the camera and then each other, or zooming the lens out for a full-length portrait and in for a close-up. As well as the usual backdrop of the venue, look for different backgrounds like coloured walls, grand features inside or nearby locations to add visual interest to the images. Don't be afraid to use different vantage points either, get low to the ground so you're shooting through the grass or tilt the camera up to get more of the sky in the scene. While you should try and get the classic shots, consider introducing some off-camera flash for a contemporary look too, if that's your style. While you may not have time to get individual shots of the bride and groom done, try to grab these when you can during the day.

Top tips

Don't forget to photograph the details: shoes, rings, flowers, centrepieces and cufflinks – they help depict the day.

Don't be afraid of taking control of the shoot and directing people in to the best light. It's your responsibility to get good images.

Shoot to sell: Capture images from different angles so the bridal couple are spoilt for choice and have to buy them all.

Always get a photo of the whole venue to help set the scene in the album.

Wedding party and groups

To some degree, every wedding requires group shots but it's up to you to put a cap on how many you'll do. You can make them as quirky and fun or as conventional as you want, especially with the bridal party, but here are a few pointers to get you started. Bring the bride and groom front and middle, having them stand naturally or adopt a pose, then ask the rest of the party to spread out behind them formally or in a way that shows off their personalities. Try opening the aperture up so the bride and groom are the only ones in focus too. Take pictures of the bride with the groomsmen and the groom with the bridesmaids, as well as them with their own party. Keep an eye on the details as they'll stand out in the pictures: jackets and ties straight, flowers pointing in the right direction, hands not looking awkward and their weight on their back foot for a relaxed stance. Use a wide-angle lens and a high vantage point to take a picture of all the guests together.

© BRETT HARKNESS P

© BRETT HARKNESS

© ESTHER LING

© STUART COOPER

Top tip

To avoid making guests wait at the ceremony venue, propose to the couple that you do the group shots at the reception venue, if appropriate. Everyone will be more relaxed once they've got a drink in their hand. It also gives you an opportunity to whisk the couple away for their 20-minute photo shoot without them worrying that their guests aren't entertained.

Speeches and reception

Emotions always run high during the speeches, you have tears, laughter and priceless looks between the bride and groom. Make sure your lens is pointing at either the person speaking or the person being spoken about to capture their reactions as well as those of the guests. When it comes to the cake, get a shot of it before it is cut and be ready for both the traditional shot of them cutting it together and the potential candid if they decide to stuff each other's faces. The first dance normally marks the end of the night. Use a wide aperture to retain the ambient light and atmosphere in the room, jaunty angles to add movement and, if you have to use flash, use a little fill or bounced flash so as not to overpower the natural atmosphere. And don't be afraid of slightly blurring the couple to create a sense of movement.

Pro insight

Brett Harkness Photography:
"People often ask us 'how long do you need for pictures?' and the truth is we don't need any time really and that's why we get the clients that we do. The more time to allocate to pictures, the less likely you are to move up the social scale. People who have money don't want to be bothered but still want the imagery, so we rarely schedule in shots. When I'm at the bride's house, for instance, we don't interfere but we'll keep them on track.
If it's a winter wedding we'll try to get pictures of the bride at the house while we still have a bit of daylight. If it's a summer wedding there won't be any posing until later in the afternoon when the light's softer. Often the first time I speak to the bride and groom is when they're coming out of the church and I'm congratulating them. We don't pose the bride in the car, do pictures of her and her dad or the signing of the register, unless they're documentary. We grab shots when we can, even if that means pulling the bride aside for a few shots as she's on the way to the toilet. The group shots and the couple pictures are usually the only time we'll ask for 20 minutes of pictures, which is often organised at the pre-wedding shoot. At one of our last weddings we had 15 minutes to do the couple's shots, the bridal party and all the family shots. With the group shots whether you meticulously pose people or place them straight in a line, we've found it doesn't make a difference to what sells. So I'd rather spend my time photographing the bridal party and the wedding couple creatively."

Professional development

If you want professional advice and help developing your technique and style, there are countless photography courses in the market for you to choose from. But be careful for this same reason. Make sure you research the photographer who is running the course to ensure they're experienced, that you like their style and source feedback from prior students. There are also some useful books by Oliver Cameron publishing and Ilex Press if you want comprehensive advice in a one-stop handbook. One of the UK's top wedding photographers, Brett Harkness, has also released a training DVD (RRP £80) that takes you through every stage of shooting a real wedding, from what equipment to use to how he photographs the bride getting ready, through to the evening reception. If you want a resource that gives you a true insight in to what it takes to shoot a wedding well and invaluable advice on lighting, posing and shooting to sell, then we highly recommend it. It may seem pricey, but when you consider the fact it contains everything you'd get from a course bar the one-to-one advice and you can watch it again and again, it's a great investment. To buy the DVD go to: www.brettharknessphotography.com

WORKFLOW & WEDDING ALBUMS

With the wedding day over, it's time for the real work to begin. As time is money, in this final section of our guide to wedding photography, learn how to shave hours off post-production without compromising on quality as we share the secrets for an efficient workflow and show you how to tackle album design

YOU'VE FINISHED SHOOTING the wedding, now what? Depending on how long you were working and how many photographers you worked with, you may have as many as 3,000 Raw files to process. With such a huge number of files to organise, categorise, back-up, edit and output, it's difficult to know where to begin, which is why having a coherent, logical and efficient workflow is crucial – the last thing you want is to lose or save over important images. You also need to remember that time is money and the less time you sit in front of the computer editing pictures, the more money will be in your pocket as profit. It's not uncommon to spend just as much, if not more, time sat processing pictures as you did taking them, which is why it was so important to factor these prospective hours in to your price at the start.

Adobe Lightroom is a fantastic tool for processing and organising large amounts of images, in fact you can do so much in it, from editing and sorting Raw files to making tonal and colour adjustments, that you may find only a few images need to make it in to Photoshop. You may wonder why we recommend you using Lightroom and Photoshop if Lightroom is so capable, but while Lightroom is ideal for processing Raw files (it has the same interface as Photoshop's Adobe Camera Raw) and managing files, Photoshop offers unparalleled editing capabilities. The main benefits are Layers and Layer Masks, which allow you to apply non-destructive changes to an image, so as not to harm the original pixels. It also means you can overlay textured layers, composite pictures and selectively tweak your adjustments. For instance if you boost the saturation of the landscape, you'll normally find the bride looks like she's got an orange tan, but using a Layer Mask you can selectively paint the areas you want to revert back to their original state, in this case returning the skin tone to its natural colour.

If you don't want to fork out for Photoshop as well as Lightroom, but still want more advanced editing tools, you might want to check out plug-ins to add to Lightroom or Aperture like those by Nik Software or OnOne Software. They offer a variety of plug-ins with various talents similar to Photoshop's but at a fraction of the price, such as skin softening and removing distracting objects. You can even add layers to Lightroom with OnOne's new software called Perfect Layers. Nik Software offers an abundance of colour and black & white filters – some of the best we've come across – in its Color Efex Pro 3.0 and Silver Efex Pro 2.0, respectively. They can also be bought as part of Nik Software's Complete Collection featuring all six plug-ins, designed to offer an all-in-one editing workflow system in conjunction with Lightroom and Aperture or Photoshop. Whatever your budget or workflow preference, there's no doubt there's something for everyone. It's just a matter of figuring out your workflow preferences and editing style, which can be fairly easy since most of the software options offer a free trial, so that you can try before you buy.

Improve your workflow

Different photographers have different ways of managing their workflow, but they all agree that you need to be ruthless with your editing. If you don't know which images are the best, the couple probably won't know either. It's easy to fall in to the trap of showing them too many pictures and too much of the same thing because you're not confident in your edits. It's going to be around image 500 when the client may start to lose the will to live at the viewing, so if you're confronted with five similar images, pick a maximum of two. Sequences, however, do look good in an album, say of the couple walking down the road, so don't be afraid to group these together and edit them the same. It's good practice to shoot with the intention of turning an image black & white or treating it in a certain way as this can add to the efficiency of your workflow.

Above all, have confidence in your decisions. If you want to give a vintage look to an image, crop it unconventionally or turn another black & white, do it. Avoid bombarding your client with too many options at the viewing as it can get confusing. Remember you're the professional and they'll be looking to you to tell them what looks good in an album, so don't be afraid to stand by your style.

Don't forget the metadata

When you import your pictures from your memory card, depending on the software you're using, you have the option of entering in basic metadata, even if it's just your name and copyright details. You may also find it helpful to input the same keywords to all the pictures as a batch, like the name of the bride and groom, the name of the wedding venue, and the wedding date in case you need to search for the files later.

To give you an idea of what a professional wedding photographer's workflow is like, we asked Stuart Cooper to describe his:

Categorise: Create a folder on your hard drive called Weddings and within that create a folder named after the year, eg 2011. Inside that create a folder for the client labelled by their first names.
Download: As soon as you return from the wedding, or even sooner if you have a portable storage device, download and back up all the Raw files to two external hard drives, calling the folder Camera Files. The hard drives should be stored in separate locations in case of a fire or flood.
Import pictures: Import the files in to your management software, in my case Lightroom, and batch name them after the client and the year of their wedding, for instance 2011Sam&Andy. Doing this means in two years' time if you need to find the pictures all you have to do is go to your Weddings folder and type in the names of the clients to find the pictures.
Edit in and out: To quickly pick the images you want to keep, set Lightroom to Grid mode (press ***G***) and then tag every image you want to keep by clicking ***P***. Then select Attributes above the images and click on the flag so Lightroom only shows those images you've flagged, hiding the ones you've rejected. Now take a second run through and press ***U*** to unflag images you want to get rid of. If you have several pictures that are quite similar, or of the same scene, and you want to quickly compare them, highlight them all and press the ***N*** key to isolate those images. Lightroom will then display them side by side and as large as it can make them on screen. Click on the images you want to

"Take three or four successive group shots as you're guaranteed that someone different is blinking in each one. Save all of them during your editing process so you can clone eyes back in to form one final image" *Esther Ling*

reject and press ***U*** to make them disappear. At each stage it gets easier to determine which images are keepers and which should be disregarded. Instead of keeping variations of images, pick one image with impact to show the client. Aim for 200-300 pictures for a six- or eight-hour wedding.

Edit: Run through the remaining pictures and batch-edit images to correct the White Balance, exposure, tone, contrast and colour if they were all taken in similar conditions and with similar settings. Next address each image individually and make any further basic adjustments. Hopefully you've used the correct settings and got most of it right in-camera, otherwise this can be a very long and laborious task. Once you're done, export them in to a folder called Colour as JPEGs. Now inside the client's folder are two files: Camera Raw and Colour. Then run through the Raw images again in Lightroom, tagging the files (by clicking ***6*** to highlight them red) that you want to convert to black & white. Apply your Lightroom preset to change them all to black & white, then repeat the process for the images you want to crop.

Export: Ideally, most of your editing will be done in Lightroom, and there may only be 50 or 60 pictures out of the 300 that you need to export to Photoshop to apply creative effects using Photoshop actions, or to clone out exit signs or clone in eyes on a group shot and so on.

Some photographers like to edit their images entirely, getting rid of blemishes and dust spots etc while others prefer to return for this more detailed retouching once the client has bought the images. It's up to you how you do it, but editing all the images ready for printing and the album design means you don't risk re-editing the pictures, interfering with the workflow of ➤

Shoot in JPEG?

If, like pro photographer Brett Harkness, you're confident and competent enough to shoot in JPEG instead of Raw, you could make your workflow even simpler by cutting out any Raw conversions. Once you've downloaded the images, select the pictures you want to show the client and then simply batch-edit the low-res versions. The only high-res pictures that Brett Harkness works on are those purchased for the album or separately. "When our couple sees the images for the first time on a slideshow the quality of viewing is quite low, so we don't need a high-res image," explains Kristie Harkness, "If I have 2,000 images and each of them is 20MB and I have five clients' slideshows to edit, my computer would probably combust! We batch process the low-res images for the slideshow but once they've picked the picture they want to buy, we process each high-res file individually."

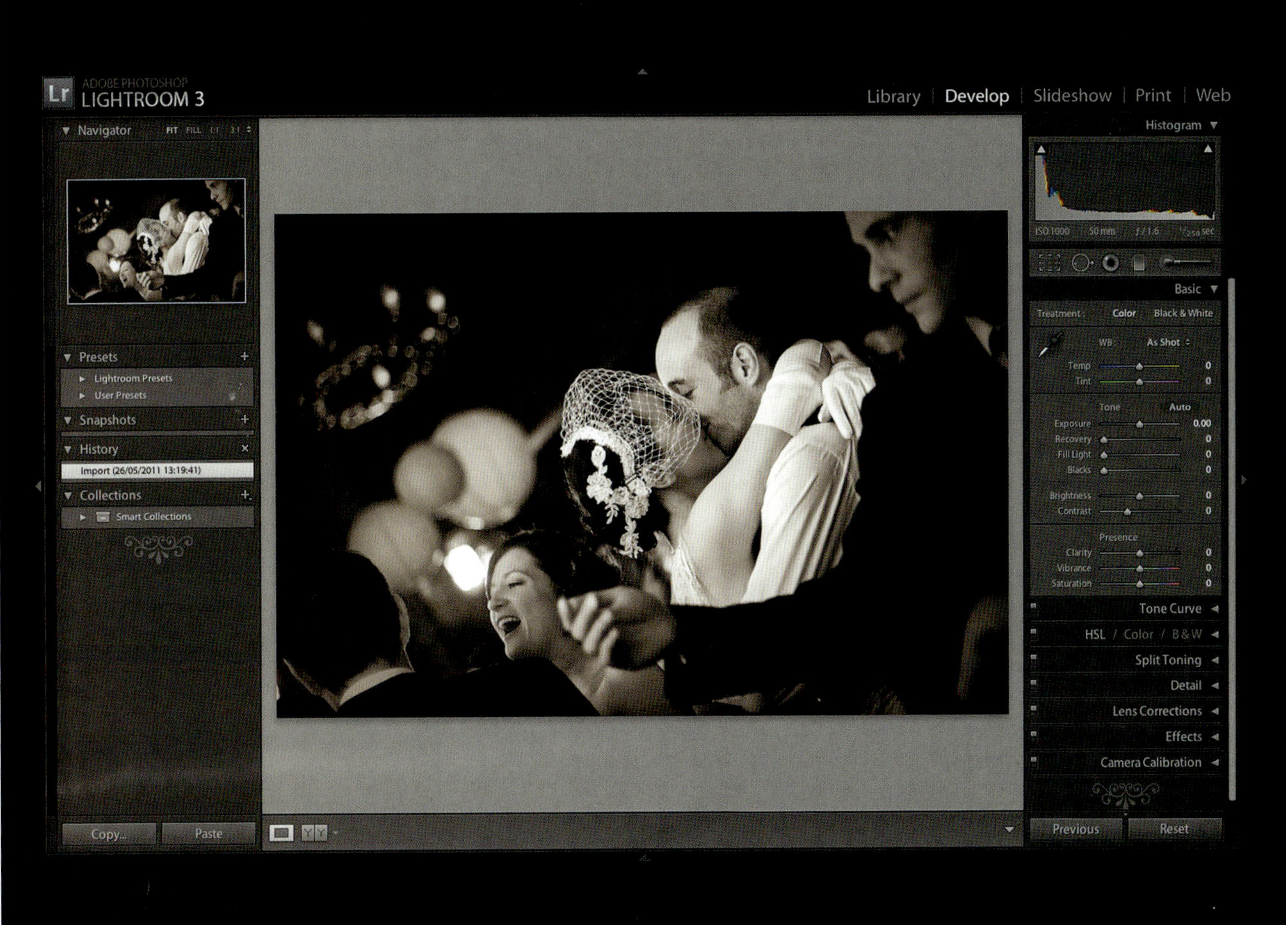

"Convert your Raw files in to DNG files (digital negatives), as in ten years' time software might not read camera-specific Raw files" *Stuart Cooper*

your next wedding. Once you've finished editing all the pictures in Lightroom, export them as JPEGs to a new folder called Edited, which is what will be used for the clients' viewing and prints. Also, save the images you've worked on in Photoshop to the same folder.

Create: Next build the slideshow, ordering the pictures to show the flow of the day. While we don't recommend you saturating your slideshow with duplicate images with different treatments, you could crop into an image differently and place it miles apart in the slideshow without the client recognising the similarities. You may find by doing this they buy both. Burn the slideshow to DVD and save the slideshow in the clients' folder in case they want access to it later. Make sure the clients' folder, which should now contain three folders and a slideshow, is backed up to at least two external hard drives, if not three.

Upload pictures: Before you finish off the wedding, create a final folder containing all the edited JPEGs that you've batch processed to make them web-friendly. Load a small selection on to your blog and all the pictures on to your client's proofing gallery on your website. ➤

An efficient workflow

Batch processing and Actions can save a lot of time, whether it's to resize, convert Raw to JPEG or apply your signature creative effect. Instead of repeating the same steps for every image, you can save hours by applying a number of adjustments to your images with one click of your mouse. You can create your own action (see below) or download a selection for free or for a small cost online. Check out Totally Rad Actions, Jeff Ascough, Red Leaf Studios and LilyBlue for some amazing actions used by many professionals.

How to record your own Action in Adobe Photoshop

☑ Pick the image you want to edit and practise the technique until you know exactly how you want the effect applied.

☑ Once you're confident in the process, revert back to the original image, and go to ***Windows> Actions*** to open the Action control panel.

☑ To create a new action either click on the *New Action* button at the bottom of the Action panel or click on the small tab in the top right corner to access the drop-down menu. You'll find *New Action* is the second option down.

☑ Give the Action a name to match the technique (for instance high-contrast black & white), select a colour to highlight the action's button, then click ***Record***. Now go through the process of applying the technique to the image and the software will record every step. This is why practising the effect is important as every adjustment you make to the image is stored so it can be applied automatically to other images with a single click of the action's button.

☑ Once you've finished the technique, click on the ***Stop*** button (square button) at the bottom of the Action panel to finish recording. Now, if you want to apply the effect to an individual picture quickly, all you need to do is open the image and select the action you want to apply from the Actions palette. As every image is different, you may find the action's effect varies, so to refine the treatment to suit the image, access the History panel (***Windows> History***) and step back in stages until you're happy with the results, or reduce the opacity of the layers treated.

☑ If you want to apply the action to a number of images, go to ***File>Automate>Batch***. Under the Play section, select the action you want to apply and the Source (where the images you want to edit are located – make sure they're all in one folder or open in Photoshop). Similarly select the Destination (where you want the edited images to be saved) and give the file a name before clicking ***OK***.

How should you up-sell for maximum profit?

The final viewing where the client selects their wedding pictures is a special time as they relive their big day, and it can be an opportunity to increase profits. Find out how to make it work for both of you

ONE OF THE HARDEST things to do as a creative is sell your own work, so unless you're a born salesperson it's much easier to let your work sell itself. Wherever you're showing the client their wedding images, take along or have samples displayed of products that they might want to buy, such as mini and parent albums, canvases, framed prints and acrylic blocks. Professional photographer Esther Ling finds it hard to sell her own work, so subconscious selling suits her better. By showing her clients what an album with 100 images looks like, she puts an idea in their head, which often leads to them buying 100 images.

When it comes to showing your client their wedding images, normally it's via a slideshow on a projector screen in your studio or in their living room, on your laptop, or in a private gallery on your website. If your clients prefer to select their images once they've seen them in print, consider getting a box of proofs printed or a proofbook, both of which are available from printing companies such as Loxley Colour, OneVision and Graphistudio. If you do choose to present the images face-to-face, make sure you ply them with tea, coffee and finger food, or take along a bottle of champagne and some cakes (but make sure they are well-presented and look special – chocolate muffins in a plastic supermarket box simply won't do). The process of selecting their pictures can take hours, so clear your diary.

Normally the clients pick all the images for the album, but it has been known for the photographer to make the executive decision, or to have the clients select their favourites while the photographer selects the rest. While the first option is obviously more appealing to discerning customers, whichever one you choose to use, just be sure it's clear to the clients at the time of booking to avoid any problems later. Most wedding packages with an album include a certain amount of images that the clients can select at no extra charge. For Esther Ling, that's the first 60, but it's often impossible to whittle them down to this number from the several hundred presented to them, which gives you the opportunity to up-sell. Esther Ling always forewarns her clients at the initial booking stage that while 60 is a good number, she'll be taking a lot more than that and her average client spends an additional 'x' amount of money, planting the seed that they may be spending more and may therefore need to assign an extra budget for it.

© BRETT HARKNESS

To help clients select the pictures, Kristie Harkness, partner in Brett Harkness Photography, has a process that's proven to work time and time again. She lets them enjoy watching the slideshow through once, then takes out the detail and venue pictures. As they won't need them all, she tells them that at the end they can pick out a few that are special to them and complement their other pictures to accent the album. She then goes through the rest of the slideshow twice, normally finding they cut out at least half of the pictures on each round. After this they're usually at the point where they struggle and it comes down to whether they have the budget to spend or not. "This is when I'll tell them the cost and try to find a compromise where they're comfortable with what they spend but still get the best out of the wedding images," she says.

It's important to be flexible and open at this stage of selling as you don't want the customer to feel fleeced or leave with buyer's remorse – but don't be too flexible. You can get customers who want to haggle on cost, but as a rule don't give them a discount. Try to find a comfortable compromise that doesn't undervalue your service by offering them product like a free parent album or if they buy four of the extra pictures they want, you'll give them the other four for free.

A common query is whether you should charge clients by the page or picture. Basically by charging a flat rate per extra image (between £20 and £30 is expected), rather than by the page, you're allowing yourself more scope for profit, and if you've priced yourself correctly in the first place, you should be able to absorb the extra cost of adding pages to the album if you need to, so it all balances out. You should use as many pages as necessary though to make the best of the pictures, rather than trying to cram them in to a set number of pages. It's all about delivering a quality product and service, so if a client spends a lot with you or you've built a special relationship with them, consider giving them a free mini album for their parents, or including a case with the album, or giving them the images they were pained to take out as a surprise and a thank you from you for their custom."

We recommend...

For professional printing products, check out Kaleidoscope Framing, Loxley Colour, OneVision and Ultimar. Each of them require you to become a professional member before you're given access to trade prices and services. While Luminati and WhiteWall also deal with the public, they offer a variety of affordable and quality products such as acrylic frames and canvas prints that also may be worth considering for your offering.

© QUEENSBERRY/ JOHANNES VAN KAN (NEW ZEALAND)

© FOLIO ALBUMS

"Look at other people's albums for inspiration to find the styles you don't like. You can't please everyone, so find the right type of album and design to reflect your tastes and style of photography"
Esther Ling

Wedding albums

Wedding albums are vehicles for retelling stories and preserving memories so they can be relived, shared and treasured forever. Although styles have changed, print media has developed and alternatives have been introduced, the popularity of the photography album seems to be unyielding, according to Ian Baugh, the director of Queensberry, a company often considered the industry's benchmark for album design and manufacturing. While for the client an album holds emotional value and is a beautiful product to hold their wedding pictures, for the photographer the quality of your albums are evidence of your position in the market. Everyone who sees them makes a judgement on what you offer, how good you are and even have an idea of how much you charge, so you need to make sure that the products live up to the standard of your photography and your service. As well as contributing to your brand, albums often give you the opportunity to double your revenue from a wedding by enabling you to devise opportunities to up-sell by selling more images and pages. If you choose the 'shoot and burn' approach (supplying high-res files on CD), while you don't have the hassle or cost of an album, you don't get the benefits of prospective clients seeing your work at its best and there's no opportunity to up-sell, as all you're selling them is a low price.

The key to designing an album is simplicity: less is more. Your clients want to treasure their album for years to come, so take a long-term view and avoid using gimmicks like overlaying images or torn borders. Let the pictures do the talking and don't overwhelm them by introducing fussy finishes and designs that may date.

Depending on what album company you choose to go with, they may offer their own design software, but if not there are dozens available to make your design process simple and effective. Once you've chosen your album company, contact their sales department and ask them for any recommendations, as there may be software that works better with their system. If they don't have any suggestions, we highly recommend Photojunction. It's free to use, created by Queensberry, and while it allows you to work within a template it enables you to break free of the 'paint by numbers' approach to take control of every aspect of the design. Most album companies have software that's free to download, even if you're not a member. But make sure you pick one that allows you to drag and drop pictures on the page as it makes designing much easier.

If you're unsure of your design skills, consider passing the work on to someone with the talent to do it for you, until you've developed the confidence. Most album companies offer a design service for an extra cost, which is relatively small once you consider the many hours you might waste trying to get the design right.

Most album companies are wholesale suppliers who sell exclusively to partner photographers, so you need to register before you can get access to pricing and restricted areas of their website or ➤

Top tips for designing an album

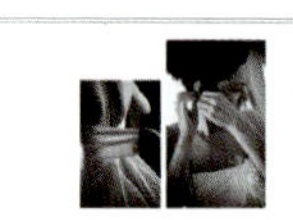

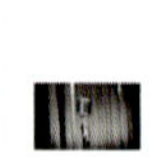

- ☑ Use the album to tell a fluid story of the day as it unfolded – keep the events in order. An album full of the happy couple looking at the camera or kissing is not story telling, you need to balance these pictures with candids, detail pictures and groups that convey the emotion, flow and atmosphere of the day
- ☑ Keep the album's style consistent throughout
- ☑ Avoid gimmicks or current trends: use a classic finish like leather and a design that's timeless and clean
- ☑ Design in spreads – consider how the images and the design of the two pages work together
- ☑ Make sure the pages are always balanced
- ☑ Combine different picture sizes on the page for more visual interest
- ☑ Give one picture more prominence on the page to focus the viewer's attention
- ☑ Use repeated patterns to provide continuity and flow to the pages
- ☑ Be aware of the space between images and use empty space to give pictures more impact
- ☑ Check alignment: make sure text, images and graphics line up for a professional finish
- ☑ Don't be afraid to fill an entire double-page spread with one image if it's got impact or to bleed an image off the edges of the page

Album companies

☑ Queensberry
Starter pack: £250 + VAT and includes swatch book, page sampler, a little digital copy album, 30% off three studio display albums with free printing and design services on your first album
Free design software: Photojunction
Bespoke in-house design: Charges per image but for a typical album would be from £100 + VAT
Website: www.queensberry.com

☑ Folio Albums
Starter pack: Cover swatches from £10 and a 25% discount on all studio sample albums
Free design software: No but recommends Photoshop, InDesign or Photojunction
Bespoke in-house design: From £149
Website: www.folioalbums.com

☑ Graphistudio
Starter pack: Free and includes one main book (any size and cover), one 20x30cm and four 10x13cm parent books and a calendar
Free design software: Graphisoftware
Bespoke in-house design: £1.80 per page
Website: www.graphistudio.com

☑ Sim2000 Imaging
Starter pack: From £209 and includes one album, A5-sized parent books, two A6-size soft and two hard-backed books. There are three different levels of starter packs, varying in content and cost, to choose from
Free design software: SimWare
Bespoke in-house design: From £240
Website: www.sim2000imaging.com

☑ Loxley Colour
Starter pack: A 40% discount on sample albums from the range of your choice
Free design software: Loxley Design Pro and Roes (Remote Order Entry System)
Bespoke in-house design: From £50
Website: www.loxleycolour.com

☑ Bespoke Photobooks
Starter pack: From £85 and includes three albums of various sizes and a swatch pack
Free design software: No but recommends Photoshop or InDesign
Bespoke in-house design: From £30
Website: www.bespokephotobooks.com

☑ Booked Images
Starter pack: From £229 and includes one Large Book and one Little Book. There are three levels of starter packs including additional products that you're able to amend to suit your needs
Free design software: Booked Compose
Bespoke in-house design: From £60
Website: www.bookedimages.com

An alternative to albums

Some photographers have found that they can save a fortune by not having a studio sample album but by emphasising to their clients that every album is bespoke. Instead they show clients album layouts on their laptop or iPad to give them a feel for what one looks like and rely on swatch books and page samplers. If you prefer to opt for sample albums, as they are a great way to show prospective clients your work, don't use a selection of pictures from various weddings, feature one wedding from start to finish for more impact.

forums. They require proof that you're a bona fide professional photographer, but that term is used loosely – usually if you can demonstrate that you do commissioned work, even if it's at weekends, and you have a professional-looking website and blog, that can be enough. Different companies ask for different levels of proof but most do understand if you're just starting out and lack an extensive portfolio. All they really want to ascertain is whether you're serious about your photography, you act professional and plan to derive an income from it – not someone who's shot a friend's wedding for free and wants an album. Often it's as simple as filling in a form on their website and they'll get back to you within a few days, but sometimes they may ask to speak to you on the phone or meet you before making a decision.

Once a company has accepted you, you'll usually have access to an overwhelming plethora of finishes, paper types, covers and sizes to pick from. Remember the feeling. If you're confused with choice, how will your client feel if you offer them everything? When you first join you'll be invited to buy a starter kit, which often contains swatch samples and studio sample albums in a finish of your choice. Pick one or two sizes and styles of album you like and want to offer your clients. In terms of size, according to Queensberry their most popular are 12x12in and 14x10in, as they're affordable and big enough to be practical for a lot of images. Folio Albums, which was formed by photographer Stewart Randall, after he couldn't find an album product to suit his needs and budget, finds it only necessary to sell albums in a 10x10in or 12x12in format with leather covers. If you prefer to shy away from the classic and lean more towards the modern, Loxley Colour and Graphistudio offer a variety of finishes from the classic Italian leather, soft silk, and hard-back to ultra-modern metallic and acrylic transparent covers.

These days most albums are flushmount digital prints, which can look beautiful but are increasingly common. This is one reason Queensberry remains the market leader as it offers a gorgeous matted finish so that every image is mounted in the album. If you use the right software, you can normally design an album in under a day, and most companies promise to deliver you the finished product within three to four weeks from the time your order is confirmed. We recommend you give your clients a lead time of ten weeks from when they select their pictures until they receive their album in case of any problems, and then try to deliver it early just to finish off your customer service, which has been exceeding their expectations from start to finish.

Get approval

Once you've designed the album, it's a good idea to have the client approve the layout before sending it to the printers. You could do this face-to-face at their home or in your studio, or use an online proofing tool like AlbumExposure (Albumexposure.com). Some album design softwares, like Photojunction, enable you to export your album as a slideshow or Quicktime file to email to your clients. While by involving your clients in the design process you risk dragging out the production time and maybe interfering with the workflow of your other weddings, we'd still advise that you have your clients proof the album layout until you build up the design experience and portfolio of albums to show clients what they'll be getting in advance. A redesign and reprint of an album if the client isn't happy with it could devour your profits.

CONNECT
YOUR
IMAGINATION
MANFROTTO 290 SERIES
A long lasting solution with a solid performance.
The ideal tripod to develop your skill and passion
for photography and video further.
Essential performance!
Increase the accuracy of your
pictures with the innovative
3-faced design column.
A rock solid and reliable support
with professional grade,
adjustable aluminum leg locks.
Manfrotto
Manfrotto
Imagine More
Manfrotto™
A Vitec Group brand
manfrotto.co.uk

ESSENTIAL KIT FOR SOCIAL PHOTOGRAPHY

WE BREAKDOWN THE KEY KIT YOU NEED TO HELP ENSURE SUCCESS

SOCIAL PHOTOGRAPHY, especially weddings, is stressful but lucrative, which is why an increasing number of photographers are attempting to make an income from this area of photography. Whether it's a family portrait shoot or a wedding day, many photographers ensure they're well prepared so that they can capture those special memories and moments perfectly; while unfortunately there are others who fail to deliver. This could be down to poor preparation or technique, but quite often it's not using the most appropriate equipment.

This section of the guide is dedicated to highlighting the gear that will help you take the best possible pictures. It covers everything from the types of cameras and lenses you should be using to the bags and pouches that allow you fast access to photo kit, plus the various accessories that ensure you're always ready for every eventuality. Whether you're a wedding photographer, a studio- or location-based lifestyle photographer, being able to manipulate light is essential, which is why we've dedicated space to covering the best selection of diffusers and reflectors on the market. We've also tested and rated the key lens that every social photographer should consider buying, or at least renting – the absolutely brilliant 70-200mm f/2.8 zoom.

We're fully aware that the tag 'wedding photographer' is a broad one and covers those that shoot it as a pastime to full-time professionals making a tidy living from it. So, to ensure that we provide indispensable information to suit every size of budget and requirement, our wedding kit guide has be broken down into two broad categories offering advice for the most common types of wedding photographer. So, whether you're just getting started, already enjoy some success or are at the stage where it's your main form of income, we have essential kit advice that could make future shoots go smoother and help you capture even better pictures. And, while we've split the kit in to two levels, there is no reason why you can't pick and mix gear from each to suit your taste and budget, plus you'll find a lot of it is applicable to lifestyle portrait photographers too.

Core kit to carry

IMAGE SENSOR CLEANING KIT

In the unlikely event of dust settling on a sensor, keep a kit handy to quickly clean it. Check out Green Clean and Arctic Butterfly products.

MEMORY CARDS

Opt for fast cards from reliable brands like Lexar, SanDisk, Kingston and Panasonic. SD users look for Class 6 or faster SD cards or CompactFlash of at least 233x or faster. Buy the best you can afford.

CARD STORAGE

Use a case for safe storage of cards. Keep unused cards facing upwards and used cards facing downwards. Check out the Lowepro Pixelpak and Gepe CardSafe.

MICROFIBRE CLOTH

Always carry a lens cloth. The most convenient is the £6 Spudtz pouch, which clips to your bag or belt. It's also 18% grey, ideal for custom White Balance in tricky lighting.

STEPLADDER

This optional extra is useful for shooting group shots or unusual perspectives.

Contacts

Ansmann
www.ansmannenergy.co.uk
Billingham
www.johnsons-photopia.co.uk
Black Rapid
www.johnsons-photopia.co.uk
Canon
www.canon.co.uk
Cullmann
www.newprouk.co.uk
Custom Brackets
www.flaghead.co.uk
Epson
www.epson.co.uk
Expodisc
www.daymen.co.uk
Gepe
www.johnsons-photopia.co.uk
Giottos
www.daymen.co.uk
Green Clean
www.flaghead.co.uk
Hama
www.hama.co.uk
Hahnel
www.hahnel.ie
Interfit
www.interfitphotographic.com
Lastolite
www.lastolite.com
Lowepro
www.daymen.co.uk
Manfrotto
www.manfrotto.co.uk
Metz
www.intro2020.com
Nikon
www.nikon.co.uk
Op/Tech
www.newprouk.co.uk
Pocket Wizard
www.johnsons-photopia.co.uk
Quantum
www.flaghead.co.uk
Rogue
www.daymen.co.uk
Sandisk
www.sandisk.com
Sanyo eneloop
www.intro2020.com
Seculine
www.intro2020.com
Sekonic
www.johnsons-photopia.co.uk
Sigma
www.sigma-imaging-uk.com
Slik
www.intro2020.com
Spudtz
www.johnsons-photopia.co.uk
Sto-fen
www.newprouk.co.uk
Tamrac
www.intro2020.com
Tamron
www.intro2020.com
Thinktank
www.snapperstuff.com
Velbon
www.intro2020.com
Westcott
www.johnsons-photopia.co.uk

'Part-time' wedding photographer

You're a very good photographer and you'd like to make money from shooting weddings, but you have a full-time job that pays the bills, so at the moment, shooting weddings is a secondary form of income. You most likely advertise yourself as a wedding photographer, mainly for local work, with the majority of the weddings you shoot at weekends, although you may well take the odd day off to shoot weekday weddings too. You fancy taking your photography further and try to save money whenever possible to allow you to upgrade your kit. Here's what we suggest you should be packing for the big day.

WHITE BALANCE AID

While your camera's Auto White Balance is reliable, in tricky light, use a WB aid for accurate colours – otherwise a bride's white dress may have a colour cast. A grey card is suitable, but a handier option is to hold an ExpoDisc up to your lens and take a quick custom reading. A 77mm ExpoDisc costs £60.

TOP-END APS-C DIGITAL SLR

If you regularly shoot weddings, you need to use as good a camera as possible. As well as improved performance, it also provides visual assurance of you as a dedicated wedding photographer. A top-end APS-C DSLR is a suitable choice, offering great handling, enhanced performance and solid build. The £1,200 Canon EOS 7D or £1,050 Nikon D300s are solid choices, as are the majority of models costing £1,000 or more.

MID-RANGE STANDARD ZOOM

Invest in a decent quality standard zoom from one of the independents like Sigma, Tamron or Tokina and you'll see significant improvement in image quality. This type of lens is ideal for group shots, scene setters and working in tight environments. The faster maximum aperture allows for handheld photography in most general situations as well as creative use of shallow depth-of-field. The £350 Sigma 17-70mm f/2.8-4 DC Macro OS HSM and £350 Tamron SP AF 17-50mm f/2.8 XR Di II VC are excellent, well-priced options that should be on your shortlist.

FLASH SOFTBOX

A softbox is popular for portraits as it gives a flattering light. Versions available for flashguns include Lastolite's Ezybox range, which attaches in mere seconds and comes in various sizes, including the £55 Ezybox Speed-Lite Mini (22x22cm) shown here. Elemental's Flashgun Softbox (50x50cm) is another good buy. Attach the flashguns on to lighting stands such as the £30 Interfit Cor750 via a dedicated mount, such as the £25 Cullmann CB2 ball & socket head shown here, and you're able to control the angle of the flash.

WIRELESS FLASH SYSTEM

An increasing number of wedding photographers are taking advantage of wireless flash systems to shoot ever more creative flash exposures during the day as well as at night. Canon and Nikon have their own dedicated systems compatible with selective DSLRs and flashguns, but they're expensive. Instead, we'd suggest you look at using independent-brand wireless triggers that will work with almost all models of flash. Hahnel offers the £50 RF Combi, Interfit has the £95 Titan-Pro transceiver, while PocketWizard, market leaders in wireless triggers, have the excellent £200 FlexTT5 transceiver and £180 MiniTT1 transmitter.

GRIP REFLECTOR

The most useful collapsible reflector you can use, especially when working alone, is the grip-type. A handle allows you (or an assistant) to angle a reflector with ease. Lastolite makes a number of TriGrip reflectors (and diffusers) in various sizes and colours, we'd recommend the £60 75cm silver/white reflector as the best first choice. Alternatively buy the £90 TriFlip set, which allows you to slip on various colours including the highly-efficient Sunfire shown here.

GADGET BAG

You need a bag that has good capacity, is comfortable to carry and is fast to access. While a backpack is a fair option, you're better off looking at shoulder bags. The Lowepro Classified series, with its easy access zip, is ideal. The Classified 250AW shown here costs £120 and holds ample kit, with smaller or larger versions available. Tamrac's £90 Pro 12 is another great option.

FLASH, DIFFUSER & BRACKET

A highly-specified and powerful flash with a bounce head allows you a greater scope of options as well as better coverage. Consider the £220 Canon Speedlite 430EX II, £240 Nikon Speedlight SB-600 or well specified independent flashguns like the £200 Metz 50 AF-1 shown here. Fit a diffuser panel like the £16 Sto-Fen Omni-Bounce over the head to soften the light. An alternative is a reflector attachment for improved bounce-flash results, such as the £35 Rogue Flashbender. If you only use a single flashgun, you're better off mounting it on a bracket rather than the hotshoe for better performance. Custom Brackets make a number of flash brackets including the £70 Folding-S shown here. Just be sure you also fit the required mount and dedicated lead (not shown).

TRIPOD & HEAD

Depending on your style of photography, you may or may not use a tripod, but it's worth having one in your car boot just in case. Opt for a solid mid-range model like the £100 Manfrotto 190ProB and a good head like the £60 Giottos MH1311 ball & socket.

MID-RANGE APS-C DIGITAL SLR

Should your primary camera develop a problem, ensure that your back-up is up for the job by opting for a mid-range model. Ideally choose as good a model as possible – often you'll find a secondhand, previous generation DSLR is good enough, such as the Canon EOS 50D or Nikon D300, or you could go for current models like the £800 EOS 60D or £600 Nikon D90.

BUDGET ULTRA-WIDE ZOOM

Extend your shooting options further by buying an ultra wide-angle lens. You probably won't use it much, so one of the more affordable lenses should do. Their very wide field of view makes it easier to shoot large groups as well as dramatic church interiors and other creative options. The £400 Sigma 10-20mm f/4-5.6 EX DC HSM and £390 Tamron SP AF 10-24mm f/3.5-4.5 Di II LD are more affordable than marque lenses but still deliver very high-quality results.

'SLING' CAMERA STRAP

Black's Rapid R-Strap slings across the shoulder and is built for speed, and is ideal for having a camera at your side while shooting with another. The £60 RS-W1B version is designed specifically for women.

MODULAR STORAGE SYSTEM

The fastest way to get to kit is to take it out of your gadget bag and on your person. Modular systems do just that, with a belt or harness holding pouches that can store lenses, filters, cards or other accessories. Shown here from Tamrac's excellent Modular Accessory System is the £20 MX5397 belt, £14 5385 Large Flash case and £15 5343 Lens Case Pro 100. Also look at Lowepro's Street & Field (shown over the page).

SPUDTZ LENS CLOTH

Clip a £6 Spudtz to your belt or gadget bag so you can clean optics with minimal delay.

In the bag...

☑ MEMORY CARDS: 5X 8GB

Take at least five 8GB cards to hold the hundreds of Raw and/or JPEG images you'll shoot over the course of the day.

☑ MID-RANGE TELEPHOTO ZOOM

You may not use a telezoom much, but there are situations when it is a great option. It's ideal for filling the frame with your subject from a distance, such as when they're walking up the aisle, and it's the perfect choice for candids too. Used at the short end, it's also good for head and shoulder portraits. Avoid budget telezooms and instead look at those with faster apertures and better optics. While 70-300mm zooms offers more pulling power, many find the 70-200mm a better choice. Lenses to consider include the £530 Canon 70-200mm f/4, £400 Nikon AF-S 70-300mm f/4.5-5.6 VR, £450 Sigma 50-150mm f/2.8 EX DC HSM II and £350 Tamron AF 70-300mm f/4-5.6.

☑ 50MM F/1.4 STANDARD LENS

The 50mm f/1.8 is a capable lens, but if you can stretch the budget, you'll find the 50mm f/1.4 offers superior optics and a near-magical fall-off in depth-of-field when used at maximum aperture. As well as the Canon EF 50mm f/1.4 USM and Nikon 50mm f/1.4G, you should also consider Sigma's 30mm f/1.4 EX DC HSM and 50mm f/1.4 EX DG HSM. It's also worth noting that Tamron's 60mm f/2 Di II Macro doubles up as a brilliant portrait lens too.

☑ RECHARGEABLE BATTERIES

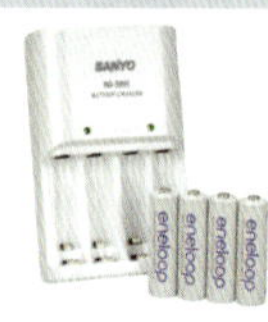

A pack of batteries aren't expensive, it's when you're constantly having to replace them that the cost starts to mount. Rechargeable batteries are the best option, as they can be used up to around 1,000 times before needing replacing. The best brands include Ansmann and Sanyo Eneloop. Although they may be slightly more expensive to buy, you'll make your money back quickly.

'Full-time' wedding photographer

Shooting weddings is becoming (or has become) a serious form of income for you. Being able to buy better quality equipment means you're able to capture a greater range of images and deliver better results, leading to lots of recommendations and further work. Investing some of your earnings from wedding photography into kit will pay dividends and gives potential customers a clear impression that you are dedicated to your wedding photography business. Our outfit covers a variety of options for when you're shooting solo or with an assistant.

BACK-UP: TOP-END APS-C DSLR

Many pros have a secondary camera fitted with a lens covering a different range to the primary outfit to hand at all times, as opting to switch cameras is often quicker than trying to swap lenses. Your second camera needs to be either a top-end APS-C DSLR or another full frame model. Many fit a telezoom to a top-end APS-C body to provide additional pulling power or instead attach a 50mm f/1.4 lens for wide-aperture portraits. Models such as the £800 Canon EOS 60D or £1,200 EOS 7D or £1,100 Nikon D300s are perfectly suited for use as secondary bodies.

FAST TELEPHOTO ZOOM

The 70-200mm f/2.8 is the telephoto of choice for wedding professionals. Boasting superb optical quality, fast AF and a wide maximum aperture, it has everything a portrait photographer working at speed needs. Some even boast image stabilisation to aid handholding in low-light. Every marque brand has at least one in their range, as do the major independent brands such as Sigma and Tamron. We test popular 70-200mm f/2.8 zooms over on the next page.

FLASH BROLLY

An alternative to the softbox is the brolly. The Westcott Umbrella Flash Kit includes a stand, vari-angle mount and a silver brolly, all for £70. You'll need a wireless trigger too, but it's a cost-effective option for studio-like portraits from your flashgun.

PRO WIRELESS FLASH SYSTEMS

Invest in a couple of top-end flashguns, such as the £370 Canon Speedlite 580EX II or Nikon's £330 Speedlight SB900 and you have a sophisticated flashgun set-up capable of great results. Use a dedicated transmitter like the £180 Canon ST-E2 or £230 Nikon SU-800 for the ultimate in wireless control. Or check out Pocket Wizard's range of sophisticated transmitters and transceivers.

TRIPOD

A sturdy tripod is required if it's to hold a full-frame DSLR with the likes of a 70-200mm f/2.8 attached. To keep the weight down, invest in a carbon-fibre model like the Manfrotto £240 055CXPRO3, £250 Slik Pro 714 CF II or the £210 Giottos MTL-8261B (shown here). A triggered ball & socket head will let you adjust camera positions quickly and come highly recommended. Manfrotto's £120 327RC2 is one of the best.

FIVE-IN-ONE REFLECTOR KIT

A silver/white reflector is a good basic option but five-in-one kits, while heavier, provides a choice of reflective surfaces. Check out the £35 Elemental 107cm kit or, £80 Lastolite Bottletop kit. Westcott's £85 Photo Basics Reflector Kit, shown here, comes supplied with a stand and bracket so you can leave your reflector set up – but watch out for wind!

LIGHT METER

Many photographers get by quite happily without them, but lots of pros still swear by ambient and flash readings from a handheld meter. The £140 Sekonic L-308s is our favourite, providing ease of use, accuracy and reliability at a very good price.

FULL FRAME DSLR

If you want to deliver the very best image quality, then you can't do much better than using a DSLR with a full frame sensor. The larger size allows for sharper images with less noise and offers better wide-angle coverage too. While the difference in image quality over the best APS-C sensors isn't massive due to the quality of the latest APS-C sensors, you're in a competitive market, so if you need your images to be as good as the competition's, you don't want to give them an edge in terms of cameras. You don't need flagship models: the £1,700 Canon EOS 5D MkII or £1,700 Nikon D700 offer superb quality as well as an excellent range of features.

FAST STANDARD ZOOM

The most popular lens for weddings is an f/2.8 standard zoom. Covering wide-angle through to short tele, this lens handles everything from head and shoulder portraits to group shots, as well as scene setters too. Due to it being the primary lens, most pros stick to using the marque lenses like the £950 Canon 24-70mm f/2.8L or £1,200 Nikon AF-S 24-70mm f/2.8G ED. If these are too expensive, you should also look at the likes of the £650 Sigma 24-70mm f/2.8 EX DG IF HSM and £380 Tamron 28-75mm f/2.8 XR Di LD as options too.

LOWEPRO STREET & FIELD

Lowepro's Street & Field system offers an extensive range of options, allowing you to pick and mix pouches to your needs. Shown here is the £23 Light Utility Belt, £28 Quick Flex Pouch 75AW, £30 Utility Bag 100AW and £25 Lens Exchange 200AW.

RECHARGEABLE FLASH PACK

If you're constantly using flash, it's worth looking into a rechargeable flash pack that provides hundreds, if not thousands, of flash bursts before needing recharging. Most slip on a belt and offer far better recycling times than standard AA batteries can manage. Quantum is the leading brand, offering different packs with dedicated leads for all major brands. The £420 Quantum Turbo SC (Slim Compact) offers fast recycling times (around 1.4 secs) and up to 400 bursts per charge used with a hotshoe-type flash.

LARGE GADGET BAG

You're carrying around a lot of kit so need a bag that's comfortable and spacious. The £220 Billingham 335 exudes quality and style and its brand suggests you're a successful photographer. Fast access isn't its strong point, but not such a problem if you wear belt pouches. A more practical option used by many wedding photographers is the Lowepro Stealth Reporter. Designed with social and press photography in mind, they're spacious, robust, comfortable and quick to get inside. Different sizes are available, but we'd recommend the £120 D650AW.

In the bag...

MEMORY CARDS: 6X 8GB

You need very fast cards to handle sequences of Raw files on a full-frame DSLR. You'll fill them up quickly, so buy at least half a dozen 8GB cards.

PORTABLE PHOTO VIEWER

Back up your images from each card on to a portable photo viewer when you get a free moment. Brands such as Vosonic and Archos make them, but the P-series from Epson are the best. They boast large sharp screens, fast transfer rates and reliability. Our favourite is the £450 160GB P-7000.

PREMIUM ULTRA WIDE-ANGLE

Full frame sensors highlight the use of inferior lenses, in particular ultra-wide zooms, so you need to look at buying a premium ultra-wide. There are several strong contenders to consider, including the £1,100 Canon 16-35mm f/2.8L and £1,300 Nikon AF-S 17-35mm f/2.8 ED.

REMOTE RELEASE

Avoiding shake is the usual reason for using a remote, but with weddings, it's also so you can fire the shutter while keeping direct eye contact while talking with subjects, for more natural and relaxed results. Check your instruction book for compatibility if you opt for the manufacturer's remote. However, we'd strongly suggest you look at remotes from Hama, Hahnel and Seculine, who all make affordable dedicated releases.

FAST STANDARD 50MM LENS

Even though you have a fast standard zoom in the outfit, it's still worth having a 50mm f/1.4 to hand, as its maximum aperture can prove extremely useful when shooting creative effects or shooting handheld in low light.

FAST ZOOM LENSES

It's the telezoom of choice for enthusiasts and professionals shooting anything from weddings to sport to wildlife. We test and rate the versatile and desirable 70-200mm f/2.8 lens from leading marque and independent brands to see which offers you the best value

THE 70-200MM f/2.8 lens is larger, heavier and far more expensive than the regular 'budget' telezooms that most of us are used to sticking on the front of our DSLRs. But it's the lens that every photographer who uses a telephoto zoom on a regular basis should aspire to own. Quite simply, it will take your photography to a new level in terms of image quality and general performance. It's the telezoom that serious enthusiasts save up for and professionals wouldn't live without. So what makes it such a special lens to use?

The main reason, of course, is the image quality it delivers. There is no 'duff' 70-200mm f/2.8 lens – every single one delivers sharpness that exceeds that of your average telezoom. We're not talking slightly better either, these lenses deliver incredibly sharp results, so when you read our reviews of models bear this in mind. The optics used in these lenses are of the highest quality and within each lens you'll normally find a number of 'special' elements such as fluorite, low dispersion or aspherical groups, all designed to reduce aberrations and distortion to give you the sharpest possible images.

The f/2.8 maximum aperture means they're very fast too, which gives maximum benefit when you're using it at the 200mm end of the zoom and need a fast shutter speed. This wide aperture setting also offers the bonus of very shallow depth-of-field, which is perfect for creative portraits and a reason why wedding photographers rate it so highly.

These lenses also offer other improved features too, namely a better autofocus performance over budget options, an image stabiliser with extra modes to suit panning and optional teleconverters. It's an expensive optic, but if you regularly shoot at telephoto settings, it's one to save up for. Our comparison test will help you make the right choice.

Tamron 70-200mm f/2.8 Di LD Macro

GUIDE PRICE: £840 / **STREET PRICE:** £630
CONSTRUCTION: 18 elements in 13 groups
MAXIMUM APERTURE: f/2.8
MINIMUM APERTURE: f/32
FILTER THREAD: 77mm
ANGLE OF VIEW: 35° – 12°
NO. OF DIAPHRAGM BLADES: Nine
MINIMUM FOCUS: 95cm
MAXIMUM MAGNIFICATION RATIO: 0.3x
DIMENSIONS: 89.5x194.3mm
WEIGHT: 1,150g
SUPPLIED ACCS: Tripod collar, case, hood
TELECONVERTERS: 1.4x & 2x SP Pro
FITTINGS: Canon, Nikon, Pentax & Sony

Handling
You're in for a surprise. Despite costing considerably less than its rivals, the build quality of the Tamron lens is excellent. The wide zoom and focus ring have textured, rubberised finish and are smooth in action, with the focus ring switching from AF to manual via a push-pull action for Canon and Nikon lenses, or an AF/M switch for Pentax and Sony versions.

Features
the Tamron lacks a number of features found on its rivals, which is to be expected for its price. It boasts the shortest minimum focusing distance of our tested models. It has three LD (Low Dispersion) elements, but lacks image stabilisation or any ultrasonic focusing.

Performance
The AF system lags behind its rivals in terms of speed and is also prone to hunting before locking on to the subject. Wedding photographers should note the AF isn't brilliant in low light. There is little to complain about in terms of its optical performance, which is excellent considering its price.

Verdict
The low price makes this a desirable fast telezoom. While it lacks features, its high-quality optics make it a fine 'budget' buy. It's a major step up from budget zooms but it has a less than perfect AF system.

Handling	★★★★½
Features	★★★☆☆
Performance	★★★½☆
Value	★★★★☆
Overall	★★★★☆

Sigma 70-200mm f/2.8 EX DG OS HSM

GUIDE PRICE: £1,540 / **STREET PRICE:** £1,000
CONSTRUCTION: 22 elements in 17 groups
MAXIMUM APERTURE: f/2.8
MINIMUM APERTURE: f/22
FILTER THREAD: 77mm
ANGLE OF VIEW: 34.3° – 12.3°
NO. OF DIAPHRAGM BLADES: Nine
MINIMUM FOCUS: 140cm
MAXIMUM MAGNIFICATION RATIO: 0.12x
DIMENSIONS: 86.4x197mm
WEIGHT: 1,430g
SUPPLIED ACCS: Tripod collar, case, hood
TELECONVERTERS: 1.4x and 2x EX DG APO
FITTINGS: Canon, Nikon, Pentax, Sigma & Sony

Handling
This Sigma feels like a premium lens although parts of the barrel have a slight plastic feel. The zoom ring has a wide, easy-to-grip finish and smooth action. The manual focus ring displays similar characteristics but is narrower – a slightly wider ring would be better.

Features
The Sigma pretty much matches what's found on marque lenses. Its Optical Stabiliser (OS) claims a four-stop benefit and settings for general use or panning. It also has internal focusing, a Hypersonic Motor (HSM), two 'F' Low Dispersion (FLD) and three Special Low Dispersion (SLD) elements.

Performance
The AF is excellent: quiet, fast and responsive. We found the OS offers around three stops benefit. The Sigma delivers a strong performance optically if you avoid the maximum aperture, where results are soft at the edges. It's very sharp at the centre of the frame and delivers excellent results from f/4-f/11 throughout the zoom range. Chromatic aberration is admirably low.

Verdict
A real alternative to marque models. Its OS works well and AF is excellent. The optical performance is fantastic and if you're a Canon user, this is a better-specified alternative to the similarly-priced non-IS Canon zoom.

Handling	★★★★½
Features	★★★★½
Performance	★★★★½
Value	★★★★½
Overall	★★★★½

Nikon AF-S 70-200mm f/2.8G ED VR II

GUIDE PRICE: £2,100 / **STREET PRICE:** £1,650
CONSTRUCTION: 21 elements in 16 groups
MAXIMUM APERTURE: f/2.8
MINIMUM APERTURE: f/32
FILTER THREAD: 77mm
ANGLE OF VIEW: 34.2° – 12.2°
NO. OF DIAPHRAGM BLADES: Nine
MINIMUM FOCUS: 140cm
MAXIMUM MAGNIFICATION RATIO: 0.12x
DIMENSIONS: 87x209mm
WEIGHT: 1,540g
SUPPLIED ACCS: Tripod collar, case, hood
TELECONVERTERS: TC-20, 17, 14 (2x, 1.7x, 1.4x)
FITTINGS: Nikon

Handling

This telezoom oozes class. Its solid magnesium-alloy barrel, weather/dust sealing and smooth controls are what you'd expect from a premium zoom. The zoom and focus rings are a good size and sport a grooved rubberised texture and smooth action.

Features

The Nikkor is kitted out with features including a focus limiter and enhanced Vibration Reduction system (VR II) with standard and panning modes. The AF boasts a Silent Wave Motor while seven Extra-low Dispersion (ED) elements are used to minimise chromatic aberration. The lens also features Nano Crystal coatings to reduce flare and ghosting.

Performance

AF is quick, quiet and accurate at locking on static or moving subjects. The VRII system is superb too and the claimed four-stop improvement is achievable. The optics deliver razor-sharp results throughout the zoom range. Chromatic aberration and distortion are well controlled but use the hood to avoid ghosting in sunlight.

Verdict

The ultimate choice for the Nikon user. Beautifully designed, robust and loaded with every feature you might need, this high-performing lens is perfect for pros or enthusiasts who can afford it.

Handling	★★★★★
Features	★★★★★
Performance	★★★★★
Value	★★★★★
Overall	★★★★★

Canon EF 70-200mm f/2.8L IS USM II

GUIDE PRICE: £2,800 / **STREET PRICE:** £1,850
CONSTRUCTION: 23 elements in 19 groups
MAXIMUM APERTURE: f/2.8
MINIMUM APERTURE: f/32
FILTER THREAD: 77mm
ANGLE OF VIEW: 34° – 12°
NO. OF DIAPHRAGM BLADES: Eight
MINIMUM FOCUS: 120cm
MAXIMUM MAGNIFICATION RATIO: 0.21x
DIMENSIONS: 88.8x199mm
WEIGHT: 1,490g
SUPPLIED ACCS: Tripod collar, case, hood
TELECONVERTERS: Extenders EF1.4xII, EF2xII
FITTINGS: Canon

Handling

Sporting a distinctive grey finish, this Canon telezoom is one of the largest and heaviest of its type. It has a robust build and moisture and dust sealing. Both the zoom and focus rings have a grooved surface and very nice actions.

Features

You've everything you could need in this Canon lens. An Ultrasonic Motor (USM) gives fast, silent AF and internal focus ensures filter users are kept happy. The Image Stabiliser (IS) has two modes (general and panning) and there is a focus limiter too. The optical set-up includes one fluorite and five Ultra low Dispersion (UD) elements.

Performance

Focusing is quiet, fast, and responsive in every shooting situation. The IS system works a treat too and our tests show a four-stop benefit is possible. The optical performance is nothing short of incredible. Wide open, it gives crisp results that improve further once the lens is stopped down. Sharpness is superb throughout the range. Colour fringing is minimal, as is distortion.

Verdict

Canon users wanting the best should buy this lens. It is feature-packed and produces a dazzling performance. Its size and weight may put off those with smaller DSLRs, but other than this and the price, it's hard to fault.

Handling	★★★★★
Features	★★★★★
Performance	★★★★★
Value	★★★★☆
Overall	★★★★★

Overall verdict

There aren't too many 70-200mm f/2.8 lenses on the market, but it's reassuring to know that all four we've tested here offer very high-quality optics, so you won't go far wrong whichever one you choose.

All are relatively big and bulky compared to budget models, due to the superior optics that they incorporate, but handle well and are a joy to use. Interestingly, the performance on APS-C and full frame sensors were very similar, an indication that lens manufacturers are taking care to ensure their lenses have universal appeal. The Tamron stands out simply because it's far more affordable than any of the other models. In terms of optics, it's not far behind the more pricey options, which makes it a very tempting proposition. Its lack of image stabilisation isn't a major handicap but it is let down by its autofocus performance, which isn't as responsive as the other models on test.

For just under £1,000, you'll find the Sigma lens, which we highly recommend. The Sigma boasts a very good image stabiliser for its price and is available in other fittings too, so represents a great investment for those who use Nikon, Pentax, Sigma or Sony digital SLRs.

This leaves the superb but expensive Canon and Nikon pairing. Are either worth their high price tag? In truth, if you're not planning on taking pictures to make money, the Sigma is probably a better buy. But the Canon and Nikon do take optical performance to new heights, so if you can afford either of these and could benefit from their extra quality, don't hesitate for a second, as they're both superb.

Lighting aids for portraits

Whether working with ambient light or shooting in a studio with flash, reflectors and diffusers are an inexpensive and versatile aid to help manipulate light. Here are the main types to consider

IT'S A COMMON misconception that you need expensive equipment to get professional-looking portraits. While a better camera and superior optics do make a difference, there are many affordable bits of kit that can lead to far better pictures if used correctly. Lighting aids such as reflectors and diffusers are two such item, proving useful whether you're using daylight, studioflash or any other form of lighting for that matter.

Any wedding or portrait photographer, studio or location-based, find lighting aids invaluable for controlling light quickly and effectively if they need to fill in shadows or diffuse light to make it more flattering.

There are different types of lighting aids available in different sizes, shapes and colours, from small handheld options to those that require a stand or assistant to hold them. This guide covers a range of products from all the popular brands to help you make the right choices and ultimately save you money.

California Sunbounce

www.theflashcentre.com

The California Sunbounce range of reflectors is a favourite with professionals thanks to their stability, build quality and light weight. The reflector panels are fitted to aluminium frames that come in various sizes and are quick and easy to assemble, disassemble and pack up for storage and transportation. There is a good choice of reflective panels available, although not every colour is suitable for every frame, but you still have several options open to you (the downloadable PDF catalogue has a very useful easy-reference table).

While you can buy extra panels to use with a frame, the difference in price for complete kits and individual panels isn't that wide, so it's often worth buying the complete outfit to save you having to swap panels while on location. As with other brands, there are silver/white and gold/white reflector options, but you'll find that there are other reflective finishes eg zebra/white (zebra is a mix of gold and silver), as well as a number of translucent diffuser options too.

As they're made for professional use, you'll find that they're relatively expensive, but are made to last for years of intensive use and are produced from the best possible materials. The Sunbounce system is extensive, so contact importers The Flash Centre if you require further details, or download the catalogue at www.sunbounce.com.

Because the number of options is huge, we've listed the different reflector ranges below and stated the price of the two most popular reflective colours. While a number of sizes are available, we'd recommend the Mini or Pro as your first choice, and the Mega (stated as Big in the catalogue) if you're a very keen enthusiast. Here are the main options:

Micro-mini: (60x90cm)
Silver/white: £106; Zebra/white: £128
Mini: (90x125cm)
Silver/white: £159; Zebra/white: £194
Pro: (130x190cm)
Silver/white: £240; Zebra/white: £281
Big: (180x245cm)
Silver/white: £377; Zebra/white: £439

While a couple of translucent panels are available for the Pro and Mega panels, for diffusing purposes, we'd recommend you check out the Sun Swatter. This is a large diffuser that is ideal for outdoor use as it can be held by a boon over the subject and outside of the image area. It's easy to assemble and designed to be used in windy conditions. There are two sizes available and a number of options for the light-reducing value of the translucent material (1/3, 2/3 or one-stop light diffusion). We'd recommend the smaller Sun Swatter with the 1/3 or 2/3-stop diffuser as a good first option.

Other specialist reflectors in the range includes the Sun-mover, which allows for additional control of the spread of light and the Sun Cage – a purpose made mobile studio for location shooting.

Sun Swatter (130x190cm)
-1/3 stop complete £235
Sun Swatter (130x190cm)
-2/3 Stop complete £245
Sun Swatter Giant (180x245cm)
-1/3 Stop complete £393
Sun Swatter Giant (180x245cm)
-2/3Stop Complete £408

Calumet

www.calumetphoto.co.uk

Calumet is a major photo retailer and has an extensive number of own-brand photo accessories, including its ZipDisc range of collapsible reflectors. These include two colour reflectors, translucent panels and four-colour sleeves (gold/silver/white/black) The ZipDisc kits are as follows:

Translucent white ZipDisc panel

The circular diffuser at the heart of its 5-in-1 kit is available on its own too.

56cm £15; **81cm** £26;
107cm £37; **130cm** £46

Zigzag gold-silver/White ZipDisc

The gold-silver side combines gold and silver for added warmth to the subject.

56cm £15; **81cm** £26; **107cm** £35

Silver/white ZipDisc

The classic handheld reflector. Supplied with a zip case.

56cm £15; **81cm** £26; **107cm** £37

ZipDisc Four-colour cover

This four-colour (gold, white, silver and black) sleeve cover can be used on any round or oval reflector.

56cm (22in) ZipDisc reversible: £14
81cm (32in) ZipDisc reversible: £22
107cm (42in) ZipDisc reversible: £32

ZipDisc holder

Calumet offers two telescopic holders to keep your ZipDisc in place while you're shooting without assistance. Choose between the standard version at £27 or, if you're shooting outdoors, opt for the heavy-duty holder at £35.

Please note that if you visit Calumet's website, you may get a little confused about the product descriptions, so if you've any queries, phone their customer service on 08706 030303.

Interfit

www.interfitphotographic.com

Interfit is one of the UK's leading brands of studio equipment and has an extensive range of reflectors, from handhelds to larger stand-supported types, so you've plenty of choice!

Soft sun/white; silver/white and silver/gold:

Round, collapsible reflectors available in three finishes and four sizes

30cm £10; **56cm** £16; **82cm** £27; **107cm** £37

5-in-1 kits

These feature a translucent reflector, with a four-colour overlay sleeve (gold, silver, black and white), supplied in a zip-up bag. They are available in three sizes as follows:

56cm £25: **82cm** £36; **107cm** £42

Easy Grip: Interfit's Easy Grip reflector has a thick handle for one-handed use and measures 90x60cm (36x24in). It is available in the following colours: sunlight/white; gold/silver; silver/white and ½-stop translucent and costs £40.

Portrait Reflector Kit: Interfit's Portrait Reflector Kit is essentially three reflector panels attached to a frame that fits easily on a lighting stand. Each 90x60cm (36x24in) panel can be individually positioned for improved lighting control. The kit is supplied with one silver/gold panel and two sunlight/silver panels and costs £100.

The Large Flat Panel Reflector: Studio-based photographers may be interested in these large reflector panels, made for full-length portraits and fashion shoots. The Large Flat Panel Reflector measures 89x178cm (35x70in) and is supplied complete with a stand and a rotating/tilting bracket for using the panel vertically or horizontally. Silver/gold and white/black versions are available for £84.

Flexi-lite 5-in-1: This stand-mounted panel reflector is aimed at pros and can be used handheld or on location. The aluminium frame has a boon arm that can be positioned at any angle. Various kits are available in medium (100x150cm) or large (150x200cm). The INT303 has a gold/silver/black/white cover and costs £307.

Lastolite

www.lastolite.com

Lastolite is one of the world's leading studio accessory brands and is particularly renowned for its lighting aids, so it's no surprise to discover it has an extensive range of products. Many are designed for specific pro uses, so due to space constraints, we've selected the products most suitable for general portrait photography. A comprehensive brochure PDF can be downloaded from Lastolite's website if you'd like to check out the entire range.

Collapsible reflectors: When it comes to collapsible reflectors, no brand has as many options as Lastolite. Its round reflectors are available in 30cm, 50cm, 76cm, 95cm and 120cm diameters and there is a huge 1.8x1.2m rectangular option too. All of these are available in the following finishes: silver/white; sunfire/white, silver/gold, sunfire/silver; gold/white and sunlite/soft silver. A two-stop diffuser is also available in all sizes from 50cm upwards. Guide prices for silver/white are as follows: 30cm £13; 50cm £24; 75cm £35; 95cm £58; 120cm £75; 1.8x1.2m £91.

Bottletops 5-in-1 kit: This includes a diffuser panel with elasticated covers. The kit comprises the diffuser panel and a gold/white and sunfire/silver cover and comes in four sizes: 50cm (£41), 75cm (£47), 95cm (£57) and 120cm (£85).

TriGrip: The original TriGrip was the first collapsible reflector to feature a handle and proved extremely popular. The design has been updated, with a new moulded grip improving handling and there are now three sizes in the range: the £47 Mini TriGrip (45cm); £62 TriGrip (75cm) and £77 Large TriGrip (1.2m). For each size, you can choose reflectors in silver/white, gold/white, sunfire/silver and sunlite/softsilver finishes, as well as a one-stop or two-stop diffuser. Accessories for the TriGrip include a support bracket and the TriFlip, a set of seven reflector covers that can be placed over a TriGrip to offer the ultimate in versatility. You can also buy a £185 TriFlip 8:1 kit that supplies a two-stop diffuser (Mini TriGrip or TriGrip) with seven colour sleeves.

Triflector: The MkII kit consists of a support frame with three collapsible panels, all easily packed away in a case weighing a total of only 1.2kg. The panels are available in the following reflective finishes: sunfire/silver, silver/white, gold/white and a 1.2-stop diffuser. A kit is £130; extra sets of panels range from £33-£45.

UpLite 4:1: A set of self-supporting 120x90cm reflector panels for use by photographers working on their own, who need to bounce light at an angle from the floor. The angle can be adjusted from 30-80° and the two panels can also be separated for handheld use. The UpLite comes in two versions: the Cool Tone has a sunlite/softsilver and silver/white reflective surfaces, while the Warm Tone has a gold/white and sunfire/silver reflective surfaces. It comes supplied with a waterproof shower cap and a carry case and costs around £120.

Skylite: Best suited for serious photographers looking for a lightweight, durable and large diffuser that can also double up as a reflector. The rigid, hollow aluminium frame supports a diffuser (0.75 or 1.25 stop) or reflector (gold/silver, silver/white, black/white or sunfire/white) via secure Velcro fastenings. The Skylite can be bought in a number of kit forms and three sizes are available as follows: Small 1.1x1.1m (1.3kg); medium 1.1x2m (2kg) and large 2x2m (2.3kg). The standard kit includes the frame, silver/white and translucent fabrics and carry bag, and are priced at around £120, £184 and £225 for the small, medium and large respectively.

JOBS IN PHOTOGRAPHY

Find out how to make money from landscapes, travel, wildlife and sports photography

LANDSCAPE PHOTOGRAPHY

If you're an outdoor photographer, sustaining an income from your images is likely to be your dream. Find out how to make it come true

REGARDLESS OF WHETHER you live in the heart of the countryside or in the middle of a town or city, you are never far from a photogenic landscape. It is this accessibility that makes scenic photography so popular among digital photographers. Whether it's a sweeping vista of rolling hills or a cityscape of skyscrapers, good images are always saleable. However, if you wish to earn cash from your captures, you first need to know which markets to approach. With no shortage of high-quality scenics available from professional and amateur photographers, this is a competitive area and, generally speaking, only well-composed, well-lit, technically-perfect images will appeal to editors and publishers. Don't let this put you off though, images that meet the above criteria could soon be earning you money.

Knowing your market saves you time and effort in the long run. Before you approach a magazine or publisher, spend time looking at the material they already use to guide you in making your picture selection. It's a good idea, at first, to specialise in photography of one county or region. An intimate knowledge of an area

LEE FROST

helps produce better images, as experience tells you where to visit in certain light or weather conditions. Don't make the common mistake of overlooking tourist hotspots and landmarks either. Many photographers disregard them as they've been shot to death, but they can always be photographed better or from a different viewpoint. Photographs of recognisable locations often sell the best, especially with calendar publishers. But while pictures of local views may prove to be your bread and butter work, also try taking dramatic or fine-art images: there's a good market for these with photo magazines, picture libraries and as limited edition prints.

Essential landscape kit

A wide-angle lens is a must-have for shooting sweeping vistas. A traditional 28mm wide-angle lens is fine for photographers with a full frame camera, but most DSLR bodies have a smaller APS-C sensor that increases the focal length by a factor of around 1.5x, therefore, opt for a wide-angle zoom covering a focal length of around 17-35mm. A telezoom is useful for cropping into the landscape.

Filters are important tools for landscape photography too. It is best to invest in a slot-in system, like the Cokin P or Lee Filter system. A polariser is a must for saturating colour and boosting blue skies and you will need a set of graduated ND filters to balance unevenly lit scenes. Invest in a good, sturdy tripod and comfortable backpack to carry all your landscape kit.

Potential markets

Prints

It's common for landscape photographers to sell prints of their most attractive images. Not only is it satisfying to know that people like your work sufficiently to display it on their walls, but it can make you some extra cash. Selling prints can also prove a door opener for other work or commissions in the future.

To give your prints an exclusive feel, it can be worthwhile limiting the number you sell of each view to a set amount – and numbering and signing them individually. Produce prints in several sizes, and sell them mounted not framed, as the majority of buyers will prefer to frame to their own taste. Visit a few local galleries, introduce yourself and show them a selection of your work. If they are interested in marketing your photography, they will advise you with how much you can reasonably charge. This can vary tremendously, but around £40-£80 is not unreasonable for a quality, mounted limited edition 15x10in or 18x12in print. Naturally, they will take a commission of the selling price, typically 15-25%. This still leaves a decent profit margin on the cost of printing and mounting your shot. You also could rent a stall at a craft or art fair, although this approach requires more time and money.

Magazines

There is a good variety of magazines that are constantly on the lookout for quality scenic images. Photographs that feature footpaths, walkers or wooden stiles appeal to walking magazines like *Country Walking* and *TGO*, while images with great technique suit photography titles. But by far the biggest market is regional magazines. Wherever you are based, there will be titles dedicated to that county or region. Pop into your local newsagents and buy copies specific to your area. Have a look at the style and quality of the images and then make an initial approach. Unless stated otherwise, send a polite, brief introductory email with a list of the locations you have available, along with an example of your work and a link to your website. Once your images are used regularly, you may find that it later leads to commissioned work.

Postcards

Millions of postcards are produced, sold and sent every year and publishers add new scenes to their range annually. They only sell for a few pence, so the profit margin on them is relatively small. Postcard publishers will normally offer a single reproduction fee of around £50- £100 for pictures they wish to use. This may not sound like much,

but they are shouldering the risk of whether the image sells well or not. Obviously, the ones that do will generate a reasonable profit, but equally publishers may not even recover their costs if the image doesn't prove popular.

Some publishers, like Judges consider images that are vibrant and suitable from anywhere in England and Wales. However, other printers, like Thomas Bennaci, specialise in images of a specific region, so do your research before making an approach. Pictures that sell best are normally of the most popular viewpoints and attractions or scenes that include significant buildings or monuments – have a look at the postcards already on sale to give you a good idea of the style and quality.

Insider view

LEE FROST

Lee Frost

LANDSCAPE PHOTOGRAPHER

Q) How did you get started?
I was a typical hobbyist photographer in my early teens and started submitting images to magazines, getting published and earning a bit of money from it. As I got myself known in photography magazines, I started to get work off the back of my submissions and eventually began writing for the titles too, which is now a part of how I make my living.

Q) How profitable are calendars, postcards and greeting cards?
It's always been a bit hit and miss. The fees you get for postcards are never great and calendar publishers that pay decent money prefer to work with as few photographers as possible. If you've got a really good library of images, featuring wide coverage of the UK, you stand a better chance of directly working with a publisher. The images of mine that are used in calendars, however, are mainly sourced through picture libraries.

Q) How do you make a full-time job out of landscape photography?
My income is split in to three categories: selling photographs, whether that be prints, via picture libraries or to magazines; writing photography books and magazine features; and operating photography tours and workshops. I don't think there's any photographer in the UK at the moment who makes a decent living just from selling photographs. Even Joe Cornish – the god of UK landscape photography – does workshops, operates a gallery that exhibits other photographers' work and publishes greeting cards by other photographers. All the renowned landscape photographers in the UK like Joe, Charlie Waite and David Ward are involved in other areas of photography to make a good living. If you're starting out, you'd be naive to think you could make decent money from just taking and selling your landscape pictures.

Q) How do you go about selling your images?
Most of my images sold for publication are done via picture libraries so I have little to do with it. I get statements through every quarter telling me what's been sold and how much for. There are so many image libraries now, many linked with Getty Images. I've been contracted to Robert Harding World Imagery since the late '80s and they're my main source of stock sales, especially since they teamed up with Getty Images. I probably make more money now from stock than I ever have. I also work with a smaller library called the Travel Library in Hampshire.

Q) What resources can you recommend?
Buy *The Freelance Photographer's Market Handbook*: it was my bible in the early years. Unfortunately, it's also the bible of anyone else trying to sell a few images so you tend to find the markets in the book are flooded, though it's still a good starting point and certainly got me going. Knowing where to send your images and what is required is the biggest hurdles.

Q) How did you start your courses?
When Charlie Waite started up Light & Land some 15 years ago, he asked me to lead some workshops and after a few years of doing this, I set up on my own as I wanted more choice over the destinations I was taking groups to. Photo Adventures has now been operating for about ten years. It wasn't easy, but being quite a well-known name in photo magazines and having written a few photography books definitely helped with business.

Q) What advice do you have for landscape photographers wanting to start courses?
You have to be realistic. For a start, there are many more photographers doing workshops and course than they used to be – a lot run by photographers who aren't particularly well known. I think many of them are photographers who see workshops as a way of making more money or newcomers to professional landscape photography who see it as a way of trying to drum up some business. Competition is quite strong. I no longer do short UK workshops anymore because the market's flooded, instead I do longer overseas workshops to places such as Cuba.

If you're passionate and talented, you shouldn't let the competition put you off but don't expect to be filling up workshops overnight if no one knows who you are. It's quite a slow process. I've been doing it for ten years, been a full-time landscape photographer for almost 20 years, and I still take every year as it comes because I never know if the next year will be as good as this one. Keep your wits about you and be aware that the industry is constantly changing, markets disappear and you have to find new ones: it's never an easy ride but equally I wouldn't want to be doing anything else.

For further details on Lee Frost's Ph[illegible] Adventures, visit: www.leefrost.co.uk

SPORTS PHOTOGRAPHY

Get to grips with what it takes to be a sports photographer and how to earn cash standing on the sideline

IF YOU LOVE sport and photography, what could be better than combining the two interests? Surely it's a dream job. Professional sports photographers get into events for free, have the best view of the event and are often within just a few metres of sport's biggest and best stars. It sounds like a cushy number, doesn't it? However, sports photography is extremely challenging. At the highest level, the expectancy and pressure is massive. You have to capture the key incidents no matter how difficult the conditions: there are no second chances.

Digital SLRs have made the life of sports photographers a little easier. ISO sensitivity can now be adjusted with the push of a button and altered quickly in changing light. No longer is there an anxious wait for film to be processed, instead pros can send their images to their agencies and publications within moments of capture via the internet and their laptop.

While images taken at major events such as Ryder Cups, Premiership games and Test matches may be the most lucrative and saleable, there are ways to make money while you build a reputation and portfolio that lets you in to those games. Not only can you take and sell pictures of local sporting events, they're also the best places to hone your skills – and you don't need a pass to take pictures at the village football club or rugby ground. Always try to pick out a shooting position that gives a clean or interesting background and separates the action from the backdrop. In addition to quick reflexes, a good knowledge of the sport you're covering helps you capture relevant, appealing, saleable images. Having captured some good snaps, approach the sports people in your shots and enquire if they would like to buy a print. Admittedly this won't make you rich, but it will allow you to earn a few quid while you learn.

Photographing local events will help you build a good portfolio of images, which in turn will enable you to take the next step. Seek permission to attend larger regional ...ts or matches, using your portfolio of ...s proof of your ability and ...proach a regional weekly ... if they have any ...reelancer. This can lead ...ou are good, be a ...ney or even a ...nocked back at ...nick skin in this ...ou believe in your ...u will be given an ...nen you do, grab it..

RICHARD PELHAM

RICHARD PELHAM

Essential sports kit

You'll require more than just a basic digital camera set-up to consistently capture frame-filling, action-packed shots. Two DSLR bodies allow you to swap from one focal length to another quickly without wasting valuable time changing lenses. Pros rely on fast optics, capable of being used indoors or in poor light. However, this type of kit isn't cheap. Ideally, you will want a good, versatile mixture of focal lengths, boasting a fast, maximum aperture of f/2.8. At least one telephoto upwards of 300mm is required for shooting distant action, while shorter focal lengths like the 70-200mm are ideal for closer action. A wide-angle lens can also be useful, producing visually strong, unusual and intimate sporting images in situations where you are able to get near to the action. A monopod is the best form of support, being easier to manoeuvre than a tripod. You'll often shoot long bursts of images, so you will need several large capacity memory cards and also a number of charged batteries. To be able to transmit images from events, a laptop is an essential tool for today's professional.

Potential markets

Stock agencies
One of the best ways to sell your images after an event is to place them with an agency. There are a few photo libraries specialising in action images, but most of the main agencies, like the Press Association, tend to have their own staff photographers or are only prepared to market the images of established professionals. Agencies like Action Images will consider speculative submissions as long as their unusual; so don't waste their time or yours by sending them anything but top-notch material.

Although agencies take a hefty commission on sales (typically 50%), they are able to reach worldwide markets that one person simply can't. Obviously, images of big sporting events or stars have greater commercial appeal and be more marketable. Eye-catching or unusual images will be highly saleable regardless of where they were taken or of whom. However, images like this may sell better on general online agencies, like Alamy or Fotolibra.

Local papers
Selling images of local sporting events or matches to the local weekly paper is one of the most common routes into sports photography. Depending on the size of the paper, they may already have a staff photographer, but it is very likely they also rely partly or fully on freelancers. To demonstrate your ability, approach the paper with examples of your work and speak only to the person who assigns the photographers. Presuming your work is sufficiently good enough, they may well be prepared to give you an opportunity. This will get you on the sidelines of fixtures that, otherwise, you wouldn't legitimately be able to attend. The money may not be great at first, but the experience will be invaluable.

Regular assignments will give you the opportunity to continue building your portfolio and with time, you will be in a position to progress to a regional daily paper and then, who knows, a national daily...

Insider view

NICK WOOD

Nick Woods

SPORTS PHOTOGRAPHER

Q) What's the state of the industry?
A few years ago, large agencies such as Getty Images went on a spree, buying up smaller agencies to dominate the field for most major sports such as football. So, as these agencies have a lot of the industry tied up with most broadsheet papers and clubs making them their first port of call, it doesn't make financial sense to target high-profile sports or teams.

Q) How can photographers look to get in to sports photography?
It can be a vicious circle to begin with as to attach yourself to an agency, you need a portfolio of decent events. But it's the clubs (who can be very selective about their photographers) and agencies that can get you the accreditation or press pass you need for these events. To help build a portfolio of published work, start off by buying a copy of your local papers over the next couple of weeks and take note of what sports the editors cover. Follow the events and send the images to the editors each week. If your images are better than what they already have, they may ask you to cover more events. Also, look for third division football teams as they will have less restrictions on taking photographs, or for more obscure events that might want exposure.

If you're willing to work part-time, approach your local paper or club and ask them to get you accreditation in exchange for use of your images for free to build a portfolio. If you can't get any big events, look out for the big names playing in lower level events as part of their rehab. A close-up on them can look great in your portfolio.

Q) What opportunities will the 2012 Olympics bring photographers?
Demand for images of less mainstream sports such a beach volleyball and handball should increase over the next year and it's unlikely the big agencies have specialists to cover them.

Q) Do I have to go freelance?
You could work on spec but be prepared for some hard times as it's getting more and more competitive as kit becomes more affordable. If you can make it work, it's very affluent, especially if you attach yourself to a local paper, but you may be up against agency workers. You could, however, try to get in with smaller agencies such as Action Images or Action Plus. They could get you the accreditation for low- level events, which helps you work towards building your portfolio for the larger agencies, such as Getty Images and the Press Association.

Q) Does success in sports photography rely on just taking great pictures?
No. Taking good pictures is only half the job. Agencies and picture desks are normally inundated with images so you have to make their job as easy as possible when it comes to selecting pictures. During a game I spend half my time in front of my laptop cropping images to agency proportions, resizing, filling in the metadata and even writing the headlines so they can immediately distribute it. If you're sending in images cold make sure you check the agencies/picture desk's website, or call them first, to find out the minimum requirements for submissions.

Q) Can you give us an idea of the financial investment?
Your income depends on image size, the type of picture and the publication. Local papers may pay £50-£100 for a reasonable event, but for backwater teams maybe £25. If you do get published, always ask for a hard copy or PDF for your portfolio as that's invaluable.

Investment wise, to start with, you'll need fast telephoto lenses, such as the 400mm f/2.8, or a telephoto zoom of a similar focal length to get close enough to the action, and perhaps a few extenders. You can always rent this equipment if you can't afford it. As you may need to move around, you'll need a monopod rather than a tripod and obviously at least one good quality digital SLR that can handle low light well with minimal noise, in case you need to shoot under floodlights.

Q) How else can I make money from sports photography?
If you want to earn money from sports, while building your portfolio in other ways, you could approach local sports clubs and schools to take photographs of the games, players and teams to sell. A great website for posting and selling pictures to the public is www.photoshelter.com.

For courses on how to become a professional sports photographer, visit: www.unshaken-photography.co.uk

WILDLIFE PHOTOGRAPHY

Find out the truth about what life's like working as a full-time wildlife photographer and how you can make some money from your hobby

WHEN YOU FIRST catch the wildlife photography bug, making cash from your camera may not be high on your agenda. However, taking pictures for pleasure can soon prove a costly business. Let's face it; wildlife photography isn't the cheapest hobby. Walk into your local camera shop and it is easy to be tempted by the latest digital SLR, long telephoto lens or tripod. Nice, shiny new kit will soon have you reaching for your flexible friend, but most of us will be working within a strict budget. So, no doubt before long you will want to try and recoup a few quid by selling your best nature snaps. The big question is... how?

Whether you prefer shooting mammals, insects or birds, there is always a strong market for good images. That said, traditionally, demand for bird and mammal pictures is higher. Critters oozing with the so-called 'aahhhhh' factor are always popular. 'Cute' animals, like hedgehogs, badgers, puffins or birds of prey are commercially appealing; juvenile animals or fledgling birds also sell well, so it's worth keeping this in mind. Pictures of big cats, safari animals and marine wildlife – like dolphins and whales – are also popular among greeting card and calendar publishers. However, if you can't afford to travel, some good close-ups can be achieved in captivity, so don't overlook visiting a safari park or zoo. So you've got the right images, now what do you do with them? Read on to find out...

Essential nature kit

Wildlife snappers need more kit than most. Two DSLRs are preferable and at least one long telephoto lens of 300mm or more is a must for shooting birds and mammals. A macro lens is also important for shooting insect and close-ups. Several large capacity cards will be needed. A PSD (Portable Storage Device) is also a good investment for use in the field. A large camera backpack is perfect for carrying all your bulky kit comfortably when walking long distances. Camouflaged clothing and a portable, collapsible hide are important too.

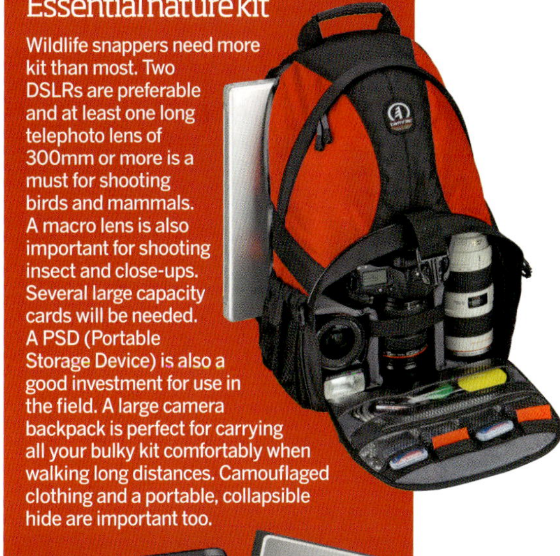

Potential markets

Calenders

Calendars are big business. Selling shots to this market not only relies on the quality of your photography, but also your ability to supply the right type of material; images that look seasonal will enhance their appeal. Do your own market research by flicking through wildlife calendars currently on sale. If you feel your images are a similar style and quality, make a note of the publisher's details and check their website for submission details, before you try contacting them via phone or email. Follow their submission details to the last letter. Calendars usually go on sale from the previous spring onwards, so publishers are working over a year in advance: many have already made picture selections for their 2012 range. Photographers need to reflect this in the timing of their submissions. £80 is the minimum fee you should expect for a calendar image. This is for single reproduction only and copyright remains with the photographer. Normally the contract stipulates that you cannot sell the picture to another calendar publisher for a year, but you are free to continue selling the images elsewhere. Look at *The Freelance Photographers' Market Handbook 2012* (www.thebfp.com) for a list of publishers.

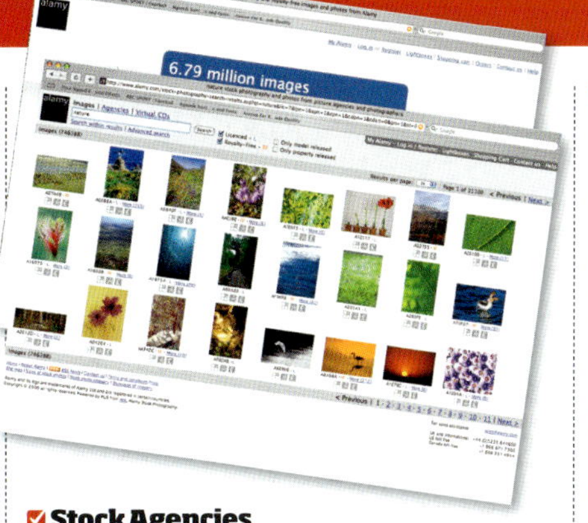

Stock Agencies

There are over 100 stock agencies in the UK and several are nature specific. Picture libraries will only accept photographers who can provide images of a consistently high standard. Contracts are very rare these days, but can be offered to photographers who can supply several hundred suitable images as an initial submission and can continue to make regular submissions. If you are unable to do this at this stage, consider an online picture library like Alamy: www.alamy.com

Nature libraries are only after strong, well-composed shots that are punchy and sharp. Unusual shots, illustrating types of animal behaviour, are often the most sought after. Stock libraries will normally take around 50% commission on images sold. This might sound steep, but a good library will reach markets in the UK and abroad that an individual won't. They can also demand higher repro fees. However, it takes time to get established and it may be a year or more before you receive your first sales report. A decent, regular income is only possible if you have thousands of images on file. There are several good, specific natural history agencies and The BFP handbook can also help you find agencies.

Magazines

There is a surprisingly small amount of magazines that are wildlife-orientated. The biggest and best is *BBC Wildlife*. It is illustrated throughout with stunning nature shots, but the standard is high. Instead, a better route might be to approach your regional magazines, where you won't be competing against such established photographers. County titles are increasingly popular and many have regular features on local wildlife. It's a starting point and photos published with them may open up other doors.

When submitting material, it is important to remember that magazines often work several months in advance. Editors will be on the lookout for seasonal shots suitable for publication in the issue they are currently working on. Therefore, there's no point sending autumnal images in October, when the editorial team will already be working on winter issues. It is often best to submit work a season in advance... so now is the time to sort through your winter images, ready to submit in the next few weeks. Confusing, eh?

Insider view

ROSS HODDINOTT

Ross Hoddinott

WILDLIFE PHOTOGRAPHER

Q) How did you get started?
I started young. I must have been just ten years old when I began shooting wildlife and knew I wanted to be a professional by the age of 17. I began by submitting images to the 'Showcase' and 'Portfolio' pages of photo magazines. This proved to be my entry route into professional photography, and one I would recommend to newcomers. I was also fortunate to win one or two quite prestigious photo competitions, such as the Veolia Environnement Young Wildlife Photographer of the Year, which definitely helped raise my profile.

Q) How can you make a full-time job out of wildlife photography?
The harsh reality is that few people do. It is one of the most popular and competitive genres of photography and it is also probably one of the lowest paid. The standard is fantastically high, so only the very highest quality material will sell. However, good images will always sell and there is a large market for nature images in magazines, books, calendars, greeting cards and prints. Like me, most wildlife photographers have to diversify in some way too; either by shooting other subjects to supplement their income, or by writing, running workshops or giving talks.

Q) How difficult is it to make a living from wildlife photography?
It is tricky – there is no point pretending otherwise. It can take many years to build a large stock of images of a sufficiently high quality that will generate a decent, regular income. When I started, the priority was to get contracted to a good, dedicated agency that would market my images. While it is still important to have work with a picture library, reproduction fees have plummeted. I'm selling more images than ever through agencies, but many of them are marketed through sub-agents for micro fees, often less than £1! It's not all doom and gloom, though, there are still good fees out there for the right material.

Q) What tips can you share?
Originality is important. While well-captured animal portraits often sell, images that are unusual, shot from a fresh perspective or illustrating behaviour or less common species have an enhanced chance. You have to be patient and determined to photograph nature but you have to be equally persistent when trying to market the results. It can be worthwhile specialising in order to achieve a reputation for a type of photography.

Q) What money making opportunities are there with wildlife photography?
Few wildlife photographers are employed; this really is a freelance profession. I generate my income from a mixture of agency sales and personal sales – selling directly to magazines and publications that I have developed a relationship with. There are opportunities to make money; you just have to look for them. Target publishers whom you feel your images would suit. Framed prints can also generate cash. Galleries will sell your images for you for a commission.

Q) How do you find your clients?
Fortunately most of my clients now approach me for images. However, originally I would email potential clients with a brief introduction and a number of example images. It can be quite disheartening at times doing this type of 'cold calling'. Often you won't receive a reply, or your work will be rejected. This doesn't necessarily mean your images aren't good enough, though. Remember, editors and picture researchers are very busy people. You just have to believe in your photography and persevere.

Q) What is a typical day as a wildlife photographer like?
In truth, there is no such thing as a typical day. Nature photographers are reliant on the weather, subject and season. Often, more time is spent looking for the subject than behind a camera. I have to do a lot of walking, visiting reserves early and late in the day when the light is best and insects are less active. Today's photographers spend more time in front of a computer than shooting. Editing, processing and captioning images takes time. Marketing work, dealing with requests and daily correspondence are also time-consuming. I work unsociable hours. I've recently done six consecutive 4.30am starts; I then may work in my office during the day, before going out with my camera again in the evening. During spring and summer, I may not get home until 10-11pm. Photography is an addiction though, and I love taking pictures.

TRAVEL PHOTOGRAPHY

Funding your travels via photography for many is a dream come true, but how do you do it and what does it really involve to be a success?

FOR MANY, the idea of trotting off around the globe taking fantastic pictures is a mouth-watering prospect. Those exotic beaches with palm trees and crystal-clear waters sound great but then reality eventually hits home. You have to consider the cost of the trip – it could easily be two grand to go to the other side of the world. Will you make enough sales to recoup your expenses, let alone make a profit? And it is profit that will keep your business going from year to year and strength to strength. Spend more than you earn and your fledgling business is eventually doomed to failure. One travel photographer we spoke to recommends you shoot everything you can locally first, as it's easy to access and has minimum overhead costs. Starting this way will give you confidence and you can fine tune your techniques – not just photographic but organising the trip, sorting out pictures and then selling the images afterwards.

If going on holiday with the family, spend some days shooting stock. Not just pretty landscapes, but the local people, road signs, kids playing on the beach or in the pool, wine glasses at sunset.

Organising your trip pays dividends for maximising your photography time, but be prepared to ditch the itinerary if something unusual or unexpected turns up. After all it's what travel photography is all about!

Use travel guides and the internet to see what pictures sell of your destination. Re-shooting places already photographed by others may seem silly but places change and shots need updating. A new building means new shots will be required by travel companies. You may also manage to take a shot that simply becomes a best-seller even though the scene has been shot a thousand times before!

Remember to get as much advice on any destination beforehand. Has a civil war just erupted? What jabs do you need? Do you need a visa? The best places to start looking for travel advice are the foreign office website www.fco.gov.uk or the dept. of health website: www.dh.gov.uk.

Essential travel kit

When travelling you must keep your gear to a minimum so keep asking the question 'Do I really need this?' The heavier your bag, the more tired you will get as the day progresses and it will become harder to decide which bit of gear you want to use. Try putting only two or three lenses and a camera in your bag for the day. A wide-angle zoom like a 10-20mm, 17-55mm and a 55-200mm should cover most situations. You could try a 70-200mm f/2.8 with a tele-converter as an interesting option but lenses with a f/5.6 aperture are much smaller and lighter! Opt for image-stabilised lenses that allow handholding in dim lighting conditions. If your budget allows, try buying several 4GB cards. Extra kit like a portable storage device to back-up your images to, spare lenses or laptop can be left in the hotel safe. Take a small, lightweight tripod that fits in your suitcase! A polariser and grey grads are essential filters.

Potential markets

☑ Calenders & postcards

Calendar companies are always looking out for new and exciting images. Some calendar concepts may be quite specific and local to one area like the Yorkshire Dales, but others may be open to images from all over. You should concentrate on shooting one region well and then start to branch out to new areas. Keep an eye out for calendars when visiting a country, you can sell to them too. Just write down their contact details rather than lugging a load of calendars around with you. Use the internet to search for calendar companies in countries you've visited and send them a CD with low-res images and a contact sheet. If you create a website using a company like www.clikpic.com you can let potential art buyers view your images in a professional and slick manner.

Postcard and greeting card companies always want new shots. Buy a single postcard from different publishing companies when out and about. Use the card as a reference for shooting new images and keep it for company contact details on the back. Spend time looking at different cards and see how yours compare.

☑ Magazines

There are quite literally thousands of travel shots being published in all kinds of magazines in any given month. Dedicated travel magazines are obvious but what about a magazine aimed at walkers, car enthusiasts or men's health? You will be surprised to learn

that many magazines run travel articles on places to visit. If you can add some text to go with your pictures you will suddenly become a travel photojournalist! You will make many editors lives much easier by giving them a finished package of words and images. Go on, give it a go! Trailfinders travel company, for example, have a magazine which uses several such short articles for every edition of their magazine. Simply get in touch with the editor and ask if they can supply a fact sheet detailing their particular requirements – number of words and how many photos to send in. You will also get a better price for a 'package' deal rather than just photos. Always keep an eye out for potential magazines to send your work to and visit the magazine stands regularly.

☑ Tourist & travel companies

Travel companies often source images from the internet and stock libraries, but there is no harm in sending them a CD and contact sheet. They often use in-house photographers or commission a pro to shoot a location or accommodation but often still need shots of the local area and people.

Local tourist boards and even local councils are always on the lookout for new material to fill their brochures with. They don't always pay top dollar but it's a good place to hone your marketing skills. Ring them up and ask to speak to the PR department and find out if they need any specific shots that you can then go out and take. It's a good way to get your foot in the door with companies.

☑ Stock libraries

Without doubt stock libraries are the life-blood for most pro travel photographers and many have several stock libraries on the go at once in different countries. Most libraries will want an exclusive deal, meaning you can't put the same shots with another library. For this reason, you should always shoot a potentially good scene from several different angles with different lenses and at different times of the day so you can maximise sales with different libraries.

Many libraries require a sizeable submission to see if you meet their criteria and often reject photographers for no good reason. Try submitting work to smaller or up and coming stock libraries. Alamy and similar libraries will usually accept work as long as you meet their strict quality guidelines.

Insider view

TIREE DAWSON

Tony West

TRAVEL PHOTOGRAPHER

Q) How did you get started?
I have a passion for travel, always have had, and combined with an interest in photography the two went hand in hand. I was in my early twenties when I discovered there were people interested in buying and publishing my images.

Q) How do you make a full-time job out of travel photography?
I think you need to target a specialised market. Taking your camera to a nice location and peddling your wares on your return, well, those days are gone. These days you need to think who might be buying your photography, think about the specialist subjects they want you to cover and then target those markets before you go. The subjects you may need to photograph could be many and varied.

Q) How difficult is it to make a living from travel photography?
I think it's extremely difficult to make a living out of just pure travel photography. So many more people are into photography and the quality is excellent. Companies use members of staff who may be handy with a camera. In the days of film and larger formats, that work would have gone to a professional photographer. These days I find myself hired to shoot the key shots in a brochure: the cover, chapter openers, that kind of thing.

Q) What tips can you share?
I trained in graphic design and was using a lot of photography in my day-to-day work. I still do a lot of business with advertising agencies and one reasons I think my images get picked is because I consider how text might be used on the picture or areas on an image that a designer might want to use. A lot of photographers don't think about where text needs to go.

In fact, some of my pictures might look a little bit out of balance, maybe with too much sky, but that's because I've shot it with a certain use in mind. You might argue that it's easy to create areas for text through manipulation, but I believe that a busy art editor in a busy production department will choose an image that needs little to no work doing to it, every time. Delivering to brief and what's needed by the client to make their job easier is very important.

Q) Where do you find your travel photography clients?
I target companies that I know will need photography from somewhere other than where they are based. An outdoor clothing manufacturer in Holland, for example, is likely to want pictures from outside of Holland. So I approach companies like that with what I think is a good idea or concept for a travel shoot for them.

Q) How much could you potentially earn from travel photography a year?
That's a very difficult question to answer. You need to take a long-term view when it comes to income from travel photography, particularly if stock is a big part of it. Sometimes you struggle to cover your expenses, on others you earn thousands by selling images to various companies. I still make sales from a trip years down the line.

Q) Give us some idea of the financial investment and return?
If I want to travel light, I take three 'workhorse' lenses: a Canon EF 70-200mm f/2.8L telephoto, a Canon EF 16-35mm f/2.8L wide-angle and a Canon EF 50mm f/1.4. I use a Canon EOS-1Ds MkIII and an EOS 5D. Then there's the accessories: flash, tripod, filters. Travel costs and accommodation all add up too. You've got to cover all those costs before you start to make any money. I try to set off on a trip with enough potential sales lined up that at least cover my expenses.

Q) What percentage of your working life is spent travelling and taking photographs?
For a two week trip, there's probably six to eight weeks of planning and selling: making calls, asking what a client is looking for, chasing product samples to take on the trip, researching the location, planning the itinerary. And then there's all the market awareness I need. I spend hours looking at what other people are doing, what's selling, what works.

After the trip I'll need to spend hours editing the pictures, sorting them for clients, maybe doing a little bit of manipulation and by that time, I'm thinking about the next trip. In with all that might be a couple of days a week shooting local travel and tourism material.

Q) What type of personality do you need to be a travel photographer?
I've come across introverted methodical types who only shoot architecture and landscapes, through to extroverts who are fantastic with people. I'm, hopefully, somewhere in the middle but I don't think you need to be a particular type of personality.
www.tonywestphoto.co.uk

PROFITABLE PROJECTS

Help fund your photography passion by trying out some of our pocket-money ideas

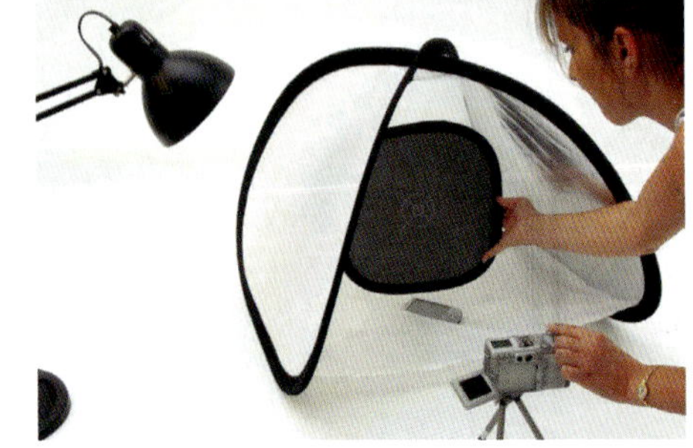

GETTING TO GRIPS WITH STOCK PHOTOGRAPHY

Selling stock is a minefield of keywords, demanding agency standards and fluctuating income, but understanding the business and what agencies are looking for can help you make a lot of money

FIRST OF ALL, let's define stock photography. Stock photography isn't usually shot with one application in mind, it could have many. A stock photograph is one that could be used in a hundred different ways by a hundred different clients. A great stock shot could make you a lot of money.

Most stock photography is sold over the internet, a practice that has revolutionised the industry. iStockphoto claims to have been the first to set up a credits-based trading platform and grew fast. The established photo agency Getty Images saw it coming and bought iStockphoto in 2006. Computer giant Microsoft had already snapped up Getty rival Corbis.

The internet has opened the door to stock revenue for thousands of photographers and brought in thousands of new clients. You could take a fabulous photograph and have it online and on sale in a couple of hours. A small business owner in Carlisle could find your image and download it for a brochure ten minutes later and it might only cost a tenner. You'd get half but there might be another fiver coming your way from a bloke in Newcastle – Australia.

So online stock photography agencies, or microstock agencies as they are known, have driven down the cost of stock photography but massively expanded the market. There are people buying images today who wouldn't have known how to 20 years ago, let alone have been able to afford it. And there are thousands of photographers serving that market, each for a very small slice of a very big pie.

Critics of microstock will tell you that its flaw is that the best photos will start to appear everywhere and clients lose the individuality that come with bespoke images. I have to tell you that this part of the market doesn't care. The business person in Carlisle couldn't care less if the image is also used in Australia. If they are in financial services, they probably don't care if a similar image is used by a dentist across the street, either. And the sheer volume of new material appearing on the sites every day helps with the churn.

Every stock agency has its own way of encouraging submissions, although when you have a go, it doesn't always feel like encouragement. Standards for submissions are very high among the biggest agencies. You will have many of your images rejected and you won't always get a full explanation why.

Simon Moran is photography director at iStockphoto and he is a bit more helpful: "Compression, poor lighting and over-filtering are the biggest problems. Years ago digital noise was a big issue but we now find that virtually all current DSLRs are fine at least up to ISO 800 as long as you get the exposure right in-camera. Shooting in Raw gives some degree of latitude to fixing mistakes in post-production, but you can only push pixels so far before they start to degrade. Your best bet is to get the exposure right at the lowest ISO you need.

> "If you want to make a lot of money from stock photography, you have to take it seriously. Treat it like a second home for your random images"

"We have many checks in the inspection process with constant feedback, updates and refresher sessions for our team of over 110 photography inspectors around the world. This rigour has helped make our collection stand out; designers know they are buying quality.

"We're inspecting just shy of 250,000 images a month right now and we accept 60-62% of those to sell. Of the files that are rejected, more than 50% will be resubmitted and accepted after the member has fixed the issues we've pointed out to them."

We asked Tom Hind, European head of content at Getty Images, what he thinks sells. "You'd be surprised!" he says. "We cater for such a range of buyers that we see a huge variety of imagery being licensed. What works for an agency today may be what's appropriate for a corporate client tomorrow. For example, backlit imagery was seen as fairly edgy a few years ago and now it's a much more mainstream choice. We work with our photographers to try and make sure they're aware of subjects and techniques that are in demand, or likely to be."

Catherine Bischoff, contributor and industry relations manager at Corbis, chooses her words carefully: "We are looking for professional images of business and finance, medicine, architecture, beauty, social issues and special events. We carefully select work of animals, agriculture, nature and travel.

"Photographers need to keep in mind that their work must be generally in demand. Our commercial photography collections are aligned around defined customer creative needs and most clearly reflect our ambition of delivering to customers a compelling spectrum of useful, inspiring and high-value photography. Our editorial photography includes commercial-ready images with high-aesthetic appeal, images with a strong breadth and depth, as well as content-specific images that can only be interpreted literally, and our news images focus on longer lead stories and are well curated."

So if you want to make a lot of money from stock photography, you have to take it seriously. Treat it like a second home for random images cluttering up your hard drive and you might pick up the odd sale, but the big money goes to the dedicated.

Simon Moran again: "Over the past decade, iStockphoto has allowed tens of thousands of hobbyist photographers to showcase and make money from their talents. Nowadays, a file is downloaded from iStockphoto every second of every day. With this kind of demand for their work, many members earn hundreds per month. A young US photographer has paid his way through medical school and was even able to buy a house with money earned through iStock. At the very top, a number of contributors earn six figures annually. A much bigger group is earning thousands each month."

Getty makes even grander claims, but Tom Hind is at pains to explain what it takes. "Some of our more successful contributors can achieve over six figures in revenue a month," he says. "In an average month we have up to 500 photographers achieving revenue of over five figures. They treat stock photography as a

business, and approach it with focus and determination. They are confident in their own vision and are persistent. They understand the market and create a point of difference for themselves through their visual approach. When this happens they can also get commissions based on the work they have online with us."

Earning potential of an image will depend partly on the way it is licensed. Getty offers two main licensing routes, 'rights managed' and 'royalty-free'. Rights-managed places more restrictions on the client. Size, position, duration of use and geographic distribution will all affect the price of an image and a client can even buy exclusivity. Rights-managed tends to suit the most specialised or individualistic images and prices tend to be higher. This is very similar to the traditional photo library business model dating back to before the days of online transactions.

Getty also operates the royalty-free model, similar to iStockphoto and many others. Royalty-free allows a client to use an image many times on many different projects without having to pay any more money. However, the rights to an image are not transferable and are non-exclusive.

Not everybody is a fan of microstock agencies. Gwyn Headley is managing director of fotoLibra, an agency that believes in maintaining the value of good photography so that more of its contributors can make a sustainable living. One of fotoLibra's services is its regular Picture Call emails sent out to members, listing specific photo requests with deadlines, sometimes allowing photographers time to go out and shoot to order. Use isn't guaranteed, but chances are improved.

"By uploading images to microstock agencies you are effectively cutting your own throat, and the throats of your fellow photographers," says Gwyn. "20 cents a sale? Come on — aren't you worth more than that?" According to fotoLibra, some areas of photography are saturated, including birds and flowers without their binomial names, trains and Big Ben. Gwyn doesn't want to see any more sunsets. "No! No! Please, no!" That'll be a 'no', then.

His advice to potential contributors is as useful as it is entertaining. It sums up fotoLibra's leftfield approach to stock photography: "Don't upload a dozen pictures of one thing from different angles. Choose only the best. Don't take pictures you hope to sell to art reference publishers on a dull, grey, drizzly day. The most important element of any photograph is not the exposure, not the subject, not the length of your lens, not the focusing, not the cost of your kit: IT'S THE KEYWORDS!"

Gwyn Headley might be taking a different approach to selling photography online, but that last piece of advice proves he knows what he's talking about. Understanding the power of keywords and how clients might be searching for images is enormously helpful. And despite their other differences, he'll get no argument from the microstock boys on that point.

Stock libraries to try

- **Alamy:** www.alamy.com
- **Fotolibra:** www.fotolibra.com
- **Getty Images:** www.gettyimages.com
- **iStockPhoto:** www.istockphoto.com
- **Jupiterimages:** www.jupiterimages.co.uk
- **Shutter Stock:** www.shutterstock.com

HOW TO MAKE MONEY FROM GREETING CARDS

Breaking into the thriving greetings card industry is a tempting prospect for any photographer, and with digital printing it's easier than ever to dip a toe in the water. We show you how to get your images noticed

NO OTHER NATION LOVES sending greeting cards as much as us Brits. We buy more cards per head than any other country, giving us the most successful industry in the world. It generates a whopping £1.47bn a year and relies on fresh content, so publishers are always on the look out for new images to use. Greeting cards are therefore a fabulous way for creative photographers to make money and to have images seen around the world. So where do you start?

The first thing you need to do is come up with some great imagery, and this can be absolutely anything. Landscapes, floral still-lifes and macro shots seem the most obvious choice, but there are as many types of photographic greeting cards as there are genre of cards. Visit local greeting card shops, art stores or chains like WH Smith, John Lewis and Hallmark to get an insight into what images are already in the market and the quality the different types of retailers are expecting. Take a note of the publisher's details on the back of the card and then go to their website looking for the tucked-away sections, usually entitled 'information for artists' or 'artist submission', for details on how to supply images. Be sure to follow them to the letter.

Publishers work a long way in advance, so you will need to plan in advance too, for instance shooting spring pictures for Easter and Mother's Day the year before you submit them. Paperhouse publishers, for instance, secured their 2012 Christmas material in June 2011 and will be looking to secure their Mothers Day range for 2013 in early 2012. While any image could potentially make a card, you'll have a better chance if you create your shots appropriately for occasions like Easter, Mother's and Father's Day and Valentine's Day. Birthday cards and blank everyday cards sell better than any other type, but don't forget about the other genres: anniversaries, new home, new job, just because, sympathy cards – the list is endless. It's worth remembering too though that 85% of greeting card consumers are women and they tend to buy based on colour or if an image triggers an emotional connection.

When shooting images, do vertical and horizontal format to give publishers options – square formats are also popular. Make sure you send images that are at least 300dpi so that publishers can accurately judge the image quality.

"Most publishers are looking for a distinctive style, creative edge, market awareness and professional quality," explains Nick Walker, the product manager at Paperhouse, which publishes ranges for National Geographic and the Royal Horticultural Society. "One of our new photographers is Assaf Frank (www.bs-factory.com), a brilliant floral photographer, but what sets him apart is his Photoshop skills. He tends to offer ten or 20 versions of the same shot that have been edited differently giving us a wide selection to pick from."

Normally publishers will get back to you within a few months if they're interested in using the images to discuss rights and agree a fee. Each company has a different way of operating; some will pay an up-front fee and a small royalty while others only pay a royalty, which on average for an independent publisher is around 5%. It can be a lot less for larger publishers though, as you'll normally be dealing with large volumes, so while the percentage is smaller the overall amount can be a lot more. It varies dramatically, but you should always make sure you get a contract and a licensing agreement and NEVER give up your copyright!

> "With digital printing, publishers no longer have to gamble a fortune on large print runs before they can get an order from a retailer"

Self-publishing

For those of you thinking of cutting out the middle-man and giving self-publishing a go, be prepared for a full-time job. If your passion is photography and not publishing, you'll find you'll spend more time on the business side of greeting cards than behind the camera being creative. Producing the images and cards isn't a problem; it's selling them and getting them into stores that's the real headache.

Jargon buster

- **Licensing fee:** The publisher has exclusive rights to an image for an agreed period. The average rate is £150 per image.
- **Flat fee:** A one-off payment that gives the publisher unlimited ownership of the picture. The fee is normally £150-£250.
- **Royalty deal:** You receive a percentage (normally 5%) of the wholesale price for every card sold. Some publishers offer a licensing fee of £100 plus a 3% royalty.
- **Sales agent:** If you decide to take the self-publishing route, you need a network of agents that can to help sell your images to retailers all over the world. They work on a commission basis.
- **Distributors:** They have a network of sales agents and are responsible for selling, marketing and distributing your card range.

"The industry is wonderful, it's really creative and dynamic but it's not growing, which means it's a mature market with more and more people coming in," explains Sharon Little, chief executive of the Greeting Card Association. "And now with digital printing, publishers no longer have to gamble a fortune on large print runs before they can get an order from a retailer. You can print quantities as small as one card at a time and work on a print-on-demand basis. Consequently the market's become flooded with very small publishers who are all against each other and the larger publishers," she adds. That's not to say you can't make a go of it though.

The best way to get started is to pick an area like the Lake District or Yorkshire Dales and get 20 or so cracking shots, have them printed up in small quantities and presented well, then get around the area's local stores and work on a print-on-demand basis. Get your order, get it printed, get paid for it and then work on getting your next order – pick stores that you can keep supplying easily. It's worth investing in a small catalogue of your range too, or at least printing off a sheet of paper with thumbnails of your designs, with your terms and conditions, order forms and sample cards, to take around shops and to see what people think. Once you've established your name locally, slowly expand it to nearby areas and regions. Photographic cards tend to get sold to independent retailers for between 60p

ALL IMAGES: JAMES GUILLIAM

and 90p, depending on the quality of the print and finish, then the retailer will give it a 100% mark-up. So although you may not make much of a profit at first, once you start doing large orders, your print costs will fall and your profits will grow. Larger retailers might even ask you to supply two orders free of charge on a sale or return basis before they commit to selling your range. It's a big gamble, as you have to invest in huge volumes and risk the cards not selling and being returned to you, but if they do sell you could stand to make a lot of money from your photography. Other investments are when you start displaying your range at trade fairs, as it could cost you around £2,000, but it's well worth it as you're putting yourself in front of retailers from all around the country. It's also where you meet other publishers and sales agents as well as making contacts that could see your images distributed across the world. You're better off waiting until your range features a minimum of 50 different cards before you look to display at trade shows though, as sales agent rarely look twice at you with anything less and their help is vital if you want to expand your business. But whether you're self-publishing or licensing images, the quality and creativity of your pictures is what will set you apart from the rest, so keep your images fresh and different and look to launch new ranges at least four times a year to keep your work competitive. ■

Recommended resources

The Greeting Card Association
- www.greetingcardassociation.org.uk

UK Trade fairs
- www.autumnfair.com
- www.homeandgift.co.uk
- www.progressivegreetingslive.co.uk
- www.springfair.com
- www.topdrawer.co.uk

Printers
- www.bonusprint.co.uk
- www.centreprint.com
- www.facemediagroup.com
- www.moo.com
- www.theimagingcentre.co.uk

Publishers
- www.abacuscards.co.uk
- www.artindesign.co.uk
- www.almanac.co.uk
- www.hallmark.co.uk
- www.images-editions.co.uk
- www.paperhouse.co.uk
- www.spottedrichard.co.uk

Case study

James Guilliam

JAMES GUILLIAM MAKES HIS LIVING FROM GREETING CARDS AND OTHER PAPER PRODUCTS, LICENSING IMAGES TO PUBLISHERS AND STOCK LIBRARIES. HE TELLS US HOW HE GOT STARTED, HOW PROFITABLE IT'S BEEN THUS FAR, AND OFFERS INVALUABLE ADVICE FOR ANYONE WANTING TO TAKE THE SAME ROUTE

"I used to work as a photographer in my early days, but wanting a change I bought a flower and garden centre in my mid-20s. It turned out that the seed company we used also owned the greeting card publisher Abacus Cards, and they were trying to get garden centres to sell their photographic greeting cards alongside their seeds. When I started selling them and a few years later, I decided to try my hand at doing my own. I took some pictures of flowers we had in the shop and sent them off to a greeting card company called Images & Editions and they immediately came back asking how big my range was and how many more could I supply. That was 15 years ago and I'm still earning a full-time income from it.

"It's difficult to say how much I earn because it varies so much. If I send an image to a publisher and it gets used once as a Mother's Day card, I might only get £50 for it, but I have some cards on the Everyday list that have earned me thousands of pounds. When you enter into an agreement with a publisher, usually it allows them to use your images on their 'paper products' and this could include anything from notebooks, greeting cards and fridge magnets to gift cards, posters and even wrapping paper. And of course every time it sells you pick up a royalty. My royalties range from 1.5% of the net price to 10%, so it can be a huge difference. I sell more images worldwide through the Photolibrary Group, which is based in Australia, than I do direct to publishers, but the royalties I receive direct are greater than I receive from card sales via the Photolibrary. Greeting cards can also spill over into calendars; I've had calendar companies see a card and want to licence the image. I've even had my images wrapped around candles in America after having seen them on cards, and then this had led to jigsaws and drink coasters.

"It's a wonderful way to make a little extra pocket money, and publishers are always looking out for new images, but you can't expect an instant return. I had images signed off for Mother's Day 2012 that were shot in spring 2010, so that's two years since they've been taken. Then, providing they're selected and put out to sale in 2012, it will be at least another six months before I see a fee. They've got to be sold, then the shops have to wait for any returned cards to be taken off the sales, then it's another quarter before you see a revenue coming in. You're looking at a minimum of two and half years from when you take an occasion picture to seeing any royalty. However, it can be quicker for Everyday cards.

"Your best chance is to study what's already out there in stores and try to find a new angle or creative twist, otherwise if you just send in similar pictures to what's already out there, you'll be struggling up against the established photographers who already have ranges and a supply-and-demand relationship with publishers."

THE MOBILE STUDIO PORTRAITIST

Setting up a mobile studio in a shopping centre to offer children and family portraits is not that difficult, which is probably why so many that do it don't want to talk to us about it

YOU CAN TELL HOW competitive a business is by how few people want to talk to you about it.

For many years, the world's finest photographers have been sharing their secrets with us. They've told us how they use their lights, how their favourite lenses work, what they do to get 'the look' – all valuable information that they are happy to share, possibly in the knowledge that it's also quite difficult and very few readers will actually pull it off.

But for the last few weeks we've been trying to get shopping centre portrait photographers to talk. You've seen them, pitched up in some retail atrium with display boards, a roll of background paper and a pouffe. They catch passing trade: mums and tots, sometimes a family group. They shoot a selection of pictures, getting the customer to pay for prints up front before supplying them through the post.

Well despite our best efforts, and we've tried pretty hard, none of the ones we asked would participate in this feature. But that's not going to stop us writing it and sharing their secrets with you.

There are no secrets. They use two medium-power flash heads with brollies or softboxes. For single portraits they use a main light in front, high and slightly to one side, and a modelling light, lower, on the other side and maybe slightly further away to save them turning the power down. You've read about this studio lighting technique a million times in this magazine. For groups they move the lights out a bit and lift the modelling light to give a strong, clean, even light across the faces. The serious ones may have a third light on the plain white background paper.

Their lenses are short telephotos: 50mm for APS-C sensor cameras, 85mm or 105mm for full-frame jobbies. Large maximum apertures for fast and accurate focusing, these guys don't mess about.

'The look' is the one that has caused independent professional portrait photographers' hearts to sink for a few years now. The look is the 'Venture' look: high-key informal portraits with a clean white background, plenty of interaction between the subjects; happy family snaps with a daring crop or composition.

The 'Venture' look has been made famous by the high street chain of the same

ALL IMAGES ISTOCK PHOTO

"If you can't walk up to 200 strangers a day and try to get them to sit for you, forget it. If you get disheartened by ten straight knock-backs, this is not for you"

name, which according to many website reviews, has left a lot of people feeling it is high in price and low on customer service. You can't deny the appeal of its style of photography, though, and huge enlargements of the company's work dominate people's living rooms all over the country.

I couldn't get any of the practitioners of this 'art' to talk about their business. Probably because it's so easy, many readers could actually pull it off.

Except.

Except that the real art to successful mobile studio work in public spaces is fantastic people skills and shameless salesmanship. If you can't walk up to 200 strangers a day, try to persuade them to sit for you, stop their children crying, make them relax and smile and get a commitment from them before they leave, forget it. If you get disheartened by ten straight knock-backs, this is not for you.

Maybe that's why the best of them don't like to share their 'secrets' and encourage others. They're all born salesmen and women, who in our experience tend to be ambitious, driven, competitive and maybe just a little bit paranoid.

If you're reading this and really do have all the personal qualities to make it work, we're surprised you're not doing it already. Or maybe you are and you just politely refused our request to take part, like the photographer who said to me: "Why would I want to encourage one of your readers to get into this game, and have them turn up next week on my patch?"

What you need

- Plain white background paper with stands. Starter kits from about £200.
- **A three-light studioflash system with umbrellas and/or softboxes. Starter kits from about £400.**
- Professional flash meter. From £150.
- **Full-frame DSLR such as the Nikon D700 from around £1,800.**
- Prime portrait lens such as the Nikon 85mm f/1.4D lens, from about £900.
- **Big screen laptop computer to display images instantly, starting from about £500.**
- A pair of stools and a counter (with bowl of sweets to entice customers).
- **Spare batteries, memory cards and a live link to the laptop so you can shoot tethered.**
- Multi-socket extension cables and gaffer/duct tape to secure cords to the floor.
- **Fabric-covered display boards for signs and samples fixed with Velcro or similar. £100 or more new, £100 or less on eBay.**
- Leaflets/flyers for handing out or pre-session marketing distribution, great deals from local printers.
- **Mobile PDQ/credit card processing machine. Charges are based on the size of business, number and size of transactions or chosen payment plan, but £15 per month for the handset, 2% on credit card transactions and 20p for debit card payments is an educated estimate. Try Cardsave.net (0808 149 5309) which will send a regional representative round to talk about your needs and advise you on the best plan for you and your business. There are also many other providers that can be found online via an internet search.**

What you need to do

Pull together everything listed in the 'what you need' list and practise, practise, practise. Making adjustments on the fly should be second nature. By the time you hit the streets, that flash meter should be all-but redundant because you will know the flash distance/power/lens aperture correlation instinctively.

Work with a professional laboratory to come up with a range of prints and products. Choose a range of sizes, have samples made up for display and work out the end cost to the customer. Your laboratory will be able to advise you on what sizes, finishes and mounts are selling well.

Plan your venues carefully. Shopping centres manage their own promotional space or work with companies like SpaceandPeople to organise it for them.

Dawn Clarke, SpaceandPeople's marketing manager, told us: "Shopping centres work very well for photographic companies as people are in a buying frame of mind. They are often in family groups and are relaxed so are more open to interaction and to offers that are put to them whilst browsing.

"Over 2.4 billion visits are made to shopping centres across the UK every year by 82% of adults and many shopping centres have a weekly footfall of over 250,000.

"We have a team dedicated to temporary traders and are able to give advice as to the best shopping centre for them, the best site within the venue to suit their needs, logistics, health and safety and legal requirements. Because we deal with venues throughout the UK, we can arrange for the company to retail in multiple venues.

"The cost of renting promotional space can vary dramatically depending on the centre and its footfall and demographics. Weekly rates can range from £500-£3,000 per week (although there will always be some that are above or below this). It is usually more cost effective to arrange the space for a week, rather than a few days because the daily rates are typically a lot higher, pro rata."

Make sure you have an electricity supply.

Just relying on passing trade might be a bit of a risk. Look at distributing leaflets telling people exactly where and when you are going to be working in the area. The flyers should feature your best work and information about any package deals and special offers. You can pay to have your leaflets inserted into local newspapers or delivered by post to all houses in specific areas. Spend some time working out which parts of town your customers live in.

Work out a system for ordering prints and decide how you want to handle payments. I think you should be as transparent as possible, with clearly displayed prices and easy-to-understand processes. You need to be able to capture customers' information, order details and cash or card payments. They will expect professional-looking paperwork, showing a permanent address and phone number, confirming what they understand to be the 'contract' they have with you.

If you're feeling really confident, you could simply shoot for free on the day, posting the results on a secure website, from which customers can order prints and products online. You will give each customer a card telling them how to access the site and when they will be able to view their images. The images need to be protected with a watermark to prevent them being copied from the website. The risk is that you will shoot hundreds of photos during the day, spend all night putting them online, but take-up of prints could be very low.

On the days of the shoot, get there early and set up. Dress smartly and go about your business with a smile. Work hard. Be nice.

If a partner or friend can help, even better. Mums and kids might respond better to a woman when asked to consider a portrait sitting. Having one person concentrating on the photography while the other deals with waiting customers will be ideal when you're busy and company for you when you're not. There will also be somebody to hold the fort when you need the loo.

HOW TO MAKE MONEY FROM A MARKET STALL

Want to supplement your main income by earning extra money from your images but don't know where to start? Why not try setting up a market stall: your own dedicated weekend store to sell your pictures from. Although the investment of time and set-up costs aren't minimal, the rewards more than make up for it

Market stalls have a huge advantage over shops. Whereas people probably only go into a shop if they are interested in buying, on a stall, you get a lot of different people walking past so even those who didn't head out with the intention of viewing your work may see something that catches their eye. Running a market stall isn't as strenuous as you might think, but it's certainly not a venture you embark on a whim: it takes commitment, time, a financial investment and, of course, a good selection of photography. However, once you've made the initial investment, you could make a profit in a matter of weeks.

Doing your market research is an important first step. Find out what local markets attract the most tourists or cater to the arts and crafts. A useful resource is the National Market Traders Federation (www.nmtf.co.uk) as it features a list of markets and what they sell in your area, so you can find one that's appropriate. Before contacting the market manager of the council for a licence and a pitch, visit the market a few times on different days to scope out any competition and to see what days attract the most people. While you'll be catering to locals who want to buy prints, you'll make many more sales if you also target local tourism too. You'll find generic images of places like London (Big Ben, London Underground signs etc) can sell very well, as do prints of the local area where the market is situated – it's funny how people will hang photos of their local area on their walls, but they do.

To work on a market stall, you at minimum need public liability insurance, which costs around £70 a year. If you join the NMTF (memberships start from £96) you get free insurance, including product, public and employers liability among many other benefits. Other set-up costs might then include equipment to display and hold your prints, clips to secure your canopy and sheets to cover the prints when it's raining, but that shouldn't set you back more than £100. If you choose to make your own frames, which involve buying a mitre saw and mouldings, this could push your costs up to around £1,000. However, it means you won't be giving your profits away every time you want an image framed and you could also reap the costs back by offering framing as an extra service to your customers. Most people feel they're getting a better deal if they get a frame included in the price, and as a result can sell really well. Canvasses are also popular as are unframed, but mounted, prints. When it comes to printing, you might want to consider doing this yourself at home using a quality inkjet printer until your sales start to take off and you can negotiate with a specialist printing company for printing in bulk.

Every market is different and rent varies dramatically, depending on whether it's privately-owned or council-owned. Typically, you can expect to pay about £90 per week to cover a weekday and a Saturday market. At some markets, you get your own stall but at others, you may just get an empty pitch. When it's the latter, you then have the extra expense of hiring a marquee. Avoid this option if you can as it will eat in to your profits.

> "You have to be quite hardy as in this country it can get very cold and wet. You also have to have a real passion about what you are trying to sell"

Over time you can learn what sells best and how to organise your stall to maximise sales, so don't expect to be racking it until you've invested time into understanding how to all works. To give you a head start though, here are a few tips: place popular images at the front to draw people in and then, when you get talking to them, show them other images that you think they might like. Also, people will walk past a stall from both directions so angle your prints so customers can get a good view of them regardless of the direction they come from. If you also do portrait photography, hand out leaflets and have examples of your work readily available. You'll be surprised by how many people book you off the back of seeing your work on the stall.

With everyone's stalls next to each other, you can't run over and hijack someone's attention, so you have to wait until they're at least looking in your direction before you engage them. Asking if there are any images that are catching their eye or if there are any colours that they are searching for prints to match up to is one way. It's best not to give the hard sell with photography as it's so subjective, allow people time to mull over their decision. This is why having a website is so important as it allows people to see your work without having to revisit the market to help them make a decision. While you can invest in a simple site but the likes of Clikpic, you can also access free websites from www.gbbo.co.uk (Getting British Businesses Online).

Having a simple pricing structure will make it easy for your customers. Selling prints in either small, medium or large is a good start, with a small (10x12in) print starting from £10 is considered reasonable. If you then move to framed prints, a good starting point is £50 for a 12x18in print. While you can make a generous profit of around 90%, if you do the framing yourself, per print remember you also need to factor in your time spent working on the stall.

According to our case study photographer, Anthony Lewis, he makes on average between £400 and £500 a week for two days trading. Quite impressive we think, although not every week is that profitable so you have to be prepared to take the good with the bad as success depends on many things, not least the weather and the time of year as this can effect how many people visit the market and how many are locals or the more seller-friendly tourists.

You have to be outgoing to do well in this business – quite hardy too as in this country it can get very wet and cold. You also have to have a real passion for what you are trying to sell. If you're the sort of person that can't get out of bed in the morning, then you're not going to do very well. Finally, you'll be lifting things all day, so a good level of fitness is definitely needed – or at least someone to help.

Market stall: Facts & figures

- ✔ **Set-up costs:** Around £900
- ✔ **Weekly expenses:** £90 per week (rent)
- ✔ **Other expenses:** £70 per year (insurance)
- ✔ **Weekly turnover:** £400-£500 (two days)
- ✔ **Average profit per image:** 90%
- ✔ **Average hours worked per day:** Ten

ALL IMAGES ANTHONY LEWIS

Case study

Anthony Lewis

AMATEUR PHOTOGRAPHER AND MARKET STALL HOLDER

"I started working on the market around two years ago, after being made redundant from my job in I.T. Having been a keen amateur photographer for a number of years, I set aside a few months to work out the best way to make money from my images. I had been selling my photos in a shop, but that wasn't going too well. The market was close by and I thought perhaps I'd have more of a chance selling my images on the market stall than in a shop.

"As soon as I started selling my images on a market stall, I was making a profit. They were selling really well, really quickly, which built my confidence up and is the reason I've stuck with it. Every month is different but, on average, half my income comes from selling at the market, while the other half comes from portrait and product shoots that I've been commissioned to do, often off the back of seeing my images on the stall. I've also had customers ask me to frame other prints that they have too.

"Every week is different, but on average a week's takings (that's two days on the market) is between £400 and £500 – but you've got to remember it's taken nearly two years to grow to this stage and there are times when I won't make anything like that. It's early mornings and long days too: I'm up at 6.45am to be at the market by 8.30am to get a pitch so I can start trading from 10am - 6pm. It's worth it though."

PROFIT FROM SHOWCASING YOUR IMAGES

Mounting your own exhibition is a fantastic feeling and may even make you a bit of cash, but it doesn't have to be in a gallery: cafés, restaurants and hotels are great platforms for selling your work

WHEN YOU BELIEVE your prints are perfect and your images are beautiful, powerful or thought-provoking, you should think about showing them to a gallery. An exhibition of your work can do wonders for your profile and confidence, and you might sell a few prints and/or win a commission or two.

Don't imagine for a minute that organising an exhibition is going to be easy. Galleries are very picky, setting their standards high to protect their reputations and keep their visitors happy. The biggest galleries are the fussiest (sorry, most discerning) and you might have to wait a while to be told your photographs aren't good enough. We would all love to see our work in The Photographers' Gallery in London, but exhibitions are scheduled two years in advance and most are 'invitation-only'. The Photographers' Gallery doesn't respond to unsolicited proposals but it does hold regular portfolio reviews and welcomes news from photographers via email. Something to aim for, perhaps.

Similarly with the Association of Photographers (AOP) Gallery, which could set you back as much as £2,500 a week for the hire of gallery space. You didn't think that because you're paying you can exhibit any old tat either, did you? The requirements are standard fare: fantastic images, artistic statement, biography, press cuttings and contact details. But they are generous enough to only take a 30% commission on any sales, unlike most galleries whose cut is 50%.

Impressions Gallery in Bradford also plans its exhibitions two to three years in advance. It sends out guidelines for unsolicited proposals to help photographers adhere to the required format. If you do get accepted, you could be one of the photographers who sell limited edition signed prints on the Impressions Gallery website for £250.

The Bristol Gallery exhibits all types of art, including work by the renowned local photographer Beezer. Holly Lopez, gallery manager, described the approach for offering your work: "We would ask the artist to submit some images and a CV to the gallery via email. We periodically assess our submissions and contact any artists whose work we feel would fit with our exhibition schedule. We would then hang the work in an exhibition and we typically take a 50% sales commission."

If this all feels like a bit of a stretch for you, there are lots of provincial galleries that do exactly the same thing on a smaller scale. A growing number of pubs, cafés and restaurants are also making wall space available to local artists. While you can't expect the same exposure or high-priced sales as you get from the major galleries, it's a great way to boost your local profile and have your work seen by different people everyday, plus you can earn some cash in the process. A lot of independent business owners are very open to the idea of selling images as they're getting free art work on their walls, plus you can offer a small commission on any prints they sell. Small establishments might be happy for a 10% commission on prints but you should be prepared to negotiate and offer no more than 20%. Gallery commissions start from 30% and they have dedicated staff selling your work. Make sure the business owner agrees to pay the cost of any damage to your work displayed on their walls too.

When choosing your images, start with local scenes that local people and visitors

"Small establishments might be happy for 10% commission on prints but you should be prepared to negotiate and offer no more than 20%"

Key contacts & resources

- **The Photographers' Gallery:** London, www.photonet.org.uk
- **Impressions Gallery:** Bradford, www.impressions-gallery.com
- **The Association of Photographers Gallery:** London, gallery.the-aop.org
- **The Bristol Gallery:** email knowledge@thebristolgallery.co.uk
- **Sylvia Adams:** www.apersonalviewphotography.co.uk

can relate to. A photograph of Brooklyn Bridge will look out of place in a Somerset tea room, but a cider orchard at dawn could sell like, erm, hot cakes. Print quality is vital, so don't cut corners with the product and think carefully about framing. A professional-quality frame that complements the image, the venue and most customers' home décor is best.

This level is a true 'pocket money' venture. You might only subsidise your hobby with income you get from the café but having your images on display in public will give you a thrill. And that's probably the best reason for giving it a go.

Case study

Sylvia Adams

LANDSCAPE AND EQUINE PHOTOGRAPHER

When a Northamptonshire pub was renovated by the new landlord, Sylvia Adams mentioned how nice one of her local landscapes would look on the wall. The landlord agreed so Sylvia came back with a 16x20in print of the nearby abandoned stately home at Lyveden New Bield. She also gave him some horseracing prints for the games room. The landlord framed and hung the prints and now keeps a stash of Sylvia's business cards behind the bar for anybody who enquires about the photographs.

She charges £75 for a signed print. "I have an Epson A3+ printer and only ever use genuine Epson inks for maximum longevity, but I explain to customers that, as for all types of printed art, they must avoid hanging them in sunlight," says Sylvia. "I cut my own deep double mounts before carefully putting them in frames from Zanart in Kettering."

The pub doesn't take any commission for sales, the landlord's just pleased to have the images. Back in 2005 Sylvia raised £1,600 for a charity trek by selling hand-made greetings cards. They were sold in the local shop, which was how the pub came to know about Sylvia's work. A member of staff in another pub took a fancy to one of Sylvia's pictures, so Sylvia promised her a free print in return for a few sales. In August, Sylvia's work will be hanging in a tea room in the village of Aldwinkle and Sylvia will pay the tea room 10% of any sales during that month. Her pictures then move to the café at Bosworth's Garden Centre in Burton Latimer, and for every print sold during September, a donation will go to charity.

It's all going very well for Sylvia. She's very busy with all types of photography but the tranquil landscapes she takes on her early morning walks with her dog are providing a steady income and growing recognition. She loves horses, and her equestrian photos, hanging in the local animal feeds store and offices have brought commissions to photograph animals.

Right now, she's probably most excited about her work appearing in a touring exhibition organised by The Photographic Angle, a charity that organises free exhibitions in vacant space around the country. "A representative from The Photographic Angle gave a talk at my camera club and encouraged us to submit work via the website," explains Sylvia. "They chose some of my travel work and that will be seen all over the country, so who knows what will come of that."

MAKE EBAY WORK FOR YOU

eBay has revolutionised online buying and selling for consumers and businesses alike, and offers great potential for photographers. Plan it right and you can make money while picking up some bargains too

SINCE ITS LAUNCH in 1995, eBay has proven to be one of the best-known and most profitable websites in the world. Offering anyone anywhere the chance to bid on and buy quite literally anything, it has proven a hit for those wishing to off-load unwanted items and get their hands on hard-to-find products. It also provides the opportunity to pick up some real bargains too. Apart from being ripped off by unscrupulous eBay members, there is very little that can be said against eBay, so if you've never tried it, we'd highly recommend giving it a go.

Becoming a member is straightforward and once you've signed up and provided your details, you can begin bidding, buying and selling items. Most major countries have their own dedicated eBay sites: eBay.co.uk for the UK, eBay.com for the USA etc, and you are able to list items for sale internationally (as well as buy from non-UK-based sellers), to appeal to a worldwide audience.

As a quick example of finding quality photo kit, we searched for a Canon EF 50mm f/1.8 lens: the six listings due to end soonest gave the chance to buy the item immediately for £69.90 (plus £10 p&p) or place bids, with the item closest to ending already at £57. Both offer decent savings.

eBay is fast and easy to use. By clicking on any item you can get further details on both it and the seller, and make a bid if you want the item. As with any auction, you should determine the maximum you want to spend and don't get carried away if another member outbids you.

As you buy and sell successfully, you'll build up and receive positive feedback from the people you deal with and this feedback score is vital. It provides other eBay members with an idea of how trustworthy you are, so ensure you provide a decent service to avoid receiving negative feedback.

Selling your photos

First things first, don't expect to make a living from selling original prints on eBay – signed or unsigned – it just won't happen. The fact is, finding high-quality photographic images on eBay isn't easy. Head to the 'Photography' category in 'Art' and you'll find the majority of images are glamour shots of 1970's Page 3 girls, nudes and other shots that in truth we were very surprised to find on eBay. While this online auction marketplace is perfect for selling most products, it seems that there is a long way to go before we can hope to be able to seriously consider selling original prints on it. The one glimmer of hope is that if you do list a high-quality image; say of a stunning landscape, it could well stand out from the crowd, as the competition is poor. But considering you have to pay for each listing (unless you start at 99p), the chances are that you'll need to pay to re-list several times before you ever sell a print. And even that's not guaranteed. Bearing in mind very few people will visit eBay to buy an image – certainly until eBay improve this area – we'd suggest you be pragmatic about the possibility of making money from selling your images on eBay.

> "eBay has proven a hit for those wishing to off-load unwanted items and get their hands on hard-to-find items. You can pick up some real bargains too"

Selling kit on eBay

If you have upgraded your camera, lens or flashgun, or have any kit that you rarely if ever use, such as spare filters, hoods, tripods or gadget bags, then listing it on eBay is a fast and easy way to exchange it for cash. Listing items doesn't take long and is quite straightforward to do, with two ways to filling in details: easy and advanced. There are also two main forms of selling on eBay. You can list an item as a Buy it Now, setting a price that you are happy with, which allows the item to be sold immediately to the first bidder. Or you can use the auction-style listing, which runs over a set period of time (one to ten days). If you like, you can set a Buy It Now price when listing the item, or set a reserve which, if not reached, prevents the item from being sold. Be aware these options all cost extra to use.

You'll need to provide basic details of the item that will appear on the listings page, upload an image, provide a description of the item that covers what it is and the condition it is in, set a price, cost of postage and the time period for the listing to run. You'll receive confirmation from eBay both when the item is listed and when/if the listing ends.

When listing items, provide an accurate description or else you may find the buyer requests a refund and may leave you negative feedback. Also, contact the buyer when you've posted the item so they're aware it's on its way.

eBay fees

eBay charges you for listing an item. It's usually free to list if the starting price is 99p or less. Should the item sell, eBay will take a small percentage of the sale. Charges are reasonable and more detail can be found on the eBay website.

How to easily shoot products to sell on eBay

Providing a decent image is essential to entice bidders to buy your item. Producing a good quality image is relatively straightforward: place your item against a white backdrop, ensure the White Balance is correct, and avoid directional light as it can cause shadows. Also bear in mind that as the file sizes that are uploaded need to be small, set your camera to shoot in JPEG, preferably at a Small/Low resolution, as this will save time preparing the image later.

With small items, you can usually get away with using a sheet of white paper near a patio door, secured to where the wall meets the floor to create a curved backdrop on which to place the item. If you plan to sell items on eBay regularly though, we'd recommend that you spend £45 on a Lastolite ePhotomaker, a white pop-up tent, with a diffuser on one side and a silver reflector on the other. It comes supplied with an EzyBalance white/grey card to ensure you set the correct White Balance for the light source used (a table lamp is suitable), as well as a mini-tripod for compact camera users. It's fast to set up and perfect for eBay.

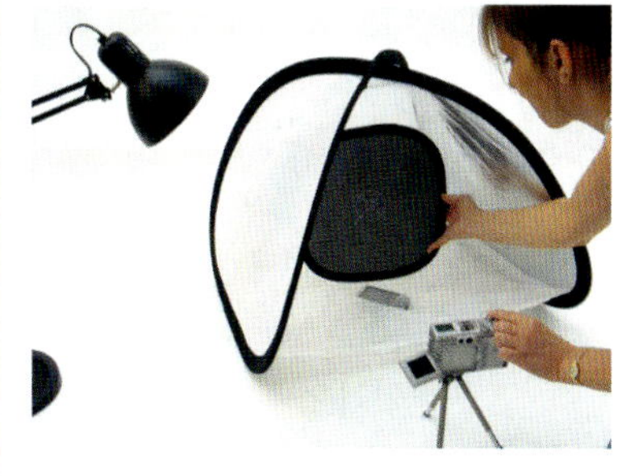

HIRE AN EBAY ASSISTANT!

If you're serious about selling photo gear on eBay, consider using a trading assistant who can sell items on your behalf. Their expertise can help sell an item for a higher price although they'll charge a fee for the service. Stuff U Sell is one of the best for shifting photo gear

Top tips for selling on eBay

- ☑ Get the basics right with your listing and it can add 10-15% to the value of your product. Text on a plain page with no pictures is the general format and can work well. But use various pictures of your product from different angles, give it a strong title and description and you could end up selling it for substantially more. Bear in mind only one image is free – creating a single multi-image JPEG in Photoshop can help you save money!
- ☑ Provide a detailed description and a decent photograph of what you're selling. Mention any damage to the product as this will build trust with the buyer.
- ☑ Write a good title. You have 55 characters and all of them are searchable terms that help them get found. Pick words you think people will use when trying to find an item.
- ☑ Time it so you're selling at a peak period so more people can see it. Aim to end listings on a Sunday night as it's the busiest time (Monday night if it's a Bank Holiday weekend). Starting Thursday and ending Sunday is a typical but an effective ten-day strategy. Or aim for a seven-day listing to start and end on a Sunday.
- ☑ For art prints, sell it as a 'Buy It Now' as you rarely get competitive bidding. But for photographic equipment, be hopeful that you have a bidding war on your hands.
- ☑ Build a good selling reputation by being accurate with your listings and providing fast and efficient delivery. Ideally dispatch within 48 hours and use Parcel2Go (www.parcel2go.com), as they're one of the best for value as they negotiate with different couriers for the best price.

Buying kit on eBay

Unless you're looking for a very specific or rare item, you can usually find what you want listed on eBay. At the time of writing, there were more than half a million items listed in the 'Photography' section of eBay.co.uk, including 19,000 digital cameras, 31,000 lenses and over 120,000 digital camera accessories. As well as lots of used items, many are new, often being sold by the eBay Store outlets of popular dealerships such as Calumet. Some great bargains can be found, so add items you really like the look of to your 'Watch list', to be sure you don't miss out. Always check a seller's feedback rating, as it's a good indication of whether they can be trusted, and don't be afraid to contact them via the 'Contact Buyer' link if you have a query. Don't assume items listed as New have a guarantee – it simply means they've never been used – so check this before bidding.

Sellers should give a good description of the item, so read this before contacting them. It should state if the item is working or faulty, lightly or heavily used, free from damage or marks and so on. If bidding on a DSLR, always ask about sensor dust and general wear and tear. If bidding on a lens, ensure optics aren't scratched or marked and are free from mould. If in doubt, don't bid. Take care if buying from overseas, such as the Far East or Africa. While prices may be lower, you may be hit with a bill for UK duty and if the item is faulty, it may not be covered under warranty. That's not to say don't buy from overseas, just be aware of any pitfalls and check all details with the seller before bidding.

eBay Apple & Android apps

If you regularly use eBay and have an iPhone or Android smart phone, or an iPad, it's worth downloading eBay's free apps. These allow you to monitor items in your watch list, bid via your mobile device, monitor how listed items are selling and reply to enquiries by potential bidders quickly and with ease.

Paypal

If you buy or sell on eBay, we'd advise you to open an account with Paypal, which provides a very smooth and one of the safest – if not the safest – online service for sending and receiving payment. Sellers incur a small fee, while both buyers and sellers benefit from Paypal's excellent protection service. The money you earn from eBay sales sit in a Paypal account and can be transferred at any time to your bank account. You can use your Paypal account to buy from eBay (and many other websites) and if your Paypal funds don't cover the total of any eBay purchase you make, Paypal will automatically retrieve the difference from your credit or debit card registered to the account. It's an excellent and trustworthy service that the eBay community respects and relies on. For further details, visit: www.paypal.co.uk

Our favourite eBay bargains

Here's items we've bought in the last year:
Canon EF 50mm f/1.8II. Used in mint condition. **£46** plus **£4** p&p. Average used price is around **£65**.
Set of Zeikos close-up filters (+1, +2, +4, +10): **£10** plus **£5** p&p. Guide price: **£40**.
Nautilus shell for still-lifes **£20** inc postage.

BUSINESS MATTERS

Learn the fundamentals of a photography business from banking to copyright law

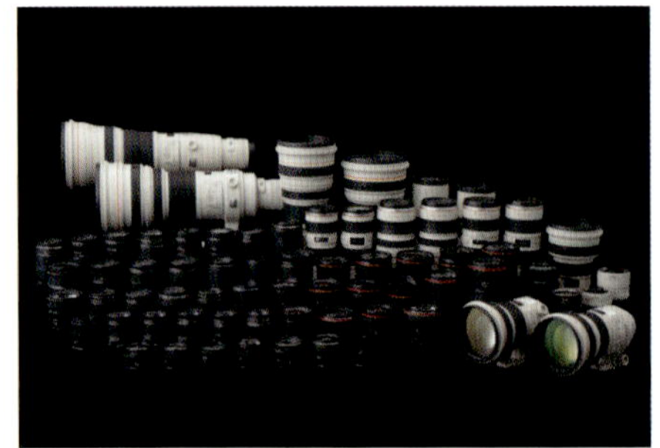

BANKING & FUNDING

You have to spend money to make money. But where can you get the money to spend and where should you put it once you've made it? Read on to find out about loans, government grants & bank accounts

YOU MIGHT IMAGINE that the best place for your money these days is under the mattress. It's not. You need a bank account if you are serious about making money from your photography. If you only earn a few hundred pounds a year, you can manage quite well with a personal account. But banks do take a dim view of people using their personal accounts for business and if they discover that you're doing so, may close the account or start applying business account charges.

Getting a business account

If you decide to create a limited company you definitely need a business bank account. The business bank account forms the hub of your accounting process and a quick glance at statements will quickly reveal what shape your business is in from one month to the next.

Bank charges are a fact of life in business. You're using the bank to run a profitable business, so the bank is entitled to charge for the service it provides to help you. Some business accounts are advertised as 'free' but this might just mean they don't have a monthly or quarterly charge. Watch out for the costs they apply to transactions.

Use an internet comparison site to choose three or four banks, go to the websites of each for the details and then arrange to meet a personal advisor. These aren't accountants or financial advisors as such, but they will be very knowledgeable about their bank's services.

According to their critics, banks aren't lending enough money to businesses at the moment. The banks deny this. As Brian Capon from the British Bankers' Association told me, banks are providing in excess of £500m of new lending to small businesses each month. Banks are still willing to lend to small businesses and around 10,000 new loans are currently being agreed each month.

"Banks look closely at applications for loans. They will need to be satisfied that the business is viable and can generate sufficient income to meet all its financial commitments as they become due. This means that businesses will need to provide the bank with three years' audited accounts, management accounts including cash flow forecasts for the business and a 'plan B' in case things don't go as expected."

So, if you think your business needs a cash injection, you'd better have a good story to tell about why you need a new computer, A1 printer and four prime lenses. The days of banks throwing money at risky business are over.

Securing grants and sponsors

If getting a bank loan is hard work, then bagging a government-funded start-up loan or grant isn't any easier.

Business Link was set up to help new businesses get access to advice, support and funding. Its website, followed by a meeting with one of its advisors, is a good place to start. Grants are limited and depend on your personal circumstances and where you live. Business Link advisor John Grange says: "Business Link doesn't provide money. It uses local advisors who know what financial support is available. We can help to write your business plan, too, which doesn't have to be 'geek-speak' or *War and Peace*."

Some parts of the country have a 'business angels' type scheme. Angels are local investors who will put money into your business if they can see a return, *Dragon's Den*-style.

The final source of funding worth considering is arts funding. Arts funding isn't just for fine-art photographers, it's there to help those whose work has a cultural or social value. If your work has social significance, enriches your region's cultural heritage or provides opportunities for deserving members of your community (such as unemployed ex-offenders, or those with learning difficulties) you can make your pitch. Your local authority will point you in the direction of local arts and community project funding. Then there's the Arts Council, whose Mathew Hanratty told us: "Photography activities that are considered eligible for funding are time-based projects that focus on personal career development of an artist. Therefore, taking part in photography exhibitions would be considered as eligible for funding."

USEFUL LINKS
www.businesslink.gov.uk
www.smallbusinesspro.co.uk
www.thisismoney.co.uk
www.artscouncil.org.uk
www.wefund.co.uk
www.uksponsorship.com
www.voluntaryarts.org

"Banks are providing in excess of £500m of new lending to small businesses each month. Banks are still willing to lend to small businesses"

The Arts Council has seen fairly dramatic cuts to its budgets, so greater expectations are being placed on corporate sponsorship. Many companies set aside money for arts sponsorship. Register your requests for funding at Uksponsorship.com or WeFund.co.uk to catch the eye of a benefactor.

So, lots to think about and, sadly, nobody's going to shower you with cash. ■

ISTOCK PHOTO

Comparison table: Business banking charges

	Free period (for start-ups)	Monthly fee	Standing orders	Auto deposits	Branch deposits	Cheque
BANKS						
HSBC	18 months	£3.15	54p per s/o	18p per credit	74p per credit	63p
Barclays	up to 24 months	£5.50	54p per s/o	15p per credit	75p per credit	59p
Natwest	24 months	£5.00	45p per s/o	22p per credit	66p per £100	71p
Lloyds TSB	18 months	£5.00	40p per s/o	20p per credit	70p per credit	65p
Alliance & Leicester*	for life	free	free	free	free	free

*Now Santander. Conditions apply to some free services, e.g. cheques limited to 100 per month.
Source: Banks' own websites on 1 December, 2010. This is intended as a guide only, please check current rates.

Other banks to consider: Clydesdale, RBS, Nationwide, Allied Irish, Bank of Scotland, Cater Allen, Co-operative Bank, Halifax, Bank of Ireland, Ulster Bank and Yorkshire Bank.

Case studies

Katherine Green

FULL-TIME DOCUMENTARY PHOTOGRAPHER

Katherine Green is a documentary photographer. In 2008 she received grants for her exhibition, *Going to the Dogs*. The project documents the closure of Walthamstow's famous greyhound stadium and its impact on the community. "The exhibition was ambitious as it consisted of two venues, 29 new pieces of work, ten oral history interviews for gallery listening posts, one interactive display of archive material, a DVD of images and audio playing on a flat-screen TV and one publication," explains Katherine. "The grants contributed to the production of the images, the framing, signage, touring costs and marketing."

So, millions, then? Er, no, not exactly. "The total grant from Arts Council England was £5,000 and £750 from Apex Arts," says Katherine. "The exhibition took one year to plan and develop. The Arts Council England application procedure is particularly lengthy and in-depth; it took approximately a month to plan and write."

Katherine has advice for other photographers: "Apply with plenty of time; meet with a funding officer; ask lots of questions and ask for feedback if you're not successful. If you are successful, be prepared to keep lots of records about the project and its development, as you will be asked for evidence in an evaluation report. "The Arts Council has specific aims and goals. It is important to be familiar with these and make sure you understand them. When applying for funding, it's important to demonstrate how the grant will help develop you and benefit others.

"My work involves and represents the community I live in. These themes chimed particularly well with the Arts Council's aims. However, this was the second time I had applied to the Arts Council. The first time I wasn't successful and the feedback I received was that this was due to lack of exhibiting experience. I managed to put that particular exhibition together on a very meagre budget so it was really exciting to be able to invest in high-quality prints and framing this time around."

© KATHERINE GREEN

TRADING STATUS

Once the money starts to roll in, you'll need to decide whether to be a sole trader or set up a limited company, not to mention dealing with the thorny issue of VAT. We guide you through this potential minefield

FOR MOST PHOTOGRAPHERS, the journey to becoming a professional is a transitional one. It begins as a hobby, leads to a few quid to cover your costs, grows into 'beer money' and ends up as a small profit. This is the kind of growth that gives people the confidence to give turning pro a go.

Simon Chaplin is the managing director of accountancy firm GreenStones in Peterborough and we asked him if there is a clear point at which someone turns pro. "Deciding when you started trading is quite hard," says Simon. "Most photographers start out taking a few snaps for friends and family and might receive a drink in exchange. Technically, that drink is taxable because it is a reward for services you have rendered! The question 'when does a hobby become a profession?' is difficult and expert advice should be taken on each individual case."

Accountants say that a lot, but he's right. Everyone's circumstances are different and although there is a lot of information available, some of it is quite complex. Expert advice doesn't have to be expensive advice. Contact Business Link and set up a meeting with an adviser in your area. Do it soon though, as the regional Business Link advisory service is being restructured from 25 November 2011.

One of the most common questions asked of Richard Hallsworth, partner at Nicholsons Accountants in Lincoln, is, "Should I form a limited company or be a sole trader? "Richard is a keen photographer and regularly blogs about photographers' finances. His response: "The easy 'tax saving' answer is yes, trade as a limited company over a sole trader and you will save tax. This is if you take a salary up to the personal allowance level and then dividends on top. The tax is saved because you don't pay national insurance on dividends extracted from the company. Based on the 2010/2011 tax rates, if you make a profit of £40,000 you would save around £2,375 of tax and national insurance by trading as a limited company. His blog goes into more detail than we can here and is a mine of useful information. Visit: www.financeforphotographers.co.uk

Limited company v sole trader

Simon Chaplin agrees with Richard: "The 'frame' for this is how much tax you save versus what an accountant will charge for the extra work. 'Zooming in' on a tax point of view, if your profits are over about £16,000 a year then your 'exposure' to tax will be high enough for you to 'focus' on becoming a company. Excuse the photo puns." Simon's also a comedian. You should see his invoices.

"Becoming a limited company also offers you the protection of limited liability, so your personal assets are safe (most of the time) and increases creditability as most people think of limited companies as more established and reliable. The downside is the extra administration involved in becoming limited: extra tax forms to file, an extra bank account, and forms to be filed at Companies House. Most people are happy to do all this admin because of the tax that they will save.

Another option to consider is a 'partnership', if you earn below £16,000 and your partner has no income. You can then share the profit and make sure all your tax allowances are used up."

Legally, you have to register a sole trader business or partnership within three months of earning your first pay cheque. You can do this either by telephoning the Newly Self-employed Helpline (see panel), registering online or posting a form to Her Majesty's Revenue and Customs (HMRC). A limited company, however, needs to be formed before you start trading, by registering it with Companies House. Both these processes are dull but relatively easy.

Before you can fill in these rather boring forms, you have another big decision to make: your trading name. This is less critical for sole traders but they can't really protect the name. They can sue for 'passing off', that is someone pretending to be them, but this might be difficult to prove.

Registering a limited company is more rigorous as it involves a search of existing companies to make sure the name is unique. The company becomes a legal entity, subject to company law and also, as Richard Hallsworth points out, to issues over privacy. "If you trade as a company, a lot of data is held about the company on public record," he says. "Details of directors, accounts, shareholdings and debentures held by finance institutions are just examples of data readily available for inspection or download from Companies House." That's a good point, Richard. Now readers can see for themselves just how much I'm struggling.

Choosing a name for your business is probably worth an article in itself. You can agonise over it the way you would the name of a baby. Things to consider include how much currency there is in your name.

> "The easy 'tax saving' answer is yes, trade as a limited company over a sole trader and you will save tax"

If people have got to know Joe Blow as a talented, reliable photographer, 'Joe Blow's Photos' should be on the list. Is location important? If so, maybe the name of your town or county should be part of the name. The same goes for any specialist services you provide such as training. (Read pXX of this guide to learn more about branding and for more on choosing the right name.)

Getting to grips with VAT

That's already quite a lot to think about for this issue, but there's just room to look at one more big decision you will face: whether or not to register for VAT. If your turnover of VAT taxable goods and services supplied within the UK for the previous 12 months is more than the current registration threshold of £70,000, or you expect it to go over that figure in the next 30 days alone, you must register for VAT.

You can also register for VAT if your turnover is less than £70,000, and there may be good reasons for doing that. Simon Chaplin again: "If your sales in the last 12 months are more than the threshold you have to register – no choice. If they are not and you take photographs for members of the public, you should not be registered. If you take photographs for business clients then you should be."

Members of the public are not in a position to claim back the VAT they pay, so if you don't charge them VAT, your services and products are cheaper. The downside is that you pay VAT on stock and business expenses but you can't claim it back.

Most business clients will reclaim the VAT they are charged, so are less concerned about the gross invoice. The other advantage of being VAT registered is that you get to reclaim the VAT you pay on supplies and services.

There is also a scheme known as 'flat rate VAT' that benefits businesses that don't hold much stock or don't have to buy lots of raw materials. The basic idea is that you charge VAT (currently at 20%) but claim back a lower percentage (currently 11% for photographers) of your total sales. It saves a lot of time on bookkeeping chores and working out what is claimable and what isn't.

It's a lot to think about, isn't it? Starting out as a professional photographer isn't about taking pictures all day, that's for sure. ■

Case studies

Charmaine Stark

BUSINESS NAME: TAKEN WITH PASSION
WEBSITE: WWW.TAKENWITHPASSION.CO.UK
MAIN ACTIVITY OF BUSINESS: WEDDING AND PORTRAIT PHOTOGRAPHY.
TYPE OF BUSINESS: SOLE TRADER.
ANNUAL PHOTOGRAPHY SALES: UP TO £16,000.
VAT REGISTERED? NO.

"I started out as a sole trader. It's not as complicated as a limited company and after all, there is only me and the less paperwork I have the better! However, now I understand the business a bit better I might stop using an accountant (who was invaluable at the start) and start doing my tax return myself, directly with the tax office, to save money. I'm not VAT registered as my turnover doesn't justify it, and I deal with the general public so I do not want to pass the cost on to them. Adding 20% to my prices, when local competition is fierce and I need my prices to be relative to everyone else, could stop clients from hiring me. I don't think it's worth the risk or the hassle of the extra paperwork at this stage in my business."

Case studies

Martyn Moore

BUSINESS NAME: NORTHLIGHT MEDIA LTD
WEBSITE: WWW.NORTHLIGHTMEDIA.CO.UK
MAIN ACTIVITY OF BUSINESS: CORPORATE PHOTOGRAPHY, WRITING AND MEDIA PRODUCTION.
TYPE OF BUSINESS: LIMITED COMPANY.
ANNUAL PHOTOGRAPHY SALES: UP TO £16,000.
VAT REGISTERED? YES, ON FLAT RATE SCHEME.

"Most of my clients are businesses. I take photographs for corporate brochures and websites. I decided to become a limited company because some of my clients are large organisations or public bodies and these guys like the 'corporate feel' of a limited company when they do business and they can claim back the VAT I charge them. I don't hold stock or buy much in the way of materials, so the flat-rate VAT scheme suits me most of the time, although I felt the pain when I moved into a new office recently. You can't claim back the full 20% VAT on purchases under £2,000."

Key contacts & resources

- **Business Link:** For personalised, free advice for how to set up and grow a business, contact Business Link: www.businesslink.gov.uk.
- **The Tax Office:** For advice on filing your yearly tax return call 0845 3000627.
- **HM Revenue & Customs:** To register as newly self-employed: 0845 9154515.
- **Companies House:** To register your business name or set up a limited company, contact: www.companieshouse.gov.uk.

HOW TO KEEP THE TAXMAN ON SIDE

Tax isn't fun. Just the very mention of the word brings most people out in a cold sweat. But if you take professional advice and keep on top of form-filling, it can all be a relatively painless process

"SHOULD FIVE PERCENT appear too small, be thankful I don't take it all. 'Cause I'm the taxman. Yeah, I'm the taxman... and you're working for no-one but me." When George Harrison wrote the lyrics for this opening song on The Beatles' album *Revolver*, he was pretty unhappy with the taxman. Back in 1966 the Beatles were paying 95% of their earnings to the Inland Revenue and Harrison made his feelings very clear in *Taxman*: "Now my advice for those who die, declare the pennies on your eyes." Angry stuff.

These days you should expect to keep more than one pound in 20. A supertax today is more likely to affect bankers' bonuses than photographers' earnings. In fact, a lot of things about the taxman have changed, apart from perhaps public opinion. It doesn't matter how helpful and reasonable the people at Her Majesty's Revenue and Customs (HMRC) are, we just don't like paying taxes.

Living in a civilised society means that we are required to hand over some of our earnings to pay for schools, hospitals, roads and the occasional excesses of our leaders. That's the way it has always been and more than likely always be.

Everyone has a tax-free personal allowance, which is the amount of taxable income you're allowed to earn each year tax-free. This year (2011–2012) that amount is £7,475. For most people, pretty much everything you earn over this amount is subject to tax.

Income tax rates change and HMRC publishes a ton of information on its excellent website. For the 2011–2012 tax year the Basic Rate of income tax is 20 % and that applies to earnings up to £35,000 a year. People who earn between £35,001 and £150,000 pay 40 % – the Higher Rate. But the biggest blow is to those people on more than £150,000 (surviving Beatles included). They're subject to the Additional Rate and pay 50 % tax and see their personal allowance reduced.

The devil is in the detail. Things like pension contributions and gift aid donations can affect these figures. Please don't wave this article under the nose of your tax inspector, crying, "but *Digital SLR Photography* magazine says it's this... "

For a typical photographer, 'earnings' are the difference between what you charge for taking photos and what it costs you to do it. Your profit is your turnover minus your expenses.

Take professional advice

This is basically how tax applies to a self-employed photographer. If you've formed a limited company and you are a director, you can pay yourself up to your personal allowance as salary tax-free (but not National Insurance-free) and then draw a dividend to which different tax rules apply. Your company will pay a 21 % corporation tax on its profits, which reduces to 20 % for financial years starting on or after 1 April 2011.

This is the shape of current UK tax law at its most basic. It doesn't cover National Insurance or VAT but it's already starting to get quite complicated. If we carry on at this rate you'll start to wonder if what you're reading is really an inspirational photography magazine.

> "For a typical photographer, 'earnings' are the difference between what you charge for taking photos and what it costs you to do it"

Get professional help. Everything you need to know is published online but sometimes talking to an expert makes it all a bit clearer. It doesn't have to be an accountant that advises you: local Business Link representatives will continue to provide a valuable service until November before the organisation is restructured. Business Link will help you to understand the principles of running a business and HMRC can give you tax advice for free. But you should consider hiring an accountant. Most of them will offer an initial consultation for free and a good accountant should be able to save you more money in tax than they charge you for doing your books.

Accountants seem to have an odd way of speaking. Simon Chaplin, head honcho at GreenStones in Peterborough, talks like this: "Whether the business is that of an individual or a company, profits are calculated so as to give a true and fair view of the business in accordance with generally accepted accounting practice and tax legislation. Business profits for individuals and companies are calculated along similar lines.

"Once business profits are calculated, the UK operates a process of 'self assessment', making it the responsibility of the taxpayer to complete an online or paper tax return declaring your income and capital gains (profits on the sale of certain assets) on the tax return, together with any claims for tax allowances or reliefs.

"There are deadlines for sending your tax return in and penalties and interest charges may be applied if it arrives late. You will always need to complete a tax return if you are self-employed, a higher rate tax payer or have untaxed income above the personal allowance."

Get to grips with form-filling

Despite this glittering repartee, you can learn a lot from people like Simon in your first year and then decide whether you want to retain their services. Lots of photographers do, because it allows them to remain focused on the business of taking pictures.

BBC news goddess Moira Stuart has been telling us "tax doesn't have to be taxing" for a few years now, and she's right. If death and taxes are the only true certainties, form-filling runs them a close third. But whether you opt to fill in a paper form or to check boxes, menus and input text online, you're entering information you should already know from your invoices, receipts, bank account and diary. The only tricky area might be deciding whether an expense is tax-deductable and the best time to claim it. There are clear rules for this and Simon Chaplin now shows us he can talk in lists as well.

"For business expenses there are two most important rules to remember," explains Simon. "The expense must be: One, wholly and exclusively for the purpose of the trade (printing paper, inks, batteries) and two, of a revenue and not capital nature (a camera would be capital whereas consumables are revenue).

"Capital expenses are treated differently, with the cost of big ticket items such as cameras, lenses and lighting claimed as capital allowances."

There isn't a lot here to separate the full-time professional and the part-time enthusiast earning a few quid at weekends. The truth is, earnings are earnings and they are subject to tax. If you have another job, you will probably have earned more than your personal allowance. An added difficulty will be working out what costs are "wholly and exclusively for the purpose of the trade". If some of your ink and paper goes on personal projects, it's hard to make that claim.

Steep penalties for tax evaders

We asked Tom Buchan, photography enthusiast and qualified tax accountant (www.tombuchan.com), how will HMRC ever know about the details? "The answer is they may never find out," says Tom. "But (and its a big but) UK tax law places the onus on you to be honest. Consequently the penalties for not being honest are steep; financially and otherwise. HM Revenue & Customs do operate a black economy unit and, as your magazine has already reported, one professional photographic body has been submitting names to HM Revenue & Customs in an effort to catch out tax evaders and maintain the integrity of the profession."

Many photographers report satisfactory dealings with HMRC. In certain cases it has paid interest on overpaid tax and will sometimes offer easy payment terms when tax has been underpaid. Like many big organisations dealing with large numbers of people, mistakes get made on both sides, and HMRC has gone to great lengths to show it can be reasonable. But you probably won't hear The Beatles singing about that. ■

Key contacts & resources

- **Business Link:** For personalised, free advice for how to set up and grow your business, contact Business Link: www.businesslink.gov.uk
- **Finance For Photographers:** www.financeforphotographers.co.uk
- **HM Revenue & Customs:** www.hmrc.gov.uk
- **Green Stones:** Peterborough-based accountancy firm: www.greenstones.co.uk

Typical accounts

A typical set of accounts for a photographer would probably include the following expenses:

- Car, van and travel expenses (parking, fuel, repairs, servicing, hotel rooms and so on)
- Repairs and renewals of equipment
- Premises expenses (either use of home as office or rent, rates, power, security, property insurance and so on)
- Business insurance costs
- Phone, fax, stationery, printing, computer software and other general office costs
- Computer and website costs
- Advertising, mailshots, free samples and so on
- Accountancy, legal & professional fees
- Bank and credit charges
- Interest on bank or other business loans
- Bad debts (invoices included in turnover but not paid)
- Trade or professional journals/ magazine subscriptions
- Membership of professional bodies

INSURANCE: A NECESSARY EVIL

Replacing all your kit if it was stolen or, worse, having to defend yourself against legal action, could finish your business before it gets off the ground. That's where tailor-made photographers' insurance comes in

INSURANCE IS THE RISK business. Both professional and semi-professional photographers need to consider insurance. The big question for all of us is "what are the odds?"

All trades have their specialist insurance brokers and photography is no exception. A number of companies offer photographers insurance cover that has been tailored to the profession. A photography specialist understands the industry and will help you to solve a problem quickly and cost-effectively through their knowledge of the business. They know how much kit is worth and the best of them will come to your rescue when you most need it.

There are many components to photographers' insurance and the right cover for you will be a combination of the elements – possibly your own unique combination. Let's find out what they are.

The easiest to understand is the cover for your kit. We own expensive equipment and the cost of repairing or replacing that equipment can be frightening. So we need insurance for our kit for the same reason we insure all our valuables against theft, loss and damage. Next is public liability. All trades should consider public liability and you shouldn't hire a plumber who doesn't have it. If one of my lighting stands take out the eye of a model, you can bet they'll see me in court. Not very clearly, but I'll still be in big trouble. Public liability insurance would offer me financial protection, but it wouldn't get me off a health and safety charge if I'd been negligent.

Photographers take on the responsibility for recording special or one-off events. If we enter into a contract, basically a promise, that we'll succeed and then we don't, we could be liable to our client for damages. This is professional indemnity insurance and it can even cover the cost of restaging an entire wedding if your memory card malfunctions.

Most insurance is discretionary, but some is a legal requirement. If you hire somebody to help you with a shoot ,you must have employers' liability insurance. The exception is if its a family member. You can find out details on the Health and Safety Executive website (www.hse.gov.uk). Employers' liability insurance provides cover if something unfortunate happens to someone as a result of them working for you and they decide to sue you.

Arranging bespoke cover

I used to work for a company where the photographers would hang out of a moving hatchback, shooting cars and motorcycles that came within inches of their wide-angle lenses. Can you imagine writing up that risk assessment?

It's difficult to say how much your insurance will cost. A landscape photographer, selling prints and carrying out the odd commission, might be a fairly low public liability or professional indemnity risk, but they have to consider travel and all the kit they take with them. Overseas travel can make quite a difference and, incidentally, the Republic of Ireland is usually considered foreign travel.

> "There are many components to photographers' insurance and the right cover for you will be a combination of all the elements"

If you own a studio, the building and its contents need to be insured, but if you hire a studio every now and then, insurance is likely to be included in the hire charges. The owner of the studio should be insured but it's always worth checking.

There are so many variables and all the specialists I spoke to offer bespoke cover, rather than a one-size-fits-all policy. This approach tends to be better for all concerned but leads to large variations in the cost of premiums. One tip, though: it's definitely worth mentioning if you're a member of a professional association like the SWPP or MPA, as you'll be eligible for a discount on your premium.

Towergate Camerasure calculates premiums on an individual basis. Hayley Luxford is Towergate's operations director. She says: "There is not just one package that will suit all. Full discussions with clients determine the exact requirements of the individual, and the policy we offer is tailored to individual needs. Our semi-professional and professional products automatically include 'all risks' cover (subject to limitations) for equipment, theft from vehicle cover and liability cover.

"A quick 'fact find' discussion with one of our handlers will establish the best level of cover together with values of equipment, your travel pattern and a few more general underwriting questions and we can usually provide you with a competitive quote. You can then arrange cover without a proposal form. A Statement of Facts form will be sent to you in the post."

David Jayne is managing director of Imaging Insurance and he lists the types of cover his company provides: "Our policy provides options for the insurance of buildings; photographic, video, computer and other business equipment; photographic, video, and film images; sound recordings; productions; business interruption; business money; public and products liability; employers' liability and professional indemnity. Depending upon a photographer's individual circumstances, all sections of the policy may be required."

Cover comes into its own

That's a lot of options and serves as a reminder of all the many things that could go wrong in business as a professional or even semi-professional photographer. Maybe instead of looking at insurance as a grudge purchase, we should look at it as an investment in peace of mind.

David agrees: "Photographers who receive a claims settlement think we've saved their bacon. For example, a recent claim for the theft of all of a photographer's equipment (worth more than £7,000) was sorted out in just three days. Our policy automatically includes cover for the hiring cost of alternative equipment until lost or damaged equipment is replaced or repaired – we aim to make sure that policyholders don't lose

any work even though they've had an incident." That's not the kind of service you'll get with a home and contents policy is it?

"Usually home contents insurance ceases to provide cover as soon as the equipment is used for business purposes or the insured starts working as a professional photographer," says David. "While normal house contents insurance may be better than none at all, if you earn any money from your equipment, house contents insurance probably won't apply. Even if you don't earn any money from photography, your kit probably won't be covered if it's stolen from your car. And there may well be restrictions on values of single items or if you go outside the UK."

Travel is also an important factor. Holiday insurance won't normally cover you if you're working abroad. We asked our specialist insurers what steps can be taken by photographers to keep their premiums down.

Towergate's Hayley Luxford again: "Premiums could be reduced by additional security measures being present that are over and above insurers' requirements. Another option is taking a voluntary excess in addition to the standard excess applied to the policy. Customers can also accumulate policy discounts for no claims and the length of time they have been a client, which will all be taken into account and can result in reductions in premiums."

David at Imaging Insurance recommends being extra careful. "Most claims result from accidental damage to equipment – so more care can mean maximising the no claims discount and saving money," he says. "You can also cover equipment for secondhand replacement cost if it is available secondhand. Try to keep the amount of equipment taken out on location to a minimum and even consider moving to a lower risk rated postcode."

Know what you're paying for

Moving home or premises might be a big ask, but there's some good advice there. It's essential that you read the small print of an insurance policy. Sorry about that, but you really ought to know exactly what you are buying. If one quote is significantly lower than all the rest, there's probably a good reason for that. And if you make a claim, you must expect your premium to rise. You're now a proven risk.

For a long time insurance companies have suffered from what some people see as a 'victimless crime' – false claims from clients who feel they have paid their premium for a few years, so are entitled to make a claim. The insurance industry will tell you that it is paying out £1.47 in claims for every £1 it collects in premiums. These numbers are not sustainable.

Insurance is not likely to get cheaper, but by dealing with a specialist who understands photography and knows the realistic risks, you're more likely to buy the cover you need. And if you do need to call on your insurer, you'll want them to react like Imaging Insurance and Towergate.

Hayley Luxford has a favourite story: "We had a very famous celebrity photographer who was on a flight to Los Angeles. The client arrived at LAX but, unfortunately, the photographic equipment didn't. All of the kit was checked in at Heathrow but mysteriously didn't make the flight. With a demanding production crew, models and celebrities waiting, we had to work rather swiftly. Thanks to supplier connections in the UK we were able to arrange the hire of replacement kit to enable the shoot to be successfully completed later that day. All of this was sorted from our offices in Hampshire and our client was over the moon." ■

THE BREAKDOWN ON INSURANCE

Navigating the minefield of insurers is tricky, especially if you don't ask the right questions. We try to make it a little easier by doing some of the legwork for you and seeking out helpful hints and advice

WE WANTED TO CALL this feature *We take the pain, so you don't have to* but I'm afraid you may still experience some slight discomfort. Nobody likes buying insurance, but like we've said before, think of it as buying peace of mind. The previous article outlined the basics of insurance, but didn't look in detail at how much time buying insurance takes or how much money it costs, so we've addressed those critical issues in this section. We promise to make it as pain-free and as helpful as possible. You will have more fun reading it than we did on the phone and analysing the quotes.

At the end of it, though, you are going to have to hit the phones and get your own quotes. While most insurers now have quote engines on their websites so you can buy your policy online, we'd still advise you pick up the phone and speak to someone to ensure the policy meets all your needs. In an attempt to give you a really useful guide to insurance policies and prices, the *Digital SLR Photography* team rang a range of photographers' insurance specialists to find out what they charge, and the policies they offer to an enthusiast and semi-pro photographer.

What we asked..

By describing our needs, we had hoped to be able to compare like with like. No dice. Put simply, the policies offered by different insurers are all different. Some offer only £50,000 or £100,000-worth of public indemnity cover, others can only quote for £75,000. We were happy to accept an excess, where we would pay the first £250 of any claim, but some companies boasted their policies are 'no excess' and wouldn't quote a cheaper price, even when we offered to pay the first 'half a monkey'.

So at the end of a long day we had a slightly frustrating set of data and a lesson for you. The lesson is shop around, ask the right questions (that we have been able to list for you) and do your best to be clear about the extent of the cover you need and find out the limitations of your cover. It's that blooming small print again.

The aim of the exercise was to establish the range of products on offer and the range of prices. We wanted to produce an approximate guide to premiums being asked for using typical profiles for our two levels of photographer (you can read the profiles in the adjacent table).

The biggest denominator was the value of kit, which we posed as £3,000 (plus £500 for computer equipment, if the insurer could include it in their policy) for the enthusiast and £8,000, including computer equipment, for the semi-pro policies. In some cases, particularly for the enthusiast policy, insurers allowed room for more kit value to be added on without having to increase the premium, which we've indicated via the Value of Kit section in the adjacent table.

"By describing our needs, we had hoped to be able to compare like with like. No dice. Put simply, the policies by different insurers are all different"

What we found out...

If you really can't be bothered working this out from our table, we don't mind telling you that the cheapest quote we got for our enthusiast profile was from Photoguard for its Select policy at £202, with professional indemnity as an extra. Photoguard, however, was the most expensive for semi-pros at £454 (Select) and £593 (Pro). Photoguard was probably hardest to understand too, separating out the professional indemnity and applying discounts to parts of the policy.

When speaking to Towergate, we didn't get a quote for £100,000-worth of professional indemnity on the phone so when the email came through with an increase of almost £300 on the premium, it was a bit of a shock for the enthusiast. The semi-pro was quoted £63.60 extra for just £25,000 of professional indemnity, which means Towergate struggles to compete on that part of the policy.

Glover & Howe were a delight to deal with on the phone, but to be fair, all the companies we spoke to were excellent. Aaduki suggested a couple of questions to ask other insurers, confident that their policy provided covers that others didn't, making Aaduki quotes very competitive with some of the best policies on offer. The same can be said for Glover & Howe.

All of these companies understand photography, so sit down and compile your own personal information, decide your own 'must-have' policy features and our list of 14 questions. Then resign yourself to making five phone calls between ten and 15-minutes long. Don't buy right away; get quotes emailed to you so you can have a good look at that small print. ■

Jargon buster

- **Employer's liability:** Protects you from claims for damages or loss made by somebody working for you, e.g. an assistant claiming for damages after receiving an electric shock from your kit.
- **Excess:** The amount paid by the policy holder in the event of a claim. Usually, the higher the excess, the lower the premium.
- **Free and open theft policy:** Covers you for the theft of unattended equipment.
- **NCD:** No Claims Discount, a reduction in premium after a period without claims, usually a year. Rewards loyalty to a company and discourages claims.
- **Policyholder:** You, after you have taken out the policy.
- **Premium:** The cost of an insurance policy, paid in an annual lump sum or in monthly installments.
- **Professional indemnity:** Cover for any loss or damages to clients caused by your professional failure, error or equipment malfunction, e.g. a corrupt memory card or damaged camera means you lose an entire shoot or a car crash prevents you from reaching the venue.
- **Proposer:** You, before you have taken out the policy.
- **Public liability:** Cover for any loss or damage to others caused by your work as a photographer, e.g. someone trips over your camera bag or lights, taking a tumble.

The enthusiast photographer

You don't earn much money from your photography, but you do shoot the occasional weekend wedding and portrait shoot. When you do a wedding your partner normally comes along for moral support and to help hold your camera bag/be a second shooter. You have a decent camera outfit based around a mid-range DSLR with an older entry-level model as a back-up, two or three lenses and the essential accessories, all totalling about £3,000. You also have a home PC and printer costing in the region of £500. Most of your shoots are local but you'd like to work outside of the UK, given the chance.

Company	Value of kit	Value of public liability	Value of professional indemnity	Overseas cover	Is hired-in kit covered?	Excess	Annual premium	Notes
Aaduki	£3,500	£2m	£75,000	up to 60 days worldwide	extra	7.5% of claim (£250 min)	£268.64	Check property security requirements
Photoguard Select	£3,000	£1m	extra	unlimited EU, up to 30 days worldwide	included	no excess	£202	£5K personal accident, pro indemnity is extra
Imaging Insurance	£3,500	£2m	£100,000	up to 60 days worldwide	extra	£150 (£250 third party)	£267.31	No item worth over £1,500, covers £600 hiring in costs
Towergate Camerasure	£4,000	£2m	£100,000	worldwide (region restrictions on pro indem/public liability)	n/a	£250	£609.50	Includes £10m empl liability, data recovery, bus interruption
Glover & Howe	£5,000	£2m	£75,000	multiple trips, up to 20 consecutive days worldwide	extra	10% of claim (£50 min and £250 max)	£266.50	

The semi-professional

You have a full-time job but you're also serious about making money from your photography, shooting up to 12 paid wedding or portrait sessions a year. You often have a second shooter or an assistant on a wedding shoot and you may have converted your garage in to a studio for portraits or you occasionally hire a studio. Your equipment is worth about £8,000, comprising the likes of studio lights, a full-frame and APS-C DSLR with a selection of fast lenses and accessories. Last year you were given a small assignment overseas and you're planning a stock shooting trip to New York.

Company	Value of kit limit for quote	Value of public liability	Value of professional indemnity	Overseas cover	Is hired-in kit covered?	Excess	Annual premium	Notes
Aaduki	up to £8,000	£2m	£75,000	up to 60 days worldwide	extra	£100-£200	£328.29	
Photoguard Select	£8,000	£1m	£100,000	UK only	included	no excess	£454	will pay 10% of replacement hire
Photoguard Pro	£8,000	£2m	£100,000	UK only	included	no excess	£593	20% of replace hire, £10K per accident, portfolio, indemnity
Imaging Ins opt 1	£8,000	£1m	£50,000	up to 60 days worldwide*	extra	£150-£250	£313.51	* liability does not include US or Canada
Imaging Ins opt 2	£8,000	£2m	£100,000	up to 60 days worldwide*	extra	£150-£250	£350.60	* liability does not include US or Canada
Towergate Semi-pro	£5,000-£8,000	£1m	£25,000 for £63.60 extra	up to 45 days worldwide	n/a	£250-£350	£272.60	
Towergate Pro	£8,000+	£2m	£25,000 included	excludes US and Canada	n/a	£150	£330	
Glover & Howe	£8,000	£2m	£75,000	multiple trips, up to 20 consecutive days worldwide	up to £2,500 value	10% of claim (£50 min and £250 max)	£324.75	

Our small print

The quotes we obtained are based on the information provided to the insurers on 14 March, 2011. We were as consistent as possible with the profiles and questions we used for every call, but there was some variation depending on the insurer's questions. Every phone quote was confirmed by email, but sometimes contained additional information not revealed during the telephone call. The quotes were only valid for a limited period of time, and that time has now lapsed. Please do not rely on these quotes as evidence of comparable cost between insurers or as an accurate representation of what you might be charged for similar requirements. Thank you.

Really good questions to ask insurers over the phone

1) If I work outside the UK, am I covered?
2) If I am covered for travel, is there a limit on the number of overseas days a year?
3) Will I get the full receipt value of my kit back, no matter how long I have owned it for (called a 'new for old policy')?
4) Can I make a claim if I don't have the original receipts?
5) Is the theft cover 'full and open', meaning I'm covered even if I've left my kit unattended?
6) Can I get an emergency replacement if my kit fails, is this an extra cost and will it be delivered to me?
7) Are there situations where my equipment might not be covered?
8) Does the professional indemnity cover me for unforeseen or unavoidable circumstances (e.g. vehicle breakdown leading to missed appointment) as well as negligence?
9) What are the consequences for making a claim? How much will my premium go up?
10) What's the cancellation policy?
11) Is it cheaper to have a higher excess? How much more is it not to have an excess?
12) What happens if I add kit to my policy after it's been taken out?
13) How flexible is the policy? For instance, if I turn professional in less than 12 months or start renting a studio how could this affect my policy and premium?
14) If I rent equipment for a shoot, do I need to temporarily add it to my policy and does this cost anything extra?
15) Is my kit covered if it's stolen from my car?

IS IT LEGAL?

More than ever, we're hearing about photographers having a brush with the law. And the differences between the law, its interpretation and public opinion have never been less clear. Time for some facts

BRITAIN IS ONE OF the most relaxed countries in the world when it comes to the freedom of photographers to take pictures. Broadly speaking, we can take photos of pretty much anyone, anything and anywhere as long as it's in public. Most of the time we can photograph policemen executing their duty, we can usually photograph other people's children playing in the street and we don't need to ask anybody's permission. We have to be careful photographing kingfishers, though.

There are restrictions and the laws change. Linda Macpherson is one of the UK's leading experts on photography and the law. She's a successful photographer and a freelance legal consultant, specialising in media and intellectual property law. On the subject of what laws should most concern photographers, she says: "The area of most general concern for amateur photographers centres on taking photographs of people, including children. And, having taken them, whether or how they can be used or published. This is a very difficult area because some of the relevant law is both vague and continually developing. The law relating to privacy rights is particularly fluid and data protection law presents a further set of issues that have not been definitively determined by any court.

"I get a lot of questions related to the general right to take photographs, both in public places and on private property and there is sometimes considerable confusion about what constitutes a public place. Issues of police powers and the law of trespass would fall within this area. It doesn't help that the law in Scotland differs from the rest of the UK in some respects."

To help photographers steer clear of trouble, Linda has written a guide called the *UK Photographers' Rights Guide*. It can be downloaded from the accompanying website at www.sirimo.co.uk/ukpr. In her introduction to the guide, Linda writes: "It is often said that there is no law against taking a photograph, but in fact there are many legal restrictions on the right to take a photograph. So it would be more correct to say that one is free to take photographs except when the law provides otherwise."

In most cases it's legal to take photographs of buildings and private property from a public place, such as the public highway, but it's an invasion of privacy to take a photo of someone in their home using a telephoto lens, even if the photo is taken from a public place. It's not illegal to take pictures of children playing in public, but a local authority's child protection policy might place heavy restrictions on photographing children at events, schools and swimming pools.

Professional commercial photography is prohibited in Trafalgar and Parliament Squares in London and in the Royal Parks, unless written permission is obtained and a fee paid. Tourist photography is allowed but a clear, sharp, well-composed 'holiday snap' of Big Ben could easily end up on a stock photography website. So it's not clear cut, is it?

It's illegal to obstruct highways, footpaths and cycleways, so expect to be moved along by the police if you set up your tripod in a busy street. Your kit may be deemed to present a risk to the health and safety of the public or just a nuisance.

> "The area of most concern for photographers centres on taking photographs of people, including children. This is a very difficult area as the law is vague"

One of the biggest areas of concern in recent years is the power given to police by the Terrorism Act 2000. Section 58A of the Act has led to misunderstandings between photographers and police officers. The section covers the offence of eliciting, publishing or communicating information about members of the armed forces, intelligence services and police that is likely to be useful to a person committing or preparing to commit an act of terrorism.

Some coppers might have interpreted Section 58A as: "You can't take pictures of me." Linda Macpherson's take on this is: "'Information' would include a photograph, and the section is very broadly drafted, as it doesn't suggest that the information needs to be intended for terrorist purposes, only that it is of a kind likely to be useful for those purposes. That might in theory include any photograph from which someone might be identified as a police officer, and some police officers seem to be interpreting it this way.

"However, the same wording about information 'of a kind likely to be useful' is contained in the original section 58. And the House of Lords has interpreted that to mean 'information of such a nature as to raise a reasonable suspicion that it was intended to be used to assist in the preparation or commission of an act of terrorism'. So, in short, no, there is no blanket legal ban on taking photographs with police in them."

Another worry related to the Terrorism Act is around powers to stop and search. It was originally covered in Section 44, which is no longer being enforced. However, its remit lives on in Section 47A, jokingly referred to in some parts of the legal community as "Section 44 reloaded". The Code of Practice relating to Section 47A can be downloaded from the Home Office website. It's a long web address, so type it carefully: http://www.homeoffice.gov.uk/publications/counter-terrorism/terrorism-act-remedial-order/code-of-practice?view=Binary

Or just go to the Home Office site and type "terrorism act s47a" into the search box. Page 19 of the code deals with concerns raised by photographers.

The Metropolitan Police Service has dedicated a page of its website to photography and although it could do with a bit of help from the Plain English Campaign people, it's very informative, especially the bit that says "Officers do not have the power to delete digital images or destroy film at any point during a search. Deletion or destruction may only take place following seizure if there is a lawful power (such as a court order) that permits such deletion or destruction."

As you might expect, there are restrictions on private property. Basically, the owner of any private space can impose their own conditions on you being allowed to enter that space. If the management company of a shopping centre says you can't take photos, well, you can't. And if a concert venue stipulates 'no photography', you will be asked to leave if you try. By breaking the conditions of entry you become a trespasser but the property owner can't confiscate your equipment or insist you delete images.

So what about the kingfishers, then? Well, although there is no restriction on taking photographs of animals and birds, the Wildlife and Countryside Act 1981

PAUL STEFAN

makes it an offence to disturb kingfishers, along with dozens of other schedule 1 protected birds, at or near their nesting places. Many wild animals, including insects, enjoy the same protection and can only be photographed near their nests or places of shelter by photographers with a licence from Natural England, Scottish Natural Heritage or the Countryside Council for Wales.

Oh, and it's illegal to photograph banknotes without written permission from the issuing bank. So if the UK is one of the most liberal countries in the world when it comes to photographers' rights, imagine what some of the others must be like. ■

Keep out of trouble

IT'S A MINEFIELD. The law as applied to photography is confusing, subject to different interpretation and it changes fairly regularly, so don't count on this feature to keep you out of trouble. Use it to learn when to be most careful. Photographers need to stand up for their rights, law enforcement agencies need to be clear on the laws they are enforcing and people should use a lot more common sense. Then maybe we could all calm down a bit. Here are a few pieces of advice from Linda Macpherson on how to keep out of trouble:

- ☑ When photographing children it is advisable to get at least verbal consent from parents.
- ☑ Even parents of children taking part in school or sports activities should inquire about child protection policies covering those events.
- ☑ When photographing riots or civil unrest, make sure the police don't think you are a participant. Move away if the police ask you to, and stay calm, or you might run the risk of being arrested for obstruction.
- ☑ Cooperate with the police. It might be irritating to be searched or questioned, but a failure to cooperate may result in detention at a police station for several hours.
- ☑ Any photographer faced with specific difficulties should seek legal advice.

PHOTOGRAPHY AND COPYRIGHT

Ignorance, carelessness and the lack of visible victims has made copyright law one of the most widely misunderstood and abused. So let's wise up and put a stop to all this nonsense

COPYRIGHT IS ONE of the most misunderstood laws affecting photography, which is strange because at the moment it is fairly simple. Copyright law deals with the intellectual property of an image – the ownership of a work by the person who created it.

So unless he or she has entered into an agreement to the contrary, a photographer owns the copyright to the photographs he or she takes. Each photo is their intellectual property and cannot be used, modified, published, copied or distributed without their permission. What's so hard about that?

One of the most misunderstood aspects of copyright is that it is perfectly possible to grant somebody else, such as a client, free use of an image in any format, forever, without giving them copyright. You can grant a licence to a client allowing them to do whatever they want with a photograph but by retaining the copyright, you can also do whatever you want with the photograph. If you surrender the copyright, you also surrender all claims to that image and any potential future uses and income. That's why you should always retain the copyright in your images.

A possible reason why there has been so much misunderstanding around copyright is that the law has changed over the years. There are different rules in different countries and territories and like many 'rights', a simple letter or contract can eliminate or override them. It used to be said that the owner or buyer of the film stock held the copyright to a photo, so that one has been consigned to the dusty heap of outdated law books in the corner. Next to the out-of-date Ektachrome.

The idea that an employer holds copyright to all images created by a photographer employed by the company still holds true, as long as the contract of employment and terms and conditions clearly stipulate that to be the case. Most employers got that one sorted years ago.

Publishers often seek to obtain copyright of commissioned images, even those taken by freelancers. The publishers' argument is that they have created the photo opportunity, they have picked up all the costs, so why shouldn't they have all rights to the image?

The photographers' argument is that they own the intellectual property, so why shouldn't they be free to use it in the future, in media not competitive to the original client. It's a good argument and both sides have a point.

The biggest challenge to copyright law is digital media. In the bad old days, every time you copied something its quality deteriorated a little. It also took time and cost money to make an inferior version. Whereas a digital copy can be identical in every respect to the original. It can be duplicated millions of times, almost instantly, and it can be transmitted anywhere in the world in a matter of seconds. It has never been easier, quicker or cheaper to use a photographer's work without permission or payment.

> "The explosion of media has made it almost impossible to find out if an image has been used without permission or payment"

Photographers go to great lengths to try to protect their digital images, from using visible watermarks or a 'proof copy' overlay, to having special webpage script to prevent the easy 'right-click' downloading of an image. Some image protection claims to embed trackable metadata in an image file, allowing its use to be detected and monitored across the internet. Most online image protection merely acts as a deterrent to would-be photo pirates; if they see an image that looks nice on someone else's site, that image can be looking nice on their own site in no time at all.

In addition, this explosion of media has made it almost impossible to find out if an image has been used without permission or payment. Print media used to be difficult to produce, but now anybody can publish a magazine or a book and it's only the responsible brands that are bothering to check rights and clearance. Everybody else takes the 'who does it hurt?' and the 'how will they ever find out?' approach.

But sometimes you will find out and, if it happens, right now at least, the law is on your side. You have to prove that an infringement of your copyright has taken place. First of all, contact the publisher and explain that an image of yours has been used without permission. Tell them how much you would like to be paid for the use of the image and on payment that will be the end of the matter. Demand a reasonable amount and you should get a reasonable response. If that doesn't work, contact a lawyer.

Notice the use of the phrase 'right now at least, the law is on your side'. The copyright law could be about to change again after the government commissioned a review, commonly called the Hargreaves report after its chairman, looking at how the UK laws can be brought into line with the demands of the digital age. There's no suggestion that photographers will have less protection in the future. One of the ideas is to create a digital rights exchange, which could help with the policing of image use and provide easier access to photographers' work for legitimate clients.

The revisions to copyright law, however, will probably lead to more misunderstandings and misinformation, so don't expect it to get any simpler to enforce this simple law anytime soon. ■

More information

- **Copyright, Designs and Patents Act, 1988:** www.legislation.gov.uk/ukpga/1988/48
- **Linda Macpherson's legal Q&A:** www.sirimo.co.uk/ukpr
- **Intellectual Property Office:** (Hargreaves Report section) www.ipo.gov.uk/ipreview.htm
- **Editorial Photographers UK and Ireland:** www.epuk.org/

ISTOCK PHOTO

How to handle the client that asks for copyright

The first thing to say is that this conversation needs to take place before a single shot is taken. You should know what you are selling before you start work. Default position should be to say 'no' to requests for full copyright. Some photographers will walk away from a job rather than give up copyright, knowing that there's a line of journeymen smudgers behind them, ready to snap it up.

You may want to control the printing of the photographs, charging extra each time copies are made. This is your prerogative and in that case you wouldn't give the client digital files, either. Explain that your business and livelihood is dependent on the revenue from prints.

If you don't make money from prints, you may just want to protect your intellectual property and be free to use it in future. So when a client attempts to secure copyright, explain that you retaining copyright need not prevent them from doing whatever they want with the photographs. You can grant them a licence to do whatever they like with the images (apart from re-selling them, perhaps) in perpetuity. Or you can draw up an agreement with terms and conditions. Maybe they can use your images only in material they themselves publish, or in print but not online, or for a fixed term such as three years. During that time you might agree to limitations on your own use of the image too, such as not to sell it to a competitor of the client, or only to sell it overseas. These are reasonable conditions that should allow both parties to get what they want.

If a client insists on full copyright, first of all ask yourself why. Is there a huge commercial opportunity for the outright owner of these images? If so, could that be your opportunity? Could you exploit that opportunity or is the client in a unique position? If the client has access to markets that you simply can't reach, consider a revenue-share with the client. If that won't work, then your price for the job should reflect the surrender of copyright.

To decide how much extra to charge for full copyright, imagine how much money you could potentially make from those images yourself. Sure, that kid in the school portrait might be a future winner of the X-Factor, but what are the odds? Then again, it's known that there was an agency that did some work for a haulage company. A photo of a random driver in a cab went on to become the first published photograph of the Yorkshire Ripper. Bought the agency boss his swimming pool, that did.

PHOTO KIT: BUY OR HIRE?

Don't overlook the option to rent rather than buy. Hiring what you need rather than buying it not only saves you money, but also allows you access to equipment you might not otherwise be able to afford

WHILE IT'S ALMOST second nature for professionals to ponder whether it's worth hiring rather than buying the gear they need, most amateur photographers rarely, if ever, consider this option. Over the following pages, we provide the answers to whether buying or hiring makes sense and where to look for the best deals.

Why should you hire rather than buy?

There are a number of reasons for hiring equipment. The most obvious is, of course, that you can potentially save a lot of money. As you'll see from our price guide table over the page, the difference between buying an expensive lens and hiring one can stretch to four figures!

What this effectively means is that you can afford to use equipment by hiring it that you simply wouldn't have the funds to buy outright. This has a number of benefits. To begin with, if you're just starting out on the road to making money from your photography and can't afford to buy expensive kit, then hiring equipment makes sense if you earn back the cost (and some profit too) from the photographs you take using it. What it also means is that by hiring, you can make use of a specific item that you only need infrequently, say a macro lens or a portable studioflash. It's a far better option than buying it and knowing you've spent a small fortune on something that spends most of its time gathering dust.

Hiring equipment also means you can 'try before you buy'. This is particularly useful if you're expecting to spend a large sum and need to be sure you're getting your money's worth. For example, many photographers thinking about upgrading a lens can hire a marque and independent lens and compare the handling, autofocus and optical performance with their current lens to see which, if any, is worth investing in. Sure, it may mean forking out £100 or more, but that's a small price to pay for knowing you've made the right choice. Especially as some firms will refund the cost of the hire if you end up buying the lens from them.

> "When it comes to camera gear, you'll find that literally anything can be hired, from an entry-level Canon EOS 400D to a top of the range Nikon D3x"

Where can you hire kit from?

There are a number of places, ranging from well-known photo retailers through to web-based firms dedicated to hiring out photo kit. Tap in photo kit hire or camera rental in Google and it brings up a number of options, but we'd suggest you stick to well-known companies, which ensure the kit they supply is regularly serviced and well stocked. The easiest way to do this is to check out the classified ads in the *Test Centre* section of *Digital SLR Photography* every issue, where you'll find several reputable firms, including Lenses for Hire, Lens Pimp and Hire a Camera.

If you want to visit a hiring centre in person, then two well-known photo retailers we'd highly recommend you contact are The Flash Centre and Calumet. Both have dedicated rental areas with extensive stock supplies and trained staff.

What sort of photo kit is available to hire?

When it comes to camera gear, you'll find that literally anything can be hired. If you need a camera body, then you'll find anything from an entry-level DSLR like a Canon EOS 400D through to top of the range models like the EOS-1Ds MkIII or a Nikon D3x is available. And let's not forget about the option of hiring a medium-format system. Ever dreamed of using a Hasselblad system? Well you might not be able to afford to buy one, but you could probably hire one for a day (albeit even a day's hire will set you back a fair bit!). ➤

Buying advice!
When buying kit, you may be asked if you want an extended guarantee to cover against damage or faults. Our advice is not to take up this option, as the odds are against you needing it

Frequently asked questions: Kit hire

We asked Calumet, one of the UK's leading suppliers of rental equipment, to answer our list of queries regarding hiring photo equipment.

Q What checks are made to hire kit so I know it's reliable?
A We test all the functions of the equipment before it leaves us to be sure it is functioning correctly, including the image sensor on digital bodies.

Q What happens if I lose or damage any hired equipment?
A We charge a 15% damage waiver fee, which covers for damage to the kit only; an excess would apply to each order where an item is damaged. If the customer has their own insurance to cover this then we would not need to charge the 15%, so long as we see the insurance policy before the goods leave us.

Q What happens if I want to take any hired kit abroad?
A That's fine. If it is outside Europe then we would charge a 20% damage waiver on the rental.

Q How far in advance do I need to reserve it?
A As far as you like! The more notice we have the more likely we'll have the item available and we can then book it in advance to avoid any disappointment.

Q What happens if it's faulty when I first receive it?
A In the unlikely event of the product being faulty on arrival or going faulty during the shoot we will do our best to have the kit replaced. (Quite often when we are informed that the kit is faulty we will talk the customer through the kit, as more often than not it is user error rather than a fault or it is something minor that can be worked around.)

Q Is the kit delivered or do I need to collect it?
A We can deliver or the customer is welcome to collect.

For further details on hiring equipment from Calumet, visit: www.calumetphoto.co.uk

Q What other equipment other than photo kit can be hired?
A It's not just photography kit that you can hire. Many rental firms include desktop computers and laptops, often bundled with software such as Lightroom and Photoshop, so it's worth enquiring if you're shooting on location and would benefit from a state-of-the-art editing facility. Many of the photo rental outlets, including Calumet, offer rental for Apple laptops for instance. For further information on hiring computers, we'd recommend you take a look at our sister titles: *MacUser*, *Computer Shopper* and *PC Pro*.

Buying your kit: How to pay

Q Why buy rather than hire?
A With so many strong arguments for hiring, it's fair enough asking why it's worth buying gear at all. The obvious reason of course is that owning kit is far more cost-effective in the long run; hiring should be a short-term measure when you can't afford to buy the kit, or simply want to use something you won't often need. For most people, paying by cash isn't an option when spending a sizeable wad on equipment, and as we highlight below, using another payment option often comes with its own rewards. Here we list the most popular buying options available to you, along with their pros and cons...

Credit cards

☑ **Advantages:** Once you've paid, you'll have a period of time, usually around 30-45 days, to pay off the balance without incurring any interest or fees. If you're saving up for the item, it's an easy way to buy it before you have the total amount you need. Some cards offer an introductory 0% interest period, which is great so long as you clear the balance before the period ends.

Benefits such as insurance for purchases, as well as extensions to the manufacturer's warranty, are available with some cards. If you're keen on travel, use a credit card that gives you Airmiles and build up points towards free flights.

☑ **Disadvantages:** Credit card companies make a fortune from interest payments, so if you don't clear your balance before the deadline, you'll end up paying interest on your purchases.

Debit card

☑ **Advantages:** If you're making an expensive purchase and don't fancy carrying around a lot of cash with you, then pay by debit card, which withdraws cash directly from your current account.

☑ **Disadvantages:** You need the balance in your bank account to avoid going overdrawn (which can incur penalty charges) or having your purchase rejected.

Payment Schemes

'Buy Now Pay Later' and pay-by-instalment schemes allow you to buy kit you currently can't afford, offering a period of time in which you pay by monthly instalments or as a lump sum on a set date in the future.

☑ **Advantages:** A relatively easy way to buy kit you haven't the money for.

☑ **Disadvantages:** High interest rates, often set at the time of purchase, means you'll be paying far more than if you pay by alternative means, so make this option a last resort. You're often better off with a bank loan instead.

For the majority of people, the chief bit of kit that they'd want to hire is lenses and thankfully there is an abundance of optics available from all the various firms. From fisheye to super-telephoto, from ultra wide-angle to a dedicated macro, you won't have any problem hiring lenses, regardless of the camera system you use.

Of course, the list doesn't stop there. Fancy shooting a portrait session but haven't any lights? No problem, just hire them. Need reflectors, stands or flash meters to use with them? Again, just hire them. In fact, if you and some friends group together, there's no reason why you couldn't all chip in, hire a comprehensive studio set-up and share the cost. And not forgetting the videographers among you, as well as hiring HD-enabled DSLRs, you can also rent dedicated HD camcorders, as well as important accessories such as microphones and rigs.

Is it expensive to hire equipment?

It depends what you want and how long you need it for. Hire an entire camera outfit with lenses and flashguns and you'll be paying well into three figures, hire a particular lens for a weekend and it may well set you back less than £100. As mentioned earlier, if the costs of hiring are covered by the fees you're charging, then you've less to worry about. But if you're taking pictures for a small fee, or none at all, you do need to be more careful. The table below give you an idea of the savings that you could make.

What are the drawbacks of hiring gear?

The most obvious is that once your hire period is over, you're back to square one, but with a slightly lighter wallet/purse. While hiring is a good short-term option, unless you're hiring equipment that helps you turn around a tidy profit, it ultimately isn't a viable route to take. Pros may be able to add the cost of rental into their fees, but if you're shooting stock images or a wedding, this isn't an option. The other factor to consider is that you might not be able to hire the equipment when you need it.

How long can I hire for?

This varies from firm to firm and usually depends on what you're hiring. As a general rule, most places have a weekend and weekly rate, some a daily rate. However, most are usually open to discussion and can often agree bespoke terms, so it's worth speaking to them to see what can be arranged. As you'll discover, the pro rata rental rate drops the longer you have the item. You should also ask about special offers as some firms charge a single day's rate for a weekend hire. ■

Comparison table: Rental prices of popular photo equipment from leading UK hire centres

	GUIDE PRICE	Calumet (Daily)	Calumet (Week)	Flash Centre (Daily)	Flash Centre (Week)	Lens Pimp (3 days)	Lens Pimp (7 days)	Hire a Camera (Daily)	Hire a Camera (Wknd)	Hire a Camera (Week)	Lens for hire (3 days)	Lens for Hire (7 days)
CAMERAS												
Canon EOS 5D MkII	£2,300	£100	£400	£95	£332	£161	£375	£70	£122	£264	-	-
Canon EOS-1Ds MkIII	£7,000	£140	£560	£125	£437	£241	£564	-	-	-	-	-
Nikon D700	£2,250	£90	£360	-	-	£161	£375	£70	£122	£264	-	-
Nikon D3x	£6,130	£135	£540	-	-	£261	£611	-	-	-	-	-
Hasselblad H3DII-39	N/A	£245	£980	-	-	-	-	-	-	-	-	-
LENSES												
Canon EF 16-35mm f/2.8L	£1,789	£36	£144	£20	£70	£23	£52	£30	£35	£74	£42	£61
Canon EF 24mm f/1.4L	£2,010	£31	£124	£25	£87.5	£28	£65	-	-	-	£37	£53
Canon EF 50mm f/1.2L	£1,910	£32	£128	£25	£87.5	£25	£57	£33	£48	£80	£44	£64
Canon EF 100-400mm f/4-5.6L	£1,940	£36	£144	£20	£20	£24	£57	-	-	-	£44	£64
Canon EF 400mm f/2.8L IS	£9,810	-	-	-	-	£72	£168	-	-	-	£165	£254
Nikon 14-24mm f/2.8G	£1,635	£36	£144	-	-	£26	£61	£30	£41	£87	£47	£68
Nikon 24mm f/2.8G	£1,950	£16	£64	-	-	-	-	-	-	-	£58	£85
Nikon AF-S 105mm f/2.8 VR micro	£765	£20	£80	-	-	£15	£34	-	-	-	£28	£39
Nikon AF-I 400mm f/2.8	£8,375	£60	£240	-	-	-	-	£57	£87	£174	-	-
FLASH												
Canon Speedlite 580EX II	£560	£16	£64	£15	£52.50	-	£33	£14	£18	£44	-	-
Nikon Speedlight SB-900	£410	£17	£68	-	-	-	£33	£14	£21	£53	-	-

HIRE WHAT YOU NEED!

As well as cameras and lenses, you can also hire studio lighting systems and accessories. And don't forget that there are a large number of well kitted out studios for hire all over the UK. Share facilities with a friend to help bring the cost down.

No question is too difficult for business journalist and photographer Martyn Moore. In this section, he sources the answers to some of your most frequently asked questions to put you on the road to success

Q) Where's the big money?

Aha! The $64,000 question. Is there any big money left? Let's see. Celebrity portraitists. Back in the 1960s the money was in taking pictures of pop stars and actors. Five or six made it very big: there was David, a couple of Terrys and one or two with royal connections. Today we live in the age of the paparazzi and you can make big money, if you're prepared to live without sleep and risk your life daily.

Glamour and fashion. There are millions of snappers out there trying to break into it. Have you seen their work? It's amazing, so what makes yours so special? And how many fashion art editors' numbers do you have stored on your iPhone? If a thousand of you went out to Milan tomorrow, I'd bet the cost of all your flights that nobody has a shot in next month's *Vogue*.

Landscapes? Forget it. Still-life studies? Satisfying but not lucrative. Aerial photography? OK if you happen to know somebody with a helicopter and the clients can afford the £1,000 an hour to keep it in the air. The big money is in people photography, although 'big money' is a relative term.

I photographed a family last month for £300 in front of a simple white background with two lights – 'Venture-style' they call it. Piece of cake, I call it. I was done in 90 minutes. Two hundred pounds an hour, that's cheap lawyer territory. They showed their neighbours, who told their friends and now a whole village has my phone number. Think of the reprints!

So if you can get in on the act of events, conferences, gala dinners, weddings, Christenings, anniversaries, graduations and dogs, you're sorted. All you need are brilliant interpersonal skills, reliable good-quality equipment, technical ability and a quick and easy system for swapping your time and prints for their cash. I hope I haven't made it sound too easy. I do have one other foolproof big money idea but I'm not going to write about it here. Send me £20 and I'll tell you all about it.

Q) Do I need an agent?

What are you, an Italian footballer? Of course you don't need an agent. Actors have agents because they don't like to talk to producers about money. Successful models have agents because they get so many offers of work, they need somebody to sort out the jobs that are 'right' for them. So, unless your art means so much to you that it feels dirty to contemplate the word 'fee', or if you have so much work offered to you that you need somebody to politely make some of it go away, you don't need an agent. Trust me.

Q) How can I tell a good photography course from a bad one?

The only people who can truly tell you what a course is like are the ones who have been on it. Look for testimonials on websites. Ask the course organiser if they can put you in touch with customers who have agreed to provide a reference. Try to find out how many delegates go back for more. A business that encourages its customers to rate the service on its website will be pretty confident of its performance.

Another way of getting feedback is to ask for recommendations on a web forum. Find out which courses other

> "There are very few activities as satisfying as passing on your skills and experience to others. And if you can get paid handsomely while you're at it, bingo!"

Digital SLR Photography readers have tried and what they thought of them. Photographers with good portfolios or memberships to associations might be lousy teachers. Sharing your skill with others is a gift that some great photographers don't possess.

The first photography courses to publish their 'net promoter rating' get my vote. The net promoter rating is based on asking customers a simple question: how likely are you to recommend this course to a friend or colleague? Various scoring systems are used, but any that come out over eight out of ten or 80% can be deemed a good bet.

Q) What's the best way of getting my photos into a magazine and is it profitable?

It's not as profitable as it used to be. Magazines, like everybody else, have to make ends meet and fees have taken a bit of a tumble. But getting work published is fantastically satisfying, and that, in a way, contributes to the problem. You should be proud to see your work in print, though, as that means it has passed a very rigorous quality-control test.

Setting aside the low pay for unsolicited work, here's how to do it. Send a disc of your very best work (no more than 50, showing wide variety. Not that one, it's soft. Bin that, it's too dark) to the editor, features editor or picture desk of your chosen magazine, together with a printed 'contact sheet' showing thumbnails. The images must be exactly right for the market the magazine operates in, so no steam engines to aviation magazines (unless it's a Flying Scotsman. Ha ha!).

Alternatively, email a link to your website, where the images intended for that magazine are presented in a smart, easy-to-use online gallery. A few weeks later, consider phoning the magazine to make sure they have seen your images and find out what they thought of them. Emphasise that you're looking for exposure rather than money. You might have to be content with picture credits and a big mug of pride for several months before you've made enough of an impression and get the call with a commission. Now it can be profitable.

Q) My clients often ask if they own the copyright to the images I've taken. Do they, and if not, should I give it to them? What are my options?

Try not to give away full copyright. What clients usually mean is "can I use this photo again and again without having to pay you more money?" and you can allow them to do this without giving them copyright. Maybe the easiest way to explain this to a client is that they can do anything they like with the image except resell it. By retaining copyright, you can even allow them to resell it as long as they at least inform you of the sale and hopefully share with you some of the revenue. Try to be clear on your contract or invoice so the client understands the limitations of use. Photographers have been forced to be much more relaxed over rights and usage in the digital age.

Q) I've been a photographer for a while now and been on a couple of courses. They're obviously a real moneymaker, should I start doing my own?

Well, as long as you can live with the old adage "those that can, do; those that can't, teach". It's all nonsense, of course, and there are very few activities as satisfying as passing on your skills and experience to others. And if you can get paid handsomely while you're at it, bingo!

A good teacher has to be a great people person. You should be blessed with strong communication skills and large reserves of patience. If you think that's you, ask a couple of other people just to check. You're probably right – good teachers tend to be confident and self-aware, too.

You also need to know photography

iSTOCK PHOTO

"None of use want to spend money when we don't have to. By submitting images to be used as stock in exchange for a credit, you've got yourself a free advert"

inside out. Nothing's worse than shelling out good money for a course to discover you know more than the tutor. I should know, I've been on both sides of that relationship. You need to be familiar with a wide variety of photography equipment, too. You will need to know how to set the ISO and image quality on various digital cameras and confidently show your students how to flip from auto to manual and around the exposure modes. You're starting to see why they're a "real moneymaker", aren't you?

So, let's assume you are made of the right stuff to teach photography. The next thing is understanding the market and considering another set of questions: do you want to specialise or can you handle studio portraits and breathtaking landscapes and wildlife? Will you include photo editing and manipulation, and what does all this mean for facilities and location?

You might consider working with other specialists to provide a broader experience for your students. And try to come up with a proposition or format that sets you apart from the other course providers out there. Pre-course get-togethers, end-of-course presentations, guest speakers, social evenings and ongoing post-course support all add value for your customers.

Let your maxim be: preparation, preparation, preparation. Try to imagine everything that could possibly go wrong and then work out how to prevent it or what you will do if it happens. One idea might be to do a dummy run. Invite friends whose opinions you trust and give them a free course on the condition that they review it as if they'd paid full price and have to tell you how it went.

While all this is going on, you should be getting a website organised with a name that will show up well in search engines. Your site should promote the benefits of your course and make it as easy as possible to contact you to make a booking.

Finally, tell the world. Send a press release to all the major photography magazines and websites and find out the cost of advertising. Invite a journalist to come along and review the course and offer a couple of free places to photo magazines as competition prizes.

All of this is just the start, of course – the real work begins now.

Q) Where's a good place to advertise?
That depends on who your customers are. If you are an aerial photographer, specialising in pictures of property and land from above, then look at trade publications like *Estates Gazette*. If you shoot weddings, consider *Brides* magazine or its local equivalent. Lots of people still look at the *Yellow Pages* and *Thomson Local*. Many towns have local or regional lifestyle magazines that carry regular wedding features and supplements. Getting adverts in suitable publications, or on websites, is a good place to start but none of us want to spend money when we don't have to. By submitting images to be used as stock in exchange for a credit, you've got yourself a free advert. I can remember when the local newspaper used to print wedding photos sent in by the photographer. Does that happen any more? Maybe that's where they've gone wrong!

Q) If I've been commissioned for a photoshoot, can I re-sell the pictures? If I can't, what if I adjusted the images so they looked different from what I supplied to the client?
Unless you have agreed otherwise, copyright remains with you and yes, you can sell the pictures to other people without adjusting them. You must consider how your commissioning client would feel though, especially if the repeat use could harm their business. These matters should be understood and

Non-professional model release form

Name of photographer..

Date..

Name of person in photograph(s)..

Rough description of photographs..

....

....

....

Contact details of model

....

I hereby grant the photographer named above and any licensees or assignees, the absolute right to copyright, sell, publish and/ or use photographic portraits or pictures of me or in which I am included, in whole or part, for advertising, trade, or any lawful purpose whatever. I waive any interest I may have in the copyright in the photographs and any moral rights I may have with regard to the photographs.

signature

ISTOCK PHOTO

"Unless the commissioning agreement restricts you and sets terms for the future use of images, you can do what you like with them. If it says you can't, you can't"

agreed in advance. You might agree not to sell images to anybody else for a year, or until a magazine issue goes off sale. You might get the client to agree that you can sell the shots straightaway but not for use in the client's market.

If the images were only made possible by the original client because they were the only people who could have created the subject or scene, they are more likely to have stipulated terms for future use by others. If they haven't, you might consider sharing any income you get with them to acknowledge their role in creating the images – then they might use you again.

If images include people, you need a model release for those people. They may be happy to appear in a toothpaste advert but not one for pile ointment. So, unless the commissioning agreement restricts you and clearly sets terms for the future use of images, you can do what you like with them. If you accepted an agreement that says you can't, you can't.

Q) I want to be a photojournalist. What's the best entry route?

Photojournalist. It's one of those words that means something different to everybody. There's a breed of photojournalist that works their way across Iraq, Jordan, Egypt, Libya and then back up to Syria with maybe a brief holiday to the site of the latest natural disaster. They live on their wits with a phone full of contacts, a laptop full of horrors and a carton of full-strength Marlboro. You need a passport and courage and/or a benevolent god. Income? Erratic. Others document life and work in the city, rural communities or the lifestyles of the rich and famous. They need a nose for a story and the means to sell it. Studying journalism at one of the NCTJ/PTC accredited universities or colleges provides a good launch pad. Approach local or regional magazines and newspapers too, offering them a story or making yourself available for editorial assignments. Learn to write in the hard news style to support your images to make the packages more saleable.

Q) I'm in the process of choosing my images and layout for my new website. Any advice?

Do a quick Google search for 'photographer websites' and you'll be inundated with sites: good, bad and the ugly. Study a selection and then work out what it is about the ones you like that caught your eye. Make a list of desirable features and decide whether you want to hit visitors in the eye with a big image, several on automatic rotation, or a selection of thumbnails. Choose images that reflect your favourite subjects, your style and your technical prowess. Draw up your first list of photos and then aim to cut it by half, rejecting any that are either sub-standard or show techniques that are better shown in other shots. Take your new shortlist and see if you can cut it by half again. Remember it's quality, not quantity. It doesn't matter that you don't put all your favourite shots on the site from day one. Good websites change regularly to remain fresh and offer repeat visitors something new.

Q) What software is good for managing my finances?

Microsoft Excel is pretty hard to beat. My accountant sends me an Excel spreadsheet for my quarterly VAT returns and it provides a good snapshot of how poor I am every 12 weeks. I type in the depressing numbers, but no software will ever make this job fun.

Excel-style spreadsheets are almost ubiquitous in accountancy and finance but you have to learn how to get the best from

them. Templates are available for almost every financial analysis you can imagine. There's also Intuit's QuickBooks, which is software specifically designed for small businesses (www.quickbooks.intuit.co.uk).

A photographer friend of mine exists almost exclusively on Apple products and uses Billings on his Mac. He uses this to time and cost jobs and it even issues an invoice via email at the end of the project. Visit www.marketcircle.com.

Q) How can I make sure I get paid on time and in full?

Get your bill in on time. You must set aside time every few days to spend on invoicing. I love invoicing, but still get horribly behind. Put your terms at the bottom of your invoice too. At the bottom of mine it says: "Payment within 14 days, please. Late payment will incur an additional charge of 10% per month. Thanks for the business."

Another alternative is to offer a discount for early payment, which is like applying your penalty up front but taking it off if the bill is paid quickly. This requires extra administration on your part and was recommended to me by an accountant who likes nothing better than messing about all day with numbers on bits of paper. But it might work for you.

Q) I always thought Photoshop was the best software for editing photos, but I keep hearing that Lightroom is the better choice for social photographers. How true is this?

I don't know. That's not very helpful, is it? So I asked Adobe's imaging guru David Marx for you: "Photoshop is the world's leading pixel manipulator. There is no other program like it for complete control over the look and feel of your digital image. No other program offers the same level of local image repair or allows such artistic creativity. If you can dream it, Photoshop can make it happen! Undeniably, Photoshop rocks but it is not an organiser of digital images. Photoshop is useless when you need to find your favourite images. Searching, sorting and organising are not part of its capabilities. This is where Lightroom's strengths lie.

"Not only can Lightroom help you organise all your files but it can help you manage the whole digital imaging workflow. Lightroom is designed to help you from start to finish. You get the most bang for your buck once you learn how to use Lightroom to empty your memory card, to sort through your files and categorise them, to set your initial Raw file conversion, make minor edits and to push the finished product out to the web or to your printer. Lightroom handles the whole chain of events with speed and grace whereas Photoshop really only functions as an image enhancer." Cheers, Dave. Now I do know. And so do you.

Q) When do I need a model release form and where can I get one?

If you plan to publish a photograph in one form or another and the person in the image is identifiable, you need them to sign a model release. The purpose of a model release form is to obtain written permission from people to use their image in your photography for whatever purpose you have in mind. It's like a little contract relating to the use of images and applies whether or not the model has been paid for the shoot. A model release form can give you permission to do anything with your images of the model, or it can be modified to restrict the use. You can request one of our model release templates by sending an email with the subject title as 'Model release form' to: dslr_eds@dennis.co.uk.

You can legally take photographs of people in public and use them in exhibitions and editorially in books or magazines without a model release form (although associating them with a derogatory article might expose the publisher to a libel action – buy me a pint and I'll tell you a very entertaining story from my own experience). But you can't use them commercially in product endorsements or advertisements.

> "Making money depends almost totally on who you know. The only exception is the talented photographer who does fine-art pictures and sells them online"

Q) If I'm not VAT registered, should I be adding tax on to the end of my clients' bills?

No, that would be illegal. Businesses charging VAT have to give that money to the taxman at the end of each quarter and for that you need to be VAT registered. If you don't meet the criteria for VAT registration it means you can keep your bills lower.

Q) What are the pros and cons of giving my client all the high-res images from a photoshoot on disk?

The pros are you won't have to mess about tracking down file numbers, designing albums, remembering print settings and doing extra prints for the client. The cons are that you won't get paid lots of extra money for doing all those things.

Be warned, though. I have a client who was supplied every image from a shoot via an internet server and sent a copy on DVD. It was an 'all in' fee because I didn't want the hassle of managing the images for the client, his ad agency, the PR company and the individuals featured in the shots. Within two months the client had deleted all the images and lost the DVD. I've resent them twice now and told the client that next time it will cost £200.

Q) Can you recommend any helpful resources to sell my images as stock?

I came across one the other day. It's called Photium and is available at www.photium.com. You can also use a Photobox gallery to sell prints and other merchandise featuring your images. The key to success with these methods is marketing your site. If you have pictures that people want and those people can find you easily enough, you can make money from stock. It sounds easy, but it isn't. The other option is to sell your images as stock through an established agency, such as iStockphoto, or one of the hundreds that come up when you type 'stock photos' into Google. They do all the marketing for you but charge low prices for images, working on volume sales. This means a low commission for you but if your photos are good enough, it can be profitable in the long run.

Q) How much does making money depend on who you know rather than what you know?

I think making money depends almost totally on who you know. The only exception I can think of is the photographer who produces fine-art pictures and sells them online or through a gallery. That photographer can be Billy Nomates and still do OK, but they have to be exceptionally talented.

The rest of us need to put ourselves about, a lot. Never go anywhere without a pocketful of business cards. Give potential clients two cards, one for them and one to pass on for you. Networking is vital. My home town holds regular business breakfasts and chamber of commerce networking evenings.

When I started out as a freelancer, I approached the organisers of these events and asked if I could come along and take pictures, telling them they could have the shots for publicity purposes for free. Once at the event, I 'worked the room', asking groups to pose for a photograph. I then gave them a business card with my web address on it and posted photos online for people to download free of charge. Each picture had my web address in the corner.

I once commissioned a photographer who put on his invoice 'If you're not happy with my work, tell me. If you are happy with my work, tell everybody'. Unfortunately, I wasn't happy with his work and told him and everybody. Your reputation is everything to your business and you must work hard to maintain it.

Talented photographers with a huge client base enjoy a kind of fame but you're only ever as good as your last job. If you mess up and handle it badly, word gets around. So if something does go wrong, use your people skills to make it right. This might mean repeating the shoot for free. Many businesses have told me that they shine in difficult situations. The way they handle their clients when it all goes wrong is what sets them apart from their rivals.

Collaboration with other people in photography is vital. Be best friends with your printer or processing lab. Find out if they are recommending your work or if they'll put your card in their reception. Work with them as a business partner.

Nurture relationships with other photographers, too. I have two friends whom I recommend to customers if I'm not available. I've also assisted other photographers, for example, doing a wedding reception for them so they can get to the next wedding ceremony on a busy Saturday. And I know for a fact that they point customers to me.

If success in business is down to who you know, the best thing you can do is get to know a lot of people. And satisfied customers will be happy to recommend you, as long as you do a good job and they like you.

Q) Should I put my prices on my website or just my contact details?

This is an excellent question. Transparency with pricing helps to build trust, which leads to long-term business relationships, but you also have to consider that every client's needs are different. If a prospective client appreciates the quality and value of your work, then they will enquire about prices, which gives you a chance to get them on the phone. Speaking with them first gives you an opportunity to show interest in what they're doing and discuss what they need, sell your business a little bit more and perhaps adjust prices appropriately.

As a commercial and corporate photographer, I work on a day rate of £300 and I don't put this on my website. Most people understand we operate in a free market economy. If I'm rushed off my feet and somebody wants to book me on my only spare day next week, I'll happily ask them for £300. If I haven't worked for five days and an interesting start-up business wants a low-cost job, I'll do it for £200 if I like the look of the job and they tell me that's all they can afford. I will tease them about what a bargain they're getting, too. If you're a social photographer, listing a few basic portrait or wedding packages could give prospective clients an idea if you're within their budget. But I might put a caveat, such as: "Every job is different, please get in touch to discuss your requirements in detail." Above all, if you do put your prices on your website, keep the packages simple and the prices for prints and products until after they see their images or request them.

The risk of putting prices on a website is that some clients will be totally put off by your expectations; the upside is that clients who are able to commission you at that level feel informed.

Q) How do I deal with an outstanding payment or a client refusing to pay?

If you are having real difficulty getting paid, you must get on the phone, asking to be transferred to the next senior person in line each time you get fobbed off. Take it to the chief executive if you have to. I rang one managing director while wearing my journalist hat and asked him if there was any truth in the rumour his company had cash-flow problems. He denied it strenuously, giving me the perfect opportunity to say, "So how about paying my flipping bill, then, before I start putting it about that you're in trouble?"

I haven't worked for the company again, but I got paid.

Disputes can arise over the quality of work and I can't really help you with that. They must be resolved through clear and sensible communication. If it goes to court you may have to show that you have acted reasonably. Last resort is to go legal: Citizens Advice Bureau, followed by small claims court.

There may even come a point where the debt is not worth the aggravation and time. Put it down to experience and move on with your life after setting fire to their offices. NO! That was a joke. Don't do that. Just move on with your life.

> "If you do put your prices on your website, keep the packages simple and the prices for prints and products until after they see their images or request them"

Q) I'm noticing that the difference between getting a job or not is whether I give them access to all the high-res images from the shoot. What's the best way to make money and give them what they want?

Give them high-res images and charge them a lot of money. That works. I give my clients permission to use the images any way they like and forever. I hold the copyright to the images, so I can use them too (but I wouldn't use specialised shots myself without asking the client first). The client pays me a very good day rate and I'm happy to shoot 'em, edit 'em, send 'em and forget 'em. One client managed to lose all the images and happily paid another £100 for me to dip into my external hard drive for them.

It's a problem if your business is built around selling prints, of course. In that case you need to explain why you can't give them the high-res version. It will help if you offer affordable prints, making it easier for the client to buy lots of prints from you. But then you're up against home PCs and desktop printers knocking them out at a few pence each. Not much mark-up opportunity there. Emphasise the print quality and archival permanence of your professional prints to help clients understand the good value that they're getting.

Q) I want to start earning a living from portraits but I can't afford to hire a studio and I don't have the space in my house to convert a room or the garage into a studio. Do you have any advice on how I could run a professional portrait business without a studio? What kit do you recommend?

Work at the clients' homes and learn to manage with whatever space they have. Or you can hire temporary space that's cheaper than a studio, such as a village hall. There are lots of two-head flash starter kits around that will easily fit in a car. Go for a 'name' and check out reviews in magazines or online. Background paper and stands aren't too expensive, either. Buy the widest rolls you can get in your car but also have some smaller backgrounds for head shots. Don't forget gaffer tape and extension cables. Make sure everything is in sturdy holdalls. Practise putting it up and taking it down. That's your studio sorted.

Q) Should I get an assistant?

What do you imagine they will do? Clean the studio and office? Make tea? That would be nice, wouldn't it? Design albums and handle emails, maybe. If you want them to do all the things you don't really like doing, you probably don't need an assistant. Running a business means doing things you never imagined yourself doing, but that doesn't mean you need an assistant so you can go to the pub instead. But if you have somebody to do all those things while you take on more paid work, or so you can do some networking and marketing, well, maybe you can make the case. Remember, an assistant will drain some resources as well as adding extra ones. You'll have to pay them, for a start, and then they'll expect training. And don't forget all that HR and employment law malarkey, either.

Assistants come in all shapes and sizes. There are the ones who want to be involved in the photography – the second pair of eyes and hands that can help to set up shots, prepare equipment and even take pictures. The true photographer's assistant will speed up sessions, make checks for you

and suggest ideas, so you can concentrate on the subject and getting the imagery.

Surprisingly, these most useful photography assistants will probably be cheaper. A recently graduated photography student will probably work for peanuts, just to get the experience. Don't forget, they will probably want your job, though. But don't let that worry you. Not too much anyway.

Someone to help you to organise groups or to hold a reflector at a wedding can be a godsend. Having someone who's competent enough to handle guests or to take pictures as people arrive so you can concentrate on the wedding party can set you apart from the competition.

Most photographers know an enthusiast who can be drafted in to be the second shooter for beer money. They can be trusted with candids of guests and might bag you the unexpected shot that would otherwise have got away.

A true photographer's assistant should be like an apprentice. They will be looking to acquire a set of skills and experience that will set them up for a career in the industry. You might have to trust them with your kit, but like an apprentice plumber, they should be acquiring their own tools as well. So, be mindful of your responsibilities. This is about giving somebody a start, not exploitation.

If you think you have a genuine need for an assistant, contact the local college and find out if there are any promising students about to be thrown out into the real world. There's a website just for wannabe assistants called www.photoassist.co.uk. Check out some of the moody student self-portraits and cheer yourself up.

Find somebody who loves photography as much as you, has some talent, and will do anything they can to get a start in this business. Then treat them well. Pay them as much as you can afford, not a penny more, and above all, keep them busy and help them learn the trade.